GEOGRAPHY 97/98

Twelfth Edition

Editor

Gerald R. Pitzl
Macalester College

Gerald R. Pitzl, professor of geography at Macalester College, received his bachelor's degree in secondary social science education from the University of Minnesota in 1964 and his M.A. (1971) and Ph.D. (1974) in geography from the same institution. He teaches a wide array of geography courses and is the author of a number of articles on geography, the developing world, and computers in social science education.

A Library of Information from the Public Press

Dushkin Publishing Group/Brown & Benchmark Publishers
Sluice Dock, Guilford, Connecticut 06437

Visit us on the Internet—http://www.dushkin.com

This map has been developed to give you a graphic picture of where the countries of the world are located, the relationship they have with their region and neighbors, and their positions relative to the superpowers and power blocs. We have focused on certain areas to more clearly illustrate these crowded regions.

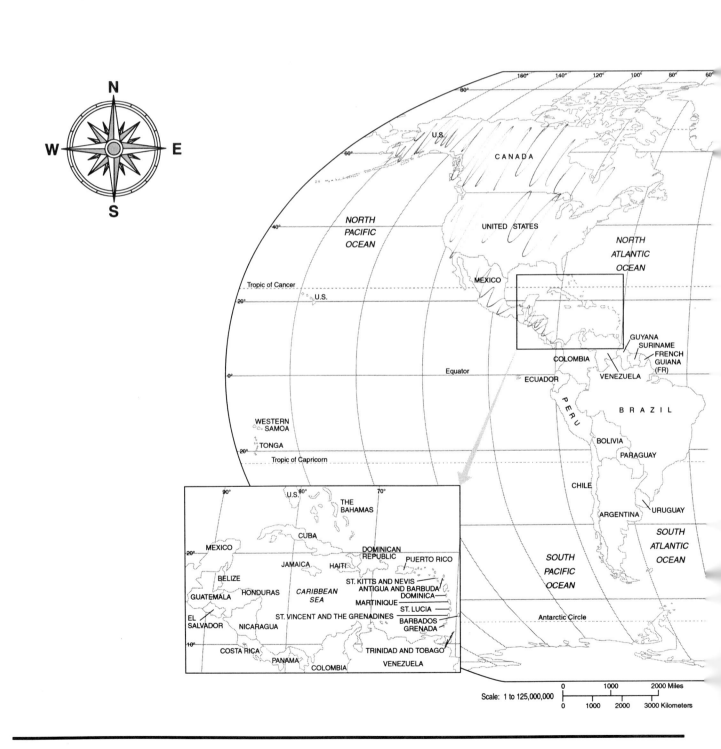

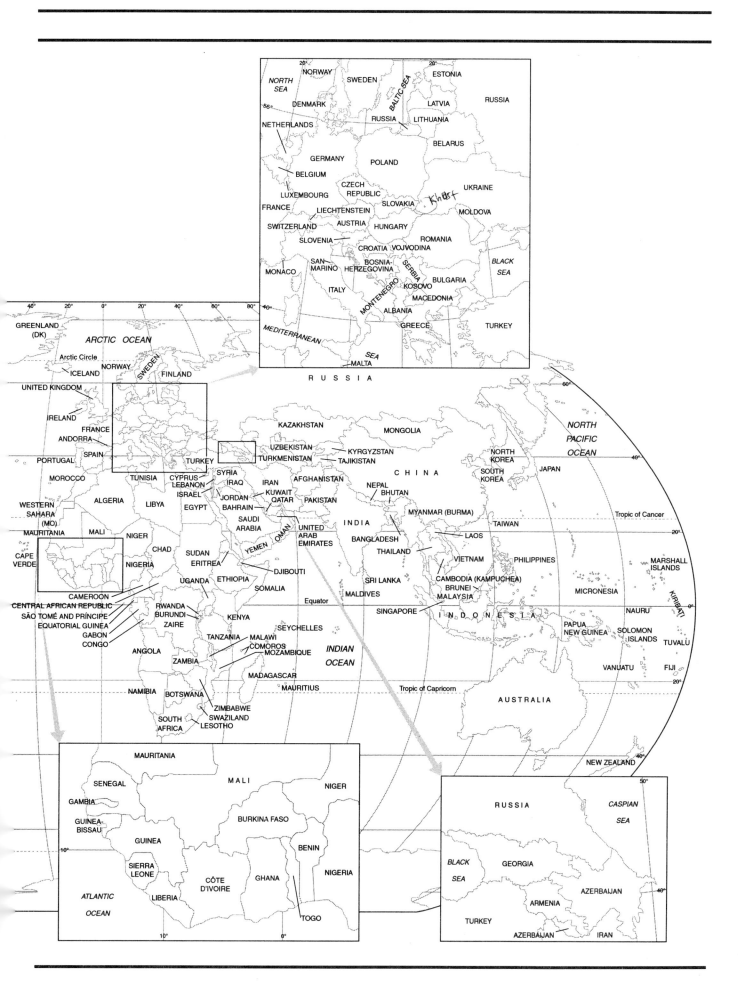

The Annual Editions Series

ANNUAL EDITIONS is a series of over 65 volumes designed to provide the reader with convenient, low-cost access to a wide range of current, carefully selected articles from some of the most important magazines, newspapers, and journals published today. ANNUAL EDITIONS are updated on an annual basis through a continuous monitoring of over 300 periodical sources. All ANNUAL EDITIONS have a number of features that are designed to make them particularly useful, including topic guides, annotated tables of contents, unit overviews, and indexes. For the teacher using ANNUAL EDITIONS in the classroom, an Instructor's Resource Guide with test questions is available for each volume.

VOLUMES AVAILABLE

Abnormal Psychology
Adolescent Psychology
Africa
Aging
American Foreign Policy
American Government
American History, Pre-Civil War
American History, Post-Civil War
American Public Policy
Anthropology
Archaeology
Biopsychology
Business Ethics
Child Growth and Development
China
Comparative Politics
Computers in Education
Computers in Society
Criminal Justice
Criminology
Developing World
Deviant Behavior
Drugs, Society, and Behavior
Dying, Death, and Bereavement

Early Childhood Education
Economics
Educating Exceptional Children
Education
Educational Psychology
Environment
Geography
Global Issues
Health
Human Development
Human Resources
Human Sexuality
India and South Asia
International Business
Japan and the Pacific Rim
Latin America
Life Management
Macroeconomics
Management
Marketing
Marriage and Family
Mass Media
Microeconomics

Middle East and the
    Islamic World
Multicultural Education
Nutrition
Personal Growth and Behavior
Physical Anthropology
Psychology
Public Administration
Race and Ethnic Relations
Russia, the Eurasian Republics,
    and Central/Eastern Europe
Social Problems
Social Psychology
Sociology
State and Local Government
Urban Society
Western Civilization,
    Pre-Reformation
Western Civilization,
    Post-Reformation
Western Europe
World History, Pre-Modern
World History, Modern
World Politics

Cataloging in Publication Data
Main entry under title: Annual Editions: Geography. 1997/98.
        1. Geography—Periodicals. 2. Anthropo-geography—Periodicals. 3. Natural resources—Periodicals. I. Pitzl, Gerald R., *comp.* II. Title: Geography.
910'.5   ISBN 0–697–37271-5   87–641715   ISSN. 1091–9937

Twelfth Edition

Cover image ©1996 PhotoDisc, Inc.

Printed in the United States of America

Printed on Recycled Paper

Editors/Advisory Board

Members of the Advisory Board are instrumental in the final selection of articles for each edition of ANNUAL EDITIONS. Their review of articles for content, level, currentness, and appropriateness provides critical direction to the editor and staff. We think that you will find their careful consideration well reflected in this volume.

EDITOR

Gerald R. Pitzl
Macalester College

ADVISORY BOARD

Staff

To the Reader

In publishing ANNUAL EDITIONS we recognize the enormous role played by the magazines, newspapers, and journals of the *public press* in providing current, first-rate educational information in a broad spectrum of interest areas. Many of these articles are appropriate for students, researchers, and professionals seeking accurate, current material to help bridge the gap between principles and theories and the real world. These articles, however, become more useful for study when those of lasting value are carefully *collected, organized, indexed,* and *reproduced* in a *low-cost format,* which provides easy and permanent access when the material is needed. That is the role played by ANNUAL EDITIONS. Under the direction of each volume's *academic editor,* who is an expert in the subject area, and with the guidance of an *Advisory Board,* each year we seek to provide in each ANNUAL EDITION a current, well-balanced, carefully selected collection of the best of the public press for your study and enjoyment. We think that you will find this volume useful, and we hope that you will take a moment to let us know what you think.

The articles in this twelfth edition of *Annual Editions: Geography* represent the wide range of topics associated with the discipline of geography. The major themes of spatial relationships, regional development, the population explosion, and socioeconomic inequalities exemplify the diversity of research areas within geography.

The book is organized into five units, each of which contains articles relating to geographical themes. Selections address the conceptual nature of geography and the global and regional problems in the world today. This latter theme reflects the geographer's concern with finding solutions to these serious issues. Regional problems, such as food shortages in the Sahel and the greenhouse effect, concern not only geographers but also researchers from other disciplines.

The association of geography with other fields is important, because expertise from related research will be necessary in finding solutions to some difficult problems. Input from the focus of geography is vital in our common search for solutions. This discipline has always been integrative. That is, geography uses evidence from many sources to answer the basic questions, "Where is it?" "Why is it there?" and "What is its relevance?" The first group of articles emphasizes the interconnectedness not only of places and regions in the world but of efforts toward solutions to problems as well. No single discipline can have all of the answers to the problems facing us today; the complexity of the issues is simply too great.

The writings in unit 1 discuss particular aspects of geography as a discipline and provide examples of the topics presented in the remaining four sections. Units 2, 3, and 4 represent major themes in geography. Unit 5 addresses important problems faced by geographers and others.

Annual Editions: Geography 97/98 will be useful to both teachers and students in their study of geography. The anthology is designed to provide detail and case study material to supplement the standard textbook treatment of geography. The goals of this anthology are to introduce students to the richness and diversity of topics relating to places and regions on Earth's surface, to pay heed to the serious problems facing humankind, and to stimulate the search for more information on topics of interest.

I would like to express my gratitude to Barbara Wells-Howe for her continued help in preparing this material for publication. Her typing, organization of materials, and many helpful suggestions are greatly appreciated. Without her diligence and professional efforts, this undertaking could not have been completed. Special thanks are also extended to Ian Nielsen for his continued encouragement during the preparation of this new edition and to Addie Raucci for her enthusiasm and helpfulness. A word of thanks must go as well to all those who recommended articles for inclusion in this volume and who commented on its overall organization. James Hathaway, Vern Harnapp, David J. Larson, Peter O. Muller, Robert S. Bednarz, Allison Gillmore, and Randy W. Widdis were especially helpful in that regard. Please continue to share your opinions by filling out the postage-paid Article Rating Form on the last page of this book.

Gerald R. Pitzl
Editor

Contents

UNIT 1

Geography in a Changing World

Eight articles discuss the discipline of geography and the extremely varied and wide-ranging themes that define geography today.

The concepts in bold italics are developed in the article. For further expansion please refer to the Topic Guide and the Index.

UNIT 2

Land-Human Relationships

Seven articles examine the relationship between humans and the land on which we live. Topics include the destruction of the rain forests, desertification, pollution, and the effects of human society on the global environment.

The concepts in bold italics are developed in the article. For further expansion please refer to the Topic Guide and the Index.

UNIT 3

The Region

Ten selections review the
importance of the region as a
concept in geography and as
an organizing framework for
research. A number of world
regional trends, as well as the
patterns of area relationships,
are examined.

The concepts in bold italics are developed in the article. For further expansion please refer to the Topic Guide and the Index.

The concepts in bold italics are developed in the article. For further expansion please refer to the Topic Guide and the Index.

UNIT 4

Spatial Interaction and Mapping

Seven articles discuss the key theme in geographical analysis: place-to-place spatial interaction. Human diffusion, transportation systems, urban growth, and cartography are some of the themes examined.

The concepts in bold italics are developed in the article. For further expansion please refer to the Topic Guide and the Index.

UNIT 5

Population, Resources, and Socioeconomic Development

Seven articles examine the effects of population growth on natural resources and the resulting socioeconomic level of development.

The concepts in bold italics are developed in the article. For further expansion please refer to the Topic Guide and the Index.

The concepts in bold italics are developed in the article. For further expansion please refer to the Topic Guide and the Index.

Topic Guide

This topic guide suggests how the selections in this book relate to topics of traditional concern to students and professionals involved with the study of geography. It is useful for locating articles that relate to each other for reading and research. The guide is arranged alphabetically according to topic. Articles may, of course, treat topics that do not appear in the topic guide. In turn, entries in the topic guide do not necessarily constitute a comprehensive listing of all the contents of each selection.

TOPIC AREA	TREATED IN	TOPIC AREA	TREATED IN
Accessibility	27. High-Speed Rail	Economic	5. Global Tide
Agriculture	23. Low Water in the American High Plains		9. Environmental Challenges in Sub-Saharan Africa
	24. Long River's Journey Ends		25. Russia and Japan
	28. Spread of Early Farming in Europe		35. Vicious Circles
	37. Assault of the Earth		39. Preventive Medicine
AIDS	39. Preventive Medicine	Ecosystem	21. Indigenous Cultural and Biological Diversity
Arid Lands	14. Threat of Encroaching Deserts May Be More Myth than Fact	El Niño	7. What's Wrong with the Weather?
Cartography	*See* Mapmaking	Environment	3. Apocalypse Soon
			8. Tortured Land
Climatic Change	7. What's Wrong with the Weather?		36. Russia's Population Sink
	12. Global Fever	Erosion	14. Threat of Encroaching Deserts May Be More Myth than Fact
Communication	20. Two-Way Corridor through History		
	26. Transportation and Urban Growth	Forests	8. Tortured Land
Computer Mapping	32. Raster Data for the Layman	Geographic Information Systems (GIS)	*See* Computer Mapping
Connectivity	27. High-Speed Rail		
Conservation	14. Threat of Encroaching Deserts May Be More Myth than Fact	Geography	2. American Geographics
			3. Apocalypse Soon
			10. Human Encroachments on a Domineering Physical Landscape
Cultural Diversity	21. Indigenous Cultural and Biological Diversity		19. Regions and Western Europe
Deforestation	9. Environmental Challenges in Sub-Saharan Africa	Geopolitical	4. Coming Anarchy
	13. Deforestation Debate		19. Regions and Western Europe
			25. Russia and Japan
Demographic Transition	35. Vicious Circles	Global Issues	5. Global Tide
	36. Russia's Population Sink		6. Has Global Warming Begun?
			12. Global Fever
Desertification	9. Environmental Challenges in Sub-Saharan Africa		17. Rise of the Region State
	14. Threat of Encroaching Deserts May Be More Myth than Fact		19. Regions and Western Europe
			39. Preventive Medicine
		Greenhouse	6. Has Global Warming Begun?
Developing World	35. Vicious Circles		
Development	35. Vicious Circles	Groundwater	23. Low Water in the American High Plains
Distance	19. Regions and Western Europe	History of Geography	1. Four Traditions of Geography
Drought	7. What's Wrong with the Weather?		
	23. Low Water in the American High Plains		

Geography in a Changing World

What is geography? This question has been asked innumerable times, but it has not elicited a universally accepted answer, even from those who are considered to be members of the geography profession. The reason lies in the very nature of geography as it has evolved through time.

Geography is an extremely wide-ranging discipline, one that examines appropriate sets of events or circumstances occurring at specific places. Its goal is to answer certain basic questions.

The first question—"Where is it?"—establishes the location of the subject under investigation. The concept of location is very important in geography, and its meaning extends beyond the common notion of a specific address or the determination of the latitude and longitude of a place. Geographers are more concerned with the relative location of a place and how that place interacts with other places both far and near. Spatial interaction and the determination of the connections between places are important themes in geography.

Once a place is "located," in the geographer's sense of the word, the next question is, "Why is it here?" For example, why are people concentrated in high numbers on the North China plain, in the Ganges River valley in India, and along the eastern seaboard in the United States? Conversely, why are there so few people in the Amazon basin and the Central Siberian lowlands? Generally, the geographer wants to find out why particular distribution patterns occur and why these patterns change over time.

The element of time is another extremely important ingredient in the geographical mix. Geography is most concerned with the activities of human beings, and human beings bring about change. As changes occur, new adjustments and modifications are made in the distribution patterns previously established. Patterns change, for instance, as new technology brings about new forms of communication and transportation and as once-desirable locations decline in favor of new ones. For example, people migrate from once-productive regions such as the Sahel when a disaster such as drought visits the land. Geography, then, is greatly concerned with discovering the underlying processes that can explain the transformation of distribution patterns and interaction forms over time. Geography itself is dynamic, adjusting as a discipline to handle new situations in a changing world.

Geography is truly an integrating discipline. The geographer assembles evidence from many sources in order to explain a particular pattern or ongoing process of change. Some of this evidence may even be in the form of concepts or theories borrowed from other disciplines. The first three articles of this unit provide insight into both the conceptual nature of geography and the development of the discipline over time.

Throughout its history, four main themes have been the focus of research work in geography. These themes or traditions, according to William Pattison in "The Four Traditions of Geography," link geography with earth science, establish it as a field that studies land-human relationships, engage it in area studies, and give it a spatial focus. Although Pattison's article first appeared over 30 years ago, it is still referred to and cited frequently today. Much of the geographical research and analysis engaged in today would fall within one or more of Pattison's traditional areas, but new areas are also opening for geographers. In a particularly thought-provoking essay, the eminent author Barry Lopez discusses local geographies and the importance of a sense of place. Nigel Thrift points

out the importance of human geography in addressing global problems. In Robert D. Kaplan's article, "The Coming Anarchy," a startling scenario is presented about the destruction of the social fabric of our planet. Then, "The Global Tide" describes the globalization of economic activity. "Has Global Warming Begun?" states that hard evidence is now accumulating that global warming is a reality.

Research into apparently abnormal weather shifts in recent years is dealt with in "What's Wrong with the Weather? El Niño Strikes Again." The next article tells of the severe environmental devastation in the once pristine Siberian region.

Looking Ahead: Challenge Questions

Why is geography called an integrating discipline?

How is geography related to earth science? Give some examples of these relationships. What are area studies? Why is the spatial concept so important in geography? What is your definition of geography?

Why do history and geography rely on each other?

How have humans affected the weather? The environment in general?

How is individual behavior related to our understanding of environment?

Discuss whether or not change is a good thing. Why is it important to anticipate change?

What does interconnectedness mean in terms of places? Give examples of how you as an individual interact with people in other places. How are you "connected" to the rest of the world?

What will the world be like in the year 2010? Tell why you are pessimistic or optimistic about the future. What, if anything, can you do about the future?

The Four Traditions of Geography

William D. Pattison

Late Summer, 1990

To Readers of the *Journal of Geography:*

I am honored to be introducing, for a return to the pages of the *Journal* after more than 25 years, "The Four Traditions of Geography," an article which circulated widely, in this country and others, long after its initial appearance—in reprint, in xerographic copy, and in translation. A second round of life at a level of general interest even approaching that of the first may be too much to expect, but I want you to know in any event that I presented the paper in the beginning as my gift to the geographic community, not as a personal property, and that I re-offer it now in the same spirit.

In my judgment, the article continues to deserve serious attention—perhaps especially so, let me add, among persons aware of the specific problem it was intended to resolve. The background for the paper was my experience as first director of the High School Geography Project (1961–63)—not all of that experience but only the part that found me listening, during numerous conference sessions and associated interviews, to academic geographers as they responded to the project's invitation to locate "basic ideas" representative of them all. I came away with the conclusion that I had been witnessing not a search for consensus but rather a blind struggle for supremacy among honest persons of contrary intellectual commitment. In their dialogue, two or more different terms had been used, often unknowingly, with a single reference, and no less disturbingly, a single term had been used, again often unknowingly, with two or more different references. The article was my attempt to stabilize the discourse. I was proposing a basic nomenclature (with explicitly associated ideas) that would, I trusted, permit the development of mutual comprehension **and** confront all parties concerned with the pluralism inherent in geographic thought.

This intention alone could not have justified my turning to the NCGE as a forum, of course. The fact is that from the onset of my discomfiting realization I had looked forward to larger consequences of a kind consistent with NCGE goals.

As finally formulated, my wish was that the article would serve "to greatly expedite the task of maintaining an alliance between professional geography and pedagogical geography and at the same time to promote communication with laymen" (see my fourth paragraph). I must tell you that I have doubts, in 1990, about the acceptability of my word choice, in saying "professional," "pedagogical," and "layman" in this context, but the message otherwise is as expressive of my hope now as it was then.

I can report to you that twice since its appearance in the *Journal,* my interpretation has received more or less official acceptance—both times, as it happens, at the expense of the earth science tradition. The first occasion was Edward Taaffe's delivery of his presidential address at the 1973 meeting of the Association of American Geographers (see *Annals AAG,* March 1974, pp. 1–16). Taaffe's working-through of aspects of an interrelations among the spatial, area studies, and man-land traditions is by far the most thoughtful and thorough of any of which I am aware. Rather than fault him for omission of the fourth tradition, I compliment him on the grace with which he set it aside in conformity to a meta-epistemology of the American university which decrees the integrity of the social sciences as a consortium in their own right. He was sacrificing such holistic claims as geography might be able to muster for a freedom to argue the case for geography as a social science.

The second occasion was the publication in 1984 of *Guidelines for Geographic Education: Elementary and Secondary Schools,* authored by a committee jointly representing the AAG and the NCGE. Thanks to a recently published letter (see *Journal of Geography,* March-April 1990, pp. 85–86), we know that, of five themes commended to teachers in this source,

The committee lifted the human environmental interaction theme directly from Pattison. The themes of place and location are based on Pattison's spatial or geometric geography, and the theme of region comes from Pattison's area studies or regional geography.

From the *Journal of Geography,* September/October 1990, pp. 202-206. © 1990 by the National Council for Geographic Education. Reprinted by permission.

Having thus drawn on my spatial area studies and man-land traditions for four of the five themes, the committee could have found the remaining theme, movement, there too—in the spatial tradition (see my sixth paragraph). However that may be, they did not avail themselves of the earth science tradition, their reasons being readily surmised. Peculiar to the elementary and secondary schools is a curriculum category framed as much by theory of citizenship as by theory of knowledge: the social studies. With admiration, I see already in the committee members' adoption of the theme idea a strategy for assimilation of their program to the established repertoire of social studies practice. I see in their exclusion of the earth science tradition an intelligent respect for social studies' purpose.

Here's to the future of education in geography: may it prosper as never before.

W. D. P., 1990

Reprinted from the *Journal of Geography*, 1964, pp. 211-216.

In 1905, one year after professional geography in this country achieved full social identity through the founding of the Association of American Geographers, William Morris Davis responded to a familiar suspicion that geography is simply an undisciplined "omnium-gatherum" by describing an approach that as he saw it imparts a "geographical quality" to some knowledge and accounts for the absence of the quality elsewhere.[1] Davis spoke as president of the AAG. He set an example that was followed by more than one president of that organization. An enduring official concern led the AAG to publish, in 1939 and in 1959, monographs exclusively devoted to a critical review of definitions and their implications.[2]

Every one of the well-known definitions of geography advanced since the founding of the AAG has had its measure of success. Tending to displace one another by turns, each definition has said something true of geography.[3] But from the vantage point of 1964, one can see that each one has also failed. All of them adopted in one way or another a monistic view, a singleness of preference, certain to omit if not to alienate numerous professionals who were in good conscience continuing to participate creatively in the broad geographic enterprise.

The thesis of the present paper is that the work of American geographers, although not conforming to the restrictions implied by any one of these definitions, has exhibited a broad consistency, and that this essential unity has been attributable to a small number of distinct but affiliated traditions, operant as binders in the minds of members of the profession. These traditions are all of great age and have passed into American geography as parts of a general legacy of Western thought. They are shared today by geographers of other nations.

There are four traditions whose identification provides an alternative to the competing monistic definitions that have been the geographer's lot. The resulting pluralistic basis for judgment promises, by full accommodation of what geographers do and by plain-spoken representation thereof, to greatly expedite the task of maintaining an alliance between professional geography and pedagogical geography and at the same time to promote communication with laymen. The following discussion treats the traditions in this order: (1) a spatial tradition, (2) an area studies tradition, (3) a man-land tradition and (4) an earth science tradition.

Spatial Tradition

Entrenched in Western thought is a belief in the importance of spatial analysis, of the act of separating from the happenings of experience such aspects as distance, form, direction and position. It was not until the 17th century that philosophers concentrated attention on these aspects by asking whether or not they were properties of things-in-themselves. Later, when the 18th century writings of Immanuel Kant had become generally circulated, the notion of space as a category including all of these aspects came into widespread use. However, it is evident that particular spatial questions were the subject of highly organized answering attempts long before the time of any of these cogitations. To confirm this point, one need only be reminded of the compilation of elaborate records concerning the location of things in ancient Greece. These were records of sailing distances, of coastlines and of landmarks that grew until they formed the raw material for the great *Geographia* of Claudius Ptolemy in the 2nd century A.D.

A review of American professional geography from the time of its formal organization shows that the spatial tradition of thought had made a deep penetration from the very beginning. For Davis, for Henry Gannett and for most if not all of the 44 other men of the original AAG, the determination and display of spatial aspects of reality through mapping were of undoubted importance, whether contemporary definitions of geography happened to acknowledge this fact or not. One can go further and, by probing beneath the art of mapping, recognize in the behavior of geographers of that time an active interest in the true essentials of the spatial tradition—*geometry* and *movement*. One can trace a basic favoring of movement as a subject of study from the turn-of-the-century work of Emory R. Johnson, writing as professor of transportation at the University of Pennsylvania, through the highly influential theoretical and substantive work of Edward L. Ullman during the past 20 years and thence to an article by a younger geographer on railroad freight traffic in the U.S. and Canada in the *Annals* of the AAG for September 1963.[4]

One can trace a deep attachment to geometry, or positioning-and-layout, from articles on boundaries and population densities in early 20th century volumes of the *Bulletin of the American Geographical Society,* through a controversial pronouncement by Joseph Schaefer in 1953 that granted geographical legitimacy only to studies of spatial patterns[5] and so onward to a recent *Annals* report on electronic scanning of cropland patterns in Pennsylvania.[6]

One might inquire, is discussion of the spatial tradition, after the manner of the remarks just made, likely to bring people within geography closer to an understanding of one another and people outside geography closer to an understanding of geographers? There seem to be at least two reasons for being hopeful. First, an appreciation of this tradition allows one to see a bond of fellowship uniting the elementary school teacher, who attempts the most rudimentary instruction in directions and mapping, with the contemporary research geographer, who dedicates himself to an exploration of central-place theory. One cannot only open the eyes of many teachers to the potentialities of their own instruction, through proper exposition of the spatial tradition, but one can also "hang a bell" on research quantifiers in geography, who are often thought to have wandered so far in their intellectual adventures as to have become lost from the rest. Looking outside geography, one may anticipate benefits from the readiness of countless persons to associate the name "geography" with maps. Latent within this readiness is a willingness to recognize as geography, too, what maps are about—and that is the geometry of and the movement of what is mapped.

Area Studies Tradition

The area studies tradition, like the spatial tradition, is quite strikingly represented in classical antiquity by a practitioner to whose surviving work we can point. He is Strabo, celebrated for his *Geography* which is a massive production addressed to the statesmen of Augustan Rome and intended to sum up and regularize knowledge not of the location of places and associated cartographic facts, as in the somewhat later case of Ptolemy, but of the nature of places, their character and their differentiation. Strabo exhibits interesting attributes of the area-studies tradition that can hardly be overemphasized. They are a pronounced tendency toward subscription primarily to literary standards, an almost omnivorous appetite for information and a self-conscious companionship with history.

It is an extreme good fortune to have in the ranks of modern American geography the scholar Richard Hartshorne, who has pondered the meaning of the area-studies tradition with a legal acuteness that few persons would challenge. In his *Nature of Geography,* his 1939 monograph already cited,[7] he scrutinizes exhaustively the implications of the "interesting attributes" identified in connection with Strabo, even though his concern is with quite other and much later authors, largely German. The major literary problem of unities or wholes he considers from every angle. The Gargantuan appetite for miscellaneous information he accepts and rationalizes. The companionship between area studies and history he clarifies by appraising the so-called idiographic content of both and by affirming the tie of both to what he and Sauer have called "naively given reality."

The area-studies tradition (otherwise known as the chorographic tradition) tended to be excluded from early American professional geography. Today it is beset by certain champions of the spatial tradition who would have one believe

that somehow the area-studies way of organizing knowledge is only a subdepartment of spatialism. Still, area-studies as a method of presentation lives and prospers in its own right. One can turn today for reassurance on this score to practically any issue of the *Geographical Review,* just as earlier readers could turn at the opening of the century to that magazine's forerunner.

What is gained by singling out this tradition? It helps toward restoring the faith of many teachers who, being accustomed to administering learning in the area-studies style, have begun to wonder if by doing so they really were keeping in touch with professional geography. (Their doubts are owed all too much to the obscuring effect of technical words attributable to the very professionals who have been intent, ironically, upon protecting that tradition.) Among persons outside the classroom the geographer stands to gain greatly in intelligibility. The title "area-studies" itself carries an understood message in the United States today wherever there is contact with the usages of the academic community. The purpose of characterizing a place, be it neighborhood or nation-state, is readily grasped. Furthermore, recognition of the right of a geographer to be unspecialized may be expected to be forthcoming from people generally, if application for such recognition is made on the merits of this tradition, explicitly.

Man-Land Tradition

That geographers are much given to exploring man-land questions is especially evident to anyone who examines geographic output, not only in this country but also abroad. 0. H. K. Spate, taking an international view, has felt justified by his observations in nominating as the most significant ancient precursor of today's geography neither Ptolemy nor Strabo nor writers typified in their outlook by the geographies of either of these two men, but rather Hippocrates, Greek physician of the 5th century B.C. who left to posterity an extended essay, *On Airs, Waters and Places.*[8] In this work, made up of reflections on human health and conditions of external nature, the questions asked are such as to confine thought almost altogether to presumed influence passing from the latter to the former, questions largely about the effects of winds, drinking water and seasonal changes upon man. Understandable though this uni-directional concern may have been for Hippocrates as medical commentator, and defensible as may be the attraction that this same approach held for students of the condition of man for many, many centuries thereafter, one can only regret that this narrowed version of the man-land tradition, combining all too easily with social Darwinism of the late 19th century, practically overpowered American professional geography in the first generation of its history.[9] The premises of this version governed scores of studies by American geographers in interpreting the rise and fall of nations, the strategy of battles and the construction of public improvements. Eventually this special bias, known as environmentalism, came to be confused with the whole of the man-land tradition in the minds of many people. One can see now, looking back to the years after the ascendancy of environmentalism, that although the spatial tradition was asserting itself with varying degrees of forwardness, and that although the area-studies tradition was also making itself felt, perhaps the most interesting chapters in the story of American professional geography were being written by academicians who were reacting against environmentalism while deliberately remaining within the broad man-land tradition. The rise of culture historians during the last 30 years has meant the dropping of a curtain of culture between land and man, through which it is asserted all influence must pass. Furthermore work of both culture historians and other geographers has exhibited a reversal of the direction of the effects in Hippocrates, man appearing as an independent agent, and the land as a sufferer from action. This trend as presented in published research has reached a high point in the collection of papers titled *Man's Role in Changing the Face of the Earth*. Finally, books and articles can be called to mind that have addressed themselves to the most difficult task of all, a balanced tracing out of interaction between man and environment. Some chapters in the book mentioned above undertake just this. In fact the separateness of this approach is discerned only with difficulty in many places; however, its significance as a general research design that rises above environmentalism, while refusing to abandon the man-land tradition, cannot be mistaken.

The NCGE seems to have associated itself with the manland tradition, from the time of founding to the present day, more than with any other tradition, although all four of the traditions are amply represented in its official magazine, *The Journal of Geography* and in the proceedings of its annual meetings. This apparent preference on the part of the NCGE members *for defining geography in terms of the man-land tradition* is strong evidence of the appeal that man-land ideas, separately stated, have for persons whose main job is teaching. It should be noted, too, that this inclination reflects a proven acceptance by the general public of learning that centers on resource use and conservation.

Earth Science Tradition
The earth science tradition, embracing study of the earth, the waters of the earth, the atmosphere surrounding the earth and the association between earth and sun, confronts one with a paradox. On the one hand one is assured by professional geographers that their participation in this tradition has declined precipitously in the course of the past few decades, while on the other one knows that college departments of geography across the nation rely substantially, for justification of their role in general education, upon curricular content springing directly from this tradition. From all the reasons that combine to account for this state of affairs, one may, by selecting only two, go far toward achieving an understanding of this tradition. First, there is the fact that American college geography, growing out of departments of geology in many crucial instances, was at one time greatly overweighted in favor of earth science, thus rendering the field unusually liable to a sense of loss as better balance came into being. (This one-time disproportion found reciprocate support for many years in the narrowed, environmentalistic interpretation of the man-land tradition.) Second, here alone in earth science does one encounter subject matter in the normal sense of the term as one reviews geographic traditions. The spatial tradition abstracts

certain aspects of reality; area studies is distinguished by a point of view; the manland tradition dwells upon relationships; but earth science is identifiable through concrete objects. Historians, sociologists and other academicians tend not only to accept but also to ask for help from this part of geography. They readily appreciate earth science as something physically associated with their subjects of study, yet generally beyond their competence to treat. From this appreciation comes strength for geography-as-earth-science in the curriculum.

Only by granting full stature to the earth science tradition can one make sense out of the oft-repeated addage, "Geography is the mother of sciences." This is the tradition that emerged in ancient Greece, most clearly in the work of Aristotle, as a wide-ranging study of natural processes in and near the surface of the earth. This is the tradition that was rejuvenated by Varenius in the 17th century as "Geographia Generalis." This is the tradition that has been subjected to subdivision as the development of science has approached the present day, yielding mineralogy, paleontology, glaciology, meterology and other specialized fields of learning.

Readers who are acquainted with American junior high schools may want to make a challenge at this point, being aware that a current revival of earth sciences is being sponsored in those schools by the field of geology. Belatedly, geography has joined in support of this revival.[10] It may be said that in this connection and in others, American professional geography may have faltered in its adherence to the earth science tradition but not given it up.

In describing geography, there would appear to be some advantages attached to isolating this final tradition. Separation improves the geographer's chances of successfully explaining to educators why geography has extreme difficulty in accommodating itself to social studies programs. Again, separate attention allows one to make understanding contact with members of the American public for whom surrounding nature is known as the geographic environment. And finally, specific reference to the geographer's earth science tradition brings into the open the basis of what is, almost without a doubt, morally the most significant concept in the entire geographic heritage, that of the earth as a unity, the single common habitat of man.

An Overview
The four traditions though distinct in logic are joined in action. One can say of geography that it pursues concurrently all four of them. Taking the traditions in varying combinations, the geographer can explain the conventional divisions of the field. Human or cultural geography turns out to consist of the first three traditions applied to human societies; physical geography, it becomes evident, is the fourth tradition prosecuted under constraints from the first and second traditions. Going further, one can uncover the meanings of "systematic geography," "regional geography," "urban geography," "industrial geography," etc.

It is to be hoped that through a widened willingness to conceive of and discuss the field in terms of these traditions, geography will be better able to secure the inner unity and outer intelligibility to which reference was made at the opening of this paper, and that thereby the effectiveness of geography's contribution to American education and to the general American welfare will be appreciably increased.

1. William Morris Davis, "An Inductive Study of the Content of Geography," *Bulletin of the American Geographical Society,* Vol. 38, No. 1 (1906), 71.

2. Richard Hartshorne, *The Nature of Geography,* Association of American Geographers (1939), and idem., *Perspective on the Nature of Geography,* Association of American Geographers (1959).

3. The essentials of several of these definitions appear in Barry N. Floyd, "Putting Geography in Its Place," *The Journal of Geography,* Vol. 62, No. 3 (March, 1963). 117–120.

4. William H. Wallace, "Freight Traffic Functions of Anglo-American Railroads," *Annals of the Association of American Geographers,* Vol. 53, No. 3 (September, 1963), 312–331.

5. Fred K. Schaefer, "Exceptionalism in Geography: A Methodological Examination," *Annals of the Association of American Geographers,* Vol. 43, No. 3 (September, 1953), 226–249.

6. James P. Latham, "Methodology for an Instrumental Geographic Analysis," *Annals of the Association of American Geographers,* Vol. 53, No. 2 (June, 1963). 194–209.

7. Hartshorne's 1959 monograph, *Perspective on the Nature of Geography,* was also cited earlier. In this later work, he responds to dissents from geographers whose preferred primary commitment lies outside the area studies tradition.

8. O. H. K. Spate, "Quantity and Quality in Geography," *Annals of the Association of American Geographers,* Vol. 50, No. 4 (December, 1960), 379.

9. Evidence of this dominance may be found in Davis's 1905 declaration: "Any statement is of geographical quality if it contains . . . some relation between an element of inorganic control and one of organic response" (Davis, *loc. cit.*).

10. Geography is represented on both the Steering Committee and Advisory Board of the Earth Science Curriculum Project, potentially the most influential organization acting on behalf of earth science in the schools.

The American Geographies: Losing Our Sense of Place

Americans are fast becoming strangers in a strange land, where one roiling river, one scarred patch of desert, is as good as another. America the beautiful exists— a select few still know it intimately—but many of us are settling for a homogenized national geography.

Barry Lopez

Barry Lopez has written The Rediscovery of North America *(Vintage), and his most recent book is* Field Notes *(Knopf).*

It has become commonplace to observe that Americans know little of the geography of their country, that they are innocent of it as a landscape of rivers, mountains, and towns. They do not know, supposedly, the location of the Delaware Water Gap, the Olympic Mountains, or the Piedmont Plateau; and, the indictment continues, they have little conception of the way the individual components of this landscape are imperiled, from a human perspective, by modern farming practices or industrial pollution.

I do not know how true this is, but it is easy to believe that it is truer than most of us would wish. A recent Gallup Organization and National Geographic Society survey found Americans woefully ignorant of world geography. Three out of four couldn't locate the Persian Gulf. The implication was that we knew no more about our own homeland, and that this ignorance undermined the integrity of our political processes and the efficiency of our business enterprises.

As Americans, we profess a sincere and fierce love for the American landscape, for our rolling prairies, freeflowing rivers, and "purple mountains' majesty"; but it is hard to imagine, actually, where this particular landscape is. It is not just that a nostalgic landscape has passed away—Mark Twain's Mississippi is now dammed from Minnesota to Mis-

souri and the prairies have all been sold and fenced. It is that it has always been a romantic's landscape. In the attenuated form in which it is presented on television today, in magazine articles and in calendar photographs, the essential wildness of the American landscape is reduced to attractive scenery. We look out on a familiar, memorized landscape that portends adventure and promises enrichment. There are no distracting people in it and few artifacts of human life. The animals are all beautiful, diligent, one might even say well-behaved. Nature's unruliness, the power of rivers and skies to intimidate, and any evidence of disastrous human land management practices are all but invisible. It is, in short, a magnificent garden, a colonial vision of paradise imposed on a real place that is, at best, only selectively known.

To truly understand geography requires not only time but a kind of local expertise, an intimacy with place few of us ever develop.

The real American landscape is a face of almost incomprehensible depth and complexity. If one were to sit for a few days, for example, among the ponderosa pine forests and black lava fields of the Cascade Mountains in western Oregon,

inhaling the pines' sweet balm on an evening breeze from some point on the barren rock, and then were to step off to the Olympic Peninsula in Washington, to those rain forests with sphagnum moss floors soft as fleece underfoot and Douglas firs too big around for five people to hug, and then head south to walk the ephemeral creeks and sun-blistered playas of the Mojave Desert in southern California, one would be reeling under the sensations. The contrast is not only one of plants and soils, a different array say, of brilliantly colored beetles. The shock to the senses comes from a different shape to the silence, a difference in the very quality of light, in the weight of the air. And this relatively short journey down the West Coast would still leave the traveler with all that lay to the east to explore—the anomalous sand hills of Nebraska, the heat and frog voices of Okefenokee Swamp, the fetch of Chesapeake Bay, the hardwood copses and black bears of the Ozark Mountains.

No one of these places, of course, can be entirely fathomed, biologically or aesthetically. They are mysteries upon which we impose names. Enchantments. We tick the names off glibly but lovingly. We mean no disrespect. Our genuine desire, though we might be skeptical about the time it would take and uncertain of its practical value to us, is to actually know these places. As deeply ingrained in the American psyche as the desire to conquer and control the land is the desire to sojourn in it, to sail up and down Pamlico Sound, to paddle a canoe through Minnesota's boundary waters, to walk on the desert of the Great Salt Lake, to camp in the stony hardwood valleys of Vermont.

To do this well, to really come to an understanding of a specific American geography, requires not only time but a kind of local expertise, an intimacy with place few of us ever develop. There is no way around the former requirement: If you want to know you must take the time. It is not in books. A specific geographical understanding, however, can be sought out and borrowed. It resides with men and women more or less sworn to a place, who abide there, who have a feel for the soil and history, for the turn of leaves and night sounds. Often they are glad to take the outlander in tow.

These local geniuses of American landscape, in my experience, are people in whom geography thrives. They are the antithesis of geographical ignorance. Rarely known outside their own communities, they often seem, at the first encounter, unremarkable and anonymous. They may not be able to recall the name of a particular wildflower—or they may have given it a name known only to them. They might have forgotten the precise circumstances of a local historical event. Or they can't say for certain when the last of the Canada geese passed through in the fall, or can't differentiate between two kinds of trout in the same creek. Like all of us, they have fallen prey to the fallacies of memory and are burdened with ignorance; but they are nearly flawless in the respect they bear these places they love. Their knowledge is intimate rather than encyclopedic, human but not necessarily scholarly. It rings with the concrete details of experience.

America, I believe, teems with such people. The paradox here, between a faulty grasp of geographical knowledge for which Americans are indicted and the intimate, apparently contradictory familiarity of a group of largely anonymous people, is not solely a matter of confused scale. (The local landscape is easier to know than a national geography.) And it is not simply ironic. The paradox is dark. To be succinct: The politics and advertising that seek a national audience must project a national geography; to be broadly useful that geography must, inevitably, be generalized and it is often romantic. It is therefore frequently misleading and imprecise. The same holds true with the entertainment industry, but here the problem might be clearer. The same films, magazines, and television features

that honor an imaginary American landscape also tout the worth of the anonymous men and women who interpret it. Their affinity for the land is lauded, their local allegiance admired. But the rigor of their local geographies, taken as a whole, contradicts a patriotic, national vision of unspoiled, untroubled land. These men and women are ultimately forgotten, along with the details of the landscapes they speak for, in the face of more pressing national matters. It is the chilling nature of modern society to find an ignorance of geography, local or national, as excusable as an ignorance of hand tools; and to find the commitment of people to their home places only momentarily entertaining. And finally naive.

If one were to pass time among Basawara people in the Kalahari Desert, or with Kreen-Akrora in the Amazon Basin, or with Pitjantjatjara Aborigines in Australia, the most salient impression they might leave is of an absolutely stunning knowledge of their local geography—geology, hydrology, biology, and weather. In short, the extensive particulars of their intercourse with it.

In 40,000 years of human history, it has only been in the last few hundred years or so that a people could afford to ignore their local geographies as completely as we do and still survive. Technological innovations from refrigerated trucks to artificial fertilizers, from sophisticated cost accounting to mass air transportation, have utterly changed concepts of season, distance, soil productivity, and the real cost of drawing sustenance from the land. It is now possible for a resident of Boston to bite into a fresh strawberry in the dead of winter; for someone in San Francisco to travel to Atlanta in a few hours with no worry of how formidable might be crossings of the Great Basin Desert or the Mississippi River; for an absentee farmer to gain a tax advantage from a farm that leaches poisons into its water table and on which crops are left to rot. The Pitjantjatjara might shake their heads in bewilderment and bemusement, not because they are primitive or ignorant people, not because they have no sense of irony or are incapable of marveling, but because they have not (many would say not yet) realized a world in which such manipulation of the land—surmounting the imperatives of distance it imposes, for example, or turning the large-scale destruction of forests and arable land in wealth—is desirable or plausible.

In the years I have traveled through America, in cars and on horseback, on foot and by raft, I have repeatedly been brought to a sudden state of awe by some gracile or savage movement of animal, some odd wrapping of tree's foliage by the wind, an unimpeded run of dew-laden prairie stretching to a horizon flat as a coin where a pin-dot sun pales the dawn sky pink. I know these things are beyond intellection, that they are the vivid edges of a world that includes but also transcends the human world. In memory, when I dwell on these things, I know that in a truly national literature there should be odes to the Triassic reds of the Colorado Plateau, to the sharp and ghostly light of the Florida Keys, to the aeolian soils of southern Minnesota, and the Palouse in Washington, though the modern mind abjures the literary potential of such subjects. (If the sand and flood water farmers of Arizona and New Mexico were to take the black loams of Louisiana in their hands they would be flabbergasted, and that is the beginning of literature.) I know there should be eloquent evocations of the cobbled beaches of Maine, the plutonic walls of the Sierra Nevada, the orange canyons of the Kaibab Plateau. I have no doubt, in fact, that there are. They are as numerous and diverse as the eyes and fingers that ponder the country—it is that only a handful of them are known. The great majority are to be found in drawers and boxes, in the letters and private journals of millions of workaday people who have regarded their encounters with the land as an engagement bordering on the spiritual, as being fundamentally linked to their state of health.

One cannot acknowledge the extent and the history of this kind of testimony without being forced to the realization that something strange, if not dangerous, is afoot. Year by year, the number of people with firsthand experience in the land dwindles. Rural populations continue to shift to the cities. The family farm is in a state of demise, and government and industry continue to apply pressure on the native peoples of North America to sever their ties with the land. In the wake of this loss of personal and local knowledge from which a real geography is derived, the knowledge on which a country must ultimately stand, has [be]come something hard to define but I think sinister and unsettling—the packaging and marketing of land as a form of entertainment. An incipient industry, capitalizing on the nostalgia Americans feel for the imagined virgin landscapes of their fathers, and on a desire for adventure, now offers people a convenient though sometimes incomplete or even spurious geography as an inducement to purchase a unique experience. But the line between authentic experience and a superficial exposure to the elements of experience is blurred. And the real landscape, in all its complexity, is distorted even further in the public imagination. No longer innately mysterious and dignified, a ground from which experience grows, it becomes a curiously generic backdrop on which experience is imposed.

In theme parks the profound, subtle, and protracted experience of running a river is reduced to a loud, quick, safe equivalence, a pleasant distraction. People only able to venture into the countryside on annual vacations are, increasingly, schooled in the belief that wild land will, and should, provide thrills and exceptional scenery on a timely basis. If it does not, something is wrong, either with the land itself or possibly with the company outfitting the trip.

People in America, then, face a convoluted situation. The land itself, vast and differentiated, defies the notion of a national geography. If applied at all it must be applied lightly and it must grow out of the concrete detail of local geographies. Yet Americans are daily presented with, and have become accustomed to talking about, a homogenized national geography. one that seems to operate independently of the land, a collection of objects rather than a continuous bolt of fabric. It appears in advertisements, as a background in movies, and in patriotic calendars. The suggestion is that there can be national geography because the constituent parts are interchangeable and can be treated as commodities. In day-to-day affairs, in other words, one place serves as well as another to convey one's point. On reflection, this is an appalling condescension and a terrible imprecision, the very antithesis of knowledge. The idea that either the Green River in Utah or the Salmon River in Idaho will do, or that the valleys of Kentucky and West Virginia are virtually interchangeable, is not just misleading. For people still dependent on the soil for their sustenance, or for people whose memories tie them to those places, it betrays a numbing casualness, a utilitarian, expedient, and commercial

frame of mind. It heralds a society in which it is no longer necessary for human beings to know where they live, except as those places are described and fixed by numbers. The truly difficult and lifelong task of discovering where one lives is finally disdained.

If a society forgets or no longer cares where it lives, then anyone with the political power and the will to do so can manipulate the landscape to conform to certain social ideals or nostalgic visions. People may hardly notice that anything has happened, or assume that whatever happens—a mountain stripped of timber and eroding into its creeks—is for the common good. The more superficial a society's knowledge of the real dimensions of the land it occupies becomes, the more vulnerable the land is to exploitation, to manipulation for short-term gain. The land, virtually powerless before political and commercial entities, finds itself finally with no defenders. It finds itself bereft of intimates with indispensable, concrete knowledge. (Oddly, or perhaps not oddly, while American society continues to value local knowledge as a quaint part of its heritage, it continues to cut such people off from any real political power. This is as true for small farmers and illiterate cowboys as it is for American Indians, native Hawaiians, and Eskimos.)

The intense pressure of imagery in America, and the manipulation of images necessary to a society with specific goals, means the land will inevitably be treated like a commodity; and voices that tend to contradict the proffered image will, one way or another, be silenced or discredited by those in power. This is not new to America; the promulgation in America of a false or imposed geography has been the case from the beginning. All local geographies, as they were defined by hundreds of separate, independent native traditions, were denied in the beginning in favor of an imported and unifying vision of America's natural history. The country, the landscape itself, was eventually defined according to dictates of Progress like Manifest Destiny, and laws like the Homestead Act which reflected a poor understanding of the physical lay of the land.

When I was growing up in southern California, I formed the rudiments of a local geography—eucalyptus trees, February rains, Santa Ana winds. I lost much of it when my family moved to New York City, a move typical of the

modern, peripatetic style of American life, responding to the exigencies of divorce and employment. As a boy I felt a hunger to know the American landscape that was extreme; when I was finally able to travel on my own, I did so. Eventually I visited most of the United States, living for brief periods of time in Arizona, Indiana, Alabama, Georgia, Wyoming, New Jersey, and Montana before settling 20 years ago in western Oregon.

The astonishing level of my ignorance confronted me everywhere I went. I knew early on that the country could not be held together in a few phrases, that its geography was ,magnificent and incomprehensible, that a man or woman could devote a lifetime to its elucidation and still feel in the end that he had but sailed many thousands of miles over the surface of the ocean. So I came into the habit of traversing landscapes I wanted to know with local tutors and reading what had previously been written about, and in, those places. I came to value exceedingly novels and essays and works of nonfiction that connected human enterprise to real and specific places, and I grew to be mildly distrustful of work that occurred in no particular place, work so cerebral and detached as to be refutable only in an argument of ideas.

These sojourns in various corners of the country infused me, somewhat to my surprise on thinking about it, with a great sense of hope. Whatever despair I had come to feel at a waning sense of the real land and the emergence of false geographies—elements of the land being manipulated, for example, to create erroneous but useful patterns in advertising—was dispelled by the depth of a single person's local knowledge, by the serenity that seemed to come with that intelligence. Any harm that might be done by people who cared nothing for the land, to whom it was not innately worthy but only something ultimately for sale, I thought, would one day have to meet this kind of integrity, people with the same dignity and transcendence as the land they occupied. So when I traveled, when I rolled my sleeping bag out on the shores of the Beaufort Sea, or in the high pastures of the Absaroka Range in Wyoming, or at the bottom of the Grand Canyon, I absorbed those particular testaments to life, the indigenous color and songbird song, the smell of sun-bleached rock, damp earth, and wild honey, with some crude appreciation of the singular magnificence of each of those places. And the reassurance I felt expanded in the knowledge that there were, and would likely always be, people speaking out whenever they felt the dignity of the Earth imperiled in those places.

The promulgation of false geographies, which threaten the fundamental notion of what it means to live somewhere, is a current with a stable and perhaps growing countercurrent. People living in New York City are familiar with the stone basements, the cratonic geology, of that island and have a feeling for birds migrating through in the fall, their sequence and number. They do not find the city alien but human, its attenuated natural history merely different from that of rural Georgia or Kansas. I find the countermeasure, too, among Eskimos who cannot read but who might engage you for days on the subtleties of sea-ice topography. And among men and women who, though they have followed in the footsteps of their parents, have come to the conclusion that they cannot farm or fish or log in the way their ancestors did; the finite boundaries to this sort of wealth have appeared in their lifetime. Or among young men and women who have taken several decades of book-learned agronomy, zoology, silviculture and horticulture, ecology, ethnobotany, and fluvial geomorphology and turned it into a new kind of local knowledge, who have taken up residence in a place and sought, both because of and in spite of their education, to develop a deep intimacy with it. Or they have gone to work, idealistically, for the National Park Service or the fish and wildlife services or for a private institution like the Nature Conservancy. They are people to whom the land is more than politics and economics. These are people for whom the land is alive. It feeds them, directly, and that is how and why they learn its geography.

In the end, then, if one begins among the blue crabs of Chesapeake Bay and wanders for several years, down through the Smoky Mountains and back to the bluegrass hills, along the drainages of the Ohio and into the hill country of Missouri, where in summer a chorus of cicadas might drown out human conversation, then up the Missouri itself, reading on the way the entries of Meriwether Lewis and William Clark and musing on the demise of the plains grizzly and the sturgeon, crosses west into the drainage of the Platte and spends the evenings with Gene Weltfish's *The Lost Universe,*

her book about the Pawnee who once thrived there, then drops south to the Palo Duro Canyon and the irrigated farms of the Llano Estacado in Texas, turns west across the Sangre de Cristo, southernmost of the Rocky Mountain ranges, and moves north and west up onto the slickrock mesas of Utah, those browns and oranges, the ocherous hues reverberating in the deep canyons, then goes north, swinging west to the insular ranges that sit like battleships in the pelagic space of Nevada, camps at the steaming edge of the sulfur springs in the Black Rock desert, where alkaline pans are glazed with a ferocious light, a heat to melt iron, then crosses the northern Sierra Nevada, waist-deep in summer snow in the passes, to descend to the valley of the Sacramento, and rises through groves of the elephantine redwoods in the Coast Range, to arrive at Cape Mendocino, before Balboa's Pacific, cormorants and gulls, gray whales headed north for Unimak Pass in the Aleutians, the winds crashing down on you, facing the ocean over the blue ocean that gives the scene its true vastness, making this crossing, having been so often astonished at the line and the color of the land, the ingenious lives of its plants and animals, the varieties of its darknesses, the intensity of the stars overhead, you would be ashamed to discover, then, in yourself, any capacity to focus on ravages in the land that left you unsettled. You would have seen so much, breathtaking, startling, and outsize, that you might not be able for a long time to break the spell, the sense, especially finishing your journey in the West, that the land had not been as rearranged or quite as compromised as you had first imagined.

After you had slept some nights on the beach, however, with that finite line of the ocean before you and the land stretching out behind you, the wind first battering then cradling you, you would be compelled by memory, obligated by your own involvement, to speak of what left you troubled. To find the rivers dammed and shrunken, the soil washed away, the land fenced, a tracery of pipes and wires and roads laid down everywhere and animals, cutting the eye off repeatedly and confining it—you had expected this. It troubles you no more than your despair over the ruthlessness, the insensitivity, the impetuousness of modern life. What underlies this obvious change, however, is a less noticeable pattern of disruption: acidic lakes, the

skies empty of birds, fouled beaches, the poisonous slags of industry, the sun burning like a molten coin in ruined air.

It is a tenet of certain ideologies that man is responsible for all that is ugly, that everything nature creates is beautiful. Nature's darkness goes partly unreported, of course, and human brilliance is often perversely ignored. What is true is that man has a power, literally beyond his comprehension, to destroy. The lethality of some of what he manufactures, the incompetence with which he stores it or seeks to dispose of it, the cavalier way in which he employs in his daily living substances that threaten his health, the leniency of the courts in these matters (as though products as well as people enjoyed the protection of the Fifth Amendment), and the treatment of open land, rivers, and the atmosphere as if, in some medieval way they could still be regarded as disposal sinks of infinite capacity, would make you wonder, standing face to in the wind at Cape Mendocino, if we weren't bent on an errant of madness.

The geographies of North America, the myriad small landscapes that make up the national fabric, are threatened—by ignorance of what makes them unique, by utilitarian attitudes, by failure to include them in the moral universe, and by brutal disregard. A testament of minor voices can clear away an ignorance of any place, can inform us of its special qualities; but no voice, by merely telling a story, can cause the poisonous wastes that saturate some parts of the land to decompose, to evaporate. This responsibility falls ultimately to the national community, a vague and fragile entity to be sure, but one that, in America, can be ferocious in exerting its will.

Geography, the formal way in which we grapple with this areal mystery, is finally knowledge that calls up something in the land we recognize and respond to. It gives us a sense of place and a sense of community. Both are indispensable to a state of well-being, an individual's and a country's.

One afternoon on the Siuslaw River in the Coast Range of Oregon, in January, I hooked a steelhead, a sea-run trout, that told me, through the muscles of my hands and arms and shoulders, something of the nature of the thing I was calling "the Siuslaw River." Years ago I had stood under a pecan tree in Upson County, Georgia, idly eating the nuts, when slowly it occurred to me that these nuts would taste different from pecans growing somewhere up in South Carolina. I didn't need a sharp sense of taste to know this, only to pay attention at a level no one had ever told me was necessary. One November dawn, long before the sun rose, I began a vigil at the Dumont Dunes in the Mojave Desert in California, which I kept until a few minutes after the sun broke the horizon. During that time I named to myself the colors by which the sky changed and by which the sand itself flowed like a rising tide through grays and silvers and blues into yellows, pinks, washed duns, and fallow beiges.

It is through the power of observation, the gifts of eye and ear, of tongue and nose and finger, that a place first rises up in our mind; afterward, it is memory that carries the place, that allows it to grow in depth and complexity. For as long as our records go back, we have held these two things dear, landscape and memory. Each infuses us with a different kind of life. The one feeds us, figuratively and literally. The other protects us from lies and tyranny. To keep landscapes intact and the memory of them, our history in them, alive, seems as imperative a task in modern time as finding the extent to which individual expression can be accommodated, before it threatens to destroy the fabric of society.

If I were now to visit another country, I would ask my local companion, before I saw any museum or library, any factory or fabled town, to walk me in the country of his or her youth, to tell me the names of things and how, traditionally, they have been fitted together in a community. I would ask for the stories, the voice of memory over the land. I would ask about the history of storms there, the age of the trees, the winter color of the hills. Only then would I ask to see the museum. I would want first the sense of a real place, to know that I was not inhabiting an idea. I would want to know the lay of the land first, the real geography, and take some measure of the love of it in my companion before stood before the painting or read works of scholarship. I would want to have something real and remembered against which I might hope to measure their truth.

Apocalypse Soon, or, Why Human Geography Is Worth Doing

Nigel Thrift

Nigel Thrift, Professor of Geography, University of Bristol, UK

A German philosopher once said that by the end of this century we would no longer be talking about how to improve the world but about how to save it. As that time approaches, so this statement rings increasingly true; we are in a race to save the world.

Is this blowing things out of proportion? The answer has to be no. Consider just the four most important global problems that currently sustain the interest of human geographers. Each one of them has serious consequences on its own. But put them together and we are presented with a truly frightening prospect. Not apocalypse now, but apocalypse soon.

The first of these problems is damage to the environment. The natural environment has been treated like a toy for so long that we are still surprised that it can bite back. Now we have to put the damage to rights or pay the consequences like global warming, loss of species and the exhaustion of finite resources. This will be a gargantuan task but it is not an impossible one. After all, nearly all damage to the environment is the result of *social* causes. In developing countries, the uneven distribution of land ownership leads to the massing of poor people on marginal land and to that land's eventual exhaustion; as more and more poor people try to eke a living from the land, so they kill both it and eventually themselves. In countries with planned economies, the result of a remorseless push to industrialize without regard to consequent problems of environmental pollution has been dead rivers and shrinking lakes. Developed countries cannot look smugly on. For example, much of the western United States has become a water welfare state. Water has been assumed to be a free and unending resource. The result is that aquifers are drying up and salt deposits are spreading.

The second problem consists of an acceptance of debt as a way of life. Since the 1960s we have grown used to a world dominated by a financial system whose chief purpose is to produce mountains of debt and then recycle them at ever greater speeds, producing more mountains of debt in the process. We tend to assume that this newest, highest and fastest-growing of all mountain ranges is somehow inevitable. But it also represents a future that has been mortgaged. Many of the developing countries found this out in the 1980s, as they battled with debts that were taking up, on average, 60 percent of gross national product (GNP). Many people, especially children, died so that the interest on these debts could be paid. Some developed countries are now in harm's way too. After a spending spree in the 1980s, the United States has a trillion dollar national debt, and another trillion dollars in liabilities is just beginning to show through. Financing these debts is going to be very difficult in a world of high interest rates caused by Japan's and Germany's increasing concern for problems in their own backyard and a corresponding lack of interest in bailing the United States out. The developing country debt crisis and the United States debt crisis are only two of many crises that have plagued the new world financial system in the last decade. The concern is that this system is now so inured to crisis that, when the big one arrives, no one will recognize it as such.

The third problem is the 'informational revolution'. We are undoubtedly going through a period of major technological change. There are epic shifts going on in the world of electronics and telecommunications that now rival in scale and importance the original industrial revolution. Instead of the growth of railways, we see the expansion of global digital highways, massive 'smart' networks of fibre-optic cables and satellite links. Instead of the growth of larger and larger industrial combines, we see the rise of 'flexible' firms, networks of subcontracts and alliances tightly co-ordinated by information technology and harnessed to flexible production systems. Instead of the growth of markets attuned first and foremost to the imperatives of production we are witness to the advent of markets where, through information technology, the consumer is truly sovereign. In each case, what defines this new industrial revolution's 'space of flows' is speed—whether it is in the form of a more rapid response to changing market conditions, more and then more truncated product cycles and more rapidly changing markets. Speed is of the essence in this brave new industrial world but it is also, because it brings with it yet higher levels of production and consumption, a problem.

The final problem is one of estrangement. We live in a world in which, through the growth of mass media like television, people are able to know more of what is going on in the world and share more experiences and signs than ever before. But the potential for greater understanding between peoples has hardly been realized: instead it sometimes seems that what are being built are new ways of identifying strangers. Blind nationalisms, ugly racisms, pathetic sexisms, and religious bigotry still persist and thrive for many and various reasons; perhaps because mutual links between people are too often reduced to a visual contact, perhaps because new forms of tolerance of others are a thinly disguised excuse for ignoring them, perhaps because old traditions of disparagement are so engrained. Whatever and wherever the case, it is clear that human difference is still treated with great suspicion.

To summarize, we live in a world that is hooked on risk. There is the risk of environmental catastrophe. There is the risk of falling into a financial abyss. There is the risk that the informational revolution will turn the world into a private playground for a few corporate giants. And there is the risk that no one will care sufficiently about what is going on elsewhere in the world to tackle these other risks. In Hans Magnus Enzensberger's (1990, p. 142) words, what we need is a 'managed retreat' from this world of risks and more risks, away from the old certainties which have only bred uncertainties.

All very dramatic. But what contributions can human geography make to this retreat? More than might be

thought, perhaps. First of all, it is these four different but interconnected risks which will form the chief areas of research in human geography over the next decade. A human geography of the environmental crisis is being formed around notions like political ecology and Gaia, one that stresses the interdependence of society and ecology (Blaikie, 1985); Emel and Peet, 1989; O'Riordan, 1989). A human geography of finance and debt is being put together, one that recognizes the monumental importance of money in the modern world, but one that is not mesmerized by the glamour of the dealing room (Thrift and Leyshon, 1987, 1992; Harvey, 1989; Corbridge and Agnew, 1991). A human geography of the informational revolution is also being constructed, one that is as aware of the spatial divisions that are being fostered by this revolution as it is of the way that the world is being drawn into a unified space of corporate flows of information (Massey, 1984; Castells, 1989; Cooke, 1989, 1990). And last but not least, a human geography of estrangement is being forged out of work on subjects like gender, race, culture and the state, one that is alive to the importance of places as a means through which people make the world and are made by it but which also recognizes that this process is no longer purely local (Jackson, 1989; Peet and Thrift, 1989; Wolch and Dear, 1989; Thrift, 1990). In the words of Frederic Jameson (1988, p. 349) human 'experience no longer coincides with the place in which it takes place'.

Another contribution that human geography can make comes from its very nature as a subject. Human geography has always been a science of difference: if there were no different people and places to describe, explain and appreciate there would be no human geography to write and draw. So human geography comes naturally to stressing the growing interdependence between places and yet, at the same time, valuing all the differences that still exist which give these places their unique worth. Concomitantly, it comes easily to the job of stressing that the differences between the people in these

places can unite as well as divide. In other words, the task of communicating about people and places, so that other people in other places realize that they exist as more than just ciphers on a screen, has become more pressing than ever.

A third contribution again comes from the nature of human geography. Human geography has always been an intensely practical project. In the past, at its worst, this made for a rather stodgy subject, frightened to move away from immediate issues and with a tendency to kowtow to authority. But the advent of a proper theoretical tradition (e.g. Gregory and Urry, 1985; Peet and Thrift, 1989) has combined with the old rough-and-readiness to produce a mixture of theoretical foresight and practical analytical skills which is well suited to the times we now live in. Human geography is now down-to-earth in the best possible sense.

To conclude, human geography is a deadly serious pursuit. The state of the world demands it. But it is important to remember that it is not all about gloom and doom. Human geography also takes from its past the sense of optimism that possessed the explorers who helped to found the subject. It is a sense that around the next corner will be something interesting, even redemptive. After all, it is important to believe that there is a way out of the current dilemmas that the world faces. What we need to do now is find the right maps.

References

Blaikie, P. 1985: *The Political Economy of Soil Erosion in Developing Countries.* London: Longman.
Castells, M. 1989: *The Informational City.* Oxford: Basil Blackwell.
Cooke, P. (ed.) 1989: *Localities.* London: Unwin Hyman.
— —1990: *Back to the Future.* London: Unwin Hyman.
Corbridge, S. and Agnew, J. 1991: The US trade and budget deficits in global perspective. *Environment and Planning D: Society and Space,* 9, 71–90.
Emel, J. and Peet, R. 1989: Resource management and natural hazards. In R. Peet and N. J. Thrift (eds), *New Models in Geography, Vol. 1,* London: Urwin Hyman, 49–76.
Enzensberger, H. M. 1990: The state of Europe. *Granta,* 30, 136–42.

1. GEOGRAPHY IN A CHANGING WORLD

Gregory, D. and Urry, J. (eds), 1985: *Social Relations and Spatial Structures.* London: Macmillan.

Harvey, D. 1989: *The Condition of Postmodernity.* Oxford: Basil Blackwell.

Jackson, P. 1989: *Maps of Meaning.* London: Unwin Hyman.

Jameson, F. 1988: Cognitive mapping. In G. Nelson and L. Grossberg (eds), *Marxism and the Interpretation of Culture,* Urbana, IL: Macmillan 347–60.

Massey, D. 1984: *Spatial Divisions of Labour.* London: Macmillan.

Models in Geography, Vol. 2, London: Unwin Hyman, 77–102.

Peet, R. and Thrift, N. J. (eds), 1989: *New Models in Geography,* 2 vols. London: Urwin Hyman.

Thrift, N. J. 1990: Taking aim at the heart of the region. In D. Gregory, R. Martin and G. Smith (eds), *Geography in the Social Sciences,* London: Macmillan.

—— and Leyshon, A. 1987: The gambling propensity: bankers, developing country debt exposures and the new international financial system. *Geoforum,* 19, 55–69.

—— and Leyshon, A. 1992: *Making Money.* London: Routledge.

Wolch, J. and Dear, M. (eds), 1989: *The Power of Geography,* London: Unwin Hyman.

The Coming Anarchy

Robert D. Kaplan

Robert D. Kaplan is a contributing editor of The Atlantic Monthly.

The Minister's eyes were like egg yolks, an after-effect of some of the many illnesses, malaria especially, endemic in his country. There was also an irrefutable sadness in his eyes. He spoke in a slow and creaking voice, the voice of hope about to expire. Flame trees, coconut palms, and a ballpoint-blue Atlantic composed the background. None of it seemed beautiful, though. "In forty-five years I have never seen things so bad. We did not manage ourselves well after the British departed. But what we have now is something worse—the revenge of the poor, of the social failures, of the people least able to bring up children in a modern society." Then he referred to the recent coup in the West African country Sierra Leone. "The boys who took power in Sierra Leone come from houses like this." The Minister jabbed his finger at a corrugated metal shack teeming with children. "In three months these boys confiscated all the official Mercedes, Volvos, BMWs and willfully wrecked them on the road." The Minister mentioned one of the coup's leaders, Solomon Anthony Joseph Musa, who shot the people who had paid for his schooling, "in order to erase the humiliation and mitigate the power his middle-class sponsors held over him."

Tyranny is nothing new in Sierra Leone or in the rest of West Africa. But it is now part and parcel of an increasing lawlessness that is far more significant than any coup, rebel incursion, or episodic experiment in democracy. Crime was what my friend—a top-ranking African official whose life would be threatened were I to identify him more precisely—really wanted to talk about. Crime is what makes West Africa a natural point of departure for my report on what the political character of our planet is likely to be in the twenty-first century.

The cities of West Africa at night are some of the unsafest places in the world. Streets are unlit; the police often lack gasoline for their vehicles; armed burglars, carjackers, and muggers proliferate. . . . Direct flights between the United States and the Murtala Muhammed Airport, in neighboring Nigeria's largest city, Lagos, have been suspended by order of the U.S. Secretary of Transportation because of ineffective security at the terminal and its environs. A State Department report cited the airport for "extortion by law-enforcement and immigration officials." This is one of the few times that the U.S. government has embargoed a foreign airport for reasons that are linked purely to crime. In Abidjan, effectively the capital of the Côte d'Ivoire, or Ivory Coast, restaurants have stick- and gun-wielding guards who walk you the fifteen feet or so between your car and the entrance, giving you an eerie taste of what American cities might be like in the future. An Italian ambassador was killed by gunfire when robbers invaded an Abidjan restaurant. The family of the Nigerian ambassador was tied up and robbed at gunpoint in the ambassador's residence. After university students in the Ivory Coast caught bandits who had been plaguing their dorms, they executed them by hanging tires around their necks and setting the tires on fire. In one instance Ivorian policemen stood by and watched the "necklacings," afraid to intervene. Each time I went to the Abidjan bus terminal, groups of young men with restless, scanning eyes surrounded my taxi, putting their hands all over the windows, demanding "tips" for carrying my luggage even though I had only a rucksack. In cities in six West African countries I saw similar young men everywhere—hordes of them. They were like loose molecules in a very unstable social fluid, a fluid that was clearly on the verge of igniting. . . .

Adapted from *The Atlantic Monthly*, February 1994, pp. 44-76. © 1994 by Robert D. Kaplan. Reprinted by permission.

1. GEOGRAPHY IN A CHANGING WORLD

A PREMONITION OF THE FUTURE

West Africa is becoming *the* symbol of worldwide demographic, environmental, and societal stress, in which criminal anarchy emerges as the real "strategic" danger. Disease, overpopulation, unprovoked crime, scarcity of resources, refugee migrations, the increasing erosion of nation-states and international borders, and the empowerment of private armies, security firms, and international drug cartels are now most tellingly demonstrated through a West African prism. West Africa provides an appropriate introduction to the issues, often extremely unpleasant to discuss, that will soon confront our civilization. To remap the political earth the way it will be a few decades hence—as I intend to do in this article—I find I must begin with West Africa.

There is no other place on the planet where political maps are so deceptive—where, in fact, they tell such lies—as in West Africa. Start with Sierra Leone. According to the map, it is a nation-state of defined borders, with a government in control of its territory. In truth the Sierra Leonian government, run by a twenty-seven-year-old army captain, Valentine Strasser, controls Freetown by day and by day also controls part of the rural interior. In the government's territory the national army is an unruly rabble threatening drivers and passengers at most checkpoints. In the other part of the country units of two separate armies from the war in Liberia have taken up residence, as has an army of Sierra Leonian rebels. The government force fighting the rebels is full of renegade commanders who have aligned themselves with disaffected village chiefs. A premodern formlessness governs the battlefield, evoking the wars in medieval Europe prior to the 1648 Peace of Westphalia, which ushered in the era of organized nation-states.

As a consequence, roughly 400,000 Sierra Leonians are internally displaced, 280,000 more have fled to neighboring Guinea, and another 100,000 have fled to Liberia, even as 400,000 Liberians have fled to Sierra Leone. The third largest city in Sierra Leone, Gondama, is a displaced-persons camp. With an additional 600,000 Liberians in Guinea and 250,000 in the Ivory Coast, the borders dividing these four countries have become largely meaningless. Even in quiet zones none of the governments except the Ivory Coast's maintains the schools, bridges, roads, and police forces in a manner necessary for functional sovereignty. . . .

In Sierra Leone, as in Guinea, as in the Ivory Coast, as in Ghana, most of the primary rain forest and the secondary bush is being destroyed at an alarming rate. I saw convoys of trucks bearing majestic hardwood trunks to coastal ports. When

Sierra Leone achieved its independence, in 1961, as much as 60 percent of the country was primary rain forest. Now six percent is. In the Ivory Coast the proportion has fallen from 38 percent to eight percent. The deforestation has led to soil erosion, which has led to more flooding and more mosquitos. Virtually everyone in the West African interior has some form of malaria.

Sierra Leone is a microcosm of what is occurring, albeit in a more tempered and gradual manner, throughout West Africa and much of the underdeveloped world: the withering away of central governments, the rise of tribal and regional domains, the unchecked spread of disease, and the growing pervasiveness of war. West Africa is reverting to the Africa of the Victorian atlas. It consists now of a series of coastal trading posts, such as Freetown and Conakry, and an interior that, owing to violence, volatility, and disease, is again becoming, as Graham Greene once observed, "blank" and "unexplored." However, whereas Greene's vision implies a certain romance, as in the somnolent and charmingly seedy Freetown of his celebrated novel *The Heart of the Matter,* it is Thomas Malthus, the philosopher of demographic doomsday, who is now the prophet of West Africa's future. And West Africa's future, eventually, will also be that of most of the rest of the world.

Consider "Chicago." I refer not to Chicago, Illinois, but to a slum district of Abidjan, which the young toughs in the area have named after the American city. ("Washington" is another poor section of Abidjan.) Although Sierra Leone is widely regarded as beyond salvage, the Ivory Coast has been considered an African success story, and Abidjan has been called "the Paris of West Africa." Success, however, was built on two artificial factors: the high price of cocoa, of which the Ivory Coast is the world's leading producer, and the talents of a French expatriate community, whose members have helped run the government and the private sector. The expanding cocoa economy made the Ivory Coast a magnet for migrant workers from all over West Africa: between a third and a half of the country's population is now non-Ivorian, and the figure could be as high as 75 percent in Abidjan. During the 1980s cocoa prices fell and the French began to leave. The skyscrapers of the Paris of West Africa are a façade. Perhaps 15 percent of Abidjan's population of three million people live in shantytowns like Chicago and Washington, and the vast majority live in places that are not much better. Not all of these places appear on any of the readily available maps. This is another indication of how political maps are the products of tired conventional wisdom and, in the Ivory Coast's case, of an elite that will ultimately be forced to relinquish power.

Chicago, like more and more of Abidjan, is a slum in the bush: a checkerwork of corrugated zinc roofs and walls made of cardboard and black plastic wrap. It is located in a gully teeming with coconut palms and oil palms, and is ravaged by flooding. Few residents have easy access to electricity, a sewage system, or a clean water supply. The crumbly red laterite earth crawls with foot-long lizards both inside and outside the shacks. Children defecate in a stream filled with garbage and pigs, droning with malarial mosquitoes. In this stream women do the washing. Young unemployed men spend their time drinking beer, palm wine, and gin while gambling on pinball games constructed out of rotting wood and rusty nails. These are the same youths who rob houses in more prosperous Ivorian neighborhoods at night. . . .

Fifty-five percent of the Ivory Coast's population is urban, and the proportion is expected to reach 62 percent by 2000. The yearly net population growth is 3.6 percent. This means that the Ivory Coast's 13.5 million people will become 39 million by 2025, when much of the population will consist of urbanized peasants like those of Chicago. But don't count on the Ivory Coast's still existing then. Chicago, which is more indicative of Africa's and the Third World's demographic present—and even more of the future—than any idyllic junglescape of women balancing earthen jugs on their heads, illustrates why the Ivory Coast, once a model of Third World success, is becoming a case study in Third World catastrophe.

President Félix Houphouët-Boigny, who died last December at the age of about ninety, left behind a weak cluster of political parties and a leaden bureaucracy that discourages foreign investment. Because the military is small and the non-Ivorian population large, there is neither an obvious force to maintain order nor a sense of nationhood that would lessen the need for such enforcement. The economy has been shrinking since the mid-1980s. Though the French are working assiduously to preserve stability, the Ivory Coast faces a possibility worse than a coup: an anarchic implosion of criminal violence—an urbanized version of what has already happened in Somalia. Or it may become an African Yugoslavia, but one without mini-states to replace the whole.

Because the demographic reality of West Africa is a countryside draining into dense slums by the coast, ultimately the region's rulers will come to reflect the values of these shantytowns. There are signs of this already in· Sierra Leone—and in Togo, where the dictator Etienne Eyadema, in power since 1967, was nearly toppled in 1991, not by democrats but by thousands of youths whom the London-based magazine *West Africa* described as "Soweto-like stone-throwing adolescents." Their behavior may herald a regime more brutal than Eyadema's repressive one. . . .

Ali A. Mazrui, the director of the Institute of Global Cultural Studies at the State University of New York at Binghamton, predicts that West Africa—indeed, the whole continent—is on the verge of large-scale border upheaval. Mazrui writes,

> In the 21st century France will be withdrawing from West Africa as she gets increasingly involved in the affairs [of Europe]. France's West African sphere of influence will be filled by Nigeria—a more natural hegemonic power. . . .It will be under those circumstances that Nigeria's own boundaries are likely to expand to incorporate the Republic of Niger (the Hausa link), the Republic of Benin (the Yoruba link) and conceivably Cameroon.

The future could be more tumultuous, and bloodier, than Mazrui dares to say. France *will* withdraw from former colonies like Benin, Togo, Niger, and the Ivory Coast, where it has been propping up local currencies. It will do so not only because its attention will be diverted to new challenges in Europe and Russia but also because younger French officials lack the older generation's emotional ties to the ex-colonies. However, even as Nigeria attempts to expand it, too, is likely to split into several pieces. The State Department's Bureau of Intelligence and Research recently made the following points in an analysis of Nigeria:

> Prospects for a transition to civilian rule and democratization are slim. . . . The repressive apparatus of the state security service . . . will be difficult for any future civilian government to control. . . . The country is becoming increasingly ungovernable. . . . Ethnic and regional splits are deepening, a situation made worse by an increase in the number of states from 19 to 30 and a doubling in the number of local governing authorities; religious cleavages are more serious; Muslim fundamentalism and evangelical Christian militancy are on the rise; and northern Muslim anxiety over southern [Christian] control of the economy is intense . . . the will to keep Nigeria together is now very weak.

Given that oil-rich Nigeria is a bellwether for the region—its population of roughly 90 million equals the populations of all the other West African states combined—it is apparent that Africa faces cataclysms that could make the Ethiopian and Somalian famines pale in comparison. This is especially so because Nigeria's population, including that of its largest city, Lagos, whose crime, pollution, and overcrowding make it the cliché par excellence of Third World urban dysfunction, is set to double during the next twenty-five years, while the country continues to deplete its natural resources.

1. GEOGRAPHY IN A CHANGING WORLD

Part of West Africa's quandary is that although its population belts are horizontal [east-west], with habitation densities increasing as one travels south away from the Sahara and toward the tropical abundance of the Atlantic littoral, the borders erected by European colonialists are vertical [north-south], and therefore at cross-purposes with demography and topography. . . . [I]ndeed, the entire stretch of coast from Abidjan eastward to Lagos—is one burgeoning megalopolis that by any rational economic and geographical standard should constitute a single sovereignty, rather than the five (the Ivory Coast, Ghana, Togo, Benin, and Nigeria) into which it is currently divided.

As many internal African borders begin to crumble, a more impenetrable boundary is being erected that threatens to isolate the continent as a whole: the wall of disease. Merely to visit West Africa in some degree of safety, I spent about $500 for a hepatitis B vaccination series and other disease prophylaxis. Africa may today be more dangerous in this regard than it was in 1862, before antibiotics, when the explorer Sir Richard Francis Burton described the health situation on the continent as "deadly." . . . Of the approximately 12 million people worldwide whose blood is HIV-positive, 8 million are in Africa. In the capital of the Ivory Coast, whose modern road system only helps spread the disease, 10 percent of the population is HIV-positive. And war and refugee movements help the virus break through to more-remote areas of Africa. Alan Greenberg, M.D., a representative of the Centers of Disease Control in Abidjan, explains that in Africa the HIV virus and tuberculosis are now "fast-forwarding each other." Of the approximately 4,000 newly diagnosed tuberculosis patients in Abidjan, 45 were also found to be HIV-positive. As African birth rates soar and slums proliferate, some experts worry that viral mutations and hybridizations might, just conceivably, result in a form of the AIDS virus that is easier to catch than the present strain.

It is malaria that is most responsible for the disease wall that threatens to separate Africa and other parts of the Third World from more-developed regions of the planet in the twenty-first century. Carried by mosquitoes, malaria, unlike AIDS, is easy to catch. Most people in sub-Saharan Africa have recurring bouts of the disease throughout their entire lives, and it is mutating into increasingly deadly forms. "The great gift of Malaria is utter apathy," wrote Sir Richard Burton, accurately portraying the situation in much of the Third World today. Visitors to malaria-afflicted parts of the planet are protected by a new drug, mefloquine, a side effect of which is vivid, even violent, dreams. But a strain of cerebral malaria resistant to mefloquine is now on the offensive. . . .

And the cities keep growing. I got a general sense of the future while driving from the airport to downtown Conakry, the capital of Guinea. The forty-five-minute journey in heavy traffic was through one never-ending shantytown: a nightmarish Dickensian spectacle to which Dickens himself would never have given credence. The corrugated metal shacks and scabrous walls were coated with black slime. Stores were built out of rusted shipping containers, junked cars, and jumbles of wire mesh. The streets were one long puddle of floating garbage. Mosquitoes and flies were everywhere. Children, many of whom had protruding bellies, seemed as numerous as ants. When the tide went out, dead rats and the skeletons of cars were exposed on the mucky beach. In twenty-eight years Guinea's population will double if growth goes on at current rates. Hardwood logging continues at a madcap speed, and people flee the Guinean countryside for Conakry. It seemed to me that here, as elsewhere in Africa and the Third World, man is challenging nature far beyond its limits, and nature is now beginning to take its revenge.

Africa may be as relevant to the future character of world politics as the Balkans were a hundred years ago, prior to the two Balkan wars and the First World War. Then the threat was the collapse of empires and the birth of nations based solely on tribe. Now the threat is more elemental: *nature unchecked*. Africa's immediate future could be very bad. The coming upheaval, in which foreign embassies are shut down, states collapse, and contact with the outside world takes place through dangerous, disease-ridden coastal trading posts, will loom large in the century we are entering. (Nine of twenty-one U.S. foreign-aid missions to be closed over the next three years are in Africa—a prologue to a consolidation of U.S. embassies themselves.) Precisely because much of Africa is set to go over the edge at a time when the Cold War has ended, when environmental and demographic stress in other parts of the globe is becoming critical, and when the post–First World War system of nation-states—not just in the Balkans but perhaps also in the Middle East—is about to be toppled, Africa suggests what war, borders, and ethnic politics will be like a few decades hence. . . .

Returning from West Africa last fall was an illuminating ordeal. After leaving Abidjan, my Air Afrique flight landed in Dakar, Senegal, where all passengers had to disembark in order to go through another security check, this one demanded by U.S. authorities before they would permit the flight to set out for New York. Once we were in New York, despite the midnight hour, immigration officials at Kennedy Airport held up disembarkation by conducting quick interrogations of the aircraft's passengers—this was in addition to all the normal immigration and customs procedures. It was apparent that drug smuggling, disease, and other factors had contributed to the toughest security procedures I have ever encountered when returning from overseas.

Then, for the first time in over a month, I spotted businesspeople with attaché cases and laptop computers. When I had left New York for Abidjan, all the businesspeople were boarding planes for Seoul and Tokyo, which departed from gates near Air Afrique's. The only non-Africans off to West Africa had been relief workers in T-shirts and khakis.

Although the borders within West Africa are increasingly unreal, those separating West Africa from the outside world are in various ways becoming more impenetrable.

But Afrocentrists are right in one respect: we ignore this dying region at our own risk. When the Berlin Wall was falling, in November of 1989, I happened to be in Kosovo, covering a riot between Serbs and Albanians. The future was in Kosovo, I told myself that night, not in Berlin. The same day that Yitzhak Rabin and Yasser Arafat clasped hands on the White House lawn, my Air Afrique plane was approaching Bamako, Mali, revealing corrugated-zinc shacks at the edge of an expanding desert. The real news wasn't at the White House, I realized. It was right below.

THE
GLOBAL TIDE

GEORGE A. LOPEZ, JACKIE G. SMITH, and RON PAGNUCCO

George A. Lopez, a Bulletin *contributing editor, is professor of government and international affairs at the Kroc Institute for International Peace Studies at the University of Notre Dame, South Bend, Indiana. Jackie G. Smith is a graduate student in government at Notre Dame. Ron Pagnucco is an assistant professor of sociology at Mount St. Mary College, Newburgh, Maryland.*

In the 1970s, babies in Third World nations were dying when they might have been thriving. The apparent culprit: ersatz mother's milk made from powder. The Nestlé Company, a Swiss-based multinational, had identified Third World mothers as a high-growth marketing opportunity. Nestlé baby formula was aggressively pushed as the "modern" way to feed infants.

In the developed world, baby formula works fine. It may not be as good as mother's milk, but it's reasonably close. As long as the bottles and rubber nipples for the formula are properly sterilized, the mixing water reasonably pure, and the mixing proportions right, babies do well on it.

But in Third World villages in the 1970s, pure water was the exception, not the rule, and the need for sterilization was hard to explain and seldom practiced. Beyond that, the formula was cheap by First World standards, but expensive by Third World reckonings. That made it fatally tempting to stretch the powder by diluting it too much, thus degrading the nutritional value.

Health care professionals and missionaries working in the Third World were outraged, and they communicated their sadness and anger to Nestlé, which did nothing, and to governments, which didn't seem to care. Nestlé had threatened no nation's security, broken no laws.

But nutritionists and activists in the industrialized world did care, and condemnation of Nestlé's marketing practices became widespread. As word got out, the cause was taken up by nearly 100 private organizations in 65 nations. A transnational economic boycott of Nestlé products was launched, coordinated by a U.S.-based transnational citizen coalition, the Infant Formula Action Committee (INFACT).

Whether the boycott had much economic effect on Nestlé's bottom line is hard to pin down. But it became a public relations nightmare for a company that liked to be known for its warm and cuddly hot chocolate and its candy-counter Crunch bars. The INFACT-led transnational campaign ultimately forced Nestlé to abandon its Third World marketing practices, and it also led to the passage in 1981 of a World Health Organization code of conduct governing the marketing and sale of infant formula.

The Nestlé boycott was arguably the first activist campaign of its type. It attracted cross-border participants who organized outside traditional diplomatic or political channels in an attempt to accomplish reform in an area outside the immediate interests of international politics. The success of the boycott,

Tomorrow's world will have borders, but fewer boundaries.

and the apparent influence of two other transnational movements of the early 1980s—the campaign against the deployment of intermediate-range missiles in Europe and the divestment campaign to end apartheid in South Africa—have inspired citizen groups around the world to organize around common cross-national interests.

Transnational social movements are one aspect of "globalization"—a term pundits use to describe the rapidly increasing cross-border economic, social, and political interactions that are not originated by national governments.

Although theorists argue about when the trend toward globalization began, few would deny that the process has been accelerating for more than two decades.

Phase 1: Interdependence

It was in the 1970s that Americans discovered—with a jolt—that the world's economy had become highly interdependent. In 1971, President Richard Nixon withdrew the dollar from the gold standard. From then on, the dollar floated against other currencies, thus facilitating—in theory—worldwide free trade.

When the Organization of Petroleum Exporting Countries (OPEC) restricted oil production and distribution in 1973, it sent a series of shock waves through Western economies. The OPEC oil embargo demonstrated that the Western nations had become shockingly vulnerable to external pressure, and their governments could do little about it.

At first, only the economies of advanced industrial states were thought to be closely interconnected, but when the entire world felt the effects of the debt crises in developing countries in the post-OPEC world, opinions were revised.

Phase 2: Intensification

Danish analysts Hans-Henrik Holm and Georg Sørensen define globalization as the intensification of economic, social, and political interaction across national boundaries.[1] Noting the dramatic increase that has occurred in both the breadth and depth of cross-border activity, they label the 1970s the decade of interdependence, and the 1980s the decade of intensification.

Superpower détente was one of the conditions that favored the increase in transnational activities that began in the mid-1970s. International contacts were no longer limited to diplomats or globe-trotting businessmen. And many of the issues that stimulated new transnational associations went beyond the political-economic and military-security issues that states traditionally concerned themselves with.

In the social and political spheres, it was becoming clear that many modern social problems were not confined within boundaries, nor did ways of dealing with issues like human rights, refugees, and environmental concerns fit neatly with notions of national sovereignty. Many of those committed to solving modern social problems were citizen-activists unaffiliated with their governments.

In the 1980s, as national leaders continued to initiate state policies and administer them through traditional diplomatic avenues, a new and diverse set of international actors gradually made their appearance in matters of "low politics," as dealing with the environment, human rights, and related issues came to be called.

The fuel of globalization

Some analysts believe that the global economy is the engine that drives social and political globalization, but it is more likely that the economy is merely the first sector to undergo the revolutionary globalization process.

The world economy began to undergo important changes more than 30 years ago. With the resurgence of Latin American and European economies, and the decolonization of Asia and Africa, American corporations began to look more widely for opportunities abroad. As the trend grew, there was a massive outward flow of U.S. investments.

In the 1980s, the intensification of global interdependence was fueled by the interaction of three major trends: the continuing internationalization of trade and money markets; the spread of cheap, high-powered technology for the production, storage, and retrieval of information; and the rise of global communications.

The growth of "multinational corporations"—a designation once reserved for a few oil and trading companies—has had a profound impact on the political, social, and economic life of nations, even as the debate continues over the social and political consequences of their increasing economic power and mobility.

For three decades nationalists have reacted to the complex set of opportunities and dilemmas presented by the globalization of production. Industrial nations fear job loss to nations where wages are lower; Third World countries rail against the unfair penetration of their economies. Shortly before becoming secretary of labor, economist Robert Reich repeated a common complaint about American-owned multinationals—that they "have no special relationship with Americans."[2]

Despite the concerns expressed in industrial and developing nations alike, between 1980 and the early 1990s, the trend continued—in 1993, 18,000 multinational corporations and their 104,000 affiliates were responsible for nearly 80 percent of international trade. Worldwide, investments in foreign markets became commonplace, increasing from $550 billion in 1980 to $1.5 trillion in 1991. Japanese overseas investment alone grew sixfold. The growth of multinationals was financed in large part by an increasingly globalized banking system, and a number of Japanese banks entered the international field.[3]

Now, in the 1990s, with the world no longer divided along an ideological fault line, the multinationals have an even broader playing field.

More recently, the greatest growth in the trade of manufactured goods appears to be regional, although there is continued rapid globalization in areas economists call the secondary and tertiary sectors—banking, investment, tourism, and services. Capital and people are more mobile, finished goods less so. These products are more likely to be traded regionally, as the trade agreements that have been signed in Europe, the Pacific Rim, and, more recently, North America, gradually take effect. In these regions, "internationalization" of production facilities is now most likely to occur when firms merge across borders.

Whether or not economic activity on a global scale is a positive development, the extent of global trade has forced businessmen to think globally, whether or not they are involved in international trade. As a matter of routine, the heads of strictly local firms must evaluate the global competition if they are going to succeed in their own marketplace. This has brought about an enormous change in thinking.

Computers: The global product

More than any other product, the computer typifies globalization. It is simultaneously a product of, and a valued tool in, the process of globalization. The inexpensive production and rapid distribution of computer equipment owes much to the diversity and mobility of globalized manufacturing. In turn, computer links have proved to be a critical tool in the globalization of the economic, social, and political spheres.

In the 1980s, the revolution in the production of communication technologies created affordable and versatile means of information processing and exchange. The dimensions of this change are close to incalculable. At the beginning of the decade, fax machines were expensive, and only a few international companies had invested in them. But by the early 1990s, these machines cost only a quarter of the 1980 price. Today, nearly 200 million fax machines have been produced in the United

States alone, and virtually every major company, government office, and voluntary association in the world communicates by fax as a matter of course.

The computer revolution is even more dramatic. In 1980, there were probably fewer than 2 million computers worldwide, and virtually all were mainframes. Today more than 150 million computers are in use, and 90 percent are personal computers—but they have greater computing power than most of the mainframes they have replaced. The number of computers in use is expected to grow by 18 to 20 million annually.

The decline in price and the widening distribution of personal computers, fax machines, and modems mean that private citizens in one corner of the world can communicate readily with others in another corner of the world. It is nearly impossible for governments to prevent the transmission of information by jamming broadcasts, instituting embargoes, or other means of control.

Human rights activists and academics were among the first to grasp that computer networks and fax machines were "technologies of freedom" that could be used to enhance democracy. For instance, Amnesty International uses the Internet to broadcast alerts about deteriorating human rights situations and to prompt its constituents to take specific actions.

Agents of change

To Robert Keohane of Harvard University, "globalization is fundamentally a social process, not one that is technologically predetermined."[4] Keohane argues that the global economy and the new communications technologies are necessary components of globalization, but they do not alone explain global social change. The critical component is the growing number of individuals with a transnational conscience who are committed to solving the pressing social and political problems of our age.

The aspirations and motives of these individuals differ from those of the international business community, as well as from those of their governments. And the activities of these private citizens are now changing the way citizens and the state relate to one another, and how each relates to the international political arena.

Of course, some mechanisms linking political and social activists outside the governments of nation-states have been with us for some time. International organizations have been created as extensions to international agreements. The oldest of these groups, the International Labor Organization, and the newer organizations created within the U.N. family,

The economy was merely the first sector to undergo the revolutionary globalization process.

are institutions that began as agents of national governments.

Since World War II, the progress made on complex and sensitive issues such as arms control, environmental cleanup, and human rights, has increasingly involved the efforts of transnational groups ranging from ad hoc networks of experts and concerned citizens to these more formal institutions. As yet, their behind-the-scenes work is largely unrecognized. As British analyst Peter Willetts writes, "Every politician and diplomat knows that in their day-to-day work as government officials they communicate with people who are not politicians, civil servants, or diplomats, yet non-governmental organizations are often omitted from written accounts of political events and usually omitted from theoretical writing about the nature of the international system." [5]

A child pumps water from a well that CARE helped her Cameroon community to build.

SHAW McCUTCHEON/CARE

Stifled by the unwillingness of nations and international governmental organizations to share decision-making, and frustrated by the failure of political institutions to bring about reform, activists began to form their own cross-border coalitions in the 1970s and 1980s. As noted earlier, three of these movements—the Nestlé boycott, the anti-apartheid campaign for South Africa, and the campaign against nuclear missile deployment in Europe—inspired, and continue to inspire, transnational social organizations today. The influence of these "non-governmental organizations"—or NGOs as they are called—should not be ignored. And these groups now number in the tens of thousands.

When its activities cross two or more national boundaries and the organization forms a centralized structure such as a secretariat, a group is categorized as an INGO—an international non-governmental organization. In 1972 there were about 2,100 INGOs. A decade later there were more than 4,200, and by 1993 more than 4,800 were registered with the Union of International Associations in Geneva.

Good or not so good?

Whether the rise of transnational agents of change benefits all humanity equally is open to debate, in part because the effects of globalization are not evenly distributed, and in part because the hub of globalization is in the West.

Holm and Sørensen argue that, although the globalization of capital may seem desirable in general, it has also meant that those who have capital and mobility have an even greater advantage over those who do not. They assert that "globalization has meant increased integration for the Organization for Economic Cooperation and Development (OECD) countries, yet this process has also involved increasing marginalization of a number of Third World countries or parts of countries. Integration in the core and fragmentation of large parts of the periphery have gone hand in hand." [6]

They agree with Keohane, who predicts that the interaction of globalization and fragmentation will eventually lead to greater regionalism, creating regional zones with sharply different standards of living. States in the North and West, with strong economies and functioning democracies, will reap the economic benefits of globalization and realize the social and political rewards of transnational movements. Life for the majority living in this zone, the "zone of peace," will be tranquil and prosperous. But for many people in Southern states, with limited resources, lesser development, and no democratic political tradition, the prospect of enjoying equal benefits will grow more remote.

Another concern about globalization is raised by those opposed to the dominance of Western ways of thinking and organizing. Sometimes we imagine that all critics of Western culture resemble the most extreme portrayals of Islamic fundamentalists presented in the Western news media. But even in cultures friendly to the West, concerns are expressed about the singular lens through which the "desirable" political, economic, and social life is portrayed in the global media. At its best, globalization should produce a synthesis of cultural views, not the triumph of one over all others.

Unfortunately, even in transnational movements that are committed to peace and justice, the goal of cultural synthesis is more frequently expressed than realized. More than three-quarters of transnational citizen groups are headquartered in Geneva, where these organizations have ready access to the U.N. community. At some point, however, more organizations should probably be located in Nairobi, Lima, or New Delhi.

A number of Western-based citizen-activists carry with them a set of assumptions that has little relevance to problems "on the ground." Often they compound the problems caused by their initial bias with a less-than-adequate willingness to listen to local groups' approaches to the problems at hand. Even old hands at transnational organizations sometimes show less sensitivity to local expertise than might be expected. Apologists say that, like their official diplomatic counterparts, many "issue and network" experts simply were not prepared for the press of work that has come their way since 1989, when the Berlin Wall came down and the Cold War ended. Many of yesterday's activists are today globe-trotting consultants—on environmental issues, human rights monitoring and advocacy, or nonviolence and conflict resolution. They had little time to prepare for their new roles.

These problems may reflect the growing pains of the transnational movement, but they provide ample ammunition to local factions who are only too willing to reject efforts to protect human rights, campaigns for demilitarization, or sustainable development under the guise of rejecting Western imperialism.

Globalization's greatest strength lies in its potential to improve the economic, social, and political life of all people. But globalization should unfold in ways that allow local groups to participate as equal partners. They are the resident change agents who understand the opportunities and obstacles in their own local-global nexus.

"Tiz-moes" do it best

More than any other social or political entity, transnational social movement organizations—TSMOs, or "tiz-moes"—may be the fullest embodiment of globalization. The majority of TSMOs are coalitions or formal federations of national or regional nongovernmental organizations (NGOs). While some TSMOs, such as the International Fellowship of Reconciliation, have been promoting peace and security issues for most of this century, most are new to the global arena. Some 94 percent of all TSMOs were formed after 1945, and their numbers have doubled since the early 1980s. Today, there are nearly 600.

A significant proportion of TSMOs are organizations of professionals committed to global betterment—Medicins Sans Frontieres (Doctors Without Borders), for instance. There is even a TSMO— and an increasingly influential one, at that—for legislators, Parliamentarians Global Action. The organization has 900 members from more than 74 nations, and through its newsletter, meetings, and briefing kits, it works for enlightened policies on disarmament and security issues.

TSMOs provide the organizational structures needed for mobilizing disparate peoples who share a common political agenda. They engage in education, lobbying, and the framing of issues in ways that would not be open to citizen groups, were they to work through the diplomatic services of their own nation-states. On human rights and environmental issues, TSMOs have played major roles in the drafting of resolutions and legal conventions for consideration by nation-state delegates to the United Nations and other international forums. Beyond that, they are widely regarded as reliable monitors of national compliance with international codes and legal agreements. In short, TSMOs are a fundamental element of a new and yet to be fully defined global governance structure that is now emerging.

—*G. L., J. S., R. P*

The dark side

Criminals have been quick to take advantage of globalization. It has been documented that complex narcotics production and trade operations in Latin America and in Southeast Asia benefit from laundering money in the global financial market.[7] Other transnational criminal activities include the international disposition of billions of dollars of stolen consumer items like VCRs, computers, and designer clothes.

But the most dangerous of globalized criminal activities may be the underground weapons trade, where diversity of demand and volume have reached staggering proportions.

For more than a decade analysts have reported that a broad array of weapons and related items are available on white, gray, and black markets. Some predicted that the demise of the Cold War would mean a steady decline in the purchase of killing technologies, but just the opposite has happened.

GREENPEACE/SMITH

Greenpeace workers and
Saudi scientists assess
damage from oil spilled during
the Gulf War at Manifah Bay,
Saudi Arabia, 1991.

At the same time that arms transactions sponsored or sanctioned by governments were reaching record levels in 1992–93, writes arms control expert Michael Klare, "Virtually all restraint had disappeared from the weapons trade; except for the continuing embargo on Iraq and a cash shortage in many Third World areas, no barriers stood in the way of prospective arms buyers in conflict-prone areas."[8]

Just as market demand varies for civilian product lines, the demand for weapons varies with the style and number of conflicts. A recent study by the American Academy of Arts and Sciences reports that local conflicts have caused an explosion in the demand for small arms and other light weapons. According to the latest *SIPRI Yearbook*, global trade in weapons totaled $22 billion in 1993.

States rarely need to buy light weapons on the black market. Buyers are usually "non-state actors"—drug cartels, minority ethnic groups like the Kurds in Iraq and Turkey, and insurgents. Light weapons are easy to market and ship. Even with a U.N. embargo in place, weapons valued at nearly $2 billion are believed to have entered Yugoslavia in 1993.[9]

Globalization and politics

However negative some consequences of globalization may be, the intensification of non-state activities has the potential to make a profound impact on politics.

Before globalization, the single non-violent route to political change involved citizens petitioning their local and national leaders for the changes they desired. Now, through transnational organizations, citizens can bring political pressure on national officials from two new directions.

"Lateral" pressure may be applied through NGOs in other countries, especially through those organizations based in countries where the "home" government is favorably disposed to the desired change.

"Downward" pressure may be exerted by INGOs. This occurs most often when transnational organizations have successfully appealed to other transnational institutions about the lack of compliance with global norms or commitments. As more private citizens in many nations take advantage of these options, it will have profound implications.

Despite the new tools that private citizens can use to influence governments, it would be wrong to conclude that the nation-state will be a less critical actor in international relations. The emergence of citizens with a transnational conscience does not guarantee that broad social movements or international non-governmental organizations will continue to thrive. These associations may be expected to be part of the changing order, but, as Keohane points out, they are still dependent on the willingness of nation-states to empower them with resources and to allow them to enter into many areas that traditionally have been the province of sovereign states. What the global citizen movements have produced is a redefined equation for how issue-based politics may be pursued and a consensus reached.

Globalization and peace

One of the most compelling questions asked about globalization is whether it will lead to a truly global civil society, which many believe is the key to world peace.

Both in reality and in its prescriptive allure, globalization is appealing. But its long-term consequences are the subject of spirited debate. Georg Sørensen notes in his review essay that some analysts, like John Naisbitt, predict that one outcome will be more direct democracy at the local level.

Other analysts, like international relations expert James Rosenau, believe that globalization is already being counterbalanced by other forces. Rosenau asserts that globalization brings with it its own self-correcting, if not countervailing, tendencies, such as fragmentation and localism.[10] For every pressure that pushes people to be or do the same things—to "act globally"—there is a distinctly local counterpressure. For example, the former superpowers and their citizens may seek new forms of global security, but local rivalries, hatreds, and wars continue.

Those whose working framework is "think globally, act locally" probably believe that Rosenau has missed the forest for the trees. What he considers a tension or a contradiction, globalist-localists are likely to see as synergy and mutual reinforcement. They believe that the transnational movements have become so powerful, and the benefits of affiliation so clear, that many groups with strictly local problems now reach out to global organizations first, because a global strategy is more likely to produce results. Today, for example, if the population living near New York's Love Canal faced the same environmental problems they encountered 20 years ago, many local citizens would be likely to seek to enlist the aid of international environmental groups like Greenpeace, Friends of the Earth, and the Natural Resources Defense Council before lobbying the New York State legislature or suing the local companies that dumped chemicals in the area.

Because citizen action is now global, there are new ways of doing politics and, as always, political structures must be adapted to economic and social change. Interdependence in the 1970s revealed the porous nature of borders. Intensification in the 1980s revealed the see-through nature of sovereignty. The 1990s may be regarded as the decade of intentional-ity, a time when those inclined to think globally have routes for action that were never before available.

The availability of new routes of action means that recruitment and membership in existing transnational organizations should increase dramatically, and the rate at which new groups are formed will also increase. Those who share a sense of global citizenship will be free to participate in a wide range of regional and global political and social entities.

There have been times—at the founding of the United Nations, or when the first pictures of the planet earth were beamed back from space—when people all over the planet were struck by the connectedness of all humanity. Now, globalization holds the hope of a constantly shared consciousness for humanity, regardless of differing political, social, and cultural realities. In this sense, the Earth *is* a new world.

1. Hans-Henrik Holm and Georg Sørensen, eds., *Whose World Order?: Uneven Globalization and the End of the Cold War* (Boulder, Colo.: Westview Press, 1995), p. 1.

2. Robert Reich, "Who Is Us," *Harvard Business Review*, vol. 90 (Jan./Feb. 1990), p. 59.

3. Trends are adapted from those listed in Charles W. Kegley, Jr., and Eugene R. Wittkopf, *World Politics: Trends and Transformations*, 4th ed. (New York: St. Martin's, 1990); Robert S. Walters and David H. Blake, *The Politics of Global Economic Relations*, 4th ed. (Englewood Cliffs, N. J.: Prentice-Hall, 1992); and Ingomar Hauchler and Paul M. Kennedy, eds., *Global Trends: The World Almanac of Development and Peace* (New York: Continuum Publishing, 1994), pp. 201–16.

4. Robert O. Keohane, "Hobbe's Dilemma and Institutional Change in World Politics: Sovereignty in International Society," in Holm and Sørensen, *Whose World Order?*, p. 184.

5. Peter Willetts, "Transnational Actors and the Changing World Order," International Peace Research Institute (Yokohama, Japan) Occasional Paper Series, no. 17, p. 3.

6. Holm and Sørensen, *Whose World Order?*.

7. Phil Williams, "Transnational Criminal Organizations and International Security, *Survival*, vol. 36, no. 1, pp. 96–113.

8. Michael T. Klare, "Adding Fuel to the Fire: The Conventional Arms Trade in the 1990s," in Michael T. Klare and Daniel C. Thomas, eds., *World Security: Challenges for a New Century* (New York: St. Martin's Press, 1994), p. 136.

9. Jeffrey Boutwell, Michael T. Klare and Laura W. Reed, eds., *Lethal Commerce: The Global Trade in Small Arms and Light Weapons* (Cambridge, Mass.: American Academy of Arts and Sciences, 1995).

10. James Rosenau, "New Dimensions of Security: The Interacting of Globalizing and Localizing Dynamics," *Security Dialogue*, vol. 25, no. 3, pp. 255–81.

HAS GLOBAL WARMING BEGUN?

Climate detectives are finally beginning to see the fingerprints of greenhouse warming on the planet.

SHAWNA VOGEL

On weather maps, it looked rather innocuous: a bubble of high pressure cruising slowly across the upper Midwest of the United States. But within it lay some of the hottest air the region had ever seen. For the millions of residents in its path this past July — especially those in Chicago — the bubble was a killer.

On July 13, the temperature in the now windless city reached 106 degrees Fahrenheit at Chicago's Midway airport, an all-time high for the city. To make matters worse, the ovenlike air mass was heavily laden with water vapor. The high relative humidity of 88 percent made the air feel like it was an incredible 117 degrees.

For the elderly, the infirm and people on medications that make it difficult for the body to dissipate heat, the scorching temperature was an extraordinary bodily insult. People began to die, and soon corpses were literally overflowing the city morgue. To handle the grisly overload, morgue officials stored the dead in refrigerated trucks pending autopsy.

By the end of the eight-day heat wave, the heat and humidity had contributed to the deaths of some 566 Chicagoans. More died as the heat wave advanced across the country before heading out into the Atlantic. The bubble could very well have been a freak occurrence, one of those rare events that reminds us that the universe is a capricious place. But it looked eerily similar to the climatic extremes that some scientists predict

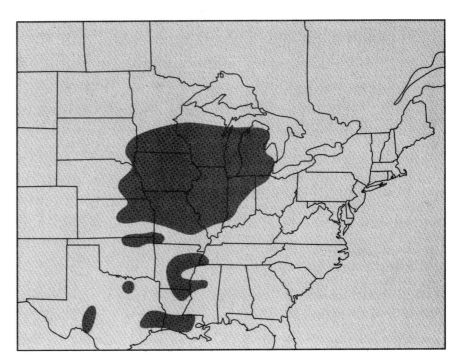

On July 13, a mass of hot, humid air lay over the Midwest, bringing dangerously high temperatures to Chicago and other cities. In this illustration, the shaded area indicates where the apparent temperature, a measure of the combined effect of heat and humidity, reached or exceeded a life-threatening 105 degrees Fahrenheit.

will be a hallmark of global warming from the greenhouse effect. And it wasn't the only event of its kind to have occurred in recent months.

Last January, David Vaughan, a glaciologist with the British Antarctic Survey, in Cambridge, England, was poring over satellite photographs of the Antarctic Peninsula when he spotted an extraordinary change in the landform's shape. A 30-mile stretch of an ice shelf in Prince Gustav Channel had collapsed and apparently drifted out to sea. Once a bridge between the peninsula and Ross Island to the

north, the ice shelf had been intact ever since people began exploring this part of the Antarctic about 100 years ago. But for the first time in recorded history, Ross Island was circumnavigable.

Six weeks later, Vaughan was amazed to find yet another shift in the peninsula's outline. "A thousand square kilometers of the Larsen Ice Shelf basically disintegrated in fifty days," he says. Floating in the midst of the broken up ice was a colossal iceberg the size of 50 Manhattans.

What's happening to Earth's climate? Has the carbon dioxide

spewing from our smokestacks and tailpipes finally caught up with us? Has this colorless, odorless gas, which causes the atmosphere to retain heat akin to the way that panes of glass trap heat in a greenhouse, finally altered the global climate?

Computer simulations, or models, of Earth's climate have predicted a variety of changes that may arise from higher levels of carbon dioxide in the atmosphere. An increased incidence of extreme weather is one such change. Alterations in rainfall patterns — some regions getting wetter, some drier — is another. But in addition to these and other regional changes, the models also predict a global increase of average surface temperatures of between 3 and 8 degrees F by the end of the next century.

Although most climate scientists are confident that the models will prove to be broadly correct, they have been reluctant to attribute individual warming trends, heat spells or weather extremes to the greenhouse effect. Future climate change is all but inevitable, they have been saying, but the evidence has not been strong enough to say whether it has already begun.

Until just recently. This year, several studies have uncovered convincing new evidence of man-made climate change — evidence that may prove as damning as a set of fingerprints found at the scene of a crime. And for the first time since the global warming debate began more than a decade ago, a good number of scientists are willing to say that man-made climate change is no longer a thing of the future.

It's probably here already.

There's no denying that the world has been kind of hot lately. On a record that extends back to the nineteenth century, the 1980s included what were then the six warmest years on record. And the trend has continued into the current decade, with 1990 and 1991 topping out as the first and second hottest years on record. After a brief cooling caused by the veil of volcanic dust and gases that erupted from Mount Pinatubo in

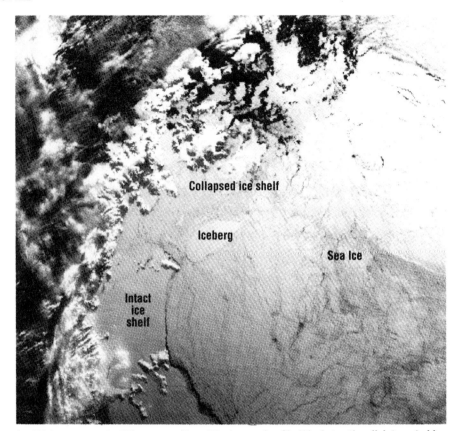

Last February, nearly 400 square miles of the Larsen Ice Shelf in Antarctica disintegrated in 50 days. The intact portion of the shelf is visible in the lower left quarter of this satellite image. To its right is fragmented sea ice, which is separated from the shelf by a large, dark crack. The dark area to the shelf's left is the Antarctic continent. The disintegrated portion of the shelf and an iceberg the size of 50 Manhattans lie above it.

June 1991, temperatures have rebounded. The British Meteorological Office in Bracknell, England, reports that 1994 was the third or perhaps the fourth warmest year on record. And even prior to this past July's lethal heat wave, temperature trends indicated that 1995 could itself turn out to be an unusually warm year in some places. Extreme midsummer heat waves in the Northeast and Southwest were certainly consistent with this.

The warmth of the 1980s and 1990s continues an even longer trend that began at the turn of the century. Slowly, a fraction of a degree at a time, average temperatures at Earth's surface have increased, most scientists agree. Climatologists have sifted through meteorological records going back to the nineteenth century and have discovered an alarming trend: According to a conservative, widely accepted estimate, average surface temperatures have risen one-half to one degree F in the last hundred

years. (Other estimates put the increase as high as 1.7 degrees.)

To some people, the message is unambiguous: Planet Earth is indeed running a fever, and we humans are to blame. But as critics of the whole notion of global warming have been quick to point out, the climate is naturally fickle. Hot spells, weird events here and there and even decade-long warming trends are all normal manifestations of natural climate variation.

Take the Antarctic ice shelf break-up. Temperatures have risen in the Antarctic Peninsula by 4.5 degrees F over the last 50 years. But elsewhere in Antarctica, the rise has been much less dramatic. Thus, the warming that appears to be at the root of the collapse is regional, not global. "Whether this is a magnification of something that's happening on a larger scale, the global warming, we just don't know," Vaughan says.

Warming trends and heat waves

The graph at right charts one estimate of changes in global temperatures from 1860 to 1994. With variations over the years, it shows an overall rise of nearly 0.7 degrees Celsius (1.5 degrees F). A more conservative estimate by a United Nations panel of scientists puts the increase at between 0.3 and 0.6 degrees C.

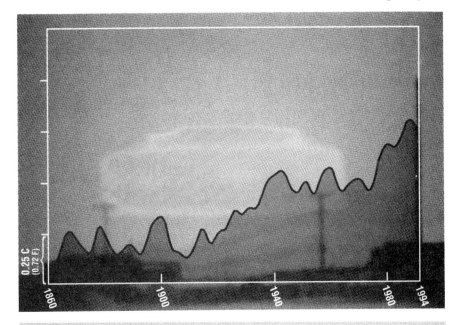

alike are part of the cycles of nature. And that's the crux of the dilemma. How can we know whether something as specific as a heat wave in the United States is the symptom of changes that we've brought on ourselves by burning fossil fuels or just a natural climatic blip?

The problem is this: During its early stages, the signs of man-made global warming should be hard to pick out against the background "noise" of natural climatic variation. This background is analogous to the static you hear on your car radio when you're cruising through deserted countryside. As you near a city, you may think you hear a change in the white noise. Is this the signal? Maybe. But it could also be a random variation in the background hiss — the unforeseeable sizzle of a transistor, perhaps. You just have to wait until you're close enough to the city for the music to stand out loud and clear.

The measured increase in temperatures of the past century has been as subtle as a change in the hiss of a car radio. Is it really global warming or is it the noise of natural variation?

As part of an effort to find out, scientists have used computer models to reproduce the climate of the past century. These simulations include the increasing amounts of carbon dioxide that we humans have been pumping into the atmosphere. In theory, if researchers could demonstrate that the changes predicted by their models matched what has actually happened in nature, then they would have evidence that carbon dioxide has been the culprit. Such a match would also provide an estimate of how much warming we should expect, and where, in the future.

As it turns out, models that predict only the effects of carbon diox-

How is Earth Like a Greenhouse?

Our planet drifts through the frigid environment of space warmed only by the rays of the sun. Most of this light is absorbed by the land, the ocean and plants. But about a third is reflected back toward space by clouds and the shiny white surfaces of glaciers and other ice masses.

If this reflection process went unchecked, Earth would be a much colder place than it actually is. However, the atmosphere contains a number of gases that, while largely transparent to sunlight, are opaque to heat. They cause warmth to be retained near the surface analogous to how panes of glass trap heat in a greenhouse.

The chief greenhouse gases are carbon dioxide, water vapor, methane, nitrous oxide and chlorofluorocarbons, or CFCs. All but the last are naturally produced, and we owe much of our planet's habitable climate to their influence. The problem is that the concentrations of greenhouse gases in the atmosphere are increasing as a result of industry, slash-and-burn agriculture and other human activities. In the past decade, concern has grown that man-made greenhouse gases may be affecting world climate.

In only the past 50 years, the concentration of carbon dioxide in the atmosphere has risen sharply, attributable in large part to increased deforestation and the burning of fossil fuels. Of all the greenhouse gases, carbon dioxide is expected to contribute the most to global warming — more than 50 percent of the total increase in temperatures by most estimates.

The next greatest contribution is expected to come from CFCs, chemical compounds used to make plastic foams, refrigerants and solvents. CFCs are potent greenhouse gases. (They have also been implicated in the destruction of Earth ozone layer, which protects the surface from the sun's harmful ultraviolet rays.) The influence of CFCs may account for about 25 percent of the observed temperature increase.

Methane originates in the intestines of cows and termites; it is also a byproduct of activities such rice farming and coal mining. The concentration of methane in the atmosphere has doubled as a result of increasing agriculture alone. And nitrous oxide has also risen, by about 8 percent, though the sources of this gas are not well-known.

Based on the known physical properties of man-made greenhouse gases and computer simulations of their impact on the atmosphere, climatologists predict that temperatures will increase steadily during the next century. — *Shawna Vogel*

Do Rising Sea Levels Mean That Global Warming Has Started?

Courtesy National Oceanic and Atmospheric Administration

EARTH: Steven G. Davis. Source: Laury Miller/NOAA

4.8 mm/year
($^3/_{16}$ inch/year)

Sea level rise (in centimeters)

1993   1994   1995

As global warming causes glaciers to melt and the surface waters of the oceans to heat up, sea level should rise. In the image at top, based on observations by the Topex/Poseidon satellite, the grey areas show where sea level has increased from 1993 through early 1995. The graph above tracks the changing sea level (grey line) compared to an arbitrary starting point (0.0 cm). Overall, ocean heights worldwide have increased at a rate of nearly 5 millimeters per year, more than twice the average rate for the current century. It's impossible to say for sure whether the rise is due to global warming or natural variation. But scientists are confident that if global warming is indeed under way, Topex/Poseidon should conclusively detect one of its effects some time within the next ten years.

ide have produced much more warming than scientists have documented: a rise in the global mean of 2.5 degrees F as opposed to the 0.5 to 1.0 degree of warming actually measured over the past century. With these results, it has been impossible to say how big a role, if any, carbon dioxide may have played in the rise in global temperatures. Moreover, the findings could mean that that there was something wrong with the models that could affect not only their estimates of past change but probably their predictions for the future.

In fact, something was indeed wrong with the models: They failed to account for the effects of sulfate aerosols. These tiny acidic droplets form when sulfur dioxide, a major by-product of fossil-fuel burning, mixes with water vapor in the air. In 1994, Joyce Penner and Karl Taylor, scientists at Lawrence Livermore National Laboratory in Livermore, California, completed the first simulations with a climate model that accounts for the effects of both carbon dioxide and sulfate aerosols.

Their study demonstrated that as sulfate aerosols float through the lower atmosphere, they create a haze that has the opposite effect of carbon dioxide: It tends to cool the climate by acting as a shield that reflects sunlight back into space. Because this shield is greatest over and downwind of industrial regions, that is where Penner and Taylor's model indicated the strongest effect. And observations have indeed shown that large areas of North America, Europe and Asia sit beneath a cooling umbrella of sulfate smog.

With the new kind of model in hand, researchers at a number of institutions worldwide took the next step in 1995: They simulated the combined effect of greenhouse gases and sulfate aerosols over the last 100 years. The models predicted a degree of warming closely resembling the actual measured climate changes of the past century. The first results of this kind were released in February by scientists at the British Meteorological Office's Hadley Centre for Climate Prediction and Research. By including both greenhouse gases and sulfate aerosols, their simulation showed a temperature increase of 0.9 degrees F over the past century, which is within the 0.5 to 1.0 degree range measured worldwide.

Not long after the British results were announced, similar modeling studies at the Max Planck Institute for Meteorology in Hamburg, Germany, and at Lawrence Livermore also produced a near match with the observed global temperature rise. With these consistent results in hand, climatologists have gained confidence that computer models can accurately mimic the way the Earth's climate machine really works. And that's strong evidence that man-made greenhouse gases,

principally carbon dioxide from combustion of fossil fuels, may already be causing surface temperatures to rise, although the effect is blunted in some parts of the world by the effects of sulfate aerosols.

But as strong as this new evidence may seem, it still is not enough to make a case beyond a reasonable doubt. Scientists who led the new modeling studies point out that it's still possible that the observed rise in global surface temperatures could have been caused by some as-yet-unknown factor and not man-made greenhouse gases. So to really nail the case, scientists would like something even more incriminating, something that specifi-

cally and convincingly points to man-made emissions as the culprit. Something like a fingerprint.

In just the past year or so, researchers have begun an intensive search for the fingerprint of man-made climate change. "The idea is that different causes of climate change have different patterns that we can recognize," says Benjamin Santer, one of the climate modelers at Lawrence Livermore. Some areas of the world have warmed more than others, whereas others have cooled. Together, these regional climate shifts form a pattern as distinct as the whorls of a fingerprint.

If man-made greenhouse gases

Linking the Oceans and Atmosphere

Courtesy Los Alamos National Laboratories and Naval Postgraduate School

Climate is intimately linked to the oceans: Currents carry huge amounts of heat, affecting the climate worldwide, and climate changes in turn affect ocean circulation. Computer simulations are helping scientists understand how currents transport heat. This may reveal key details about feedbacks between the climate and oceans, thereby improving scientists' ability to predict climate change from greenhouse gases. The image above shows a computer simulation of ocean circulation by researchers at the Los Alamos National Laboratory in New Mexico and the Naval Postgraduate School in California. The fastest-moving water is shown in black, the slowest in dark grey. The curling features reveal a pattern of currents called eddies.

have altered the climate, then the pattern of temperature changes should match the patterns generated by climate models that simulate the effects of these gases, Santer says. Climatologists believe that such a match would be powerful evidence that man-made greenhouse warming has begun. Yet efforts to find a match with models that take only greenhouse gases into account have failed to produce that critical evidence.

The current crop of improved models, simulating the effects of both sulfate aerosols and carbon dioxide, presented an opportunity to try again. Santer and his colleagues at Lawrence Livermore employed the model developed by Penner and Taylor in their

This image shows the results of recent computer model simulations of the combined influence of carbon dioxide and sulfate aerosols on surface temperatures worldwide. Arrows indicate areas of maximum cooling and black indicates regions of maximum warming. In the simulations, a rise in global average temperature was partially offset by cooling from the sulfate aerosols. The particular pattern seen here, possibly a "fingerprint" of global warming, closely resembles the pattern of climate change actually observed in the past 50 years.

search for a global warming fingerprint. The team first used the model to estimate the total effect on the current climate of the carbon dioxide and sulfates pumped into the atmosphere since pre-industrial times. They found that sulfate aerosols by themselves had a cooling effect confined mainly to the Northern Hemisphere. In contrast, carbon dioxide showed its greatest warming effects over the poles.

Together, however, carbon dioxide and sulfate aerosols produced a unique pattern of temperature changes, with some areas that had warmed and others that had cooled. "It's a very complex pattern," says Santer, "and it's sort of difficult to see how other factors, like natural variability or volcanoes, could have given you such a specific pattern of change."

Armed with the global warming fingerprint generated by the model, the Lawrence Livermore team compared it to the pattern of temperature changes that has emerged in the meteorological record over the past 50 years. And, indeed, the observed pattern of climate change showed striking similarities to the one predicted by their model. Moreover, the closer to the present the scientists looked, the stronger the link grew between the model and reality, implying that the effects of carbon dioxide and sulfate

aerosols have grown stronger over time. Such a trend is not likely to arise by chance, Santer says.

Other fingerprint studies at the Hadley Centre and at the Max Planck Institute have produced similar findings. Thus, having successfully reproduced the motley pattern of warming and cooling that has occurred over time — even as the whole planet gradually inched toward higher temperatures — these climatologists have uncovered the first convincing fingerprints of man-made warming on the climate as a whole.

But this is just the beginning of fingerprint research. The pattern of temperature change that Santer and his colleagues modeled was painted with a broad brush — they showed changes in climate across large swaths of territory. Scientists would also like to be able to simulate the smaller-scale effects of global warming on the weather. And if a model simulating the effects of man-made greenhouse gases could accurately reproduce past changes in weather patterns, then researchers would be that much more certain that humans have already begun to alter the global climate.

With this in mind, Thomas R. Karl and his colleagues at NOAA's National Climatic Data Center in Asheville, North Carolina, recently took a look at climate in the

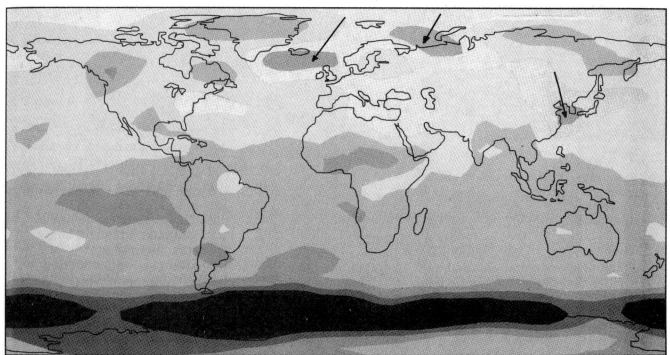

United States to see if the regional changes predicted by a number of climate models had begun to take hold. The team had at their disposal detailed weather records in North America collected since 1910, including records of climatic extremes such as drought, heat waves, cold snaps and periods of unusually high rainfall. Climate models have long predicted that in a greenhouse future such weather extremes could increase as the workings of the world climate machine are disturbed.

Karl and his colleagues devised a "climate extremes index" to assess the percentage of the United States that has experienced extremes in temperature and precipitation since the turn of the century. Overall, they discovered, the U.S. climate has become more extreme, especially in recent decades. Since 1976, the percentage of the country affected has increased by 1.5 percent as compared to the previous 65 years.

However, this in itself doesn't prove that man-made global warming has begun to affect U.S. climate—only that the climate has become more extreme. To find out if man-made greenhouse gases may be the culprit, the scientists checked the record to see how much of the country has experienced specific climate shifts that, according to models, global warming is likely to cause. These effects include increases in average temperatures (especially during the cold months), more severe and longlasting droughts and increased winter precipitation. Their "greenhouse climate response index" suggests that more and more of the United States is experiencing the kinds of weather attributable to the greenhouse effect—a 3.5 percent increase in the area affected from 1980 to 1994, in fact.

Karl cautions that it's not known with certainty if this apparent increase in severe weather is permanent, that it is not simply a short-term blip in world climate. On the other hand, he says, "the increase is of sufficient magnitude to suggest that greenhouse warming has already impacted U.S. climate, especially in the last ten to fifteen years."

Thunderstorms bloom high into Earth's atmosphere in this photo taken from the space shuttle. Since the industrial age began more than a century ago, the burning of fossil fuels has raised the concentration of carbon dioxide — the most important greenhouse gas — by about 27 percent. At the present rate, carbon dioxide concentrations may double over pre-industrial levels by the middle of the next century.

The new findings from fingerprint research by the Lawrence Livermore team, Karl and others make a powerful case that global warming has already begun, but there are some important caveats. Santer emphasizes that the degree to which he and other modelers can be confident that they have indeed detected the fingerprint of global warming rests on how accurately they have estimated the climate's natural variability — how much it wanders from the mean in a given period.

Climate models show clearly that we cannot continue to pump such a large amount of carbon dioxide and other greenhouse gases into the atmosphere without having some effect.

Detailed temperature records don't go back far enough for researchers to assess natural climate drift with total confidence. Climate modelers get around this by running their models over long periods of time without including the effects of man-made greenhouse gases. Then they compare this background variation to the results of a model run that does include greenhouse-induced changes. The Lawrence Livermore team performed this test on their model and discovered that the global-warming fingerprint it generated had not simply been the result of the model's own built-in, random variability. The fingerprint was due to the impacts of sulfur dioxide and carbon dioxide gas. Still, a cautious Santer notes that the climate's natural variability may be much larger than models have suggested. "If that's the case, then we would have much less confidence in our results," he says.

In addition, various uncertainties still lurk in the models themselves. For instance, Santer says, climate models do not realistically simulate the effects of cloud cover on the lower atmosphere; nor do they deal well with the effects of sulfate particles on the formation, lifetime and reflectivity of clouds. And modelers have not yet ruled out the possibility that volcanic dust and gas, slight changes in the sun's output or some other natural process has caused the climate changes revealed in the recent fin-

gerprint studies. So although climate models have reproduced the observed pattern of climate change, they may have done so based on faulty assumptions or incomplete knowledge. Uncertainties like this make it difficult for researchers to have complete confidence in their model predictions.

Despite the caveats, the new studies have already helped change attitudes among many doubting scientists. In 1988, climatologists were shocked when James Hansen of the Goddard Institute for Space Studies in New York told Congress that he believed man-made greenhouse gases had already begun to warm the world. Now Hansen's colleagues have begun to catch up with him.

Long a global-warming skeptic, Thomas Karl has grown more confident in light of recent findings. "If you had a jury and you wanted to make a conviction you'd have to have all twelve jurors say the greenhouse is the guilty party," he says. "I would say based on statistical analysis that you might have ten or eleven of the jurors saying the greenhouse is guilty, but still one or two would like to see a little

more evidence. Which means waiting a few more years."

Climatologists may continue for some time to stop just short of declaring unequivocally that global warming has begun. But the members of the scientific jury now generally agree that it would take an extraordinary array of evidence to prove the opposite case: that the observed rise in global temperatures has not been caused by man-made greenhouse gases. And the best climate models available show clearly that we can't continue to pump such a large amount of carbon dioxide and other gases into the atmosphere without having some effect.

For that reason, absolutely scientific certainty may be a luxury that we can't afford. While policy makers wait for the final word on how much warming to expect, carbon dioxide levels continue to rise. Any changes we make in carbon dioxide emissions will take several decades to show up as a reduction in atmospheric levels. Therefore the longer we wait to take action, the larger the impact that man-made greenhouse warming will have on our future climate.

Shawna Vogel is the author of the book Naked Earth, _which_ Earth _excerpted in the August 1995 issue._

What's Wrong with the Weather?
EL NIÑO
STRIKES AGAIN

Keay Davidson

Keay Davidson is a science reporter for the San Francisco Examiner. His story on the origin of deep earthquakes appeared in the November 1994 issue of Earth.

Noah might have been impressed by the deluge that hit California this past January. For about two weeks, torrential rains marched in from the Pacific Ocean, killing at least nine people and causing more than $1.3 billion in damages. Roads and communities were inundated as rivers breached their banks, 30-foot waves slammed into the coastline, waterspouts whirred off the coast and mud slides buried cars and closed roads in mountainous areas. In the Northern California town of Guerneville, nearly eight inches of rain fell in less than one day. Elsewhere in the state, skiers were delighted: By mid-January, the Lake Tahoe basin in the Sierra Nevada had received more than twice its normal snowfall for that point in the season.

At the same time, however, skiers in the northeastern United States were mourning. Because of the abnormally warm weather, even the snow machines couldn't keep enough powder on the slopes. And the weird weather wasn't confined to California and the Northeast. On average, temperatures in the United States were more than six degrees above normal, making it the warmest January on record. Meanwhile, Australia, the Caribbean and parts of Central America were beset by drought.

What's wrong with the weather? What's wrong is El Niño, a warming of the equatorial Pacific Ocean that disrupts weather patterns across vast stretches of the globe. Typically, El Niños occur every three to seven years when warm water in the upper reaches of the western Pacific drifts eastward and pools up off the coast of South America. This mysterious warming becomes noticeable around Christmas, which is why people on the coast of Peru and Ecuador dubbed the phenomenon El Niño, "The Child," in reference to the infant Jesus.

The California rains dramatically demonstrated that El Niño's reach can extend far beyond the equatorial Pacific. As the warm water drifted toward South America, it spawned thunderstorms further east than usual.

This shifted the path of the southern jet stream, a current of air that flows from west to east over the Pacific. Instead of coming ashore further north as usual, the jet stream slammed straight into California, carrying moisture and storms. Rain was not necessarily the only possible outcome. In some previous El Niños, changes in the jet stream brought drought to the same region.

Researchers emphasize, however, that El Niño did not *directly* cause the weird weather seen last winter. Instead, the Pacific warming altered the circulation of the atmosphere and ocean in a way that made stormy weather more likely. El Niño "stacks the deck a bit, changes the odds, so that certain [weather] patterns become more likely," explains meteorologist Stephen Zebiak of Lamont-Doherty Earth Observatory in Palisades, New York.

Atmospheric scientists have developed sophisticated programs, or models, that can predict the onset and effects of El Niño with fair accuracy. They can point with pride, for instance, to the successful forecast of the 1986-1987 El Niño, which arrived, peaked and then subsided as expected.

But forecasters' crystal balls

The Pacific Ocean:
Normal Conditions

Strong trade winds blow west along the equator (white arrows), causing warm surface water to pool in the western Pacific. Warm, moist air rises from the ocean surface, spawning thunderstorms. As the trade winds push surface water away from the South American coast, cold water rises to fill the void (black arrow) and the thermocline—the boundary between deep, cold water and the warmer layer above—dips sharply to the west.

The Pacific Ocean:
El Niño Conditions

Trade winds slacken, allowing warm surface water to flow east (white arrows) from the western Pacific. Upwelling along the South American coast diminishes as the thermocline levels somewhat (black arrow). Thunderstorms, which normally remain in the western Pacific, follow the warm pool of water across the ocean. This alters the normal pattern of atmospheric circulation. One result of these changes is a redirection of jet streams, which upsets the weather in North America.

EARTH: Steven G. Davis

have turned cloudy in recent years. In 1991, El Niño conditions began to develop in the Pacific, again as expected. The warming peaked in November and had all but disappeared by summer 1992. But then, in January 1993, El Niño resurged, peaking again by late spring. Conditions in the Pacific were back to normal by the winter of 1993-94. But then in the spring of 1994, yet another El Niño began to develop. By the time California experienced its catastrophic rains, the warming

was in full bloom — for the third time in four years. What's more, the latest satellite observations of the ocean indicate that this most recent El Niño was *twice* as strong as the last.

This repeated warming of the equatorial Pacific is unusual, but it is not the only new wrinkle in the science of El Niño. Recently, a team of researchers detected a moving region of abnormally warm water in the North Pacific they believe is the echo of the powerful 1982-1983 El Niño. An-

other team has linked the Pacific El Niño to a similar warming pattern in the Indian Ocean. This suggests that to forecast El Niño reliably, scientists may have to take into account the influence of past El Niños and climatic events thousands of miles from the Pacific Ocean.

Despite these complications, researchers remain confident that forecasts of the onset, timing and effects of El Niños will continue to improve. And that's important because lives and economies are at stake. Communities dependent on skiing or agriculture can be hurt badly by unseasonable warmth or rain. Reliable, accurate forecasting of El Niño and its effects might help those communities to cut their losses. A forecast of drought, for example, might convince farmers to plant crop varieties adapted to dry conditions.

The historical roots of El Niño research lie in the early 20th century, when British meteorologist Sir Gilbert Walker noticed that the local barometric pressures on the eastern and western sides of the Pacific Ocean had a tendency over many years to see-saw back and forth. Atmospheric scientists call this the Southern Oscillation.

Walker attempted to link this barometric see-saw to changes in weather as far away as the United States and Canada. At least one of his contemporaries ridiculed him for suggesting that regional changes in the atmosphere could have global effects. We now know that Walker was onto something: The flip-flop of the Southern Oscillation is the hallmark of El Niño and the ultimate reason warm water drifts to the eastern Pacific.

Between El Niños, high pressure prevails in the east, causing the trade winds to flow briskly westward across the tropical ocean (see diagrams, page 27). These winds drag warm surface water into the western Pacific, raising sea level there by as much as 24 inches. This westward drift robs warm water from the surface of the ocean off South America. In response, colder water wells up from below, loaded with nutrients and tiny creatures called phytoplankton. This is a favorite meal for fish, which is why the west coast of South America is normally such a good place to cast a net.

But when El Niño conditions develop, the catch of the day begins to diminish. For reasons as yet unknown, atmospheric pressure rises in the western Pacific and falls in the east, weakening the trade winds. This allows warm water in the western Pacific to drift back eastward. The result: A pool of unusually warm water extends across the equatorial Pacific.

As the upwelling of plankton-rich water decreases, the local fisheries begin to fall off drastically. This is why fishermen there could spot El Niños long before the advent of satellites and modern oceanography. As people in California well know, El Niño also has a dramatic effect on the atmosphere: Warm, moist air rushes upward from the surface of the ocean, spawning thunderstorms. As a result, the central Pacific becomes a rain-spattered corridor of storms.

El Niño is *supposed* to develop every three to seven years and confine itself to the equatorial Pacific. But the more scientists study El Niño, the more it defies previous assumptions. Scientists have some new problems to solve.

For example, why has El Niño returned three times in the past four years? Some blame a general warming of the atmosphere caused by the buildup of carbon dioxide and other "greenhouse gases." By raising global temperatures, the greenhouse effect may somehow disrupt the atmosphere in a way that makes El Niños more likely to develop. This explanation for more frequent El Niños is "a reasonable hypothesis that needs to be looked at," says Kevin Trenberth, a scientist who studies El Niño at the National Center for Atmospheric Research (NCAR) in Boulder, Colorado. "There are definitely unprecedented things happening."

For instance, he says, the temperature of the atmosphere in the tropical Pacific has been rising since the late 1970s. Trenberth speculates that the ocean isn't

cooling off as much as it once did between El Niños because it is absorbing more heat from the greenhouse-warmed atmosphere. This could conceivably diminish the length of the interval between ocean warmings and bring more frequent El Niños.

But some atmospheric researchers are skeptical, if not dismissive, of this explanation. "I don't believe it for a minute," says meteorologist James O'Brien, director of the Center for Ocean-Atmospheric Prediction Studies at Florida State University in Tallahassee. "This has happened before, so I'm not going to attribute it to some scary monster called greenhouse warming." Records of ocean temperatures, O'Brien says, show that El Niño returned repeatedly between 1939 and 1941.

Trenberth insists, however, that something has changed in the Pacific. In the last 20 years, there have been six El Niños. At the same time, he notes, there have been fewer periods in between of below-normal ocean cooling. These are known as La Niña, "the girl." To Trenberth, the scarcity of La Niñas means an overall warming trend in the Pacific Ocean. This could explain the repeated El Niños of the last four years.

The role of global warming is not the only topic of debate among El Niño researchers. Gregg Jacobs, an oceanographer at the Stennis Space Center in Mississippi, and colleagues at the University of Colorado say they've detected the relic — a kind of heat echo called a Rossby wave — of an El Niño that ended 12 years ago. They suspect the remnants of past El Niños may still roam the seas and perhaps even affect the climate.

Rossby waves aren't anything like ordinary, wind-driven surface waves, however. A Rossby wave is simply an abnormally warm region of the ocean, like an El Niño but not nearly as large. When El Niño's warmth encounters a continent, part of it bounces back, creating a Rossby wave.

According to Jacobs and his

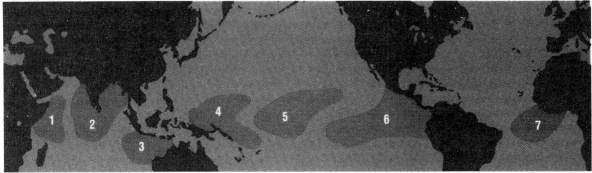

EARTH: Steven G. Davis

Source: Yves M. Tourre, Columbia University Lamont-Doherty Earth Observatory

El Niño warming does not seem to be confined to the Pacific Ocean, as shown in this illustration. As an El Niño progresses, a pool of warm water moves east across the Indian Ocean (1 through 3) at about the same time a similar pool moves across the Pacific (4 through 6). Twelve to 18 months later, an additional warm pool (7) develops in the Atlantic Ocean. Left: A map of sea surface temperatures measured last November shows warm pools of water (darkest areas) building in the Pacific and Indian oceans—the beginnings of this year's El Niño.

colleagues, the Rossby wave they've found was set in motion by the infamous El Niño of 1982-83. Often called "the El Niño of the century," the Pacific warming that struck in 1982 devastated marine life and brought disastrous droughts or torrential rains to various parts of the world. Some scientists consider it the greatest disturbance of the ocean and atmosphere in recorded history.

The researchers detected the Rossby wave using satellite observations of water movements in the Pacific Ocean. In their scenario, part of the warm pool that struck the Americas during the 1982-83 El Niño headed northwest after bouncing off the coast of North America. Right now, this elderly Rossby wave is headed toward Asia like an echo in an immense canyon. The researchers say it has already had

a measurable effect on the ocean: The Kuroshio Extension, a current that normally flows east away from the coast of Japan, may have been deflected considerably north of its normal path in a collision with the Rossby wave.

If Rossby waves from long-gone El Niños are still rolling around the Pacific, then it's anyone's guess how they might affect the atmosphere and ocean. Some researchers have suggested that Rossby waves might introduce random "noise," like the background hiss of a radio, into the circulation of the ocean and atmosphere. This might explain why El Niño occurs at irregular instead of fixed intervals.

Even more intriguing, some scientists have raised the possibility that heat from this old Rossby wave could even influence the weather — that it may

have actually played a role in the 1993 Mississippi floods. But NCAR's Trenberth has grave doubts about the whole basis of this speculation. In the first place, he doubts the wave is as old as Jacobs thinks. And if a Rossby wave from the 1982-83 El Niño can persist for so long, then why isn't the ocean cluttered up with the echoes of other El Niños? "I don't want to say it's not possible," he says, "but it's not proven."

O'Brien is more enthusiastic about Jacobs' work. "It's a new way to think about the memory of the ocean," he says. He found the satellite observations particularly convincing. "If they hadn't had the satellite confirmation, nobody would have believed it, including me," he says.

On a broader front, scientists are also trying to understand El Niño's apparent long-distance connections outside the Pacific basin. For example, Yves Tourre of Lamont-Doherty Earth Observatory and Warren White of Scripps Institution of Oceanography in La Jolla, California, have recently completed the most detailed study yet of a warming in the Indian Ocean that appears to move in sync with the Pacific El Niño.

Scientists have known about this Indian Ocean El Niño for a while, but Tourre and White are the first to take its temperature below the surface — to a depth of 1,300 feet (400 meters), in fact. This measurement tells the researchers how much heat is stored beneath the surface of the ocean, and this information is useful in forecasting: the more heat stored, the longer and more severe an El Niño can be. Until this study, the Indian Ocean warming had been observed by satellites that could sense only the temperature of the ocean surface.

Tourre and White traced the movement of this warming based on ocean temperature data collected from 1979 to 1991 by cargo ships, fishing boats, research vessels and warships. These measurements showed that during the Pacific El Niños of 1982-83 and 1986-87, warm water off Africa's east coast drifted to the center of the Indian Ocean at the same time a warm pool reached the central Pacific. Then, as the warming in the Indian Ocean reached the Timor Sea, north of Australia, the Pacific El Niño reached its mature stage off South America.

Tourre and White also detected a warming and cooling cycle in the Atlantic Ocean that appears to be linked to the Indian and Pacific El Niños. At the peak of these warmings, winds blowing from the east over the Atlantic grew stronger. This cooled the topmost layer of the ocean off the coast of Africa. Twelve to eighteen months later, the winds died down, allowing the Atlantic waters to warm up.

The Pacific and Indian ocean El Niños behave as if connected by unseen processes in the atmosphere and ocean. Right now, Tourre and White admit, those links are far from clear. But the recognition of these warming and cooling patterns outside the Pacific might still prove useful in forecasting regional weather.

Like its counterpart in the Pacific, the Indian Ocean warming can drastically affect the atmosphere. It seems to suppress the summer monsoon rains farmers rely on for their livelihood. If dry summers in India and Australia could be forecast, says Tourre, it might give people time to prepare. Similarly, changes in ocean temperature and wind speed in the Atlantic are important because they affect the weather on adjacent continents. Again, establishing links between the Atlantic warming and cooling to weather patterns might provide better long-range forecasts.

Tourre and White's study only reiterates how much scientists' views of El Niño have changed. Once thought of as a regional warming that settled off the Pacific coast of South America every so often, El Niño is now regarded as only one aspect of a phenomenon that reaches virtually around the entire equatorial realm and has the ability to affect weather from San Francisco to Sydney.

ronically, even if El Niño researchers achieve their ultimate goal — a complete model of the ocean and atmosphere that can help them predict this chronic catastrophe — forecasters would still be wrong some significant fraction of the time. This is because the weather is driven by processes that don't progress in a highly predictable manner, like the falling of a line of dominoes. Instead, the weather is influenced by inherently unpredictable "nonlinear" processes.

That means that some degree of uncertainty may always plague the computer models used to forecast El Niño's effects on the weather. "The system is simply so complicated," says Nicholas Graham of Scripps Institution of Oceanography. "It's got some profound nonlinearities in it — billions of moving parts, connected by billions of springs and moving levers."

Despite the remaining questions and uncertainties about El Niño, researchers are pleased with the progress they've made since severe El Niños in the 1970s and 1980s demonstrated the phenomenon's great and far-reaching destructive potential. "If you go back seven or eight years ago, we couldn't predict El Niño very reliably," says Eric Barron of Pennsylvania State University, who chairs a National Research Council committee on climate research. "But the last several Niños have been [forecast] months in advance. I wouldn't say we've got the timing down cold, but we've made real progress."

Michael McPhaden, director of the Tropical Atmosphere Ocean Array project at the Pacific Marine Environmental Laboratory in Seattle, also sees a bright future for model-based forecasting of El Niños. "Given the dramatic progress in the past 10 years, I'm very optimistic the models are going to improve with time — significantly."

Real success will come when scientists can anticipate El Niño's effects on regional weather as well as its time of arrival or departure. To that end, scientists such as Ants Leetmaa of the National Weather Service's Climate Analysis Center in Camp Springs, Maryland, is studying possible links between U.S. weather and the time of El Niño's peak warming.

Even though it may not be possible to flawlessly anticipate the behavior of an inherently unruly beast such as the atmosphere, "at the rate knowledge is advancing, we should be able to predict whether you're going to get excess drought *or* rain," says Florida State's O'Brien. That's because enough El Niños have been studied that meteorologists have identified some general trends in its effects on climate.

Consequently, once El Niño begins to show itself, the future becomes somewhat more predictable. Partly because of this increased understanding of El Niño, the National Weather Service has announced that it will begin issuing national forecasts of seasonal average temperatures and precipitation a full year in advance, four times the previous limit of three months.

If this confidence is justified, then the summer of 1995 will bring unseasonably warm temperatures in the eastern and western United States and unusually cool temperatures in the South. The El Niño that set in last year is expected to peak in the spring, cool down a bit and then linger for the rest of the year, tired but untamed.

And if the scientists are wrong? Then it's back to the drawing board.

The Tortured Land

An epic landscape steeped in tragedy, Siberia suffered grievously under communism. Now the world's capitalists covet its vast riches

EUGENE LINDEN YAKUTSK

SIBERIA HAS COME TO MEAN A land of exile, and the place easily fulfills its reputation as a metaphor for death and deprivation. Even at the peak of midsummer, a soul-chilling fog blows in off the Arctic Ocean and across the mossy tundra, muting the midnight sun above the ghostly remains of a slave-labor camp. The mist settles like a shroud over broken grave markers and bits of wooden barracks siding bleached as gray as the bones of the dead that still protrude through the earth in places. Throughout Siberia, more than 20 million perished in Stalin's Gulag.

Siberia is much, much more, however, than the locus of past political evil. For every person sent unwillingly to exile in its arctic wastelands, many others came to hunt, trap, fish, log or mine. The harsh life drove many back, but others stayed, captivated by the sublime beauty of earth's greatest northern landscape. Vitali Menshikov, an oceanographer by training, came to the Kamchatka peninsula in the Far East 27 years ago. He has returned to Leningrad only once; instead, he has used his vacations to take expeditions—61 so far—on ski and foot through this breathtaking land of volcanoes, geysers, forests, lakes and meadows.

Kurilskoye Lake, in the southern part of the peninsula, offers a glimpse of a paradise lost elsewhere on the planet. Sockeye salmon choke the mouths of streams, huge brown bears and their cubs feed on cloudberries in the surrounding sun-dappled meadows, while a giant stellar sea eagle rides the thermals on the flanks of one of the volcanoes ringing the lake. Boulders made of porous volcanic rock float at the edge of the lake, seemingly defying gravity. George Schaller, the renowned and famously dour American wildlife biologist, who is visiting the region to study brown bears, looks out over the natural bounty, and a broad smile splits his face. "Bears never had it so good," he says. "Isn't it nice to go somewhere and find good news?"

No one would disagree, but, as Schaller knows, the comforting image of Siberia as the world's last pristine northern frontier also misses the mark. Kamchatka is but a tiny piece of Siberia, and elsewhere this continent-size region has been grievously wounded, and continues to be wounded today. "Let's say you decide to get away from it all in Siberia," says Alexei Yablokov, Russia's leading environmentalist and once President Boris Yeltsin's top adviser on ecology. "You travel up the Yenisey River toward the Arctic. You look across the empty tundra and think you are alone in nature, miles upon miles from the nearest person, and you decide to stretch out on the riverbank. Unfortunately, you are lying in sands contaminated by plutonium from three upstream nuclear reactors whose radioactive wastes have been carelessly dumped for over 40 years."

Under 70 years of communist rule, Siberia became not only a place of punishment but also a punished place, and nuclear trauma was but one of the tortures visited on the land. Possibly the largest single source of air pollution in the world is a complex of smelters in Norilsk in central Siberia; it pumps 2 million tons of sulfur, along with heavy metals and other poisons, into the air each year, contributing heavily to a noxious arctic haze that plagues residents of the northern latitudes as far away as Canada. Siberian industrial emissions contribute heavily to the threat of global warming, which in turn may come back to burn the region. Nearly two-thirds of the region lies atop permafrost. Climate models estimate that even a small temperature rise globally would be exaggerated in the north, and could melt the upper parts of the permafrost, turning huge areas of Siberia into mush and toppling the thousand of Soviet-era buildings erected on stilts sunk into the ice. The price for ridding Siberia of ugly Stalinist architecture, however, would be that the meltdown would release enormous amounts of methane, exacerbating climate change.

The perverse genius of the Soviet system was its ability to maximize the problems associated with modern industrial societies without producing many of the benefits. Perhaps never has so vast a territory been so despoiled so rapidly. Now the question is whether the capitalism of the new Russia will save Siberia and its reeling ecosystems or finish them off. The stakes could not be higher, involving the future of earth's grandest northern landscape and the political stability of a nuclear superpower.

The expanse and the magnitudes of Siberia are mesmerizing. Officially Siberia is the territory east of the Ural Mountains and west of the Russian Far East, which includes the maritime provinces of Khabarovsk and Primorski on the Pacific coast; however, convention has labeled as Siberia all Russian lands east of the Urals—an area that covers more than 5 million sq. mi. Within these boundaries are nearly the entire lengths of four of the longest rivers on earth—the Yenisey, the Ob, the Lena and the Amur, which constitutes most of Siberia's border with China. Yakutia, now designated the Sakha Republic and the largest of Siberia's dozens of political divisions, is more than seven times the size of California. Magadan is three times; Krasnoyarsk is nearly six Californias. The entire region is frigid

From *Time*, September 4, 1995, pp. 42-48, 49, 51-53. © 1995 by Time Inc. Magazine Company. Reprinted by permission.

in winter. Oimyakon in Yakutia is often cited as the coldest inhabited settlement on earth, with winter temperatures dropping to −94°F. The summers are so short that plants rush wildly to take advantage of the brief heat and light. In some parts of Kamchatka, grasses grow up to 3 in. a day. During that season, bugs proliferate and clouds of mosquitoes, dubbed *gnusy* (the vile ones), can turn brief strolls into interludes with the vampires.

The vast expanses contain natural oddities and wonders. In the far north, climate and physics conspire to defy common sense. Lakes wander up to 10 ft. a year as their waters accumulate summer heat and melt the edges of their permafrost boundaries. Summer melting of the upper layers of the permafrost also allows leaves frozen since the Pleistocene era to return to their slow-motion decay. For years scientists were puzzled by the age of methane gases released from arctic lakes, which radiocarbon dating revealed to be more than 10,000 years old. Mammoths that strode the earth in millenniums past are still discovered almost perfectly preserved in the permafrost meat locker. Many believe the present-day Yakutian horse is itself a throwback to the era of the ice ages. With such conflation of past and present, it seems almost reasonable when one Russian ecologist, Sergei Zimov, suggests that a "Pleistocene Park" could be established using the DNA magic of its Jurassic movie counterpart. Some scientists believe the mammoth could be brought back by inserting readily available, naturally refrigerated mammoth DNA into an elephant embryo.

The natural wonders of Siberia inspire the imagination of scientists and tourists; its vast riches beckon others. The taiga, the word used to describe the region's enormous forests, in particular has captured the attention of both foreigners and Russians. Japan, Korea and the U.S. covet the rich forests of southern Siberia. The Russian government sees its timber as a quick source of cash to prop up an economy that continues to flounder. Fearful of an economic collapse that might once again bring to power a hostile, nuclear-armed totalitarian regime, the U.S. is trying to promote the responsible exploitation of the region's resources, in part through a series of agreements on trade and technology negotiated by U.S. Vice President Al Gore and Russian Prime Minister Victor Chernomyrdin. Argues Gore: "It is unlikely that you are going to see an area larger than the U.S. ruled off limits to forestry by a nation struggling for hard currency to make the transition to democracy and free markets. If that is so, doing it the right way rather than the wrong way is an advantage."

FORESTS, HOWEVER, ARE JUST one item in Siberia's bulging portfolio of natural resources. Soviet exploitation managed to poison and degrade 35,000 sq. mi. of the vast republic, but that only scratched the surface of its mineral wealth. Bob Logan, an economist at the University of Alaska, has made trips to Yakutia to study the region's economic prospects, which he describes as "staggering." As much as 20% of the territory is known to have oil and gas deposits that could make it the Saudi Arabia of the north. The area is one of the world's leading sources of diamonds, and Logan notes that 80% of the gold produced there comes from riverbeds and ancient gravel banks, an indication that the republic has barely begun to tap its underground veins.

The world looks upon all these resources and salivates. Texaco, Exxon, Amoco, Norsk Hydro and other transnational oil companies are setting up joint ventures to tap into the enormous oil and gas reserves scattered through Siberia, including the Timan Pechora basin above the Arctic Circle (where the recoverable reserves are estimated at nearly 4 billion bbl.). Canadian, American and other Western mining companies are prospecting for gold and other minerals. Norwegian and Japanese interests are negotiating to increase shipping between Europe and Asia by way of arctic waters north of Siberia.

Russia wants to realize income from the region's resources as fast as possible. Russian environmentalists, however, say they need time to put in environmental safeguards. Buying time for one purpose will inevitably come at the expense of the other.

Environmentalists have reason to be wary. In recent years, the decline in law and order in the former U.S.S.R. has led to a tremendous increase in poaching, particularly of the Amur tiger. Tigers once roamed Russia from the Caspian Sea to the Pacific and from the Chinese border to the Arctic. Now only the Amur subspecies remains, hemmed in to the forests of Primorski province by the Pacific Ocean and the Chinese border.

No one knows how many tigers are left, but today Primorski province is estimated to have between 180 and 200, down from 350 in 1990. Vasili Solkin, the head of the Russian environmental group Zov Taigi, which means Roar of the Taiga, estimates that in 1993 alone, 75 to 80 tigers were killed, representing more than one-quarter of the remaining population. When traditional East Asian apothecaries ran out of sources for tiger skin and bones, which are used as medicine, among the places to which they turned for new sup-

plies was Siberia. At the same time enforcement efforts collapsed as budgets for ranger patrols disappeared and corruption flourished, driven by stagnant salaries and hyperinflation.

Nevertheless, market chaos and international attention appear to have alleviated the crisis somewhat. In 1994 poaching began to drop dramatically. Solkin says that last year between 25 and 30 tigers were killed, about the level of poaching during the Soviet period. He argues that as many as 40% of the tigers killed in the early 1990s were never sold because of the anarchic marketplace and fear of being caught, and notes that drug dealers who dabbled in the illegal wildlife trade have backed off because trouble over a tiger skin could jeopardize an established channel for moving drugs.

The tiger-poaching crisis also showed the degree to which Russians can control an environmental problem when they have the resources. Russia has many dedicated game rangers who were thrown out of work by the collapse of the U.S.S.R. A group of international organizations led by American environmental investigator Steven Galster cobbled together the funding to put rangers back to work, and the newly formed patrols have been in the field since January 1994. The so-called Amba patrols have been working to disrupt poachers and their trade networks. Amba was given a boost this summer when Prime Minister Chernomyrdin issued a decree calling for a national strategy to protect tigers and their habitat. Unfortunately, protecting the forests that are home to tigers and other creatures is one environmental problem that is literally out of control.

According to environmentalist Yablokov, the problem can be traced to the waning days of the U.S.S.R. when the parliament, seeking to circumvent the power of the central government, passed laws that gave local authorities enormous power over resources, as well as the implied right to contravene federal regulations protecting ecosystems. Nonetheless, it was thought that the strong central government could still maintain the balance of power. Then came the August 1991 attempted coup against President Mikhail Gorbachev and the rapid unraveling of Soviet authority. With no federal checks on local power, according to Yablokov, these laws became the legal basis for the devastation of natural resources. Local politicians are quite happy with this situation because it gives them a free hand to turn a profit.

Loggers take pains to lend a pretense of legality to their ventures, but loopholes and lack of enforcement make it easy to bend the law in ingenious and profitable ways. In the district of Khabarovsk, the government tried to impose environmental controls on logging but allowed officials to exempt concessions smaller than 5,000 acres from strict review. Alexander Kulikov, chairman of the Khabarovsk Wildlife Foundation, says that just before they leave office, local officials hand out dozens of concessions, often to friends and relatives. He says that in the Khor River watershed, a region of about 12,000 sq. mi., more than 90 forest enterprises are operating with almost no oversight from the government. "What is the solution?" asks an exasperated Yablokov. "Chechnya? Send troops to Novosibirsk?"

Vice President Gore's answer is to send U.S. experts. Were U.S. involvement confined to sound environmental practices, American expertise might actually help. But U.S. initiatives are a tangle promoting contradictory programs: the U.S. is sponsoring a project to protect biodiversity in the Khor River watershed while at the same time giving grants to study the feasibility of logging in the region. Moreover, critics point out that the U.S. has a less than thrilling record preserving its own forests. The U.S. has less than 5% of its ancient forests and suffers from a timber shortage; Russia has roughly 25% of its original forests intact.

Kulikov is dubious about these American initiatives. He fears that sound forestry practices will be sacrificed early on because they have not yet proved profitable anywhere in the region. And even in the best of circumstances, U.S. solutions may not work. Says Yuri Dunishenko, the vice chairman of Khabarovsk's Wildlife Research Institute: "We have different soils and a much harsher climate than the U.S. What works in the U.S. may not work here."

A consequence of the various forestry initiatives may be a surge in anti-Western feeling, the very thing Gore hopes to prevent. While communism ravaged the land, the Soviet commissars did leave a powerful legacy: a conviction that forests and other resources are owned by all Russians and not some favored élite. Consequently, the wholesale sell-off of Siberia has aroused great bitterness among Russians. "You own us now," says an official sarcastically. Ordinary people are frustrated by corrupt courts, by self-dealing and favoritism and by confiscatory taxes that force honest businesspeople to become cheaters. Increasingly, their ire is directed against the new order. When asked to name the greatest threat to Russia's wildlife, Vladimir Shetinin, the head of the Amba patrols, responds with one word: "Democracy." It is a widely shared opinion.

WHILE THE LIQUIDATION OF FORESTS PREOCcupies Siberia's south, the northern regions are obsessed with the dream of better transportation links to the outside world. In giant

Siberia Undercover

I am sitting in the sparsely furnished living room of an Udege house in southeastern Siberia while the owner tries to sell me a tiger skin and bones. My cover is that I am part of a group of American businessmen here for a week of bird watching. The other "bird watchers" consist of Steven Galster, an environmental investigator, Anthony Suau, a TIME photographer, and Sergei Shaitarov, a Russian environmentalist who works with Galster. My ludicrously rudimentary disguise consists of a borrowed pair of binoculars. If the tiger trader asks me to name one species of local bird, we are sunk.

The impromptu undercover operation was a piece of serendipity. Galster had come to the village of Krasny Yar to encourage the Udege to set up an antipoaching squad. Galster is the executive director of a private environmental-security organization called the Investigative Network, which helps fund the antipoaching team. Seeing a group of Americans in Krasny Yar, Leonid, the poacher/trader, had approached Sergei and offered his services as a hunting guide. After a short conversation it turned out that Leonid had a tiger skin and bones he wanted to sell. Sergei arranged for us to see the skin later.

Nongovernmental environmental investigators like Galster, who was trained in intelligence techniques, are really rare birds and fun to watch. In 1993 Galster tracked shipments of rhino horn from Mozambique to Taiwan to Hong Kong. The operation ultimately brought Galster to a warehouse in Wuchuan, China, that contained the horns of more than 500 dead black rhinos worth $13 million.

The sellers, who worked for a state medicine company, were part of a dangerous syndicate. Rebecca Chin, a Taiwanese colleague who carried a concealed video camera in a shoulder bag, was trembling so badly that the film was unusable. Galster and Chin fabricated a reason to see the horn again and produced a damning videotape that landed the officials in jail and called international attention to the scale of the threat Asian trade poses to black rhinos.

Six months later, again pretending to be buyers, the two followed a trail of tiger and bear parts from Vladivostok, Russia, to Harbin, China. Using a camera concealed in the buttonhole of a gaudy sport jacket, Galster had the pleasure of videotaping the bandits as they told him they had to be careful because they had read about an American man and Chinese woman who had busted a rhino-horn ring in Wuchuan.

The poacher Leonid was not in the same league as the Chinese syndicates. Preparing to meet the tiger seller in Krasny Yar, Galster had taken the precaution of taping over the recording indicator on his video camera so that he could film even when the camera appeared to be off. This turned out to be unnecessary, since the poacher even offered to pose with the skin of the year-old tiger he was selling. As we chatted, Leonid remarked that killing a tiger was a very bad thing among the Udege, but that it was O.K. for him to sell the skin because he had not killed the animal. "They all say that," said Galster later.

After pretending to examine the remains for quality, we got down to bargaining. Leonid asked for 50 million rubles (about $11,000) for the skin and bones. Following a rehearsed script, I said it was a lot of money and wanted to think about it. Galster gave the poacher my binoculars as a gesture of good faith. Later Galster reported Leonid to a local biologist and was told that this was not his first transgression. As we left Krasny Yar, Galster pondered the delicate problem of telling Vladimir Shetinin, the head of the Amba antipoaching team, that he had given his binoculars to a tiger poacher.

—By Eugene Linden/Krasny Yar

Yakutia, officials speak of the benefits of a sea route across the top of the continent that will open their territories. They long to be free of extortionate transportation mafias that saddle the region with what may be the highest shipping costs in the world. The fees are so high that merchants in Cherski often find it more economical to import food products from Alaska than buy from elsewhere in Russia—and Alaska has the highest

food prices in the U.S. The northern passage has been used by the military and some Russian shippers for decades. According to Norwegian economist Trond Ramsland, who has analyzed the costs and benefits of the northern sea route, it can provide a link between East Asia and Europe, vastly shorter and cheaper than the present voyage through the Suez Canal. Ramsland argues that shippers could move goods at an average cost of

$35 a ton, as much as $10 a ton cheaper and 11 days faster than shipping through the Suez.

Since the northern sea route was opened to commercial foreign traffic in 1992, however, only one vessel has made the complete trip. Big insurers are loath to underwrite these ventures, given the severity of the northern weather and uncertainty over Russia's ability to keep the route open. Indeed, instead of charging minimal fees to grab market share, the Russian authority responsible for the sea route set the administration fees at $6 a ton, eating up most of the savings that might come from taking the route.

Market pressures and the demands of the Russian economy may eventually make the route financially viable. That is a moment many environmentalists dread. Tankers are likely to be the chief users of the route, and oil spills could do unimaginable harm to arctic ecosystems. Dorothy Childers of Greenpeace points out that the sea route follows the easiest path through the polar ice, the same path taken by migratory birds and marine mammals. Will development be worth the risk?

YAKUTIA, WHICH SUFFERED HORRIBLY from radioactive fallout from nuclear tests and chemical pollution during the Soviet era, has shown itself to be farsighted in dealing with some environmental issues. The delta of the Lena River lies atop reserves of oil and gas. It is also a diverse ecosystem created in part by the meeting of the great tectonic plates that lie under North America and Eurasia. Mindful of Siberia's sorry record of leaky oil pipelines and catastrophic spills, the republic was

hesitant to open this vulnerable area to drilling. Says Vasili Alekseev, the Minister of Ecology: "Since there is no truly clean technology to extract those reserves, we felt it better to create the Lena Delta Biosphere Reserve and protect the area. Perhaps in 50 or 100 years there will be a new technology for extraction, and then, if we still need oil and gas, future generations can decide whether to review the reserve's status." This is a perspective that Yakutia's arctic neighbors in Alaska might consider, as oil and gas interests clamor to open the great Arctic National Wildlife Refuge for drilling.

South and East of Yakutia, jutting 750 miles into the Pacific Ocean, lies the Kamchatka peninsula, the only major piece of the former Soviet Union to survive decades of communism relatively unscathed. A peninsula larger than North and South Korea combined, Kamchatka has stunning treasures to preserve: active volcanoes, wild rivers, hot springs, floating boulders and other natural wonders. It was spared the forced march of Soviet-style economic development. Because of its strategic location, it was sealed off from foreigners and most Russians for 65 years. With only 450,000 people, most of whom live in and around the capital, Petropavlovsk, the region is probably the largest pristine northern territory in the world. "We are aware that there are not many untouched places like Kamchatka in the world," says Boris Sinchenko, first vice governor of the Kamchatka region administration. "We have looked at what mining has done elsewhere, and we will not go the route of Magadan and Yakutia." Nor does he see Alaska as a model, noting that it has been "spoiled" by mining and

oil development. Instead he sees future growth coming from fishing, tourism and some mining in tightly controlled circumstances. The authorities in Kamchatka know how to act decisively. In 1994, after a binge of poaching and sport hunting halved the number of brown bears in just five years, wildlife officials clamped down on the use of helicopters during hunts. The bear population has stabilized at around 5,000.

Kamchatka, however, must contend with the same pressures as the rest of Russia. Sinchenko admits that the government is under great pressure to replace the subsidies and remittances that ended with the collapse of the Soviet Union. Ecologists are worried that the local government will finance those expenses on the back of the environment by opening Kamchatka's rich mineral reserves to development. David Gordon of the Pacific Environment Resources Center, a California-based environmental group that has focused its efforts on threats to Siberia, notes that even now an American-Russian joint venture is preparing to mine gold in an area near two salmon rivers that was once intended to be part of a reserve. He fears that the way in which the project is being rammed through—without proper environmental review—sets a troubling precedent. Kamchatka has more than 300 other potential mine sites, many of them near existing or proposed nature reserves.

DURING THE SOVIET ERA, THE GOVERNMENT used coercion, monetary inducements and subsidies to populate Siberia because of the region's strategic importance. Now that the subsidies have disappeared, people are leaving in search of jobs elsewhere. Of the Kamchatka peninsula's 450,000 people, 320,000 live in two cities. The rest of the peninsula has less than one person per 4 sq. km. But still, people are leaving. The peninsula has lost 40,000 people, nearly 10% of its population, since 1985. In Yakutia, the Arctic city of Cherski, near the mouth of the Kolyma River above the Arctic Circle, has lost nearly half its population in just the past two years. (Recently, though, it has had a reported influx of Russian mafia hit men who use the town as a "riverbed"—slang for a hiding place—to cool off between assassinations.)

The outflow from Siberia helps put to rest one of the most enduring myths about the region—that it is virtually empty. The number of humans is in fact low in absolute terms. Currently Siberia has 30 million inhabitants, with the largest concentrations in cities like Novosibirsk (pop. 1.4 million) and Vladivostok (pop. 640,000). The entire Russian Far East, covering 2.4 million sq. mi., has 8 million people, less than the population of Moscow. But Siberia is not empty; it is not even underpopulated.

Perhaps the most vivid example of the complex demographics comes from Primorski province in the heart of a vast and pristine watershed. When told that the outside world views their forests as empty, four Udege hunters laugh uproariously. They argue that too many people are already using the forest. A study shows that only half the watershed's nearly 5,000 sq. mi. ot forest produces enough sable, deer and elk to support hunters. And a single tribal hunter must roam a territory as large as 75 sq. mi.—about the size of the Caribbean island of Aruba—to trap enough fur and hunt enough meat to live on. That allowance is calculated to provide wildlife the space and opportunity to reproduce and maintain stable populations. The Bikin Valley has 47 hunters licensed to hunt full time in the territory, which already presses the limits of the available productive forests. Add to that 90 other permitted hunters who enter their grounds to hunt for meat and, as the region opens up, sport hunters and poachers, and the ecological calculus for the survival of species goes completely awry.

STILL, THE SMALL HUMAN POPulations of Primorski, Kamchatka, Khabarovsk, Yakutia and the other republics and provinces of Siberia are a luxury shared by few other places on earth. They give the region the opportunity to restore the ecological balance. And while it is tempting to draw parallels between the ecological standards of Siberia and those of most of the Third World, there is a tremendous body of environmental expertise and activism among the Russian people. For every profiteer who would make a quick buck off the fire sale of Siberia's assets, there are many who decry the theft of national patrimony. What Russia does not have is time and money, and the paradoxical nature of its plight is that it must sell its resources in order to stabilize its economy and thus create a democracy in which rules can be enforced regulating the exploitation of those resources.

As of now many major corporations are still poised on the sidelines. Russia's tax laws and the mercurial nature of its legal system still discourage major investment. For instance, some months after Yakutia passed its first constitution, Russia imposed a number of changes on the document. Says economist Logan: "Nobody is going to make investments looking 25 or 30 years into the future in a country where changes can be imposed at the constitutional level by fiat." Nevertheless, Russia is struggling to resolve these problems, and when it does, the real land rush will begin.

When that moment comes, neither the problems nor the solutions will be Russia's alone. Those who are pushing the clanking machines toward the forests' edge and those who will profit from the Siberian harvest need to be responsible and restrained. The high technology and efficiency of the West can help reduce rampant waste and pollution, but they can also speed destruction.

Land-Human Relationships

The home of humankind is Earth's surface and the thin layer of atmosphere enveloping it. Here the human populace has struggled over time to change the physical setting and to create the telltale signs of occupation. Humankind has greatly modified Earth's surface to suit its purposes. At the same time, we have been greatly influenced by the very environment that we have worked to change.

This basic relationship of humans and land is important in geography and, in unit 1, William Pattison identified it as one of the four traditions of geography. Geographers observe, study, and analyze the ways in which human occupants of Earth have interacted with the physical environment. This unit presents a number of articles that illustrate the theme of land-human relationships. In some cases, the association of humans and the physical world has been mutually beneficial; in others, environmental degradation has been the result.

At the present time, the potential for major modifications of Earth's surface and the atmosphere is greater than at any other time in history. It is crucially important that the consequences of these modifications for the environment be clearly understood before such efforts are undertaken.

The first selection in this unit deals with serious environmental problems in sub-Saharan Africa. The next piece draws on literature to detail the experiences in encountering cold environments. Then, changing land use is examined by William Meyer, and Eugene Linden's article points out that more disease may be the outcome of global warming.

Can the rain forests of Earth be saved? What is the climatic impact of their wholesale destruction? Richard Monastersky, in "The Deforestation Debate," discusses a NASA program to improve the assessments of global de-forestation. William Stevens reports on recent studies indicating that desertification may not be as serious a problem as originally believed. The last unit article reports on the Chernobyl nuclear catastrophe ten years after the event.

This unit provides a small sample of the many ways in which humans interact with the environment. The outcomes of these interactions may be positive or negative. They may enhance the position of humankind and protect the environment, or they may do just the opposite. We human beings are the guardians of the physical world. We have it in our power to protect, to neglect, or to destroy.

Looking Ahead: Challenge Questions

What are the long-range implications of atmospheric pollution? Explain the greenhouse effect.

How can the problem of regional transfer of pollutants be solved?

The manufacture of goods needed by humans produces pollutants that degrade the environment. How can this dilemma be solved?

What would be the climatic effect of losing the tropical rain forests?

Where in the world are there serious problems of desertification and drought? Why are these areas increasing in size?

What will be the major forms of energy in the next century?

How are you as an individual related to the land?

Can humankind do anything to ensure the protection of the environment?

What is your attitude toward the environment?

UNIT 2

The Environmental Challenges in Sub-Saharan Africa

Akin L. Mabogunje

Akin L. Mabogunje is chairman of the Development Policy Centre in Ibadan, Nigeria, and a former professor of geography at the University of Ibadan.

Sub-Saharan Africa suffers from some serious environmental problems, including deforestation, soil erosion, desertification, wetland degradation, and insect infestation. Efforts to deal with these problems, however, have been handicapped by a real failure to understand their nature and possible remedies. Conventional wisdom views the people of this region as highly irresponsible toward the environment and looks to the international community to save them from themselves. It tends to blame all of the region's environmental problems on rapid population growth and poverty. Yet, there is no conclusive evidence that Africans have been particularly oblivious to the quality of the environment, nor has the international community shown any genuine concern for it until recently. Clearly, protecting the environment of sub-Saharan Africa is an issue that needs to be examined more carefully and incorporated into an overall strategy of sustainable economic development.

Formulating such a strategy will not be easy: In the closing years of the 20th century, virtually every country in this region is slipping on almost every index of development. The heady post-independence period of the 1960s and early 1970s, when development was considered simply a matter of following a plan formulated by Western experts, has now been succeeded by a time of fiscal crises and international marginalization. The region now finds itself afflicted by the consequences of inappropriate policies, as well as by almost endemic political instability, an inability to manage its economies effectively, and an increasingly hostile external economic milieu. As simple survival has become more problematical, it has become increasingly difficult to avoid overexploiting natural resources and degrading the environment. Analysts are now concerned that this will compromise the prospects for sustainable development in the near future.[1]

To understand the full dimensions of the problem, it will first be necessary to examine the factors that pre-dispose sub-Saharan Africa to serious environmental degradation. This will permit a detailed investigation of the environmental problems cause by humans in both rural and urban areas, along with a suggestive and comparison between those problems and ones caused solely by nature. It will then be possible to look at the question of environmental protection in terms of sustainable development in the region and to suggest the roles that the state and international assistance ought to play.

The present situation offers an important opportunity to redirect development strategy in ways that will not only improve the social and economic well-being of people in this region but also enhance the quality of the environment in which they live.

Factors Predisposing to Environmental Degradation

There are three factors that strongly increase the threat of environmental degradation in sub-Saharan Africa: its demographics, its heavy burden of foreign debt, and the absence of democracy. Throughout the region, the end of the colonial period saw a tremendous expansion of social services, especially in the areas of education and healthcare. This led to a sharp decline in infant mortality and to a rapid increase in population. During the last 25 years, annual growth rates of 2.5 to 3.5 percent have caused the population of sub-Saharan Africa to double (to 570 million); at the current rate of increase, it should double again in the next 25 years.[2]

An increase of this magnitude within a relatively short time span implies a rising proportion of children in the population and thus a heavier burden on those who must care for them. This has led to mass migration to the cities

From *Environment*, May 1995, pp. 4-9, 31-35. © 1995 by the Helen Dwight Reid Educational Foundation. Reprinted by permission of Heldref Publications, 1319 Eighteenth Street, N.W. Washington, DC 20036-1802.

(particularly by adult males) and other efforts to supplement family income through nonfarm employment. As a result, there has been less time for farm work, and more labor-saving but environmentally harmful shortcuts are being taken. In forested areas, for instance, cleared land is used continuously, even though allowing it to lie fallow from time to time would result in greater productivity and less degradation. In dryland regions, cultivation has been extended into marginal lands that are more easily cleared and cultivated.

Turning to the second factor, countries in sub-Saharan Africa incurred large foreign debts in their efforts to industrialize and to provide their rapidly growing populations with modern social services. Most of these loans have been long-term ones from official sources and on concessional terms; as the need for borrowing has become more urgent, however, countries have turned increasingly to private, short-term loans at market rates. Thus, while in 1970 the region's total official debt (excluding that of South Africa and Namibia) was slightly more than $5 billion (U.S. dollars), by 1990 it had risen to nearly $140 billion. Total private debt, which was zero in 1970, was more than $20 billion in 1990. (With other external loans, the total indebtedness of the region was more than $171 billion by 1990.[3])

The problem, however, lies not so much in the rising level of debt as in the region's dwindling ability to service it. High dependence on the export of primary products left sub-Saharan African countries vulnerable to the long decline of commodity prices that began in the late 1970s. The total value of the region's agricultural exports has fallen dramatically, with the decline averaging 0.8 percent a year from 1975 to 1980, 2.9 percent a year from 1980 to 1985, and 2.5 percent a year from 1986 to 1988. (For some countries the decline has been even more pronounced.[4]) As a result, the burden of debt has risen markedly for most countries in the region. Between 1980 and 1989, the total external debt rose from 27 percent to 97 percent of gross national product and from 97 percent to 362 percent of exports.[5]

Not unexpectedly, most countries in sub-Saharan Africa have had to undergo major structural adjustments. This has entailed not only a drastic compression of imports and a sharp devaluation of national currencies but also the retrenchment of a sizable portion of the wage- and salary-earning population. As living conditions deteriorated, more people turned to survival agriculture, both in urban and rural areas. At the same time, sharply rising prices for imported energy products forced many families to fall back on wood and charcoal for their domestic energy needs. Clearly, these developments put acute strain on the environment everywhere in the region.

There is a growing realization that economic reforms cannot be achieved without a much greater degree of decentralization and democratization in the political process.

The performance of most African governments in implementing the reforms necessary to turn their economies around has also been a source of serious concern. The international community spent the years immediately following independence rationalizing (and sometimes applauding) the necessity for authoritarian one-party or military rule. Over time, these regimes have become inordinately corrupt and have managed the countries' economies without due concern for transparency and accountability. In most countries, this has led to a high level of political instability and social alienation that has impaired both development efforts and environmental protection. There is a growing realization that economic reforms cannot be achieved without a much greater degree of decentralization and democratization in the political process.

Much of the debate about sustainable development in sub-Saharan Africa has focused on the region's severe poverty. There is no question that poverty has become widespread. The World Bank estimates that between 1985 and 2000, the number of persons living below the poverty line will rise from 180 million to 265 million.[6] By 1990, the combination of rapid population growth and an economy in crisis had lowered per capita gross national product to $340, making this region one of the least developed in the world.

For neo-Malthusians, this poverty stems directly from overpopulation; in their view, the two will inevitably lead to an increase in land fragmentation, overutilization of agricultural and grazing land, more frequent famines, lower life expectancy, and considerable environmental degradation.[7] By contrast, the renowned agricultural economist, Ester Boserup, and others argue that population growth need not result in such dire consequences. In their view, population growth can promote more intensive agricultural practices and induce more favorable attitudes toward technological and organizational innovation that will not only increase productivity but improve environmental quality as well.[8]

Two considerations suggest that the second view is more applicable to the situation prevailing in sub-Saharan Africa. First, over the period 1600 to 1900, this region lost a large part of its population to internecine warfare and the slave trade. As a result, by 1900 the region was more sparsely populated than it had been earlier. Second, at 23 persons per square kilometer, the region's current population density is still low compared to that of Asia or Europe.

This is not to imply that there is no cause for concern about the environment in sub-Saharan Africa. One needs to keep a sense of perspective in addressing the question, however. The proper focus is on the region's poverty per se (as opposed to its population growth) and on the impact this has on the environment in both rural and urban areas.

2. LAND-HUMAN RELATIONSHIPS

Poverty and the Rural Environment

Despite its pervasive poverty, sub-Saharan Africa has substantial natural resources in its rural areas, including forests and grasslands, wetlands, cultivable soils, and other biological resources.[9] Although only 40 percent of the total land area is under cultivation or used for pasture, much of it is threatened by one form of damage or another.

Three types of environmental damage are occurring in sub-Saharan Africa: deforestation, degradation, and fragmentation. Deforestation is defined as "the temporary or permanent clearance of forest for agriculture or other uses, resulting in the permanent depletion of the crown cover of trees to less than 10 percent."[10] Degradation, on the other hand, refers to the temporary or permanent deterioration in the density or structure of vegetation cover or species composition.[11] It results from the removal of plants and trees important in the life cycle of other species, from erosion, and from other adverse changes in the local environment. Fragmentation arises from road construction and similar human intrusions in forest areas; it leaves forest edges vulnerable to increased degradation through changes in microclimates, loss of native species and the invasion of alien species, and further disturbances by human beings.

While there is no doubt that all three processes are taking an increasingly heavy toll on the forest and woodland areas of sub-Saharan Africa, there is considerable controversy over the exact rate at which this is occurring. Estimates based on the subjective judgment of experts or on data from low-resolution sensors on weather satellites are generally higher than those based on the more accurate data from high-resolution sensors on the Landsat and Spot satellites.[12] Until more of the latter data are available, the actual extent of deforestation will remain uncertain.

The United Nations Food and Agriculture Organization (FAO) estimates that forested land was converted to agricultural uses at increasing rates over the period 1981 to 1990 and that such changes accounted for 25 percent of the changes in forest cover during the period.[13] These changes were concentrated in the moist and dry forest lowland areas, where the average annual conversion rate was higher than in tropical rain forest areas. Except for the dry forest areas, however, conversion rates in sub-Saharan Africa are lower than those in Latin America and the Asia-Pacific region.

Degradation and fragmentation involve a much larger area than deforestation and pose a greater threat to the diversity of plant and animal life. Selective logging and the failure to pursue a systematic program for forest regeneration (either natural or artificial) are the two major factors promoting rapid degradation of the forest and woodland environment. Owing to the desperate need for foreign exchange, the rate of logging in sub-Saharan Africa rose more than 34 percent between 1979 and 1991, compared with a global average of only 19 percent. Similarly, the lack of foreign exchange to purchase petroleum has led to a rapid rise in the production of fuelwood and charcoal.[14]

There are no firm estimates of the harm resulting from degradation and fragmentation in the region. Two factors suggest that it is considerable, however: First, the ratio of forest regeneration to deforestation is as low as 1:32 in sub-Saharan Africa, compared with ratios of 1:2 in Asia and 1:6 in Latin America.[15] Second, one out of every six species in the tropical moist forests has some economically valuable, nontimber use.[16]

Nowhere is this loss of biological resources more marked than in the region's wetlands. These wetlands include river floodplains, freshwater swamps and lakes, and coastal and estuarine environments. They provide a number of valuable resources, including wood; foraging, hunting, and fishing opportunities; and land for crops and pasture. They also contribute significantly to aquifer recharge and flood control, as well as providing habitat for migratory birds and other organisms.

Degradation of these wetlands is due not to population growth or poverty but to modern development, principally the construction of major dams on important rivers. These dams control water flow over much of the rivers' length and impair the agricultural value of wetlands both by lowering water quality and by altering the extent and timing of floods.[17] In Nigeria's Benue floodplain, for instance, the reduction in flooding caused by the Lagdo Dam led to a 50 percent reduction in the area used for environmentally friendly flood-recession sorghum farming in the dry years of the mid-1980s.[18] Similarly, the Diama Barrage on the Senegal River, built to prevent incursion of salt water during periods of low river flow, is expected to cause the loss of some 7,000 tons of shrimp and fish, while Manantali Dam is expected to greatly reduce the fish catch in that river.

If wetlands are being degraded by inappropriate development, grasslands and other relatively dry areas are being degraded by both rapid population growth and inappropriate technology and land-use practices. Recent studies, however, highlight the resilience of dryland ecosystems and caution against confusing natural changes due to recurring droughts with the long-term degradation caused by human activities.[19] They also argue against the simplistic application of the general concepts of overgrazing and carrying capacity in dryland environments.

This is not to say that such factors as overgrazing, overcultivation, and excessive use of wood for fuel have not contributed to the degradation of drylands. Rather, it is to stress that degradation occurs only where these activities lead to detrimental changes to the soil system itself as well as to plant cover. Damage to the soil system results either from erosion or from physical and chemical changes in the soil itself. Erosion by wind or water is a serious problem in dryland areas because the naturally thin soil and its slow rate of formation make recovery difficult. Such erosion accounts for nearly 86 percent of the total degradation of dryland area in sub-Saharan Africa.[20] The remainder is primarily due to the loss of nutrients from excessive cultivation and lack of fertilization.

Estimates based on the GLASOD (Global Assessment of Soil Degradation) approach indicate that by 1992 nearly 320 million hectares of drylands in sub-Saharan Africa had degraded soils, ranging from light and moderate (77 percent) to strong and extreme (23 percent).[21] These estimates, however, represent a considerable (almost two-thirds) reduction in the area previously thought to be suffering desertification as a result of human activities. Improved monitoring capabilities are making it increasingly clear that climatic variations are responsible for much of the degradation of soils in the region.

Even so, the loss of biological diversity—due to habitat destruction, the introduction of exotic species, overharvesting, pollution, and other activities that affect natural ecosystems—is a growing problem in sub-Saharan Africa. This is especially significant because biodiversity is greatest in the tropics. According to one estimate, between 40 and 90 percent of all plant and animal species are found in tropical forests.[22] Based on current trends in habitat destruction, as many as 11 percent of total species may become extinct during every 10-year period from 1975 to 2015.[23]

Despite international agreements such as the Convention on International Trade in Endangered Species of Flora and Fauna (CITES), hunting of elephants, rhinoceroses, and alligators is still a major problem in some African countries. The situation is even more serious in the case of birds, because widespread pollution is destroying their habitats, often in imperceptible ways. Tragically, although most endangered species are technically under government protection, as a practical matter they are resources free for the taking.

Poverty and Urban Environments

Although sub-Saharan Africa is the least urbanized region in the world, its urban population is growing quite rapidly. In 1965, urban areas accounted for only 14 percent of the total population of the region; by 1990, however, such areas accounted for 29 percent, and by 2020, the figure should be more than 50 percent. Already, there are 27 metropolitan areas with populations greater than 1 million and 1 (Lagos) with a population of at least 10 million.[24]

Consequently, even in urban areas, the widespread poverty exerts a strong negative impact on air, water, and land resources. The ongoing economic crisis has intensified the level of air pollution in most countries. Most households can no longer afford to use petroleum or gas products for fuel and are relying increasingly on charcoal or wood. This has greatly increased the amount of carbon dioxide generated by cities in the region. While in 1991 the region accounted for just 2 percent of global carbon dioxide emissions from industrial processes, its total contribution to global carbon dioxide emissions (from both urban and rural areas) was 19 percent.[25] Also contributing to the problem is the increased use of substandard industrial equipment and motor vehicles, made necessary because the region lacks the funds to invest in more environmentally responsible devices. Thus, three countries in the region—South Africa, Zaire, and Nigeria—are now ranked among the top 50 countries in terms of their 1991 contributions to global greenhouse emissions.[26]

Air pollution, both indoor and outdoor, exposes the population to serious health hazards, especially from suspended particulate matter and lead. Most sub-Saharan African cities do not yet suffer from serious outdoor pollution. Nonetheless, the increased use of wood and charcoal in household kitchens is exacerbating indoor air pollution and heightening the risk of acute respiratory infections, particularly among infants and children. In some areas, lead pollution from substandard vehicles is also starting to increase the risks of hypertension, heart attacks, and strokes.

Access to clean water is also a major problem throughout sub-Saharan Africa. Although the region as a whole has large water resources, a number of countries in the drier areas have experienced serious shortages. Within these countries, some 35 percent of the urban population has no source of drinking water within 200 meters of their homes. For 13 of the 18 countries for which data are available, the proportion of the population with ready access to water has declined since the 1970s[27]; in countries without data, the situation is probably worse.

Safe water, however, is at a premium everywhere in the region. Water pollution, largely from human waste, has become a serious health hazard because the economic crisis is preventing most countries from providing adequate water treatment. Diseases such as typhoid, cholera, and diarrhea are spread by drinking contaminated water, while bilharzia, guinea worm, roundworm, and schistosomiasis are spread by bathing in it. Water pollution thus exacts a tremendous toll on the population of sub-Saharan Africa, raising infant mortality rates and impairing the health of all age groups.[28]

Degradation of land resources, mainly from improper disposal of solid and toxic wastes, is another problem. Although the volume of such wastes is much lower than in industrial countries, most of the region lacks even rudimentary collection and disposal facilities. Refuse is simply dumped along roads and other public places or into waterways, contributing to the spread of disease. Although toxic wastes are not yet widespread and exposure is fairly localized, there is fear of surreptitious trade in and dumping of such wastes in some countries.

Natural Disasters

In addition to human-induced degradation, geophysical events (such as droughts, floods, tornadoes, windstorms, and landslides) and biological events (such as locust and pest invasions) greatly affect the environment and the well-being of people in sub-

Saharan Africa. The two most important geophysical events are probably drought and floods. Drought is defined as a period of two or more years during which rainfall is well below average.[29] In ecological terms, it is simply a dry period to which an ecosystem may be adapted and from which it often recovers quickly. Drought should be distinguished from dryland degradation, which, as pointed out earlier, is brought about by inappropriate land-use practices under delicate environmental conditions.

Unlike dryland degradation, however, drought inflicts acute distress on human beings and animals, forcing mass migrations from the affected areas. Given the region's poverty and its inability to invest in new techniques, plant strains, storage facilities, and so on, the capacity to deal with drought is severely limited. As a result, many countries have become dependent on international assistance; this is especially true for small countries, but even large ones like Ethiopia (where a drought occurred in the midst of a prolonged civil war) have needed significant help. However, once normal rainfall resumes, recovery takes place quickly and people tend to return to their native areas.

Floods, on the other hand, stem from periods of heavy rainfall, either

Although sub-Saharan Africa is the least urbanized region in the world, its urban population is growing quite rapidly.

in the immediate locality or upstream of it. They are most common in river valleys and floodplains. In rural areas, their effects can be beneficial as well as harmful. Although flash floods destroy crops, livestock, and settlements, they provide ideal conditions for certain fish and for cultivating crops such as paddy rice, millet, sorghum, and vegetables. In urban areas, however, especially where there has been indiscriminate building on floodplains

or where channels are blocked, floods pose a real danger to life and property. In Ibadan, Nigeria, for instance, the flood of 31 August 1980 claimed about 200 lives, displaced about 5,000 persons, and damaged property worth millions of dollars.[30]

Insects are the most important biological hazard in sub-Saharan Africa. According to Thomas Odhiambo, the leading African entomologist, "The insect world in tropical Africa is a rich and diverse one."[31] Although some species confer benefits such as pollinating trees and other plants, many others are pests to plants or serve as vectors in the transmission of disease. Serious study of insects began only recently. The initial emphasis has been on combatting plant pests through heavy pesticide use—with all the deleterious environmental consequences this implies. Fortunately, most farmers in the region cannot afford to use pesticides to any great degree.

As the entomology of the region becomes better understood, there is growing appreciation of the potential for biological control of pests. The best example so far is the cassava mealybug program. Mealybugs were inadvertently introduced into sub-Saharan Africa from South America in the early 1970s. Within less than a decade, they had cut cassava yields by two-thirds in most parts of the region. However, biologists eventually found a natural enemy of the mealybug; specially bred in laboratories and distributed throughout cassava-growing areas, it has brought losses substantially under control. Thus, this program not only saved a staple on which so many people depend but also prevented major harm to the environment.

The Potential For Sustainable Development

Three points stand out clearly from this review of environmental challenges in the rapidly growing but poor countries of sub-Saharan Africa. First, the development strategy pursued in most of these countries has wrought serious havoc on the environment without necessarily improving the average person's standard of living.

Given the region's poverty and its inability to invest in new techniques, plant strains, storage facilities, and so on, the capacity to deal with drought is severely limited.

Second, this has taken place despite the region's relatively ample natural resources. Third, and perhaps most important, knowledge about the region's environment and its degradation remains inadequate.

Nowhere is this last point more true than in the attempt to explain environmental degradation in terms of population growth. This Malthusian argument depends on there being a "carrying capacity" beyond which the environment will inevitably suffer. But as already pointed out, in most of sub-Saharan Africa the population density is relatively low. Furthermore, some prime agricultural lands are clearly "undersettled," while areas less suited to agriculture are densely populated.[32]

A recent study of the relationships among population growth and density, the intensification of agriculture, and the implications for sustainability offers some useful insights on this issue.[33] The study focused on 10 areas with relatively dense populations (ranging from 150 to more than 1,000 persons per square kilometer). Five of these were in East Africa (in Kenya, Rwanda, Uganda, and Tanzania), while the remaining five were in West Africa, mainly Nigeria. In all of these areas, the study found that "contrary to much conventional wisdom that portrays the African smallholders as wrecking their physical resources, particularly in the face of land-intensive conditions . . . farmers . . . made considerable investments in resource-based capital, thereby protecting their farms from major environmental deterioration and the negative impacts of intensification and production that usually follow."[34]

Similar conclusions have been

reached regarding other aspects of the population-environment equation in sub-Saharan Africa. Contrary to conventional wisdom, detailed field investigations in Nigeria have found that the rising demand for fuelwood has not led to greater deforestation or desertification. Far from "overcutting their trees," farmers have been maintaining their tree stocks by planting and by protecting spontaneous seedlings. The area studied showed "a 2.3 percent per annum increase in tree density between 1972 and 1981, in the wake of the disastrous drought of the late 1960s and early 1970s when pressure on woody vegetation from human and natural sources must have been very intense."[35] Field investigations in Uganda and Mali drew similar conclusions.[36]

This is not to imply that there have been no instances of severe environmental degradation. These have only occurred under three special circumstances, however: where the population density was greater than 500 per square kilometer; where the area itself was physically or biologically vulnerable; and where socioeconomic conditions impeded the implementation of conservation measures. Indeed, decreases in well-being (indicated by reduced food availability) are attributable not to rapid population growth but to the persistence of customary land tenure arrangements, misguided macroeconomic policies, and inadequate infrastructure. According to the World Commission on Environment and Development, chaired by Gro Harlem Brundtland in 1987, sustainable development is "a process of change in which the exploitation of resources, the direction of investments, the orientation of technological development, and institutional change are *in harmony* [emphasis added] and enhance both current and future potential to meet human needs and aspirations."[37] Included in the concept of harmony, of course, is the access of producers to the various factors of production, especially land.

The problem of land tenure, like many of the other problems besetting the development process in sub-Saharan Africa, probably stems from the region's incomplete transition from one mode of production to another.

Colonialism attempted to shift the economies of these countries from a precapitalist mode of production (based largely on kinship relations) into a global capitalist mode (based on "commoditized" factors of production whose prices were subject to the forces of supply and demand in a self-regulating market). Though praiseworthy in many ways, these efforts failed signally in the one major area where they could have made a real difference: the patterns of land ownership in rural areas. By and large, colonial administrators left the traditional patterns intact, thus introducing a major contradiction into the development process.

While capitalism requires well-established individual property rights, most smallholders in sub-Saharan Africa have no such rights, even though they have longstanding rights to the use of communal land. Smallholders thus have no "economic assets" in the conventional sense of the term.[38] Second, they have no real collateral against which to borrow and thus no access to the credit they need to invest in improved farm infrastructure, new cultigens, and modern technologies generally. When one considers the heavy investment that went into producing the polders of the Netherlands or the wheatlands of North America, the disability under which African farmers labor becomes readily apparent.

Consequently, much as colonial and post-colonial governments tried to make farmers more market oriented, the fact that one of their major inputs lies outside the market system has always limited the success of this effort. In many cases, farmers have chosen simply to "opt out" of the system, especially now that governments make little attempt to ensure that they receive fair prices for their output.[39] The unnecessary liabilities under which farmers labor probably account for a large part of the poverty in sub-Saharan Africa.

Other aspects of the macroeconomic policies pursued by most African governments simply served to deepen the poverty under which the majority

of their rural populations labored and exacerbated the negative impact of their activities on the environment. Widening budget deficits eroded the value of national currencies, fuelled inflation, undermined peoples' real income, and encouraged excessive exploitation of natural resources to maintain even a subsistence level of existence.

The Roles of the State and International Assistance

It is clear that the environmental challenges in sub-Saharan Africa are more complex than the simple model linking environmental degradation to population growth and inappropriate macroeconomic policies indicates. Because of this complexity, no easy solutions are available. But whatever policies are adopted, to succeed they must increase peoples' interest in protecting the environment by involving them directly in the process; reduce the incidence of poverty to reduce the pressure on natural resources; and show people how a high level of resource use can go hand-in-hand with the maintenance of environmental quality.

The state can play an important role in promoting sustainable development and improvement of the environment. By setting the correct investment priorities, it can provide needed infrastructure, services, and education. In urban areas, it should focus on providing safe water, collecting and disposing of solid wastes, and improving the physical layout of congested places; in the rural areas, it should focus on health education and basic sanitation.

Regulatory measures, however, may be more important than public investment. In this regard, the state should set environmental standards that are realistic in terms of the country's particular socioeconomic circumstances. For example, setting strict standards for indoor air pollution when most people cannot afford less-polluting energy sources simply makes enforcement impossible. Regulatory measures should also aim to remove those distortions in the economy that tend to penalize producers and/or promote overconsumption. Important examples include underpricing agricultural commodities and subsidizing public goods and services, both of which favor the urban population at the expense of the rural population. Such distortions, of course, are partly responsible for the economic collapse of many countries in sub-Saharan Africa. Although structural adjustments now taking place may improve matters, the governments' lack of commitment has left the situation far from satisfactory.

Conservation measures have been important in protecting most natural resources from excessive use or degradation. Through its power of eminent domain, the state has been able to set aside sizable tracts of land to protect watersheds, prevent soil erosion, allow natural regeneration to take place, and preserve habitats, species, and biodiversity. As of 1993, there were 663 public reserves or parks in sub-Saharan Africa, totalling 125.2 million hectares.[40] This, however, is no more than 4.6 percent of the total land area of the region, much less than the 6 percent of the world as a whole. Moreover, the 1992 Caracas Action Plan of the World Parks Congress set a goal of protecting at least 10 percent of each of the world's major biomes; sub-Saharan Africa currently falls far short of this standard.

Simply setting land aside, however, does not mean being able to manage it properly. Many governments in the region lack the staff or financial resources to administer their protected areas, much less invest in new ones. Innovative strategies, such as involving private groups and nongovernmental organizations, are being considered and may provide another option for conservation management. Such groups are believed to be better able to raise funds to purchase land, to support conservation activities in existing parks and reserves, to incorporate the local population in management decisions, and to negotiate land-use disputes within and between communities.

Important as public investment, regulation, and conservation are, however, it is institutional development that offers the most hope for alleviating poverty and protecting the environment. Three aspects of institutional development are paramount: promoting democracy, expanding individual property rights, and increasing the knowledge base.

Decentralization and democratization must go down to the community level and must entail not only giving people a voice in decisions but also ensuring that they can raise the revenues necessary to translate their desires into reality. It is this that will promote transparency and accountability in government and foster a proprietary interest in the quality of the environment.[41]

The importance of expanding property rights was made clear earlier. Although it is often claimed that land tenure in sub-Saharan Africa is so complex that nothing can be done about it, it is difficult to believe that meaningful reforms cannot be introduced. The most serious mistake that

---

The unnecessary liabilities under which farmers labor probably account for a large part of the poverty in sub-Saharan Africa.

---

many governments have made, however, was to resort to nationalization.[42] From a conservation standpoint, nationalization often fails to distinguish between traditional communal property systems (which promote sound management of natural resources) and open-access systems (which result in excessive exploitation). When land and water have been nationalized and sound management practices disturbed, the environmental consequences have often been very severe.[43]

Nationalization has also led governments to give short shrift to titling and registration. Yet, until such procedures clearly define rights to land (on either a freehold or a leasehold basis), much of the region's natural resources are bound to be treated as common property and therefore suffer degradation and "the tragedy of the commons."

The third aspect of institutional development relates to the knowledge available for making decisions on environmental matters. People in sub-Saharan Africa have been adapting to the region's various environments for thousands of years. In the process, they have accumulated valuable information that should be incorporated into more formal analyses of sustainable development.[44] Along with such knowledge, of course, must go the collection and analysis of field data by modern techniques. This is necessary to correct the "hallowed but mistaken" notions of conventional wisdom and to give governments in the region better appreciation of the causes and effects of environmental damage as well as the costs and benefits of different policy options. In this regard, independent commissions provide a useful way for governments to draw on technical expertise both within and outside of their countries; they can also be instrumental in bringing the results of advanced research to bear on local problems.

As mentioned earlier, current knowledge of the ecology of tropical forests and grasslands is still rudimentary. The rich biological resources of these areas—and the ways in which humans relate to them—have yet to receive as much study as they deserve. Given the shortage of funds and trained personnel in most sub-Saharan African countries, this is an area where bilateral and multilateral assistance could make a real difference. The Convention on Biological Diversity, signed by 153 countries at the 1992 United Nations Conference on Environment and Development (UNCED) in Rio de Janeiro, is correct in insisting that tropical countries be compensated for protecting biological diversity from which others benefit.[45] If such compensation became the order of the day, some of it should be used to finance futher study of tropical ecosystems.

Poor countries in sub-Saharan Africa could also use international assistance in reforming their environmental laws and in selecting optimal strategies for environmental management. Not enough emphasis has been given to the role of law in alleviating poverty and protecting the environment. Particularly in the area of pollution charges, the experience of developed countries could be invaluable. But countries in the tropics that are being asked to protect biodiversity and genetic resources partly for the benefit of others also need technical assistance in legally defining and protecting their rights regarding these resources.

Consequently, management strategies must go beyond assessing the impact of individual projects, as this tends to address the symptoms rather than the root causes of environmental problems. Such strategies must pay greater attention to broader issues and recognize intersectoral links and intergenerational concerns. This would entail integrating natural resource management with national economic planning as well as tailoring international assistance to specific aspects of resource conservation. To implement such strategies, African countries must strive to secure broad consensus and support, both nationally and internationally.

Conclusion

In the closing years of the 20th century, most countries in sub-Saharan Africa find themselves almost returning to the drawing board. Three decades of trying to drive their economies according to Western models have left them prostrate, their people wallowing in poverty, and their environment exposed to many hazards. More importantly, the international indebtedness of these countries and their present unattractiveness to foreign investors are forcing them to rethink the whole question of development.

The next 25 years thus offer real opportunities for improvement, beginning with population control. At the household level, the economic crisis is

inducing a reassessment of the viability of large families; at the governmental level, political inertia and indifference to family planning programs are being replaced by more effort and initiative. Already, fertility has begun to decline in some countries, such as Zimbabwe, Kenya, and Cameroon.[46] Although the future remains uncertain, there is every likelihood that this trend will spread across the region.

A decline in fertility, however, will not completely eliminate the momentum that has built up in the years of rapid population growth. The number of people will continue to increase, raising the population density all over the region. But as already emphasized, there is growing evidence that the African environment is more resilient than conventionally thought and can probably support a higher level of population and more intensive agriculture. Technological innovations and institutional developments are thus more important to maintaining a sound environment in sub-Saharan Africa than are efforts to reduce population pressure. If the focus of development shifts from mere economic growth to eradicating the widespread poverty, the people as a whole can play a more decisive role, not only in turning the economic fortunes of their countries around but also in enhancing the quality of the environment.

NOTES

1. World Bank, *Sub-Saharan Africa: From Crisis to Sustainable Development: A Long Term Perspective Study* (Washington, D.C., 1989), 22.

2. United Nations Centre for Human Settlements, *Global Report on Human Settlements 1986* (New York: Oxford University Press, 1987), table 1.

3. World Bank, *World Development Report 1992* (New York: Oxford University Press, 1992), 258–59.

4. W. B. Morgan and J. A. Solarz, "Agricultural Crisis in Sub-Saharan Africa: Development Constraints and Policy Problems," *Geographical Journal* 160, no. 1 (1994): 57–73.

5. World Bank, note 3 above, pages 250–51.

6. World Bank, *World Development Report 1990* (New York: Oxford University Press, 1990), 139.

7. A. S. MacDonald, *Nowhere to Go But Down? Peasant Farming and the International Development Game* (London: Unwin Hyman, 1989).

8. E. Boserup, *The Conditions of Agricultural Growth* (Chicago: Aldine, 1965); and E. Boserup, *Population and Technological Change: A Study of Long-Term Trends* (Chicago: University of Chicago Press, 1981). See also R. W. Kates and V. Haarmann, "Where

the Poor Live: Are the Assumptions Correct?" *Environment*, May 1992, 4.

9. World Bank, note 3 above, page 201.

10. A. Grainger, "Quantifying Changes in Forest Cover in the Humid Tropics: Overcoming Current Limitations," *Journal of World Forest Resource Management* 1 (1984): 3–63.

11. World Resources Institute, *World Resources 1994–95* (New York: Oxford University Press, 1994), 133. See also A. Grainger, *Controlling Tropical Deforestation* (London: Earthscan Publications, 1993).

12. A. Grainger, "Rates of Deforestation in the Humid Tropics: Estimates and Measurements," *Geographical Journal* 159, no. 1 (1993): 33–44.

13. Food and Agriculture Organization, *Forest Resources Assessment 1990: Tropical Countries*, FAO Forestry Paper 112 (Rome, 1993), 38.

14. World Resources Institute, note 11 above, page 310.

15. A. D. Jones, "Species Conservation in Managed Tropical Forests," in T. C. Whitmore and J. A. Sayers, eds., *Tropical Deforestation and Species Extinction* (London: Chapman and Hall, 1992), 3.

16. J. Davidson, *Economic Use of Tropical Moist Forests,* Commission on Ecology Paper No. 9 (Gland, Switzerland: International Union for Conservation of Nature and Natural Resources, 1985), 9.

17. B. R. Davies, "Stream Regulation in Africa," in J. V. Ward and J. A. Stanford, eds., *The Ecology of Regulated Streams* (New York: Plenum Press, 1979). For more information on one such project in Botswana, see the review by C. W. Howe of *The IUCN Review of the Southern Okavango Integrated Water Development Project, Environment*, January/February 1994, 25.

18. C. A. Drijver and M. Marchand, *Taming the Floods: Environmental Aspects of Floodplain Development in Africa* (Leiden, the Netherlands: University of Leiden, 1985).

19. A. Warren and M. Khogali, *Assessment of Desertification and Drought in the Sudano-Sahelian Region 1985–1991* (New York: United Nations Sudano-Sahelian Office and United Nations Development Programme, 1993).

20. D. S. G. Thomas, "Sandstorm in a Teacup? Understanding Desertification," *Geographical Journal* 159, no. 3 (1993): 318–31. See also United Nations Environment Programme, *World Atlas of Desertification* (London: Edward Arnold, 1992).

21. D. S. G. Thomas, note 20 above, page 328.

22. P. H. Raven, "Biological Resources and Global Stability," in S. Kawano, J. H. Connell, and T. Hidaka, eds., *Evolution and Coadaptation in Biotic Communities* (Tokyo: University of Tokyo, 1988), 16–23.

23. W. V. Reid, "How Many Species Will There Be?" in T. C. Whitmore and J. A. Sayers, note 15 above, table 3.2.

24. United Nations Centre for Human Settlements, note 2 above, table 6. See also G. McGranahan and J. Songsore, "Wealth, Health, and the Urban Household: Weighing Environmental Burdens in Accra, Jakarta, and Sao Paulo," *Environment*, July/August 1994, 4.

25. World Resources Institute, note 11 above, pages 362–65. See also K. R. Smith, "Air Pollution: Assessing Total Exposure in Developing Countries," *Environment*, December 1988, 16.

26. World Resources Institute, note 11 above, page 201.

27. United Nations Development Programme, Environment & Natural Resources Group, *The Urban Environment in Developing Countries* (New York: United Nations, 1992), 29.

28. D. Satterthwaite, "The Impact on Health of Urban Environments," *Environment and Urbanization* 5, no. 2 (1993): 87–111. For another side of this, see J. Briscoe, "When the Cup is Half Full: Improving Water and Sanitation Services in the Developing World," *Environment*, May 1993, 6.

29. D. Wilhite and M. Glantz, "Understanding the Drought Phenomenon: The Role of Definitions," in D. Wilhite and W. Easterling, eds., *Planning for Drought* (London: Westview Press, 1987), 1130.

61

30. A. B. Oguntola and J. S. Oguntoyinbo, "Urban Flooding in Ibadan: A Diagnosis of the Problem," *Urban Ecology* 7 (1982): 39–46.

31. T. R. Odhiambo, "Insect Pests," in E. S. Ayensu and J. Marton-Lefevre, eds., *Proceedings of the Symposium on the State of Biology in Africa* (Washington, D.C.: International Biosciences Network, ICSU [International Council of Scientific Unions]), 115.

32. A. J. Dommen, *Innovation in African Agriculture* (Boulder, Colo.: Westview Press, 1988), 115–17.

33. B. L. Turner II, G. Hyden, and R. Kates, eds., *Population Growth and Agricultural Change in Africa* (Gainesville, Fla.: University Press of Florida, 1993).

34. Ibid., page 422. See also M. Mortimore and M. Tiffen, "Population Growth and a Sustainable Environment: The Machakos Story," *Environment*, October 1994, 10.

35. R. A. Cline-Cole, H. A. C. Main, and J. E. Nichol, "On Fuelwood Consumption, Population Dynamics and Deforestation In Africa," *World Development* 18 (1990): 522–23. The conventional view is presented in E. Eckholm, G. Foley, G. Barnard, and L. Timberlake, *Firewood: The Energy Crisis that Won't Go Away* (London: Earthscan, 1994); and E. Eckholm and L. Brown, *Spreading Deserts: The Hand of Man*, Worldwatch Paper 13 (Washington, D.C.: Worldwatch Institute, 1977).

36. H. P. Andersen, "Land Use Intensification and Landscape Ecological Changes in Budondo Sub-County, Uganda," (Master's thesis, University of Oslo, 1993); and T. A. Benjaminsen, "Fuelwood and Desertification: Sahel Orthodoxies Discussed on the Basis of Field Data from the Gourma Region of Mali," *Geoforum* 24, no. 4 (1993): 397–409.

37. World Commission on Environment and Development, *Our Common Future* (New York: Oxford University Press, 1987), 46.

38. World Bank, note 6 above, pages 31–32.

39. A. O. Hirschman, *Exit, Voice and Loyalty* (Cambridge, Mass.: Harvard University Press, 1990); see also G. Hyden, *No Shortcuts to Progress: African Development Management in Perspective* (London: Heineman, 1983).

40. World Resources Institute, note 11 above, page 316.

41. See R. L. Paarlberg, "The Politics of Agricultural Resource Abuse," *Environment*, October 1994, 6.

42. A. L. Mabogunje, *Perspective on Urban Land and Urban Management Policies in Sub-Saharan Africa,* Technical Paper No. 196 (Washington, D.C.: World Bank, 1992), 15–22.

43. World Bank, note 3 above, page 12.

44. P. Richards, *Indigenous Agricultural Revolution: Ecology and Food Production in West Africa* (London: Hutchinson, 1985).

45. J. A. Tobey, "Toward a Global Effort to Protect the Earth's Biological Diversity," *World Development* 12, no. 12 (1993): 1931–45.

46. World Resources Institute, note 11 above, page 30. See also the articles in the January/February 1995 issue of *Environment*.

Human Encroachments on a Domineering Physical Landscape

Linda Joan Paul

Linda Joan Paul is a lecturer, Department of Geography, at the University of Regina, Regina, Saskatchewan.

. . . To a geographer, the geographical overtones of Claire Mowat's *The Outport People* (OP in text page citations) and Aritha van Herk's *The Tent Peg* (TP in text page citations) are immediate. Both novels are introduced through the use of a map. The maps help to set the atmosphere of the books and also suggest the characters' anticipated relationship with the environment. In addition, they introduce the region the characters are about to confront. These environments, although similar in many ways, are viewed differently by the authors. While Mowat has fallen in love with the map of Newfoundland and all that it is anticipated to represent (*OP*, 1), to van Herk, the map suggests a foreboding, dangerous, deceptive, and powerful landscape.

J.L., the female protagonist in *The Tent Peg*, watches Mackenzie, the leader of the summer geologists' camp, trace the flight route with his finger on the map. We soon learn that "the lakes below are an impelled deception; if you raise your eyes for one moment, you become instantly lost," that the land is "an unending hesitation of sameness . . . and yet ever-changing . . . Skull teeth gleam through an invitation; the tundra can both restore and maim. No man lives to presume its power" (*TP*, 1987, 7). On the other hand, Mowat holds a romantic preconception of what Newfoundland will be like: "I used to stare at the Newfoundland map, entranced by the icon of that distant island of cool winds surrounded by the blue Atlantic . . . I could feel the salt spray on my face and hear the foghorns bleating." Like Lucy Maud Montgomery's Anne's House of Dreams, Mowat has her windblown island of her dreams.

For geographers, vivid and detailed descriptions of physical, cultural, and regional landscapes expand our comprehension of place. Mowat and van Herk paint detailed pictures of the Newfoundland and Yukon environments, certainly through the prism of their own experiences and visions, but also through the perceptions of their characters as well.

Setting often is not an important as other elements of a story—plot, character, and theme. A setting's importance depends on the purpose of the story. If the author wants his or her story to be universal, elements of the story will not be so strongly localized or obvious. Sometimes, however, authors want to stress local rather than universal themes. In this essay, local elements of setting will assume importance (Berlinguette 1989). *The Outport People* and *The Tent Peg* are regional novels that constantly refer to regional settings.

Interestingly, the novels have many elements in common. The protagonists, both female, decide to leave a mundane urban environment for isolated and more simple locations. For J.L., the particular destination was not important. "I did it deliberately. I wanted this job, I wanted to head for nowhere and look at everything in my narrow world from a detached distance" (*TP*, 23). On the other hand, the Mowats chose a specific locale:

> We decided, irrationally and passionately, to live there . . . it was going to be so much cheaper to live in an outport where houses were half the price they were in Ontario, and without roads we wouldn't need a car. We planned to eat a lot of fresh fish and wild berries. I would make my own bread and my own clothes. We would be as far away as possible from the vexations of the urban, managed world. (*OP*, 3)

Both protagonists left regional capitals: J.L. escaped from Edmonton, while Claire Mowat's flight was from Toronto. Both chose hinterland locations as their end-points. Within these hinterlands, they chose locales so isolated they could not be reached by road. For Mowat's Newfoundland outport Baleena, a weekly scheduled supply ship was the umbilicus that linked "forty isolated coastal communities with the rest of the world" (*OP*, 2). In *The Tent Peg*, what eventually becomes known as Fort Chaos can only be reached by air. "I'm the pilot that [*sic*] flies them fuel, food and mail once a week, Wednesdays. It's a long flight from Mayo, but I don't mind, it's beautiful country" (*TP*, 78). The frail transportation connections suggest there are human encroachments in these isolated spots but that the natural environments of both regions make these inroads difficult.

To many, their environments are considered harsh. The situation in the Arctic is considerably more extreme that in Newfoundland. In *The Tent Peg*, the first planned geological survey site was in the Northwest Territories. "Nothing but tundra and lakes, lakes and tundra. Once you're out there, in amongst the moss and the occasional outcrop, you melt right down in the barrens. Not a dot of anyone anywhere" (*TP*, 10).

2. LAND-HUMAN RELATIONSHIPS

But Mackenzie liked it that way. J.L.'s thoughts follow similar patterns, " . . . thinking of the barrenlands, that shivering silence stretched out over the pale flatness, treeless and unashamed."

Preparations for a summer camp at the first site are abandoned when company headquarters anticipate a uranium find in the Wernecke Mountains of the eastern Yukon.

> The cold surface of the water reflects inlaid turquoise against a dull overhang of mountains. You might believe that the ice has melted but it's only sunk, green and congealed, to the bottom of the lake where it will hover all summer, chilling the water. That damn lake will never be warm enough to swim in.
>   The snow too lies scattered and torn in patches on the moss . . . We're here . . . in an alpine valley that never feels summer, just varying shades of winter. Nothing to break the angry gusts coming off those mountains. We're above the tree line, above everything. (*TP,* 42)

Mowat describes grey granite outcrops, steep, rocky slopes, marsh, the barrens, and the North Atlantic, stormy and cold. The force of the wind is so strong that even trees adapt, stunted and bending, to its onslaught. These scenes contrast sharply with Squire's depiction of Montgomery's Prince Edward Island as a pastoral idyll and Lucius O'Brien's portrayal of landscape in *Sunrise on the Saguenay* as sublime.

Within a lazy day's sail from Baleena, Mowat waxes poetic as the entrance to Rosey (Enragée) River, a fjord, comes into view.

> The cover . . . was spectacular. We were surrounded on three sides by a deep evergreen forest, that rose almost straight up the side of a steep cliff. Far above us we could see a fresh-water stream, the seemingly weightless drops splattering and sparkling as they fell down to the sea. North of us a landscape of glacier-worn rocks marched into the distance, and below us the water was so clear. (*OP,* 168)

At times, then, both authors describe the majesty of their surroundings. Straying from their campsite, only a few miles downstream, Mackenzie, in *The Tent Peg,* guides Thompson to a new world, surprisingly different for its proximity. The air is hot and thick, and they leave the stony bare landscape for trees, almost forgotten, and the steady whine of mosquitoes! After a walk, they hear

> a long, far-away roar that grows larger as we walk, louder and stronger until it overtakes and conceals the sounds of the forest.
>   And then, without warning, we are standing at the edge of a narrow gorge that is creased hundreds of feet deep into the rock. Over it roars a mountain stream that, in its fall, unleashes itself to brilliant life. (*TP,* 197)

In both books, there are elements of danger. For Mowat danger appears sporadically. For van Herk it is omnipresent. Mowat writes:

> One day we decided to climb to the top of the cliff that loomed above our little hideaway. It was our intention to find the source of the waterfall. We climbed, with considerable difficulty, for nearly two hours, up over the vertical rocks and slippery boulders, clinging to feeble little spruce trees as we went. When we reached the crest of this isthmus which divided the inland waterway from the sea, we could once again see the Atlantic Ocean stretching into infinity to the south of us. We were ecstatic—the way Cortes must have felt where no men, and certainly no woman, had ever stood before . . .

> Then we started to consider our trip back down, and wondered what would happen if one of us fell and broke a leg amid the jagged crevices of this landscape that was more suited to eagles than to people. (*OP,* 169–70).

Interestingly, aboriginal people undoubtedly inhabited the environments portrayed by both authors long before Europeans arrived on the scene. Yet these possible intrusions are scarcely alluded to by either writer.

In *The Tent Peg,* foreshadowing keeps the elements of the environment in the mind of the reader. Both Mackenzie and J.L. hear the mountain beginning to shift. But when the massive overhang finally lets go, only J.L. is awake to sense it:

> I felt the mountain rumble, I felt it stir and I was instantly awake, listening with every bone arched . . . I'm clear of the camp, moving up the valley. The cirque rests at the neck of the mountain, it creeps upward, lifts itself against the moment of upthrust time that left it there to wait . . . I hear the splash of a pebble bouncing from a cliff. The sound seems to fade but then it's joined by the smaller chinks and spatters of stones, a trickle that gradually cascades . . . begins to sing, to surge, to roar, and finally to rumble . . . the whole side of the mountain caught in a torrent of itself . . . The east side has let go and slid down into our valley. Where once was an even slope rises a raw gap. (*TP,* 120–21)

The camp crew, who are a hundred yards from being hammered to death by boulders, are stunned. Danger is imminently present, although no deaths occur. The foreboding results of the rock slide lie adjacent to the camp for the rest of the summer, constantly reminding the team of nature's engulfing power.

The harsh environment extends beyond the inanimate. On more than one occasion, J.L. confronts a grizzly bear, which again spooks the men. References to and sightings of grizzlies foreshadow the possible event. J.L. and Ivan spot a grizzly and her two cubs from the helicopter. Jerome carries his Magnum and brags about what he will do if he encounters it. Cap says he's horny, and J.L. tells him to find a grizzly bear. Eventually a grizzly lumbers into camp. Cap reports, "I have to blink to focus on what I see. And then I cannot move, I am absolutely pillared in place" (*TP,* 108). The bear roars, J.L. confronts it and stares it down. Both the she-bear and J.L. turn and move in opposite directions. The bear and the rock slide are such powerful symbols it is hard, at one level, to take these events at face value; both of them represent the formidable danger of the Yukon.

In the two novels, the descriptions of and feelings for the landscape vary with the perceptions of the characters. Natural environments can induce or reflect mood. Weather is an obvious barometer of characters' moods. Sometimes they react to it mentally, sometimes they describe it dispassionately. It is, however, a regional force to be reckoned with.

One of Claire Mowat's objectives in writing her book was to explain, describe, and interpret Newfoundland's outports and all their intricacies to the rest of Canada. The reader is guided with humour, and warmth, on a laywoman's geographical tour of the region. The weather, always different from Toronto's scorching and humid summer heat, became a fascination for Mowat, a significant regional contrast. (Similarly, Squire, in chapter 11, notes Montgomery's juxtaposition of the idyllic P.E.I. rural landscape and Toronto's dingy streets.)

Indeed, for Mowat, weather was a marker of the passing days. Changeable, penetrating, it was often a domineering physical force in the natural landscape. Most noticeable were the storms.

> Rain turned to snow and back to rain again and at night the glass in our bedroom window rattled ominously. Almost every week a gale blew with such ferocity that in the more popular places of this world it would have made headline news. Winds of fifty, sixty, and seventy knots were commonplace, and gusts reaching a hundred knots were not infrequent. At the railway terminal at Port-aux-Basques, empty freight cars were blown right off the track at least once every winter.
>
> Fortunately these hurricane winds didn't come without warning. We watched the southern sky gradually turn from pale grey to the colour of school blackboards. We bolted our doors against it and waited. It was known locally as a "blow"—surely one of the greatest understatements in the English language. (*OP*, 18–19)

She later comments that wind, rather than cold, was the chief peril of winter. Often the temperature hovered around the freezing point, and freezing rain, known locally as "glitter storms" (*OP*, 19), was a common occurrence.

Perils extended beyond the land. Obvious were the dangers for fishermen caught at sea in a storm. More obscure dangers existed as well, such as ships being crushed in the ice. On sunny winter days, the sea, often a deep indigo blue, deceptively resembled the inviting Caribbean, giving no hint that it could freeze a person to death within minutes. However,

> whatever kind of weather we got, it didn't last very long. Mingled with those tempestuous winter days . . . we had plenty of "civil" days. They dawned sunny and unexpectedly serene and mocked the calendar that told us it was December. On such sunny days in March, every clothesline in Dog Cove was laden with undulating sheets. (*OP*, 72)

These sunny days are interspersed with endless days of drizzle and fog. "It was June, the month of everlasting fog. Fog is no one's friend. It doesn't water the garden, it doesn't fill up the well and you can't skate or ski on it. It is the bane of all seafaring men" (*OP*, 123).

Weather was a less prominent aspect of the geology crew's life, undoubtedly because their season in the Arctic was for the short summer months only. Still, when arriving in the Territories, J.L. was fascinated by sun dogs.

Dramatically, the dangers of the spring break-up were brought to the fore. Mackenzie, his airplane having previously landed on weakening ice, takes a running leap from the lake shore to the Cessna and falls partially through the ice. His leg and clothing instantly freeze.

Although winter storms are over for the season, rain, especially, affects the morale of the survey crew.

> It's been raining for a week. Cold rain that chills you right through. Puts everybody in a foul temper. When I fly the men out, the helicopter is full of curses and the smell of steamy rain suits. And the mist. It obscures the mountains . . . At night everyone's wet and muddy and snarling. They drink more. In the morning they're late getting up. (*TP*, 131)
>
> The pilot is bitchy as hell; they don't like flying in break up. Use skis and you'll need floats; use floats and you'll need skis.

> Who can tell? It's that kind of country, changes her mind the minute your back is turned. (*TP*, 11)

As with the Newfoundland outport, a shift in the weather can brighten spirits: "The crew is pleased as can be . . . the rain has stopped, it looks like a good day, sunshine and a breeze. Every one of them feels good, you can tell by the way they stomp around" (*TP*, 144). Hearne, a photographer, reiterates this enthusiasm during a clear day when he feels he can capture the texture of rocks which form the massive landslide.

Environmental perception also varies with the outlook and mood of the characters, as does the sense of isolation, similarly described by Paul and Simpson-Housley with regard to Ostenso's *Wild Geese*. Mackenzie, the party chief and veteran Arctic surveyor, remarks of the Northwest Territories, "I like it out there alone. Alone with nothing around but tundra and quiet, the two of them holding each other down against the sky at their own expense." (*TP*, 12). Later, at the Yukon site, J.L. comments of Mackenzie, "He's glad to be out here, away from town, the transition accomplished. This is his world, he moves effortlessly, the moss under his feet natural and yielding."

Milton, the Mennonite, has ambivalent feelings towards this mountainous, isolated environment: "I figured you could get closer to God up here, but He feels farther away" (*TP*, 66). Later he comments of the mountains, "They are an example of God's glory" (*TP*, 66). In contrast, Hudson, the upper-class Englishman, finds the isolation anything but glorious: "God's glory. They look murderous to me" (*TP*, 67). To him, the remote, pressing mountains were like glinting teeth.

Milton also compares the Yukon to his permanent home: "Every night now we have a fire, we gather sticks and burn them . . . It's eerie, the sparks against the solid darkness. The mountains lie uneasy after the slide, they're not peaceful and far like the prairie is. I miss the prairie, the unrolling land" (*TP*, 148).

Roy, the pilot, feels that three months of isolation in the Yukon mountains would drive a saint mad. Yet by the summer's end, most of the crew have come to terms with the campsite and the foreboding mountains. Their perceptions change and this environment becomes part of an accepted way of life. Drying tundra moss on her tent floor, J.L. summarizes this eventual feeling of acceptance, suggesting the summer was worth the stay, just for the scent of the moss.

"Maps are seductive" (*OP*, 1). In this first sentence of her novel, Claire Mowat suggests how she perceived Newfoundland's isolated outports. Later, however, as Mowat's sojourn in Baleena lengthened, she was willing to admit that if they hadn't lingered until it was too late to move on, they might never have become infatuated with the place. In general, the Mowats like the isolation. Yet they seemed surprised when others, as urbane as themselves, chose a similar lifestyle. Of the fish plant owners, the Drakes, Mowat was to inquire, rhetorically, why a couple who kept an impressive wine cellar and read magazines like *Gourmet* and *Vogue* should choose to live in this remote outport. Later she answered part of the question herself. Freeman Drake seemed content when hunting and fishing in the back country. The Mowats also liked hiking into the back country and taking long walks in varying weather: "One brave little boy ventured to tell me that there were t'ousands blueberries up t'river. We eventually discovered that up the river was the source of a lot of things that made for a pretty nice life—salmon, trout, moose, caribou, ptarmigan, wild berries and firewood" (*OP*, 161).

Although domineering, both physical environments allow human encroachments. In neither place, however, is it easy to carve out a permanent cultural niche. Mowat describes her first impression of her home-to-be in Baleena.

> We rounded a small island of grey granite topped with a pelt of tawny grass, and suddenly there is was, lonely as a lighthouse, the house we had impulsively bought . . . Our new home stood apart from its neighbours, its clapboard walls painted a pristine white in contrast to the turquoise, yellow and green of the other houses. Behind it was a steep rocky slope, with a marsh below, and beyond that only the cold and stormy North Atlantic. (*OP*, 5) There wasn't a single passenger car for two hundred miles. Nor was there a foot of pavement.
>
> Baleena appeared to be a haphazard scattering of small tidy houses connected by pathways and bumpy trails. Houses seemed to grow together in clusters in those places where massive boulders and rocks did not. (*OP*, 3)

Similarly, van Herk paints a scene of a physical environment unwilling to yield to human encroachment easily: "The snow too lies scattered and torn in patches on the moss. In between, our boxes and bags, our summer's survival, seems lost, inadequate" (*TP*, 42). There are perpetual reminders of their transient visit. The wind carries the voices of the crew, who are setting up the Storm Haven tents, clustered close together so as to ward off the chill. As the helicopter appears, Mackenzie states,

> I wave my arms in a circle to signal a flat landing spot . . . The machine needles closer and closer to the ground, dust and dry winter moss blowing up from the cushion of air under the skids, when suddenly the Storm Havens billow and lift, struggle olive and canvas and alive against their puny ropes and pegs . . . Huge crippled kites, they green the chilly air like blossoming sails for one wild escaped moment, only to hesitate and then collapse in heaps of inert canvas on the gray moss. (*TP*, 42–43)

Jerome, another surveyor, does not like the scattered layout of the tent village: "The Jutland's set up facing the lake so the wind will hit that tent square every night. The Storm Havens aren't in a row, they're just any old way . . . The garbage pit's too close and the shitter is too far away. Somebody's decided to build a shower" (*TP*, 54).

In both these rugged environments, settlements are scattered insignificantly, yet are colourful and bold, perhaps to announce that humans do exist there.

Human imprints in the survey camp are minor, impermanent adaptations to the environment—radio antenna hung with bright flagging, paths worn to the garbage dump and latrines, or two dozen brown bottles cooling at the edge of the lake. The day the campsite is established, Thompson is already discussing the anticipated sadness the crew will feel at the end of the summer when they leave their temporary home. The only significant landmarks, after the crew has left, will be the stakes, testament to the Yukon's two-post system for staking mine claims for mineral rights. After their discovery of gold, regulations allowed each person to stake eight claims. Thus, a total of eighty claims would be staked, an initial and end post, 1,500 feet apart, indicating the length of each claim. Each person was required to strike his or her own claims, which they did by hammering posts into the ground and heaping stones around the base to give more support.

But little human evidence exists to indicate the intense activity of a summer's work. Frequent comments show the crew's awareness of their stay's impermanence. At the close of the season, the campers dismember their cultural landscape, everything from worn or torn clothing to the table used for food preparation. As they do this, J.L. still feels the mountains hover above them, awaiting their departure.

In Baleena, human encroachments on the natural landscape were somewhat more permanent, since Euro-Canadians had inhabited the area for a longer period of time in this outport, which, though officially one community, was in fact really five. A government wharf, a freight shed, a few old trucks (though not a single passenger car), two churches, a few stores, and a post office created an artificial environment. The only industry was the fish plant, "a series of plain wooden buildings that sprawled along the shore of the deep harbour of The Gut" (*OP*, 21). In addition, transient vessels, such as those carrying fish to ports in New England, anchored at Baleena. A few prominent buildings could be found, such as the doctor's Edwardian mansion and the Anglican church constructed like an inverted ship.

Though not designed as such, one boat became a temporary home. "Frank . . . lived in the tiny forepeak of his trap boat, which he had rigged out with a narrow bunk and a small coal stove" (*OP*, 8). Other boats were put to new uses as well. The refrigerator ship carrying fish products south had been a minesweeper in the Second World War. Change of form, function, and environment did occur. But in general, most people believed a good life was possible without continual change. These outports did not rush headlong into the twentieth century, grabbing and transforming, adapting to the continually changing technology that was so evident in Central Canada.

Interestingly, Baleena and Fort Chaos shared some common cultural features—worn pathways and territorial claims. Fishing was territorial, as were claims staked for gold. And as with the surveyors' camp, supposedly pristine water bodies around Baleena collected the garbage of higher civilization.

> The end of winter is the best season for beachcombing. As the ice and snow melt, the bounty that has been hurled ashore by months of storms begins to appear. Driftwood and sea shells were everywhere, along with the occasional fragment of whale bone, the skeletons of birds and a lot of other mysterious jetsam . . . Less intriguing were the hundreds of fragmented plastic bottles and bags that were altogether too easy to identify. (*OP*, 83)

Transience was evident in Baleena too. Stretched out "like an aerial photograph . . . were the long-deserted settlements of Outer Island and Offer Land, with only the collapsing stick fences of their cemeteries as barely visible reminders of the human lives they once harboured" (*OP*, 82–83). In 1919, the families of Outer Island decided to abandon their island homes to move to less remote outports like Baleena. Some had dismantled their houses, board by board, and then rebuilt them at Round Harbour. Near the end of the Mowats' stay at Baleena, the nearby outport of Grand Anse was to be relocated and two hundred people would be moving to Baleena. Dismantling came in other forms too. The house of the Roses, the Mowats' neighbours, typified an alteration commonly resorted to by elderly couples whose children had grown up and left home. To reduce heating costs and housework, the house was decapitated of its second floor.

Eventually even Baleena could not hold the twentieth century at bay. A television transmitter was under construction, and surveyors were planning the route of the eventual Trans-Canada Highway. The isolation, their simple lifestyle that had so attracted the Mowats to Newfoundland, was quietly slipping away (*OP*, 236–37). Thus, the Mowats bid farewell to that windswept rock which they had called home.

Before we turn to the final theme of this chapter, one other symbolic geographical feature should be discussed, an occurrence found in *The Tent Peg*. Some of the characters are names after early Canadian explorers—Mackenzie, Franklin, Hearne, Hudson, and Thompson. Their importance to the geographical discovery of Canada has long been recognized. Mackenzie, Thompson, and Hudson have great Canadian rivers or water bodies names after them. Place names are an integral part of the cultural geography of languages. In a novel representing the gigantic physical forces and spaces of Canada's northern regional hinterland, their quests into unknown regions cannot be overlooked. In her book, these five characters all symbolize exploration in the physical and spatial sense. The search for minerals in the Wernecke Mountains is a major theme of the book. However, exploration can be sensed at more than one level.

J.L. describes Mackenzie as an explorer who loved his work and who loved rocks and maps and the way the earth had given birth to herself. Thompson was still deciding, still on the edge. Franklin analysed everything. Hearne was a photographer who liked colour and textures (*TP*, 138). Hudson, the Englishman, was incongruent, a smooth diamond in a rough world. For the most part he hated the isolation. Yet he was willing to take a risk, to confront the unknown, difficult as it was. None of these men had stopped questioning, exploring, discovering. Thus, new worlds and spaces, physical and mental, were opened to them.

One significant difference between the two books concerns the symbolic literary landscape. While van Herk uses the landscape very symbolically, Mowat responds to the Newfoundland landscape much more matter-of-factly, with no hidden symbolic agenda. Her purpose is to describe the outport life from her point of view, but nonetheless as accurately as possible. She knows that a unique lifestyle may soon disappear. The final subject to be examined in this chapter, then, centres on the major symbolic theme of *The Tent Peg*—the confrontation of stereotypes and the ties that bind (women especially, but also men), those conventions in society that inhibit freedom. This is not a new phenomenon. In fact, the original story of Deborah, a prophetess and judge, and Jael, wife of Heber the Kenite, is found in the Book of Judges in the Old Testament.

First written in prose (chapter 4) and then in poetry (chapter 5), these chapters from the Book of Judges recount a story of conquest, ultimately under the direction of and then at the hand of women.

The people of Israel, at the time, were facing a long and difficult struggle to gain possession of the promised land. In *The Tent Peg*, van Herk symbolically asks whether there is a promised land for women. Judges were chosen by God to lead the Israelites. Deborah was one of these charismatic leaders, gifted with wisdom and prophetic insights (Duncan 1989). Judging Israel at the time, she called Barak, leader of the Israelites' army, saying God commanded him to gather his army at Mount Tabor, traditionally the mountain of the transfiguration. God, she continued, would also draw Sisera, captain of the Canaanite army, with his chariots and men, and would ultimately "deliver him into thine hand" (Judges 4:6, 7). "And she said, I will surely go with you: nonetheless, the road on which you are going will not lead to your glory, for the Lord will sell Sisera into the hand of a woman" (Judges 4:9). This story on conquest relates directly to the force of two women—Deborah, who prophesied the battle, and Jael, who killed Sisera, the Canaanite general. Indeed, *The Interpreter's Bible* described the first ten verses of chapter 4 as "The Power of Women" (1953, 711). The two armies fight. Sisera and the Canaanites are routed. Sisera escapes to the tent of Jael. As peace had previously existed between Jabin, his king and the house of Heber, Sisera trusted Jael. She promised him refuge, gave him milk, covered him with a rug so he could sleep. "For Jael the wife of Heber took a tent peg, and took a hammer in her hand, and went softly to him and drove the peg into his temple, till it went down into the ground, as he was lying fast asleep from weariness. So he died" (Judges 4:21).

Chapter 5 recounts the deeds of Deborah, Barak, and Jael in a long poem known as "The Song of Deborah (Nunnally-Cox 1981, 49). "Most blessed of women be Jael, the wife of Heber the Kenite, of tent-dwelling women most blessed" (Judges 5:24). And the land had peace for forty years (Judges 5:31).

Throughout *The Tent Peg*, the symbolism of this episode is referred to constantly, continually reminding the reader of the analogy. J.L. lives in a tent. The men in the survey crew, weary from a day's work, sleep in their tents through the catastrophic event of the rock slide. At various times, they come to J.L.'s tent for comfort and counsel. Nails are driven into the ground (temple of the earth) as tent pegs or as stakes in the gold claim. Men's visions are pierced without their being aware of the change in their perceptions. This leads to their freedom, but more importantly perhaps, to J.L.'s, to her emancipation as a woman. As a result, new geographical relationships and a new spatial organization can be forged. J.L.'s struggle for and final acceptance in the new territory of a male-dominated survey camp in the Yukon is a prime example of this.

At one point, Cap summarizes the major symbols of the novel:

> This summer gets stranger and stranger. First she, J.L., hits right in the middle of that target, even though she's never shot a gun before. And if I hadn't seen her talking to that bear with my own eyes, I wouldn't have believed it . . . Then she sees a rockslide that stops just short of camp. Even worse, the rest of us don't hear a thing, just sleep right through tons of falling rock that practically roll right over us. (*TP*, 125)

2. LAND-HUMAN RELATIONSHIPS

Hitting the bull's eye symbolizes J.L.'s recognition of the problems of stereotyping she must face. In confronting the she-bear, a grizzly, J.L. gains the initiative and strength to remain in the wilderness, to confront and challenge the men who do not want her to overstep conventional women's bounds within society. J.L. interprets the grizzly as her friend, Deborah, acting out the role of a prophetess in the twentieth century. And finally there was the rock slide, massive and terrifying. Only J.L. was awake at the time. Only she witnessed it. The men were asleep in their tents, their temples to the ground. This event was to mark a turning-point in the novel. Their temples had been pierced. Gradually, all but Jerome accepted J.L. and her position within the camp, and thus her new equal position within society. As they accepted her, J.L. also changed, willing to see men and her relationship to them in a new light.

At the close of the book, as J.L. dances above the fire, her last night in camp, she summarizes her perceptions of the summer. She alludes to the symbol of Mount Tabor, traditionally the mountain of the transfiguration, as she refers to her and the men's transfiguration: "For a moment I can pretend I am Deborah celebrating myself, victory, peace regained. And in their faces I see my transfiguration, themselves transformed, each one with the tent peg through the temple cherishing the knowledge garnered in sleep, in unwitting trust. (*TP,* 226).

And so, "I leap free," at face value, *of the fire;* on another level, *of society's bonds.* Her last words are, "They can rest now, we can all rest." Men and women are free to choose new directions in time and space.

Two novels, Claire Mowat's *The Outport People* and Aritha van Herk's *The Tent Peg,* describe domineering, harsh physical landscapes in Canada, isolated regions that have been ignored by and to a large extent have been unknown to the majority of Canadians. They are powerful, rugged, unyielding. In both books, the encroaching cultural landscape has a tenuous hold at best. All traces of van Herk's temporary summer camp could evaporate if the site is neglected for a few years. The outports could last longer, but through relocation, many of these could gradually disintegrate, transforming into a non-human environment once more. Often Claire Mowat regards her isolated outport region with affection. However, the towering mountain and its massive landslide thundering to the tip of the tarn where the geology camp is situated symbolize the respect the Yukon always demands of its human encroachers. Juxtaposed in this essay are two dominating landscapes. Their authors' perceptions and the reactions of their human intruders show diverging responses to their power.

REFERENCES

Berlinguette, Lorna. 1989. Personal comment, October.
Biblical references. 1952. *Revised Standard Version.* Toronto: William Collins and Sons.
Duncan, Reverend Mary. 1989. "Women of Faith: Deborah." Unpublished sermon, Wesley United Church, Regina.
Eliade, Mircea. 1961. *The Sacred and the Profane.* Translated by Willard R. Trask, New York: Harper Torchbooks.
The Interpreter's Bible. Vol. 11. 1953. Nashville: Abingdon Press.
Montgomery, Lucy M. 1922. *Anne's House of Dreams.* Toronto: Seal Books.
Mowat, Claire. 1983. *The Outport People.* Toronto: Seal Books.
Nunnally-Cox, Janice. 1981. *Foremothers: Women of the Bible.* New York: Seabury Press.
van Herk, Aritha. 1987. *The Tent Peg.* Toronto: McClelland & Stewart, New Canadian Library. (First published by McClelland & Stewart/ Bantam, 1981).

Past and Present Land Use and Land Cover in the USA

WILLIAM B. MEYER

Dr. William B. Meyer is a geographer currently employed on the research faculty of the George Perkins Marsh Institute at Clark University in Worcester, Massachusetts. His principal interests lie in the areas of global environmental change with particular emphasis on land use and land cover change, in land use conflict, and in American environmental history.

L and of many uses," runs a motto used to describe the National Forests, and it describes the United States as a whole just as well. "Land of many covers" would be an equally apt, but distinct, description. *Land use* is the way in which, and the purposes for which, human beings employ the land and its resources: for example, farming, mining, or lumbering. *Land cover* describes the physical state of the land surface: as in cropland, mountains, or forests. The term land cover originally referred to the kind and state of vegetation (such as forest or grass cover), but it has broadened in subsequent usage to include human structures such as buildings or pavement and other aspects of the natural environment, such as soil type, biodiversity, and surface and groundwater. A vast array of physical characteristics—climate, physiography, soil, biota—and the varieties of past and present human utilization combine to make every parcel of land on the nation's surface unique in the cover it possesses and the opportunities for use that if offers. For most practical purposes, land units must be aggregated into quite broad categories, but the frequent use of such simplified classes should not be allowed to dull one's sense of the variation that is contained in any one of them.

Land cover is affected by natural events, including climate variation, flooding, vegetation succession, and fire, all of which can sometimes be affected in character and magnitude by human activities. Both globally and in the United States, though, land cover today is altered principally by direct human use: by agriculture and livestock raising, forest harvesting and management, and construction. There are also incidental impacts from other human activities such as forests damaged by acid rain from fossil fuel combustion and crops near cities damaged by tropospheric ozone resulting from automobile exhaust.

Changes in land cover by land use do not necessarily imply a degradation of the land. Indeed, it might be presumed that any change produced by human use is an improvement, until demonstrated otherwise, because someone has gone to the trouble of making it. And indeed, this has been the dominant attitude around the world through time. There are, of course, many reasons why it might be otherwise. Damage may be done with the best of intentions when the harm inflicted is too subtle to be perceived by the land user. It may also be done when losses produced by a change in land use spill over the boundaries of the parcel involved, while the gains accrue largely to the land user. Economists refer to harmful effects of this sort as *negative externalities,* to mean secondary or unexpected consequences that may reduce the net value of production of an activity and displace some of its costs upon other parties. Land use changes can be undertaken because they return a net profit to the land user, while the impacts of negative externalities such as air and water pollution, biodiversity loss, and increased flooding are borne by others. Conversely, activities that result in secondary benefits (or *positive externalities*) may not be undertaken by landowners if direct benefits to them would not reward the costs.

Over the years, concerns regarding land degradation have taken several overlapping (and occasionally conflicting) forms. *Conservationism* emphasized the need for careful and efficient management to guarantee a sustained supply of productive land resources for future generations. *Preservationism* has sought to protect scenery and ecosystems in a state as little human-altered as possible. Modern *environmentalism* subsumes many of these goals and adds new concerns that cover the varied secondary effects of land use both on land cover and on other related aspects of the global environment. By and large, American attitudes in the past century have shifted from a tendency to interpret human use as improving the condition of the land towards a tendency to see human impact as primarily destructive. The term "land reclamation" long denoted the conversion of land from its natural cover; today it is more often used to describe the restoration and repair of land damaged by human use. It would be easy, though, to exaggerate the shift in attitudes. In truth, calculating the balance of costs and benefits from many land use and land cover changes is enormously difficult. The full extent and consequences of proposed changes are often less than certain, as is their possible irreversibility and thus their lasting significance for future generations.

WHERE ARE WE?

The United States, exclusive of Alaska and Hawaii, assumed its present size and shape around the middle of the 19th century. Hawaii is relatively small, ecologically distinctive, and profoundly affected by a long

---

"The adjustments that are made in land use and land cover in coming years will in some way alter the life of nearly every living thing on Earth."

---

and distinctive history of human use; Alaska is huge and little affected to date by direct land use. In this review assessment we therefore survey land use and land cover change, focusing on the past century and a half, only in the conterminous or lower 48 states. Those states cover an area of almost 1900 million acres, or about 3 million square miles.

How land is *used*, and thus how *land cover* is altered, depends on who owns or controls the land and on the pressures and incentives shaping the behavior of the owner. Some 400 million acres in the conterminous 48

states—about 21% of the total—are federally owned. The two largest chunks are the 170 million acres of western rangeland controlled by the Bureau of Land Management and the approximately equal area of the National Forest System. Federal land represents 45% of the area of the twelve western states, but is not a large share of any other regional total. There are also significant land holdings by state governments throughout the country.

Most of the land in the United States is privately owned, but under federal, state, and local restrictions on its use that have increased over time. The difference between public and private land is important in explaining and forecasting land use and land coverage change, but the division is not absolute, and each sector is influenced by the other. Private land use is heavily influenced by public policies, not only by regulation of certain uses but through incentives that encourage others. Public lands are used for many private activities; grazing on federal rangelands and timber extraction from the national forests by private operators are the most important and have become the most controversial. The large government role in land use on both government and private land means that policy, as well as economic forces, must be considered in explaining and projecting changes in the land. Economic forces are of course significant determinants of policy—perhaps the most significant—but policy remains to some degree an independent variable.

There is no standard, universally accepted set of categories for classifying land by either use or cover, and the most commonly used, moreover, are hybrids of land cover and land use. Those employed here, which are by and large those of the U.S. National Resources Inventory conducted every five years by relevant federal agencies, are cropland, forest, grassland (pasture and rangeland), wetlands, and developed land.

- *Cropland* is land in farms that is devoted to crop production; it is not to be confused with total farmland, a broad land use or land ownership category that can incorporate many forms of land cover.

- *Forest land* is characterized by a predominance of tree cover and is further divided by the U.S. Census into timberland and non-timberland. By definition, the former must be capable of producing 20 cubic feet of industrial wood per acre per year and remain legally open to timber production.

- *Grassland* as a category of land cover embraces two contrasting Census categories of use: pasture (enclosed and what is called improved grassland, often closely tied to cropland and used for intensive livestock raising), and range (often unenclosed or un-improved grazing land with sparser grass cover and utilized for more extensive production).

- *Wetlands* are not a separate Census or National Resources Inventory category and are included within other categories: swamp, for example, is wetland forest. They are defined by federal agencies as lands covered all or part of the year with water, but not so deeply or permanently as to be classified as water surface *per se*.

- The U.S. government classifies as *developed* land urban and built-up parcels that exceed certain size thresholds. "Developed" or "urban" land is clearly a use rather than a cover category. Cities and suburbs as they are politically defined have rarely more than half of their area, and often much less, taken up by distinctively "urban" land cover such as buildings and pavement. Trees and grass cover substantial areas of the metropolitan United States; indeed, tree cover is greater in some settlements than in the rural areas surrounding them.

By the 1987 U.S. National Resources Inventory, non-federal lands were divided by major land use and land cover classes as follows: cropland, about 420 million acres (22% of the entire area of the 48 states); rangeland about 400 million (21%); forest, 390 million (21%); pasture 130 million (7%); and developed land 80 million (4%). Minor covers and uses, including surface water, make up another 60 million acres (Table 1). The 401 million acres of federal land are about half forest and half range. Wetlands, which fall within these other Census classes, represent approximately 100 million acres or about five percent of the national area; 95 percent of them are freshwater and five percent are coastal.

These figures, for even a single period, represent not a static but a dynamic total, with constant exchanges among uses. Changes in the area and the location of cropland, for example, are the result of the *addition* of new cropland from conversion of grassland, forest, and wetland and its *subtraction* either by abandonment of cropping and reversion to one of these less intensive use/cover forms or by conversion to developed land. The main causes of forest *loss* are clearing for agriculture, logging, and clearing for development; the main cause of forest *gain* is abandonment of cropland followed by either passive or active reforestation. Grassland is converted by the creation of pasture from forest, the interchange of pasture and cropland, and the conversion of rangeland to cropland, often through irrigation.

Change in wetland is predominantly loss through drainage for agriculture and construction. It also includes natural gain and loss, and the growing possibilities for

Land Use and Cover in the Conterminous U.S.		
Land Class	Area in Million Acres	Fraction of Total Area
Privately Owned (shown in diagram below)		
Cropland	422	22.4%
Rangeland	401	21.3
Forest	391	20.8
Pasture	129	6.9
Developed	77	4.1
Other Catagories[1]	60	3.2
Federally Owned[2]	404	21.4
TOTAL[3]	1884	100%

[1] Other minor covers and surface water
[2] Federal land is approximately half forest and half rangeland
[3] Included in various catagories is about 100 million acres of wetland, covering about 5% of the national area

Table 1 Source: U.S. 1987 National Resources Inventory, published in 1989. U.S. Government Printing Office.

wetland creation and restoration are implicit in the Environmental Protection Agency's "no *net* loss" policy (emphasis added). Change in developed land runs in only one direction: it expands and is not, to any significant extent, converted to any other category.

Comparison of the American figures with those for some other countries sets them in useful perspective. The United States has a greater relative share of forest and a smaller relative share of cropland than does Europe as a whole and the United Kingdom in particular.

2. LAND-HUMAN RELATIONSHIPS

Though Japan is comparable in population density and level of development to Western Europe, fully two-thirds of its area is classified as forest and woodland, as opposed to ten percent in the United Kingdom; it preserves its largely mountainous forest area by maintaining a vast surplus of timber imports over exports, largely from the Americas and Southeast Asia.

Regional patterns within the U.S. (using the four standard government regions of Northeast, Midwest, South, and West) display further variety. The Northeast, though the most densely populated region, is the most heavily wooded, with three-fifths of its area in forest cover. It is also the only region of the four in which "developed" land, by the Census definition, amounts to more than a minuscule share of the total; it covers about eight percent of the Northeast and more than a quarter of the state of New Jersey. Cropland, not surprisingly, is by far the dominant use/cover in the Midwest, accounting for just under half of its expanse. The South as a whole presents the most balanced mix of land types: about 40 percent forest, 20 percent each of cropland and rangeland, and a little more than ten percent pasture. Western land is predominantly rangeland, with forest following and cropland a distant third. Wetlands are concentrated along the Atlantic seaboard, in the Southeast, and in the upper Midwest. Within each region, of course, there is further variety at and below the state level.

WHERE HAVE WE BEEN?

The public domain, which in 1850 included almost two-thirds of the area of the present conterminous states, has gone through two overlapping phases of management goals. During the first, dominant in 1850 and long thereafter, the principal goal of management was to transfer public land into private hands, both to raise revenue and to encourage settlement and land improvements. The government often attached conditions (which were sometimes complied with) to fulfill other national goals, such as swamp drainage, timber planting, and railroad construction in support of economic development.

The second phase, that of federal retention and management of land, began with the creation of the world's first national park, Yellowstone, shortly after the Civil War. It did not begin to be a significant force, however, until the 1890s, when 40 million acres in the West were designated as federal forest reserves, the beginning of a system that subsequently expanded into other regions of the country as well. Several statutory vestiges of the first, disposal era remain (as in mining laws, for example), but the federal domain is unlikely to shrink noticeably in coming decades, in spite of repeated challenges to the government retention of public land and its regulation of private land. In recent years, such challenges have included the "Sagebrush Rebellion" in the

rangelands of the West in the 1970s and 1980s calling for the withdrawal of federal control, and legal efforts to have many land use regulations classified as "takings," or as exercises of the power of eminent domain. This classification, where it is granted, requires the government to compensate owners for the value of development rights lost as a result of the regulation.

Cropland

Total cropland rose steadily at the expense of other land covers throughout most of American history. It reached a peak during the 1940s and has subsequently fluctuated in the neighborhood of 400 million acres, though the precise figure depends on the definition of cropland used. Long-term regional patterns have displayed more variety. Cropland abandonment in some areas of New England began to be significant in some areas by the middle of the nineteenth century. Although total farmland peaked in the region as late as 1880 (at 50%) and did not decline sharply until the turn of the century, a steady decline in the subcategory of cropland and an increase in other farmland covers such as woodland and unimproved pasture was already strongly apparent. The Middle Atlantic followed a similar trajectory, as, more recently, has the South. Competition from other, more fertile sections of the country in agricultural production and within the East from other demands on land and labor have been factors; a long-term rise in agricultural productivity caused by technological advances has also exerted a steady downward pressure on total crop acreage even though population, income, and demand have all rise.

Irrigated cropland on a significant scale in the United States extends back only to the 1890s and the early activities in the West of the Bureau of Reclamation. Growing rapidly through about 1920, the amount of irrigated land remained relatively constant between the wars, but rose again rapidly after 1945 with institutional and technological developments such as the use of center-pivot irrigation drawing on the Ogallala Aquifer on the High Plains. It reached 25 million acres by 1950 and doubled to include about an eighth of all cropland by about 1980. Since then the amount of irrigated land has experienced a modest decline, in part through the decline of aquifers such as the Ogallala and through competition from cities for water in dry areas.

Forests

At the time of European settlement, forest covered about half of the present 48 states. The greater part lay in the eastern part of the country, and most of it had already been significantly altered by Native American land use practices that left a mosaic of different covers, including substantial areas of open land.

Forest area began a continuous decline with the onset of European settlement that would not be halted until the early twentieth century. Clearance for farmland and harvesting for fuel, timber, and other wood products represented the principal sources of pressure. From an estimated 900 million acres in 1850, the wooded area of the entire U.S. reached a low point of 600 million acres around 1920 (Fig.1).

It then rose slowly through the postwar decades, largely through abandonment of cropland and regrowth on cutover areas, but around 1960 began again a modest decline, the result of settlement expansion and of higher rates of timber extraction through mechanization. The agricultural censuses recorded a drop of 17 million acres in U.S. forest cover between 1970 and 1987 (though data uncertainties and the small size of the changes relative to the total forest area make a precise dating of the reversals difficult). At the same time, if the U.S. forests have been shrinking in area they have been growing in density and volume. The trend in forest biomass has been consistently upward; timber stock measured in the agricultural censuses from 1952 to 1987 grew by about 30%.

National totals of forested area again represent the aggregation of varied regional experiences. Farm abandonment in much of the East has translated directly into forest recovery, beginning in the mid- to late nineteenth century (Fig. 2). Historically, lumbering followed a regular pattern of harvesting one region's resources and moving on to the next; the once extensive old-growth forest of the Great Lakes, the South, and the Pacific Northwest represented successive and overlapping frontiers. After about 1930, frontier-type exploitation gave way to a greater emphasis on permanence and management of stands by timber companies. Wood itself has declined in importance as a natural resource, but forests have been increasingly valued and protected for a range of other services, including wildlife habitat, recreation, and streamflow regulation.

Grassland

The most significant changes in grassland have involved impacts of grazing on the western range. Though data for many periods are scanty or suspect, it is clear that rangelands have often been seriously overgrazed, with deleterious consequences including soil erosion and compaction, increased streamflow variability, and floral and faunal biodiversity loss as well as reduced value for production. The net value of grazing use on the western range is nationally small, though significant locally, and pressures for tighter management have increasingly been guided by ecological and preservationist as well as production concerns.

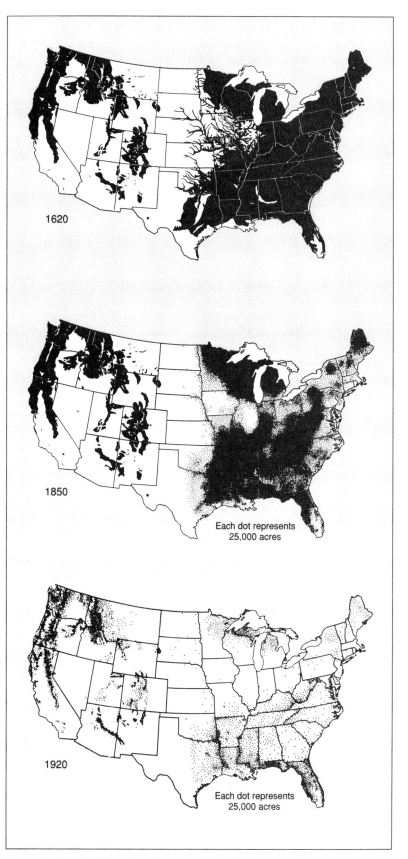

Figure 1 Area of virgin forest: top to bottom 1620, 1850, and 1920 as published by William B. Greeley, "The Relation of Geography to Timber Supply," Economic Geography, vol. 1, pp 1-11 (1925). The depiction of U.S. forests in the later maps may be misleading in that they show only old-growth forest and not total tree cover.

2. LAND-HUMAN RELATIONSHIPS

Wetland

According to the most recent estimates, 53% of American wetlands were lost between the 1780s and the 1980s, principally to drainage for agriculture. Most of the conversion presumably took place during the twentieth century; between the 1950s and the 1970s alone, about 11 million acres were lost. Unassisted private action was long thought to drain too little; since mid-century, it has become apparent that the opposite is true, that unfettered private action tends to drain too much, i.e., at the expense of now-valued wetland. The positive externalities once expected from drainage—improved public health and beautification of an unappealing natural landscape—carry less weight today than the negative ones that it produces. These include the decline of wildlife, greater extremes of streamflow, and loss of a natural landscape that is now seen as more attractive than a human-modified one. The rate of wetland loss has now been cut significantly by regulation and by the removal of incentives for drainage once offered by many government programs.

Developed land

As the American population has grown and become more urbanized, the land devoted to settlement has increased in at least the same degree. Like the rest of the developed world, the United States now has an overwhelmingly non-farm population residing in cities, suburbs, and towns and villages. Surrounding urban areas is a classical frontier of rapid and sometimes chaotic land use and land cover change. Urban impacts go beyond the mere subtraction of land from other land uses and land covers for settlement and infrastructure; they also involve the mining of building materials, the disposal of wastes, the creation of parks and water supply reservoirs, and the introduction of pollutants in air, water, and soil. Long-term data on urban use and cover trends are unfortunately not available. But the trend in American cities has undeniably been one of residential dispersal and lessened settlement densities as transportation technologies have improved; settlement has thus required higher amounts of land per person over time.

WHERE ARE WE GOING?

The most credible projections of changes in land use and land cover in the United States over the next fifty years have come from recent assessments produced under the federal laws that now mandate regular national inventories of resource stocks and prospects. The most recent inquiry into land resources, completed by the Department of Agriculture in 1989 (and cited at the end of this article), sought to project their likely extent and condition a half-century into the future, to the year 2040. The results indicated that only slow changes were expected nationally in the major categories of land use and land cover: a loss in forest area of some 5% (a

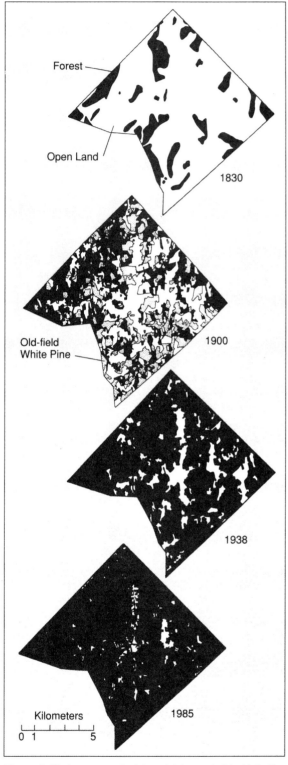

Figure 2 Modern spread of forest (shown in black) in the township of Petersham, Massachusetts, 1830 through 1985. White area is that considered suitable for agriculture; shaded portions in 1900 map indicate agricultural land abandoned between 1870 and 1900 that had developed forest of white pine in this period. From "Land-use History and Forest Transformations," by David R. Foster, in *Humans as Components of Ecosystems*, edited by M. J. McDonnell and S.T.A. Pickett, Springer-Verlag, New York, pp 91-110, 1993.

slower rate of loss than was experienced in the same period before); a similarly modest decline in cropland; and an increase in rangeland of about 5% through 2040. Projections are not certainties, however: they may either incorrectly identify the consequences of the factors they consider or fail to consider important factors that could alter the picture. Because of the significant impacts of policy, it's role—notoriously difficult to forecast and assess—demands increased attention, in both its deliberate and its inadvertent effects.

Trends in the United States stand in some contrast to those in other parts of the developed world. While America's forest area continues to decline somewhat, that of many comparable countries has increased in modest degree, while the developing world has seen significant clearance in the postwar era. There has been substantial stability, with slow but fluctuating decline, in cropland area in the United States. In contrast, cropland and pasture have declined modestly in the past several decades in Western Europe and are likely to decline sharply there in the future as long-standing national and European Community agricultural policies subsidizing production are revised; as a result, the European countryside faces the prospect of radical change in land use and cover and considerable dislocation of rural life.

WHY DOES IT MATTER?

Land use and land cover changes, besides affecting the current and future supply of land resources, are important sources of many other forms of environmental change. They are also linked to them through synergistic connections that can amplify their overall effect.

In most of the world, both fossil fuel combustion and land transformation result in a net release of carbon dioxide to the atmosphere.

Loss of plant and animal biodiversity is principally traceable to land transformation, primarily through the fragmentation of natural habitat. Worldwide trends in land use and land cover change are an important source of the so-called greenhouse gases, whose accumulation in the atmosphere may bring about global climate change. As much as 35% of the increase in atmospheric CO_2 in the last 100 years can be attributed to land use change, principally through deforestation. The major known sources of increased methane—rice paddies, landfills, biomass burning, and cattle—are all related to land use. Much of the increase in nitrous oxide is now thought due to a collection of sources that also depend upon the use of the land, including biomass burning, livestock raising, fertilizer application and contaminated aquifers.

Land use practices at the local and regional levels can dramatically affect soil condition as well as water quality and water supply. And finally, vulnerability or sensitivity to existing climate hazards and possible climate change is very much affected by changes in land use and cover. Several of these connections are illustrated below by examples.

Carbon emissions

In most of the world, both fossil fuel combustion and land transformation result in a net release of carbon dioxide to the atmosphere. In the United States, by contrast, present land use and land cover changes are thought to absorb rather than release CO_2 through such processes as the rapid growth of relatively youthful forests. In balance, however, these land-use-related changes reduce U.S. contributions from fossil fuel combustion by only about 10%. The use of carbon-absorbing tree plantations to help diminish global climate forcing has been widely discussed, although many studies have cast doubt on the feasibility of the scheme. Not only is it a temporary fix (the trees sequester carbon only until the wood is consumed, decays, or ceases to accumulate) and requires vast areas to make much of a difference, but strategies for using the land and its products to offset some of the costs of the project might have large and damaging economic impacts on other land use sectors of the economy.

Effects on arable land

The loss of cropland to development aroused considerable concern during the 1970s and early 1980s in connection with the 1981 National Agricultural Lands Study, which estimated high and sharply rising rates of conversion. Lower figures published in the 1982 National Resource Inventory, and a number of associated studies, have led most experts to regard the conversion of cropland to other land use categories as representing something short of a genuine crisis, likely moreover to continue at slower rather than accelerating rates into the future. The land taken from food and fiber production and converted to developed land has been readily made up for by conversion of land from grassland and forest. The new lands are not necessarily of the same quality as those lost, however, and some measures for the protection of prime farmland are widely considered justified on grounds of economics as well as sociology and amenities preservation.

Vulnerability to climate change

Finally, patterns and trends in land use and land cover significantly affect the degree to which countries and regions are vulnerable to climate change—or to some degree, can profit from it. The sectors of the economy to which land use and land cover are most critical—agriculture, livestock, and forest products—are, along with fisheries, among those most sensitive to climate variation and change. How vulnerable countries and regions are to climate impacts is thus in part a function of the importance of these activities in their economies, although differences in ability to cope and adapt must also be taken into account.

These three climate-sensitive activities have steadily declined in importance in recent times in the U.S. economy. In the decade following the Civil War, agriculture still accounted for more than a third of the U.S. gross domestic product, or GDP. In 1929, the agriculture-forest-fisheries sector represented just under ten percent of national income. By 1950, it had fallen to seven percent of GDP, and it currently represents only about two percent. Wood in 1850 accounted for 90 percent of America's total energy consumption; today it represents but a few percent. These trends suggest a lessened macroeconomic vulnerability in the U.S. to climate change, though they may also represent a lessened ability to profit from it to the extent that change proves beneficial. They say nothing, however, about primary or secondary impacts of climate change on other sectors, about ecological, health, and amenity losses, or about vulnerability in absolute rather than relative terms, and particularly the potentially serious national and global consequences of a decline in U.S. food production.

The same trend of lessening vulnerability to climate changes is apparent even in regions projected to be the most exposed to the more harmful of them, such as reduced rainfall. A recent study examined agro-economic impacts on the Missouri-Iowa-Nebraska-Kansas area of the Great Plains, were the "Dust Bowl" drought and heat of the 1930s to recur today or under projected conditions of the year 2030. It found that although agricultural production would be substantially reduced, the consequences would not be severe for the regional economy overall: partly because of technological and institutional adaptation and partly because of the declining importance of the affected sectors, as noted above. The 1930s drought itself had less severe and

dramatic effects on the population and economy of the Plains than did earlier droughts in the 1890s and 1910s because of land use, technological, and institutional changes that had taken place in the intervening period.

Shifting patterns in human settlement are another form of land use and land cover change that can alter a region's vulnerability to changing climate. As is the case in most other countries of the world, a disproportionate number of Americans live within a few miles of the sea. In the postwar period, the coastal states and counties have consistently grown faster than the country as a whole in population and in property development. The consequence is an increased exposure to hazards of hurricanes and other coastal storms, which are expected by some to increase in number and severity with global warming, and to the probable sea-level rise that would also accompany an increase in global surface temperature. It is unclear to what extent the increased exposure to such hazards might be balanced by improvements in the ability to cope, through better forecasts, better construction, and insurance and relief programs. Hurricane fatalities have tended to decline, but property losses per hurricane have steadily increased in the U.S., and the consensus of experts is that they will continue to do so for the foreseeable future.

Shifting patterns of land use in the U.S. and throughout the world are a proximate cause of many of today's environmental concerns.

CONCLUSIONS

How much need we be concerned about changes in land use and land cover in their own right? How much in the context of other anticipated environmental changes?

As noted above, shifting patterns of land use in the U.S. and throughout the world are a proximate cause of many of today's environmental concerns. How land is used is also among the human activities most likely to feel the effects of possible climate change. Thus if we are to understand and respond to the challenges of global environmental change we need to understand the dynamics of land transformation. Yet those dynamics are notoriously difficult to predict, shaped as they are by patterns of individual decisions and collective human behavior, by history and geography, and by tangled economic and political considerations. We should have a more exact science of how these forces operate and how to balance them for the greatest good, and a more detailed and coherent picture of how land in the U.S. and the rest of the world is used.

The adjustments that are made in land use and land cover in coming years, driven by worldwide changes in population, income, and technology, will in some way alter the life of nearly every living thing on Earth. We need to understand them and to do all that we can to ensure that policy decisions that affect the use of land are made in the light of a much clearer picture of their ultimate effects.

FOR FURTHER READING

Americans and Their Forests: A Historical Geography, by Michael Williams. Cambridge University Press, 599 pp, 1989.

An Analysis of the Land Situation in the United States: 1989-2040. USDA Forest Service General Technical Report RM-181. U.S. Government Printing Office, Washington, D.C., 1989.

Changes in Land Use and Land Cover: A Global Perspective. W. B. Meyer and B. L. Turner II, editors. Cambridge University Press, 537 pp, 1994.

"Forests in the Long Sweep of American History," by Marion Clawson. *Science*, vol. 204, pp 1168-1174, 1979.

GLOBAL FEVER

Climate change threatens more than megastorms,
floods and droughts. The real peril may be disease

EUGENE LINDEN

FLOODS. DROUGHTS. HURRICANES. Twisters. Are all the bizarre weather extremes we've been having lately normal fluctuations in the planet's atmospheric systems? Or are they a precursor of the kind of climactic upheavals that can be expected from the global warming caused by the continued buildup of CO_2 and the other so-called greenhouse gases? Scientists are still not sure. But one of the effects of the unusual stretch of weather over the past 15 years has been to alert researchers to a new and perhaps even more immediate threat of the warming trend: the rapid spread of disease-bearing bugs and pests.

Climate change, whether natural or man-made, may already be spreading disease and pestilence, according to a host of new studies, including a major report being prepared by the World Health Organization and other international institutions for release this summer. Malaria, for example, has been flourishing in recent years owing to unusually hot weather. Similarly, climate disruptions may be giving new life to such ancient scourges as yellow fever, meningitis and cholera, while fostering the spread of emerging diseases like hantavirus.

Underlying all these outbreaks is the same Darwinian mechanism: unusual weather such as dry spells in wet areas or torrential rains in normally dry spots tends to favor so-called opportunistic pests—rodents, insects, bacteria, protozoa, viruses—while making life more difficult for the predators that usually control them. Episodes of extreme weather are routinely followed by outbreaks of plagues, both old and new. Among the most recent examples:

CHOLERA. In 1991 a freighter coming from South Asia emptied its bilges off the coast of Peru. Along with the wastewater came a strain of cholera that found a home in huge algal blooms stimulated by unusually warm ocean waters and abundant pollution. The microbe then made its way into shellfish and humans. So far, the epidemic has infected over half a million people and killed at least 5,000.

HANTAVIRUS. In 1993 a six-year drought followed by heavy rains produced a tenfold increase in the population of deer mice in the American Southwest, leading to an outbreak of a deadly form of pulmonary hantavirus. The disease, which first appeared on a Navajo reservation, has since spread to 20 states and killed 45 people, nearly half of those infected.

PLAGUE. In 1994 a long monsoon in northern India followed by 90 consecutive days of 100°F heat drove rats into the cities. In Surat, they caused an outbreak of pneumonic plague. The ensuing panic killed 63 people and ultimately cost India $2 billion.

DENGUE FEVER. The coastal mountain ranges of Costa Rica had long confined dengue fever, a mosquito-borne disease accompanied by incapacitating bone pain, to the country's Pacific shore. But in 1995 rising temperatures allowed *Aedes aegypti* mosquitoes to breach the coastal barrier and invade the rest of the country. Dengue also advanced elsewhere in Latin America, reaching as far north as the Texas border. By September the epidemic had killed 4,000 of the 140,000 people infected.

Of all the infectious diseases humans will have to contend with as the world gets warmer, malaria may be the worst. Malaria is already the world's most widespread mosquito-borne illness. Rising temperatures will not only expand the range of *Anopheles* mosquitoes, but make them more active biters as well. Paul Epstein, an epidemiologist with the Harvard School of Public Health, notes that a temperature rise of 4° F would more than double mosquito metabolism, forcing them to feed more often. A 4° rise in global temperatures could also expand malaria's domain from 42% to 60% of the planet. When temperatures rise above 104° F, mosquitoes begin to die off—but at those temperatures, so do people and the crops on which they live.

Humans often make matters worse for themselves by the changes they make in their local environments. Unusually warm waters played an important role in the cholera epidemic that hit Latin America in 1991, but the outbreak was also exacerbated by sewage poured into the waters off Asia and Latin America, the destruction of pollution-filtering mangroves in the Bay of Bengal and overcrowding in the cities.

The same synergies that empower microbes also weaken our defenses against them. Heat, increased ultraviolet radiation resulting from ozone depletion, and pollutants like chlorinated hydrocarbons

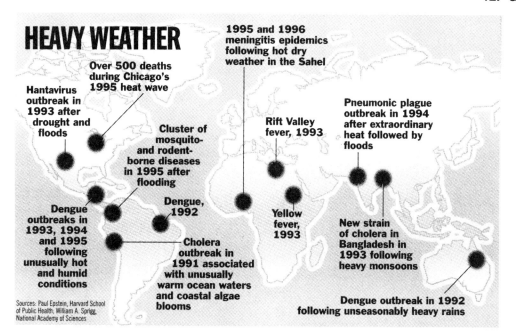

HEAVY WEATHER

1995 and 1996 meningitis epidemics following hot dry weather in the Sahel

Over 500 deaths during Chicago's 1995 heat wave

Hantavirus outbreak in 1993 after drought and floods

Pneumonic plague outbreak in 1994 after extraordinary heat followed by floods

Cluster of mosquito- and rodent-borne diseases in 1995 after flooding

Rift Valley fever, 1993

Dengue, 1992

Dengue outbreaks in 1993, 1994 and 1995 following unusually hot and humid conditions

Yellow fever, 1993

New strain of cholera in Bangladesh in 1993 following heavy monsoons

Cholera outbreak in 1991 associated with unusually warm ocean waters and coastal algae blooms

Dengue outbreak in 1992 following unseasonably heavy rains

Sources: Paul Epstein, Harvard School of Public Health; William A. Sprigg, National Academy of Sciences

all suppress the disease-battling immune systems—both for humans and for other animals. Epstein, who is one of the principal authors of the upcoming WHO study, notes that in recent years variants of the class of viruses that includes measles have killed seals in the North Sea, lions in the Serengeti and horses in Australia—three very different animals widely scattered around the globe.

A common denominator in each case: abnormal weather had caused malnutrition, weakened animal immune systems and spurred the reproduction of viruses. Epstein also notes that once ordinarily benign microbes invade weakened animals, they can become sufficiently deadly to invade healthy populations. The real threat

for people, says Epstein, may not be a single disease, but armies of emergent microbes raising havoc among a host of creatures. "The message I take home," he says, "is that diseases afflicting plants and animals can send ripples through economies and societies no less disastrous than those affecting humans."

A small but persistent group of critics, many of them supported by the oil and coal industries, still don't buy it. S. Fred Singer, president of the industry-funded Science and Environment Policy Project, argues that Epstein and his colleagues fail to note the positive health benefits of warmer nights and winters. Others, like John Shlaes, executive director of the Global Climate Coalition, suggest that

when the world is faced with pressing health problems stemming from overcrowded cities and the collapse of sanitation systems, the threat of disease caused by climate change may seem like a minor concern.

No one disputes the role of poverty and overpopulation in spreading disease. That is no reason to ignore the warnings sounded by Epstein and his colleagues, however. Scientists first raised alarms about climate change in the late 1980s, but the international community has taken few concrete steps to address the problem. The world is gambling, in effect, that problems in the future will not be serious enough to warrant inconvenience in the present. With each passing year, the future gets closer and that bet gets bigger.

The Deforestation
D · E · B · A · T · E

Estimates vary widely over the extent of forest loss

RICHARD MONASTERSKY

As tales of burning forests captured headlines in the late 1980s, a string of rock stars, movie actors, and even ice cream makers joined the fight to save tropical woodlands, helping to transform the awkward term "deforestation" into a household word. But recent studies have produced markedly different estimates of the pace of clearing, raising questions about the accuracy of deforestation figures that have floated around policy circles in recent years.

While tropical forests are certainly vanishing at a disturbing rate, the widespread disagreement over deforestation estimates makes it difficult for government officials and scientists to assess the problem. That, in turn, hampers efforts to gauge the threat of related issues, such as habitat destruction and global warming.

Concerns about previous deforestation estimates emerged in the last few years as researchers from a number of countries looked into the problem, often using more reliable methods than before. Most recently, a study published in the June 25 SCIENCE confirmed suspicions that several earlier assessments had drastically overestimated the rate of forest destruction in the Brazilian Amazon basin, thereby inflating some global estimates.

The Brazilian case provides a dramatic example of how different researchers can arrive at markedly divergent conclusions concerning the extent of deforestation. In 1988, Alberto Setzer of Brazil's National Space Research Institute (INPE) used data collected by infrared sensors on a U.S. weather satellite to gauge the number and extent of fires within the legally defined Brazilian Amazon — an area that includes only part of Brazil's tropical forests. Assuming that 40 percent of the fires occurred on recently cleared forest,

Setzer's team calculated that 8 million hectares of forest were cleared during 1987 within the legal Amazon — an almost unfathomable amount equal to 2.2 percent of the forest.

Although contested by other researchers, that alarming number found its way into several global deforestation estimates at the time. In particular, the Washington, D.C.-based World Resources Institute (WRI) included Setzer's Amazon figure in a 1990 worldwide assessment. The high number for Brazil drove up WRI's global estimate for tropical forest loss, which was calculated at 16.4 to 20.4 million hectares per year.

Despite the controversy over the Brazilian estimate, WRI's global total seemed to agree with a provisional number issued by the United Nations Food and Agriculture Organization (FAO), which put tropical deforestation at 17 million hectares per year for the period 1981 to 1990 (SN: 7/21/90, p.40).

Brazil emerged from the WRI study and others looking like the ultimate forest destroyer, responsible for roughly one-third to one-half of the global deforestation total. That triggered a round of international finger-pointing, focusing criticism on Brazil for allowing such rapid clearing of the Amazon. Brazil, however, complained that the estimates were inaccurate and that deforestation rates had never reached such heights, says Jayant A. Sathaye, an energy and forestry analyst at the Lawrence Berkeley (Calif.) Laboratory.

More recent studies have backed up Brazil's claims. In the last few years, researchers at INPE and the National Institute for Research on Amazonia, based in Manaus, Brazil, challenged Setzer's fire-counting technique and began gauging deforestation by mapping cleared areas on images taken by Landsat satellites. Studies that relied partly on this technique indicated that deforesta-

tion within the Brazilian Amazon averaged 2.1 million hectares per year between 1978 and 1989 and 1.4 million hectares from 1989 to 1990.

The newest estimate for Brazil goes even lower. David Skole of the University of New Hampshire in Durham and Compton Tucker of NASA's Goddard Space Flight Center in Greenbelt, Md., studied some 200 Landsat images covering the entire Brazilian Amazon for 1978 and 1988, allowing them to map the extent of forest and cleared land for those two years. The images showed that deforested areas covered 7.8 million hectares in 1978 and 23 million hectares in 1988, implying an average annual loss rate of 1.5 million hectares, Skole and Tucker report in their recent SCIENCE paper.

Conventional wisdom holds that Brazil's deforestation slackened dramatically after peaking in 1987, in part because the country's economy slowed, reducing the land speculation that had motivated people to clear forest for new farms or rangeland. If true, that standard theory could explain why Setzer and others found so much more deforestation going on at the peak period than others have seen in the last four years.

But Skole dismisses that explanation. "A lot of people are using it as a convenient excuse for being wrong," he contends. Although he, too, finds that deforestation rates have dropped in Brazil, he says the average for the late 1980s did not range much above 2 million hectares per year — not high enough to explain the earlier estimates.

If Brazil's actual rate of forest loss is so much lower than studies had previously suggested, how accurate are the various global estimates? Skole, for one, has little faith in the sea of numbers. "All of the published global studies do not use a systematic approach," he says. "They use secondary and tertiary sources, anecdotal reports, different time periods, different methodologies, different terminology. It's the state of affairs right now in deforestation monitoring. It's kind of a sad state of affairs, but people are using whatever resources they have, which are not adequate."

Before deforestation gained widespread attention in the late 1980s, most researchers relied on an estimate by FAO, which concluded in 1981 that tropical deforestation worldwide averaged 11.3 million hectares per year during the late 1970s. That number stood uncontested because it was the only figure available.

Since 1989, FAO has been working to update that global estimate. In 1990, it released a provisional figure of 17 million hectares of deforestation per year; but this March it lowered the global total to 15.5 million hectares per year for the period 1981 through 1990. K.D. Singh, leader of FAO's forestry assessment team in Rome, explains the change by saying that his organization's 1981 study overestimated the amount of forest remaining in the tropics at that time, a mistake that had inflated its 1990 estimate.

By all accounts, the latest FAO assessment represents the most comprehensive global study to date, having collected scattered data from individual countries or provinces and woven them together using a mathematical model based on information about forest conditions, population density, and ecological zones. Singh says his team has striven to find the best data available, although the quality and type of data vary from one region to another. Some local and national governments have conducted forest surveys using satellite images, while others have used ground-based approaches for estimating deforestation.

The success of the FAO effort remains uncertain, however. Forestry researchers cannot yet check the new global assessment against other studies because FAO released only regional deforestation estimates and has not yet issued tallies for individual countries.

For instance, the FAO numbers reported in March include 6.2 million hectares of forest lost annually in tropical South America from 1981 through 1990. That region includes Brazil and six other nations. To some researchers, the South American total appears unrealistically high. If FAO chose the best data available at the time (the Brazilian estimates of 2 million hectares lost annually in the legal Amazon during the 1980s), that would leave more than 4 million hectares cleared each year outside the Brazilian Amazon.

Where, then, is all that missing South American deforestation? That is precisely the issue raised by an international

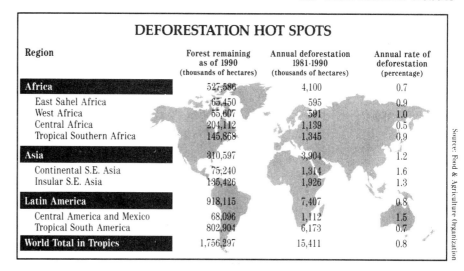

DEFORESTATION HOT SPOTS

Region	Forest remaining as of 1990 (thousands of hectares)	Annual deforestation 1981-1990 (thousands of hectares)	Annual rate of deforestation (percentage)
Africa	527,586	4,100	0.7
East Sahel Africa	65,450	595	0.9
West Africa	55,607	591	1.0
Central Africa	204,112	1,139	0.5
Tropical Southern Africa	145,868	1,345	0.9
Asia	310,597	3,904	1.2
Continental S.E. Asia	75,240	1,314	1.6
Insular S.E. Asia	135,426	1,926	1.3
Latin America	918,115	7,407	0.8
Central America and Mexico	68,096	1,112	1.5
Tropical South America	802,904	6,173	0.7
World Total in Tropics	1,756,297	15,411	0.8

Source: Food & Agriculture Organization

committee of researchers called the Intergovernmental Panel on Climate Change. In a 1992 report, the panel questioned FAO's South American estimate (which has since decreased slightly), saying, "This seems to ascribe a very high proportion (about 70 percent) of the total deforestation in South America in the late 1980s to the region outside the Brazilian Amazonia, even though this region accounts for very little of the total amount of forest on the continent."

But FAO's Singh says researchers have not appreciated the extent of South American deforestation in the open forest outside of the rainforest of the Brazilian Amazon. "This has been one of our main findings — that the deforestation outside the legal Amazon basin is quite high," he told SCIENCE NEWS. The open forest faces a greater threat because it is more accessible and because more people live there than in the rainforest, Singh says.

Beyond those hints, Singh says he cannot respond fully to criticisms of the new deforestation assessment until FAO publishes its more complete report, which will include a breakdown of figures for individual countries. The report should come out in late summer, he says. Singh also hopes to submit the study to a panel of scientists for peer review.

Some researchers, however, wonder whether the FAO will delay releasing the long-awaited numbers, perhaps indefinitely, in hopes of avoiding the intense scrutiny that will descend on this study. Ken Andrasko, chief of a forestry section in the Environmental Protection Agency's climate change division, suggests that deforestation studies have acquired political significance in the wake of last year's Earth Summit in Rio de Janeiro, where countries signed treaties on biodiversity and climate change. The climate change convention requires all countries to provide an inventory of their greenhouse gas emissions, including

those caused by deforestation. Since future treaties may call for all countries to limit their emissions, the deforestation estimates will partly determine how much a country needs to cut back.

"It's going to be increasingly difficult to publish those individual country [deforestation] estimates. If the number is higher or lower, it has very real political consequences now," Andrasko says.

That lesson was not lost on Brazil, which released its own deforestation data on the eve of the Rio summit. Such studies, as well as the one by Skole and Tucker, show that while Brazil may still be number one, it no longer sits in a category of its own, far and above every other nation on the list of forest destroyers.

Although the FAO did not provide estimates for individual countries, the data released earlier this year clearly indicate that tropical forests are shrinking worldwide. Indeed, parts of other continents are losing a greater percentage of their forests than is South America, which has much more intact forest than other parts of the globe. According to FAO, the highest percentages of deforestation during the 1980s occurred in southeast Asia, Central America and Mexico, and West Africa.

Looking beyond the problem of absolute deforestation, experts say fragmentation and degradation of remaining forests also present substantial threats, especially to the diversity of plant and animal life in some of the most biologically rich habitats on Earth. Indeed, Skole and Tucker found that the area of disturbed habitat surrounding cleared areas grew by more than 4 million hectares per year in Brazil's Amazon, much faster than the pace of deforestation there. "Even though the rate of deforestation was much lower than previous estimates, the effect on biological diversity was much greater," says Tucker.

To address such concerns, the second phase of the FAO study will examine the extent to which people have broken up forest or removed trees without stripping an area bare. As part of this work, Singh's team has purchased high-resolution satellite images for 117 randomly selected regions corresponding to about 10 percent of the forest-covered land in the tropics. For quality control, his group also used these satellite images in the first phase of the study to improve its deforestation estimates.

Ideally, FAO would purchase satellite images for the entire tropical belt. But Singh says the organization cannot afford the thousands of images needed to cover the tropics.

An ongoing NASA project may help complete the picture. In a program called Landsat Pathfinder, NASA is funding the purchase of satellite photos covering some three-quarters of the world's tropical rainforest. According to Skole, a participant in the project, it will provide the most accurate assessment of deforestation to date. As with the Brazilian case, the research done with satellite data could show that past estimates have been inflated. But Skole says the new study may also uncover much more deforestation than had been suspected.

The NASA effort does have some critical limitations. Because it focuses mostly on tropical rainforest, it will not include all open forests and dry forests, which cover just as much territory as do rainforests. Moreover, the project is a one-shot deal, not to be repeated. Experts say periodic updates are needed, not only to assess the changing deforestation threat but also to gauge the resulting increase in concentrations of carbon dioxide.

Despite its drawbacks, however, the NASA project should finally provide a means of checking the global estimates. "I feel confident," says Skole, "that in the next two to three years, as our work comes forward, we will have a much better idea because we are applying a consistent method."

Threat of Encroaching Deserts May Be More Myth Than Fact

William K. Stevens

Common wisdom has it that the deserts of the world are on the march, steadily expanding, permanently converting pastures and croplands to sand dunes, and that human mistreatment of the drylands that flank the deserts is responsible.

But scientists using the most up-to-date investigative techniques have found no evidence that this is true, at least in the case of the Sahara and its immediate environs, everyone's favorite and most serious example of what is called "desertification." In view of the lack of evidence, many experts suspect that the threatening image of encroaching deserts may be more myth than fact.

The findings, based largely on satellite measurements, are forcing a reassessment of just what is happening in the arid and semi-arid drylands along the desert's perimeter, which have turned out to be more resilient than once thought. And even as talks on a multinational treaty to deal with desertification enter an important phase at the United Nations this week, some leaders of the international effort to halt drylands degradation have backed away from the idea that deserts are expanding. In fact, they and others say, the very term desertification confuses the issue and obscures what is really going on in the drylands.

No one denies that what is taking place in the drylands is serious. As in much of the rest of the world, growing population and economic pressures are depleting the soil, damaging vegetation and natural ecosystems, depressing agricultural yields and threatening the future survival of those who live in the regions between deserts and more humid grasslands. Drylands' sparse rainfall and inevitable droughts make them more vulnerable than more humid regions.

The degradation is serious enough to the 900 million people who live in these regions, which cover a quarter of the earth's land mass. But are the drylands turning into permanent deserts? Not likely, according to the emerging scientific evidence.

Images obtained by the National Aeronautics and Space Administration from meteorological satellites show that from 1980 through 1990, the boundary between the Sahara and the Sahel drylands region on its southern border—actually a vegetative transition zone rather than a sharp line—did not move steadily south, as conventional wisdom would have it.

Rather, the vegetation line moved back and forth in conjunction with rainfall patterns, creeping northward in wetter years and southward in drier ones. The shifts from one year to the next ranged from 30 to 150 miles along the border, but no overall trend could be discerned one way or the other.

Swedish scientists at the University of Lund, combining a variety of data collected by satellites and aircraft with ground observations, examined the Sahara-Sahel border in the Sudan for the period 1962 to 1984, when the border was thought to be moving southward. The studies found that this was not happening. The Swedish scientists also found, contrary to what some had argued, no evidence that patches of desert were spreading outward from villages and water holes within the drylands area of the Sahel. And they found no changes in vegetation cover and crop productivity that could not be explained by variations in rainfall.

Major oscillations between extended dry and wet climate patterns are a normal and governing fact of life in the drylands, said Dr. James E. Ellis, an ecologist who heads the Center for Environment and Sustainable Agriculture, a research group in Morrillton, Ark., run by the Winrock Corporation, a private voluntary organization.

Long-term rainfall records show that the climate in Africa's drylands has shifted back and forth between periods of extended drought and higher rainfall for at least the last 10,000 years. On the basis of long-term studies in Kenya, Dr. Ellis believes that climate keeps the drylands in a continual state of disequilibrium, and is a bigger influence on the dynamics of drylands ecology than people are.

Role of Climate

While the evidence taken together suggests that climate is the major influence on crops and natural ecosystems in the Sahel, it does not yet prove the case. The scientific record is too sparse and short at this point, says Dr. Compton J. Tucker of the space agency's Goddard Space Flight Center, who conducted the 1980–1990 satellite studies. Forty to 50 years of observations may be necessary to determine for sure whether the desert is spreading and, if so, whether climate or human activity is most responsible.

The evidence does not mean that deserts are not spreading, but simply that "we can't find it," says Dr. Ulf Hellden, the leader of the Swedish team. Nevertheless, he said, "our hypothesis is that climate is responsible for whatever land degradation is taking place" in the Sahel. "We know we can explain 70, perhaps 80 percent of the food productivity variability with rainfall statistics, which leaves another 20 to 30 percent we cannot explain," he said.

The prime candidate for explaining that 20 to 30 percent is human activity, argues W. Franklin G. Cardy, a Canadian who directs the Nairobi-based desertification control program of the United Nations Environment Program, or UNEP, which has led the struggle to halt drylands degradation. Scientists have identified a number of factors contributing to land degradation in the Sahel and other arid regions. Cattle, camels and goats overgraze the land. Excessive grazing and cultivation by fast-growing populations reduce vegetation and encourage soil erosion by wind and water. In wet years in some localities, herders move farther north in search of new stretches of greener grass. Farmers move in behind them and plow up the land. When dry years return, the herders return to find the land plowed up, while the farmers cannot get a crop and the soil blows away, just as it did in the American dust bowl of the 1930's.

"There is no doubt in my mind" that excessive grazing and cultivation are causing serious land degradation in drylands, said Dr. David Hillel, an environmental scientist, hydrologist and soil expert at the University of Massachusetts at Amherst.

Not least of the problems is that when precipitation does return to degraded land, it takes only a little rainfall to cause much erosion. One problem, Mr. Cardy said, is that it is "extremely difficult" to measure land degradation scientifically.

"It's invisible, essentially," he said. "The farmer knows he or she has less and less crop, knows that it's not going to be sustainable. The farmer will tell you, but not quantifiably."

Lack of Rain

In the Sahel, the problem has been exacerbated in the last 25 years by below-average rainfall, according to the conclusions of international experts who met in Sweden to examine the situation in 1990. This has led some experts to wonder whether any concern over desertification would have emerged had the last quarter-century been a wet cycle rather than a dry one.

The group that met in Sweden also concluded that scientific evidence did not confirm any human-made trend toward desert-like conditions. Rather, it supported the view that dryland ecosystems are resilient and bounce back after a drought. The scientists noted that population growth could reduce this resilience, but they added that outward migrations when conditions got bad enough could allow the land to recover. The scientists did not rule out the possibility of a future trend toward desert conditions as a result of human activity.

The proposition that deserts are expanding dates to the early years of this century. The idea that regenerating drylands on the edge of the deserts would stop the spread emerged at about the same time. Over the years, anecdotal evidence convinced many scientists, development experts and much of the public that deserts were indeed advancing. By the 1970's, this view had long since moved into the mainstream; in 1972, the United States Agency for International Development asserted that the Sahara was moving southward at 30 miles a year. But many scientists in time came to see the anecdotal evidence as unconvincing. Go to the drylands in the dry season of a drought year, they pointed out, and the land will certainly look like a desert. But in many cases, they added, the same land would look different in a wet year.

As the new evidence has emerged in the last decade, UNEP, for one, has modified its view considerably. Mr. Cardy calls the concept of expanding deserts and advancing sand dunes "largely invalid." And he believes, along with Dr. Hillel and others, that the term "desertification" should be jettisoned.

It persists, Mr. Cardy and others say, mainly as a political artifact, a way to call attention to one regional expression of the global problem of land degradation, and thereby attract financial assistance. African countries, in fact, extracted the promise of a desertification treaty at the 1992 Earth Summit in Rio de Janeiro as the price of their support of other countries on other issues.

And so the term desertification hangs on, though its definition was enlarged in Rio to encompass more than human activity as a cause of deterioration of drylands. The definition adopted by the Rio delegates reads: "Desertification is land degradation in arid, semi-arid and dry subhumid areas resulting from various factors, including climatic variations and human activities." No mention of desert encroachment.

A Proposed Strategy

Definitions aside, Mr. Cardy said, the practical issue is what to do about human impact on the drylands, whatever the influence of climate and whether or not the desert is advancing. Some experts say that if the drylands are mostly hostage to climate, it might be best to concentrate resources and effort on improving wetter, more productive lands where the costs would be lower and the returns in terms of agricultural yields would be much greater.

"That's a good economic argument," Mr. Cardy said, "but where are the people who live in the drylands going to go? As populations grow, are we going to say that because it's tough we'll turn our backs on them? It doesn't make sense. People have been making a living in those areas for millennia."

Until now, Mr. Cardy acknowledged, efforts to stem drylands degradation have had mixed results at best. One reason, he says, is that solutions have too often been imposed from above and from outside, ignoring the experience and perceived needs of the people who live there.

Dr. Ellis provides an especially telling example. "In the past," he said, "we've attempted to intervene in these systems in ways consistent with our perspectives on North America." Specifically, herders have been encouraged to attach themselves to a single piece of land, on the model of North America, where greater rainfall keeps growing conditions relatively stable. But in the unstable ecology of the drylands, in times of drought herders must be able to move their animals freely across wide expanses, as they traditionally did, to take advantage of scarce grass wherever and whenever it appears.

An emerging new philosophy on management of the drylands seeks to tailor aid more closely not just to the climatic and ecological realities of the region but to local peoples' traditional strategies and tactics for coping with them. Mr. Cardy said these solutions could be as simple as the donkey cart provided to villagers in

---

Climate seems to have more influence on drylands than people do.

Burkina Faso so they could haul stones to create terraces to prevent erosion.

Where there are successes, he said, they usually build on locally generated efforts to rehabilitate land. Aid might be partly directed simply toward helping inhabitants of dry-lands in these efforts and assisting them over rough spots by extending credit, for example, or by providing seed for the next growing season if drought forces families to eat everything they grow.

Rehabilitation of Lands

There is apparently no great secret about how to rehabilitate arid lands. Soil conservation, erosion control and protecting slopes are all "standard stuff," well illustrated by the rehabilitation of the American dust bowl, Mr. Cardy said. And some strategies to beat drylands drought have precedents at least as old as the Bible: Dr. Hillel cites Joseph's building of the granaries to tide Egypt over its seven lean years.

Before any solutions can be adopted, scientists say, it is essential to understand the drylands for what they are. But the full picture remains elusive, given the gaps in knowledge that still exist and the lack of definitive proof about desert expansion and the causes of drylands degradation.

Unless the characteristics of the drylands are documented according to scientific standards, said the scientists who met in Sweden in 1990, "there is a risk that the desertification issue will become a political and development fiction rather than a scientific fact."

The Decade of Despair

DAVID R. MARPLES

David R. Marples is a professor of history and directs the Stasiuk Program on Contemporary Ukraine at the Canadian Institute of Ukrainian Studies at the University of Alberta. His most recent book is Belarus: From Soviet Rule to Nuclear Catastrophe *(1996).*

The Chernobyl accident on April 26, 1986, was the world's worst disaster at a civilian nuclear power plant. It is also one of the most widely known and controversial industrial disasters of all time. Wildly exaggerated claims have been made about the accident's impact; equally wild assertions have been made in dismissing its effects. Objective assessments are few. The truth about Chernobyl has been bent from the start—the Soviet Union wanted to protect the reputation of its ambitious nuclear power program, and the nuclear industry everywhere wanted the public to believe that a similar disaster "could not happen here."

In the Soviet Union, "Chernobyl" became a battle cry for anti-Moscow protest, and for an assault on an industry with a poor record. (Ironically, its record was no poorer than that of other Soviet energy industries; both the coal and oil industries had suffered higher casualty rates, and the coal industry had caused terrible air pollution for years.)

Scientists have attempted definitive studies of the effects of Chernobyl, but they have invariably fallen short of the mark, mainly because of the lack of adequate or reliable data.

In August 1986, when the Soviet delegation to the International Atomic Energy Agency (IAEA) in Vienna reported its findings on the accident, there was a widespread tendency to praise the new openness of Mikhail Gorbachev's presidency. The Soviets emphasized that the disaster was caused by "human error," and a show trial was staged the following July in the contaminated town. The hapless plant director, absent at the time of the experiment that caused the accident, received a ten-year sentence. His colleagues got lesser penalties (two to five years). Repudiating this staged nonsense, Valery Legasov, the leader of the Soviet delegation to the IAEA, hanged himself nine months later, on the second anniversary of the accident. By all accounts, Legasov was plagued with guilt about the design faults and technical shortcomings of the Soviet-made reactor.

Ten years later, there is no consensus on the number of victims or the overall health impact of Chernobyl, nor has the accident engendered a new safety consciousness at the nuclear plants in the newly independent states. In the meantime, the Soviet Union has collapsed, replaced by 15 new republics, most of which are waging a battle for economic survival, with an inadequate supply of energy as a critical element in the struggle. Under these circumstances, the importance of nuclear power, even in Ukraine, the site of the Chernobyl station, has increased.

Still, after a decade, it should be possible to view the event without the emotions that have shaped many earlier discussions. In reviewing various aspects of the disaster, I will try to provide a reasoned discussion of the number of the accident's direct casualties, its long-term health effects, and its meaning to an industry that relies on Soviet-made nuclear power reactors.

Direct casualties

One of the most controversial arguments about the accident concerns the number of direct casualties. The official Soviet toll rose from two to 31 during the summer of 1986, where it remained thereafter. Several Western scientists have adhered to that number, and it is a staple of Chernobyl stories in the Western press. The "official" casualty report has developed into something of a truism—if something is repeated often enough, people begin to accept it.

But the figure of 31 direct fatalities at Chernobyl is as mythic today as it was in 1986. During the early cleanup phase, it was clear there would be many more victims, particularly among the crews decontaminating the plant, those flying helicopter sorties over the roof of the gaping reactor in a flawed attempt to stop radiation from leaking into the atmosphere, and those working at the reactor scene at a variety of other hazardous tasks.

By 1990, at least 5,000 decontamination workers had died, although not all their deaths can be attributed to Chernobyl.[1]

For the most part, these people were not volunteers. They were military reservists, brought in from various parts of the Soviet Union. Most were in their 20s and 30s, but some were older. One of their missions was to fill in the great hole in the reactor roof—workers on the roof flung shovelfuls of radioactive graphite into the hole and, wearing heavy shielding, made their way as quickly as possible to safety. Radiation levels were so high that geiger counters, which were in inadequate supply, went off the scale.

Contrary to regulations, some of the workers remained in the "Exclusion Zone," an area around the damaged reactor with a 30-kilometer radius, for six months or longer, accumulating potentially fatal doses of radiation. Many were cavalier about safety. When I traveled by car to the Chernobyl plant in the summer of 1989, I saw reservists sitting in ditches above which had been posted signs declaring, "Danger! Radiation!" Wearing only overalls, they were evidently taking a smoke break. A friend at the German magazine *Stern* showed me one of his prize photographs: it was of cleanup crews taking a lunch break at the site of the damaged reactor. They wore no protective headgear or clothing as they sat on the ground eating their sandwiches, with the roofless reactor looming behind them.

Any estimate of direct casualties involves supposition and guesswork. I have encountered totally undocumented estimates as high as 125,000.[2] Even "official" sources are wildly inconsistent—how can one reconcile statements from Ukraine's health ministry and the Chernobyl Union that thousands of union members have died—with an official report from Belarus that only 150 of the 66,000 decontamination workers from that republic have died? In Belarus, the names of the workers are known and their records have been preserved.

Is it possible to make a reasonable estimate of the number of direct casualties of Chernobyl? The National Committee for Radiation Protection of the Ukrainian Population recently issued what appear to be far more reliable figures, indicating that 5,722 cleanup workers, or "liquidators" have died.[3] To this total must be added approximately 100 plant personnel, Pripyat residents, local farmers, coal miners, and officials who died in the immediate aftermath of the disaster. This number may be low, because it is very difficult to obtain accurate information about those who were evacuated. Still, total deaths directly related to the Chernobyl accident must be in the region of 6,000. To say more is to enter the realm of the unknown. Nevertheless, I believe that 6,000 represents the *minimum* possible number.

Fallout

The Chernobyl reactor spewed highly radioactive fallout over a vast area, but only in the spring of 1989 was detailed information about fallout made available to the public. The accident contaminated an area of more than 100,000 square kilometers (about the size of the state of Kentucky), and lower levels of contamination affected many parts of Europe, particularly eastern Poland, southern Germany, and Scandinavia. The worst hit regions were in the then-Soviet republics of Belarus, Ukraine, and Russia.

Of the radionuclides released, the most harmful were iodine 131, cesium 137, and strontium 90. Because the latter two have much longer half-lives than iodine, they received most of the initial attention. The iodine,

> A decade after Unit 4 exploded, there is no consensus on the number of victims, nor are Soviet-style reactors any safer.

The explosion spread varying degrees of radioactive contamination over much of Europe; the most heavily contaminated areas (in gray) are in Ukraine, Belarus, and eastern Russia.

however, appears to have traveled the farthest and to have had the most severe repercussions in terms of health.

Scientists disagree about the effects of low-level radiation on humans. In Ukraine, claims made by scientists affiliated with the newly established Center for Radiation Medicine (administered at first by the Academy of Medical Sciences in Moscow) varied widely from statements made by environmentalists, political figures, doctors, local scientists, and journalists. While visiting Chernobyl and Kiev in 1989, I was told by specialists at the center that none of the thyroid problems of Ukrainian children were a result of the release of radioactive iodine. They attributed all sicknesses to "radiophobia" or to sensational journalism. On the other hand, the film *Mi-kro-fon!*, co-produced by journalist V. Kolinko, claimed that birth defects found in livestock 300 miles away were caused by fallout.[4] Both sides seem to have indulged in gross distortion.

A similar debate arose over the amount of radiation the human body could tolerate. On one occasion, a prominent Ukrainian politician remarked that one week after the accident radiation levels in the city of Kiev were 100 times above the maximum permissible. What he probably meant to say was that levels were 100 times above natural, or background, radiation.

After the accident—and with the approval of international authorities—the Soviet medical authorities declared that the population could tolerate a level of 35 rem above background over a natural life span of 70 years. This decision was immediately attacked by Ukraine's Green World environmentalists because it ignored the amount of radiation that evacuees and cleanup crews had already received. In 1991, the level was lowered from 35 to 7 rem, or 0.1 rem (1 millisievert) per year. (The background level in Ukraine is considerably lower than in Finland, which is generally about 6 millisieverts per year.)

The area hit hardest is a zone that embraces about 20 percent of Belarusian territory, from the Brest region in the southwest, to the Mogilev and Gomel regions in the east and southeast; a large portion of north-central Ukraine, including the Kiev, Zhitomir, and Chernigov regions; and in southern Russia, the Bryansk and adjoining areas. Cesium contamination is widespread. An estimated four million people live in areas where the soil is contaminated with more than 1 curie per square kilometer, which could result in additional radiation to the human body of 1 millisievert per year. Approximately 60 percent of this territory is in Belarus, 30 percent in Ukraine, and 10 percent in Russia. Because the region is predominantly agricultural, most families continue to rely on the food they produce on their private plots. Most of the local population has been consuming contaminated food for nearly a decade.

I visited the Chausy district in Belarus in spring 1995. This region, which is 250 miles north of Chernobyl, has not received much public attention. Radiation levels range from 1 to 15 curies per square kilometer. Contaminated wells have been boarded up and local factories have closed down. The local economy is depressed and the local stores stock little food. Families must provide for themselves. In one house, an elderly man was even raising pigs in his kitchen.

Is the health of the local population at risk? The opinion of the villagers was mixed, but most were fatalistic. Children from local villages were being sent by a Minsk charitable organization to Europe and North America for summer vacations, in the hope that it might improve their generally poor health.

Evacuation is a controversial and much debated affair. About 116,000 people were evacuated immediately after the accident, all from the Exclusion Zone. In addition, both the Soviet and post-Soviet authorities have had a policy of immediately evacuating residents in other areas with cesium contamination of 15 or more curies per square kilometer.

Less urgent evacuation is based on 5–15 curies, and those living in areas with 1–5 curies—especially families with children—are considered eligible for evacuation if it should become impossible to obtain uncontaminated supplies of food and water. A much wider area than the original 30-kilometer zone was evacuated in 1989. There was a great clamor for evacuation between 1986 and 1990, but this sentiment has been less in evidence since then.

The declining interest in evacuation may be a reflection of the plight of evacuees in their new surroundings. The Belarusian press is filled with evacuee complaints—they are often unable to find employment and their new housing is shoddy, often lacking hot water (or just water). Sewerage is often inadequate. Many would-be evacuees prefer to wait in the zone, hoping to be moved to Kiev or Minsk. In some cases, though, the authorities have simply failed to act: A recent Ukrainian report noted that 2,000 families had been waiting to be evacuated from the Poliske district, just west of Chernobyl, for more than five years.[5]

One family moved from the contaminated zone in Belarus to a "clean" area in Ukraine. At their new destination they were shunned by their neighbors, who feared the newcomers would contaminate them. Their children were ostracized at school for the same reason. The situation became so intolerable that the family decided to return to Belarus.

In Minsk, a group of newly constructed

apartment blocks at the far north of the city is occupied almost exclusively by evacuees, who sit outside the apartments in rural style, conversing, smoking, and drinking. It has been difficult for the evacuees to adjust suddenly to their new environment. As one reporter said, "There is a lot of drinking there," and people are nostalgic for their native villages.

Many elderly people chose to remain in the zone. A 1991 study commissioned by the IAEA notes the strains caused by evacuation, but my visits to the zone suggest that staying behind is also a strain—few of those who remained receive an adequate or nutritious food supply.

Both Ukraine and Belarus have had to make deep cuts in spending for post-Chernobyl problems. Before 1994, Chernobyl-related expenditures—mainly for evacuating and providing housing and amenities for the resettled—swallowed 13 percent of the Ukrainian government's budget. Severe cost-cutting began in 1994 and 1995, and funding was cut to 3.4 percent. The chairman of the parliamentary committee that deals with Chernobyl-related problems states that this amount is totally inadequate. In Belarus, funding has been cut from a high of more than 20 percent of the budget to about 10 percent. Neither republic can afford to provide adequate funding on a long-term basis.

Both Ukraine and Belarus have depended on international aid, and on charitable assistance in particular. In Minsk Hospital No. 3, I saw testing equipment for diabetes and other items that had been sent from Germany to the Belarusian Charitable Fund's "For the Children of Chernobyl." At one time, 38 charitable organizations were devoted to assisting children in Belarus who were affected by Chernobyl. But it would be a mistake to think that these organizations are generously supported. Most are struggling for survival. As time passes, it becomes more difficult to raise funds.

Long-term health consequences

Few questions have been debated more heatedly than the effect of Chernobyl on the long-term health of the population. At one end of the spectrum is Anatoli Romanenko, the Ukrainian health minister, who announced in June 1986: "Medical services are keeping a close eye on health protection of everyone involved in relief work at Chernobyl. . . . The main thing is to preserve people's health. There is no cause for alarm whatsoever in the rest of Ukraine's territory [outside the 30-kilometer zone]. . . . Doctors have checked tens of thousands of people, and thousands of tests have been carried out in the laboratories.

Their results give us grounds to say that there is no danger to people's health."[6]

At the other end of the spectrum is the current Ukrainian health ministry, which issues statements that require careful analysis. One communiqué noted that the health of those in the contaminated zones was deteriorating. By 1991, only 28–32 percent of adults and 27–31 percent of children were said to be in good health.[7] Such astonishing figures reflect mainly heightened rates of respiratory diseases and diseases of the blood and nervous system.

These conflicting statements show how variable a single institution has been throughout the course of the disaster. The later claim—surely exaggerated—is the antithesis of the attempt to cover up in the first months after the accident.

Health information was classified during the Soviet period, and apart from a single and nearly unreadable volume issued by the Soviet Academy of Medical Sciences in 1989, little was forthcoming other than the proceedings of scientific conferences. Before Chernobyl, little research was conducted on the kinds of problems a Chernobyl-type accident would produce.

In 1992, the Institute of Psychology of the Russian Academy of Sciences produced a major psychological study, noting that the field was new and little researched.[8] Dr. A. Guskova of the Russian Institute of Biophysics observed: "The psychological damage is clearly the most important. . . . [I] feel that it is very important to realize that this factor is due not so much to a conviction that danger exists or does not exist, but rather to an uncertainty, a lack of constructive plans for the future."[9]

During a tour of hospitals and clinics in Minsk in December 1992, I was told that, before Chernobyl, diseases of the blood received little attention in the medical community in Belarus. A study of the incidence of leukemia was undertaken after Chernobyl, but a dispute was evident between the director of the Institute of Hematology and several of his leading researchers over the validity of reports of pre-Chernobyl rates. Today's numbers might be reliable, but statistics from the 1970s were probably the result of guesswork. Some researchers are now using the average European incidence as a baseline.

We do know that in general health and health care is problematic in both Belarus and Ukraine, and that in recent years, health statistics have taken an alarming turn. (In part, that may reflect a notable improvement in disease detection.) The infant mortality rate is more than double that for Europe as a whole, and cases of infectious diseases have risen markedly over the past four years. Both Ukraine and

Not all liquidators have been monitored on a regular basis, and information from official Ukrainian sources is unreliable.

Belarus have experienced negative population growth in recent years. Diseases like tuberculosis and diphtheria, once thought to be under control, are back; vaccination rates have dropped. In southern Ukraine, 400 cases of cholera occurred last summer as a result of polluted water.

U.S. bone marrow specialist Robert Gale, speaking at the Eurochernobyl-2 conference in Kiev in 1991, remarked that although Kiev's hospital beds were full, he doubted that the occupancy rate was specifically related to Chernobyl. More recently, the deputy chief of Minsk's Children's Hospital No. 3 told me that there has been a dramatic increase in congenital diabetes. "Before Chernobyl," he added, "we had no such problems." By 1995, according to the Belarusian State Information Agency, the lung cancer rate among the 32,000 evacuees was four times the average of the rest of the capital's population.[10]

These reports present the observer with a predicament: Which current health problems are related specifically to fallout? There is no known or previously suggested link between congenital diabetes and radiation or the consumption of irradiated products. Yet the largest number of cases of childhood diabetes emanate from Gomel province, the most heavily contaminated region.

As a group, the cleanup crews, or liquidators, have clearly been affected the most. They suffer from a variety of diseases, particularly skin ailments. But not all liquidators have been monitored on a regular basis, and information from official Ukrainian sources is unreliable. Even the number of those who took part in cleanup is uncertain, with reports varying from 600,000 to 660,000. But the number seeking aid from the government has declined.

One reads indifferent and even callous statements denying that the accident has caused major health problems, even as more deaths are reported.[11] But exaggerated statements from ostensibly responsible bodies like the Ukrainian Health Ministry mean that reality is often overlooked, especially in the skeptical international community.

In 1991, some reliable data were provided by V. G. Baryakhtar, the vice president of the Ukrainian Academy of Sciences. He reported that about 129,000 cleanup workers were living in Ukraine, but precise data were available for only 56,000 who had received radiation doses of 100–200 millisieverts. This number excluded 187 local residents who suffered from acute radiation sickness, and another 1,000 who had radiation burns as a result of the accident. About 80 percent of those examined had an impaired immune response. The rate of thrombosis was increased in cleanup crews,

and about one-third of this group had experienced a loss of libido. About 40 percent of those studied had marked hearing impairments. Medical authorities in Minsk also report that people in areas where the radiation dose is estimated at 10–30 rem have an impaired immune response. Significant chromosomal aberrations are found in the population in all affected areas.[12]

Has Chernobyl had adverse genetic consequences for the human population? Of the three republics most affected, only Belarus has a program that monitors the incidence of congenital deformities. Using the period 1982 to 1985 as a baseline, the overall rate of congenital defects rose 24 percent from 1987 to 1992; in areas where the cesium contamination of the soil was 1–5 curies per square kilometer, the increase was 30 percent; and in areas with more than 15 curies per square kilometer, the increase was 83 percent. On February 1, 1991, the Belarusian parliament established the "National Preventive Program of Genetic Consequences of the Chernobyl Accident."[13] Unfortunately, this study, like many others, has been plagued by a shortage of funds.

After the atomic bomb was dropped on Hiroshima in 1945, the rate of leukemia increased within 18 months, and the number of cases peaked within four to five years. Given the Japanese experience, it was anticipated that an increase in the rate of leukemia would be a major consequence of the Chernobyl accident.

Although it may take as long as 15 years after exposure to develop the disorder, there has not been a significant increase in leukemia in the Chernobyl-affected areas so far. Levels have risen somewhat in Ukraine and Belarus generally, and the leukemia rate is at the upper end of the European average. But the rate of leukemia seems to be lower than it was in the 1970s. In Minsk, which has the highest incidence of leukemia, there were 48 cases per million children from 1986 to 1991, compared to the reported 72.5 cases per million in 1979.[14]

Evgeni Ivanov, the chief hematologist in Belarus, asserts that the main cause of leukemia in that republic is industrial pollution, not radiation from the Chernobyl accident. His position is disputed by some of his own colleagues, who argue that it is not backed by scientific data; they add that Novopolotsk and Svetlagorsk, for example, are more heavily polluted than Minsk but have a lower incidence of leukemia.[15] It may be premature to say that the Chernobyl accident has not resulted in increased cases of leukemia, but one can say that original predictions have not materialized.

In contrast, the rate of thyroid cancers in children has increased dramatically, and the increases appear to correlate closely with the areas that received the most radioactive fallout. These cancers may be attributed to the radioactive iodine in the atmosphere in the first days after the accident, or to the consumption of contaminated milk, which affects infants far more than adults.

One 1993 Ukrainian study predicted that, of the 89,000 people exposed to radioactive iodine in Pripyat and other heavily contaminated regions, there would be a maximum of 530 cases of thyroid cancer in children, of which 50 would be incurable; and 290 cases in adults, of which 30 would be incurable.[16]

In a letter to the author, John Jagger, a retired U.S. radiation expert, predicted that from 1989 to 2000 the number of cases of childhood thyroid cancers would be double the number recorded between 1989 and 1994, and would decline thereafter, with the rate of incidence following a bell-shaped curve. According to Jagger, a total of 932 cases could be expected.[17] There is no evidence, however, that the disease has reached its peak, or that its appearance in the population follows Jagger's model or the mathematical model adopted by the Ukrainian scientific team.

According to an October 1994 article in *Nature*, 527 cases of thyroid cancer had appeared in children in Belarus, Ukraine, and Russia; more than 65 percent were in Belarus. At a November 1995 meeting of radiation scientists sponsored by the World Health Organization, these cases were directly attributed to fallout from Chernobyl. One expert who has written widely on the subject, Dillwyn Williams of Cambridge University's Addenbrooke's Hospital, stated that in heavily contaminated regions one in every 10 children could conceivably develop thyroid cancer. Some cases have occurred as far as 300 miles away from Chernobyl.[18]

Evgeni Demidchik, head of the Minsk Thyroid Tumor Clinic, has monitored the incidence of the disease in Belarusian children since 1966. Before the Chernobyl disaster, he saw an average of one case per year. "Excess" cases began to appear in 1990, and from 1993 to 1995, the number of new cases rose from 79 to 91 per year. By 1994, Belarus alone had reported that 424 children had thyroid cancer. Contrary to expectations, the number of cases has continued to rise each year.

Somewhat more than half of all cases came from the heavily contaminated Gomel province, and another 23 percent were reported in eastern areas of Brest province, near Pinsk; 11 percent occurred in Minsk. According to Demidchik, only seven cases have been reported in northern Vitebsk province, the only region of Belarus not affected by fallout.

Almost all of the afflicted children were born or conceived before the Chernobyl accident.[19] Because of the close correlation of cases with the pattern of fallout and the ingestion of radioactive iodine, it seems probable that, of the 91 cases of thyroid cancer in Belarusian children in 1994, some 90 percent were radiation-induced.

Belarus also reports an increase in the rate of non-cancerous tumors in children. Before the Chernobyl accident, the average rate was one a year; now the annual rate exceeds 60.[20]

The increased incidence of both benign and cancerous tumors is a discernible and disturbing consequence of the Chernobyl accident. It is reasonable to conclude that Ukraine and Belarus had serious pre-existing health problems and that those problems have been exacerbated by the Chernobyl accident.

Nuclear power

The disaster at Chernobyl caused many countries, and most particularly the Soviet Union, to review the status of their nuclear power plants. On the surface, the newly independent republics have made notable improvements, and information about the operation of the nuclear power industry is more available. The IAEA visits the most potentially problematic plants. International attention has focused on other Chernobyl-type reactors, graphite-moderated RBMKs. RBMK plants include the reactors at Sosnovi Bor (St. Petersburg), Kursk, and Smolensk, in Russia; and the Ignalina plant in Lithuania.[21]

The Chernobyl reactor that was destroyed was a second-generation RBMK-1000. Although little could be done to improve the other reactors on the site—to eliminate their instability if operated at low power or to fortify their inadequate containment—some improvements were implemented: Shutdown time was reduced; uranium enrichment was increased; and strict rules were introduced regarding the disabling of safety mechanisms and the conduct of experiments.

Nonetheless, the state of the nuclear power industry in the newly independent states is a cause for concern, if not alarm. Several first-generation units are considered obsolete and unsafe. An Armenian reactor, now re-started, is located in an earthquake-prone area. In addition, there are concerns about technical aspects of later generations of reactors. And despite its problems, Russia has announced an ambitious reactor-building program that would expand its nuclear power industry greatly.

Cost overruns and financial shortages have also contributed to problems in the nuclear industry. In 1994, it was reported at an international conference in Monterey, California, that safety regulators in Ukraine were not being paid on a regular basis, and that nuclear industry personnel were generally dissatisfied.[22]

Overriding this disturbing picture is the protracted debate between the G7 industrial nations and Ukraine over setting a date for the closure of the Chernobyl station and the construction of a new iron and concrete shell to cover the now-decaying sarcophagus in which Chernobyl's Unit 4 is encased.

The Chernobyl station's future

The Ukrainian government maintains that international concern about safety at Chernobyl is unwarranted; that the complex is safer than other RBMKs, and safer than plants with the other major Soviet reactor type, the VVER (water-water-pressurized reactor). Ukraine's VVERs have a poor safety record; incidents occur regularly at the giant station near Zaporozhe.[23]

Ukraine and the G7 countries finally agreed in December 1995 to set the target date for the shutdown of Chernobyl as the year 2000.[24] Ukraine was basically forced to accept this agreement by the G7's threat to withhold future credits. Ukraine was also formally accepted into the Council of Europe in November 1995 and it did not wish to endanger this hard-won status. In exchange for the shutdown, Ukraine will receive $500 million in grants and $1.8 billion in loans—just over half of what the government estimates is needed.

Left hanging is the funding needed to place a new shell, sometimes called the *Sarkofag-2*, over the sarcophagus in which Unit 4 was encased in December 1986. The first sarcophagus was visibly deteriorating by the late 1980s, and it is not expected to last more than another decade. It cannot be repaired from inside because of dangerously high radiation levels—10,000 roentgens per hour, according to one source.[25] After the new cover is in place—a yet-unfunded project that would cost upwards of a billion dollars—technicians could conceivably begin to disassemble the fragmenting first cover. Because Chernobyl Unit 3 will have to be shut down during construction of the new sarcophagus, Ukrainian authorities would like to delay the process as long as possible.[26]

G7 loans will be used to help Slavutich, a new town of about 28,000 that was built about 45 miles east of the Chernobyl station to house plant employees and their families, and to purchase a new source of energy to compensate for the loss of Chernobyl. Within Ukraine, there is a debate about whether it would be better to build a gas- or a coal-fired plant, or to commission two new reactor units at Rovno and Khmelnitsky.[27]

The Slavutich region is constantly monitored because the soil was contaminated by Chernobyl's fallout. The choice of coal would simply compound the area's environmental problems. On the other hand, neither Rovno nor Khmelnitsky has a particularly good safety record.

Greenpeace has proposed an alternative solution that would involve a stringent program of conservation. Primarily by reducing the activities of its machine-building and metallurgical industries, Ukraine might be able to reduce its energy use by as much as 65 percent.[28] This plan would be unpopular because it would increase unemployment. However, the Greenpeace suggestion was highlighted in the parliamentary newspaper, suggesting that it is being taken seriously.

Statements from the Ukrainian nuclear industry and the Chernobyl plant suggest that the lessons of Chernobyl have been forgotten in some quarters. Sergei Parashin, the plant director, has frequently said that Chernobyl is much safer than other RBMK stations. His remarks were echoed in late November by Chernobyl press officer Valeri Idelson, who declared that the station was "the safest nuclear plant in Ukraine and one of the best among the [former Soviet] countries."[29] The Chernobyl plant sponsored the publication of a book claiming that the station could operate effectively and safely far into the future.[30]

Facing the future

Daunting problems await. The roof over the destroyed reactor is cracked and its longevity is doubted. The situation has been aptly described by a Ukrainian expert who stated that virtually all the problems engendered by Chernobyl still remain, including the destroyed reactor and over 100 radioactive burial sites nearby.[31] In spite of their financial and safety problems, both Ukraine and Russia have decided to continue to commission new nuclear power plants. Ukraine cannot afford to finance a new sarcophagus, and the aid the G7 group has proposed will cover only a small part of the expense.

In retrospect, the one major international study of the health consequences of the accident, the International Chernobyl Project, was inaccurate. Its conclusions have been contradicted as better information became available about thyroid cancer, casualties among liquidators, the incidence of congenital defects, and the general rise in morbidity that is sometimes termed "Chernobyl AIDS." Few long-term safety lessons appear to have been learned. If anything, the chance of a major nuclear accident in the region is greater today than in 1986.

Several recent nuclear incidents could, potentially, have been serious, and one resulted in the loss of life. Of most immediate concern is the giant nuclear edifice on the Dnieper River at Enerhodar, near the industrial city of Zaporozhe, where there were two incidents in the first week of December 1995. Ironically, every accident there or at another VVER station bolsters the case for keeping Chernobyl open, on the theory that since 1986 it has been relatively accident-free.

Meanwhile, the Ukrainian nuclear industry has lost a number of specialists to Russia, where wages are higher and economic conditions are somewhat better. Over 8,000 nuclear workers left Ukraine between 1993 and 1995 alone, and the economic crisis has meant that many employees in the industry have worked for extensive periods without receiving wages.[32] Small wonder that nuclear workers are described as "demoralized."

Ukraine's situation is not unique. The collapse of the Soviet Union created an energy-rich Russia and Turkmenistan, and energy-hungry countries everywhere else. With an urgent need for energy, the basic rules of safety have been pushed into the background. On one occasion I heard a Ukrainian nuclear official being lectured by a U.S. specialist about this sorry state of affairs. The response was angry, and can be paraphrased as follows: "It's all very well for you energy-rich capitalists to sit in your armchairs and lecture our people, who shiver in frozen apartments. But if you were in our position, what would you do?"

All the problems engendered by Chernobyl remain.

1. David R. Marples, "Revelations of a Chernobyl Insider: An Interview with Yuri Risovanny," *Bulletin of the Atomic Scientists*, Dec. 1990, pp. 16–21.

2. Ukrainian Ministry of Health, cited in *The Ukrainian Weekly*, April 30, 1995.

3. *Holos Ukrainy*, June 7, 1995, p. 4.

4. *Molod Ukrainy*, Feb. 26, 1989.

5. *Holos Ukrainy*, Oct. 4, 1995.

6. Radio Kiev, Broadcast to Europe, June 2, 1986.

7. *Rabochaya gazeta*, May 12, 1993.

8. M. I. Bobneva, ed. *Chernobyl'skiy sled: mediko-psikhologicheskie posledstviya radiatsionnogo vozdeystviya*. 2 vols. (Moscow: Votum, 1992.)

9. The International Chernobyl Project, *Proceedings of an International Conference: Assessment of Radiological Consequences and Evaluation of Protective Measures ["The ICP"]* (Vienna: International Atomic Energy Agency, 1991), p. 40.

10. Interview with V. V. Glod, editor-in-chief, Belarusian State Information Agency, Minsk, April 1995.

11. For example, see the account of a visit to the Chernobyl zone by Sir Bernard Ingham (Margaret Thatcher's press secretary) in *Nuclear Forum*, Autumn 1994, pp. 7–9.

12. *The ICP*, pp. 41–44; interview with Evgeni Konoplya, Director, Institute of Radiobiology, Belarusian Academy of Sciences, Minsk, April 14, 1993.

13. G. I. Lazyuk et al., "Geticheskie posledstviya katastrofy na Chernobyl'skoy AES i puti ikh minimizatsii." *Il Mizhnarodny Kanhres 'Svet paslya Charnobylya'* (Minsk: Belarusian Charitable Fund "For the Children of Chernobyl," 1994, pp. 19–20.)

14. Cited in David R. Marples, *Belarus: From Soviet Rule to Nuclear Catastrophe* (New York: St. Martin's Press, 1996), ch. 4.

15. Ibid.

16. I. A. Likhtarev et al., "Ukrainian Thyroid Doses After the Chernobyl Accident," *Health Physics*, vol. 64, no. 6 (June 1993): p. 598.

17. John Jagger, letters to author, Jan. 4 and 11, 1996.

18. "Health Consequences of the Chernobyl and Other Radiological Accidents," sponsored by the World Health Organization, Geneva, 1995. Cited in Michael Balter, "Chernobyl's Thyroid Cancer Toll," *Science*, vol. 270, Dec. 15, 1995.

19. E. P. Demidchik, "Osobennosti klinicheskogo techeniya i khirurgicheskogo lecheniya raka shchitovidnoy zhelezy u detey." Unpublished paper, Minsk, 1993.

20. E. P. Demidchik, letter to author, Feb. 2, 1996.

21. The U.S. Energy Department lists Ignalina as one of the ten most dangerous nuclear power plants in the world.

22. Nikolay Steinberg, former chief engineer at Chernobyl and chief of safety operations for Ukrainian nuclear power stations.

23. Reuters, Dec. 7, 1995.

24. *Holos Ukrainy*, Dec. 21, 1995, p. 4.

25. Mikhail Umanets (former Chernobyl plant director and until recently chairman of the State Committee of Ukraine for the Use of Nuclear Energy), cited in *Holos Ukrainy*, April 1, 1995, p. 5.

26. *Holos Ukrainy*, March 21, 1995, p. 4.

27. Ibid., Sept. 5, 1995, p. 6.

28. Ibid., Dec. 2., 1995, p. 4.

29. *Intelnews*, Dec. 4, 1995.

30. Ibid.

31. *The ICP*, p. 62.

32. *Holos Ukrainy*, Feb. 15, 1995, p. 4.

The Region

The region is one of the most important concepts in geography. The term has special significance for the geographer, and it has been used as a kind of area classification system in the discipline.

Two of the regional types most used in geography are "uniform" and "nodal." A uniform region is one in which a distinct set of features is present. The distinctiveness of the combination of features marks the region as being different from others. These features include climate type, soil type, prominent languages, resource deposits, and virtually any other identifiable phenomenon having a spatial dimension.

The nodal region reflects the zone of influence of a city or other nodal place. Imagine a rural town in which a farm-implement service center is located. Now imagine lines drawn on a map linking this service center with every farm within the area that uses it. Finally, imagine a single line enclosing the entire area in which the individual farms are located. The enclosed area is defined as a nodal region. The nodal region implies interaction. Regions of this type are defined on the basis of banking linkages, newspaper circulation, and telephone traffic, among other things.

This unit presents examples of a number of regional themes. These selections can provide only a hint of the scope and diversity of the region in geography. There is no limit to the number of regions; there are as many as the researcher sets out to define.

Paul F. Starrs's thought-provoking essay on the importance of place and the concept of region leads this unit. Then, "The Rise of the Region State" suggests that the nation-state is an unnatural and even dysfunctional unit for organizing human activity. In "Megacities: Bane–or Boon?" a series of short articles from World Press Review report on the boom in global urbanization and the rise of megacities.

Barry M. Brunt proposes an up-to-date approach to the concept of region, a mainstay in geographical analysis. "Two-Way Corridor through History" discusses plans for commemorating the Camino Real, the historic trail linking Mexico and New Mexico. Next, Bruce Wilcox and Kristin Duin present a report on a study linking cultural diversity and biological ecosystems in Latin America. "Does It Matter Where You Are?" considers aspects of geographical location principles in the context of the new global economic systems. "Low Water in the American High Plains" focuses on mismanagement of a valuable water resource in the United States.

"The Long River's Journey Ends" covers hydroelectric development in the Three Gorges area of China's Yangtze River. Finally, the ongoing dilemma facing Japan and Russia over ownership of four islands in the Kurils is discussed.

Looking Ahead: Challenge Questions

To what regions do you belong?

Why are maps and atlases so important in discussing and studying regions?

What major regions in the world are experiencing change? Which ones seem not to change at all? What are some reasons for the differences?

What regions in the world are experiencing tensions? What are the reasons behind these tensions? How can the tensions be eased?

Why are regions in Africa suffering so greatly?

Discuss whether or not the nation-state system is an anachronism.

Why is regional study important?

UNIT 3

The Importance of Places, or, a Sense of Where You Are[1]

In this mobile society where every shopping mall has the same stores, can we really say there are differences among the country's regions?

Paul F. Starrs

Paul F. Starrs is professor of geography at the University of Nevada.

"A time and a place for everything" goes a well-weathered adage. The meaning of time in this spare phrasing has never warranted a second thought. Unvarying since the sundial, time is a comfortable given governed by planetary rotation and counted through the cycle of seconds, hours, days and months. If the exact interval captured by a throwaway term like "just a moment" fluctuates depending on whether you're Hopi, Huron, Hasidic, a homeboy, 3 years old or 102, a clock nonetheless ticks through 24 inviolable and orderly hours in a day.

But consider again that initial sentence: While time is known, it is without doubt "a place" that is less defined. Can the region—a place broadly construed—really have any universal meaning, or is it just a vaguely named sacrament in the church of location? What are regions, and how should we receive them in an ultra-modern era of mass communication?

A thoughtful mention of any "region" immediately takes on a burden of complicated assumptions. Europe is a vexatious and fitting example. That it exists is incontestable. And yet, what exactly is Europe? A separate continent surely Europe is not; a uniform economic organization also assuredly no. True, Europe counts as its own a motley collection of highly assorted, if generally Caucasian, peoples (Basque, Catalan, Friesian, Welsh, Walloon), with a presumptive (if hardly universal) Christian religious heritage, and claims can be made to a very grossly familiar linguistic heritage. Beyond that, Europe is an eclectic assemblage whose political sovereignty is in essence a status deigned by United Nations recognition—Norway, Ireland, Portugal, the Netherlands, San Marino, Bosnia, Macedonia, Greece. These disparate parts amount to a decidedly unseemly whole. So if Europe is genuinely a single region, then what is the binder for its constituent parts? Obvious answer: "Europe" is, in fact, a convention, a useful ploy hearkening to a generally common history that includes the World Wars, the Holy Roman Empire, Jenghis Khan's depredations, the Neanderthal and the European Economic Community (except for the countries that have not been allowed to join or elect not to). With such a messy match, Europe as a region is more organizing thought than any demonstrable fact.

While the "new regionalist" geographers, the breed of scholar whose domain generally is said to include places and regions, have of late been self-eviscerating like a sea cucumber over just what constitutes "a region," most essayists and geographical scholars agree that the region as a unit of analysis and description is basic and not to be rubbished. Remaining as a category fluid, elusive and mutable, regions are entrenched in common thought and vernacular speech.[2]

As with fashions for couture and academe, regions erratically fall in and out of favor. They are today's hot ticket, especially as renewed in the guise of "regionalism," which last peaked in the United States during the 1940s heyday of the Tennessee Valley Authority, when economic needs were thought best explored in a great restructuring of the country into socioeconomic regions that had their own distinctive personalities

(Odum & Jocher 1973; Campbell 1968; Dorman 1993; Archer 1993).[3]

Global forces both dismember and contribute to regional identity. In the 1990s, a major point of contention in academic geography is how to parse, map and understand the connections of regions to booming inter-regional phenomena: The globalization of finance (capital), information (cyberspace), communications (cellular, FAX, satellite), transportation (frequent flier flights and high-speed rail), language (the hegemony of American English), or culture otherwise construed (MTV, grunge, CNN, Rupert Murdoch's newspapers, music).[4] An accurate rendering would show the globe slashed by vast arrows of movement that reshape and deform, describing essential and ongoing patterns of geographical change. While post-modernists like Doreen Massey are able to write intelligently of "a new burst of time/space compression," a skeptic would reply that this "burst" is merely an acceleration of the same foreshortening of the world's borders, a death of certainty and control, which started in 1492.

For all the glitz of global systems and parlance about the world economy, regions remain vital. Teasing out the singularities and generalities of places are among the foremost skills that anyone, from politician to market researcher to planner, can trot out to make sense of the planet. If the Earth is not simply made up of nugget-like places that embody perfectly consistent traits, the region amounts to the most resourceful, utilitarian and creative of lies.

WHEN YOU'RE THERE, YOU'LL KNOW

Regions are, in general, more useful than real. What often are taken to be time-honored physical wholes—like the Southwest, the short-grass prairie, the Midwest and the Middle East—turn out to have sloppy edges (Meinig 1971, Said 1979, Shortridge 1985). If a mental map, an image of shared traits and cultural stereotypes, is firm, when it comes actually to mapping boundaries and attributes the cartography of any region loses exactness. An old-time regional geographer could counter by saying that ephemera like planning districts, culture areas and homelands are hardly regions at all. By conservative reckoning, the only region is something with a self-evident physical presence. While for some of the tire-kicking school there remains a real pleasure toiling to map the Basin and Range physiographic province, imprecision is hardly a fatal flaw. Mathematicians working with fractals, physicists with sub-atomic particles and philosophers charting the ideological canyons of the mind are quick to admit that fuzziness can be more useful than the obsession of an accountant or a scientist with calculator exactitude. As with the edges of forests, deserts, tundra or other ecotones, the margins of a region frequently have the highest diversity and interest, and all borderlines say much of what lies inside.

As organizational structures rather than geographical certainties, regions embody events, emotions, physical similarities, human activity, or history and economy. Find one unity or several, and the geographic elaboration of a region begins. Many of the "new regionalists" argue regions are social constructions, revealing economic or class practices. Regions, which are interesting primarily as a physical setting for social interactions, suffice, in essence, as a game board (Goldfield 1984, Thrift 1990, Pudup 1988). Others are content if a regional description stockpiles plenty of room for change, which regions do (Gilbert 1988). All regions are effective manipulations of nature, casting and organizing human practice and gathering up bundles of traits to make sense of our presence on earth. If regions did not exist, they would have to be invented. And because we need to know where and what the manifold human creations are, we have regions. There is poignancy to this metaphysics, as with any discussion of scholarship's fastidious fashions.[5] The reality is straightforward: Regions exist because we want, need and relish them.

The inherent problem with regions is as simple as it is true. Geographers, like the sociologists, conservation biologists, anthropologists and historians who have joined in the traffic of places, worry about criteria used to identify a region (Hough 1990). Are the keys solely economic? Religious? Ethnic? Territorial? Do regions originate in history or are they entirely contemporary? If an area where overlapping attributes meet forms a region, then the edges are a pronounced problem. Are places defined by watersheds and biological life—bioregions—a valid means of defining a region? Do the world's nations, discrete groupings of peoples that exist within and among the larger political entities that convention calls "countries" (think of Navajo, Provencal, Scots or Zulu territory), constitute regions? (Nietschmann 1993).

But regional characterizations allow each and every person to make sense of the world, and the categories developed often are remarkably acute in their capturing what is important about people who are, after all, geographically located on a discrete part of the earth.

Predictably, questions raised are more persistent than easy. How should we contend with larger social and structural forces defining a region? Each place is linked to others. From the Internet to the global economy, from the tracing of transnational money flows to the Hollywood movies that bully the French cinematic self-identify, even the smallest Appalachian hollow, Mormon village and South Central Los Angeles gang are connected to additional parts of the world. The most erudite sort of formulations discussing the relationship between the local and the global admit that regions are indispensable (Lipietz 1993).

There is space aplenty for flourishing skepticism. Whenever a region is identified it is easy to carp about the criteria used to single it out.[6] Regions are ultimately a state of mind, a convention. They exist in untold numbers, interwoven and overlapping. And while scholars squirm about the squishy boundaries, if you're there, you generally know. Having a sense of where you are is not just street smart, it is a survival trait through human history and geography.[7]

Debate over regional structure turns around a problem that social theorists call reification, or, in clinical terms, setting a region in stone (Jameson 1981). Places are no more uniform than the people within them. Talking about the West or the Bible Belt or the Colorado Plateau or the Chicken Fried Steak Line is no more defensible than prattling on about what "American Catholics believe," or "Cuban Americans argue," or "environmentalists claim." Catholics, Cubans and environmentalists are many and diverse. By the same token, people who fall into a designated region do not all hold to whatever is being attributed to them. But regional characterizations allow each and every person to make sense of the world, and the categories developed often are remarkably acute in their capturing what is important about people who are, after all, geographically located on a discrete part of the earth.

Regions literally hold together. But each region is also part of larger processes and interactions. A secondary lesson is, then, simplicity itself: Always examine the meaning and assumptions behind any region. Almost certainly the region is real. How have those come to be, and what do they mean? Much elegant prose is devoted to the description of regions. In fact, some of the best writing, going from Joel Garreau to Jan Morris to John McPhee to Gretel Ehrlich, delves deeply into regions and their sumptuous character. But analyze always, for a region can be developed as a scientific fact as easily as an emotional and poetic necessity.

THE USES OF REGIONAL IDENTITY

Modern politics is replete with examples of regions created in an attempt to control problems too large for the traditional political structures of towns, cities and counties. Thrown together of opportunism and necessity, these utilitarian creations have become essential political and economic facts. There are regions, however, that are literary and spiritual so much as real. Places do have life, and regions have identity—as, for example, has the American South (Cash 1941; Odum 1947; Wilson & Ferris 1989). The range of forms and purposes behind singling out regions illustrates problems of the age. Regions meet an impressive assortment of ends. The past uses, boundaries and creators of regions prove as illuminating as where and how regions today are constituted. A region always accommodates its particular time and is built within the limitations of available space. For all that, there are six regional categories that are characteristically contemporary, and a few words on each will suggest why regions are likely to stick around. What distinguishes them is that each have to be mapped to have any meaning: Regions are pure and simple geographic creations, and however their charter may be construed, for each, the map is the territory, and the accuracy of the map directly reflects on the capacity and vigilance of the creator.

THE ECOSYSTEM

After a century of trying to manage natural resources according to boundaries that have far more to do with political accident, land division history and convenience than with biological necessities, government resource managers and scientists are attempting to piece together large coherent natural bodies. Unsurprisingly, this generally occurs in areas that are in some degree of crisis. Designated "ecosystems" have obvious value. While two—the Greater Yellowstone Ecosystem and the Everglades Ecosystem—are built around national parks, there are other prominent attempts, including the Forest Service-developed "Sierra Nevada Ecosystem Project" (SNEP, more commonly), which is struggling to bound and understand a swarming human presence in the Sierra Nevada foothills of California and Nevada. Ecosystem studies try to transcend politics, seeking biological and planning alternatives to the threats of unbridled growth in environments that are subject to an unusual degree of hazard, and which cannot be planned within the older city or county boundaries.

These vaunted "ecosystems" are by and large the creations of scientists-cum-managers, and they therefore fulfill and reinforce their own public credibility. Ironically, what the scientific land managers keep rediscovering is an old Alfred Korzybski line, "the map is not the territory, and the name is not the thing named" (Bateson 1979). Sadly, naming an ecosystem and designating experts to study it goes only a teeny distance toward solving crises often political, social and economic in nature. In being so vexedly human, problems are rarely readily accessible to the gimlet eye of control by scientific edict. Other recognizable ecosystems have not fared well—Amazonia, the Sahara, the

Aral or the Caspian sea—in part because they extend into multinational space. Considering that earnest efforts like the "Biosphere Preserves" program of UNESCO are well-intentioned, it is obvious that conservation efforts within countries are far easier to develop and enforce than protections offered under international treaties or covenants.

THE REGIONAL AUTHORITY

Among the most successful regions are those embraced by regional authorities, which are created to handle questions ranging from transit problems, sewage, and hazard abatement to conservation districts, water systems, and comprehensive area planning. These umbrella agencies, as they are often called, have on occasion met with surprisingly good results. An experiment extending back decades, successful regional authorities accommodate themselves to political reality, but also can weather storms that might dislodge more local agencies.

Like corporations after passage of the 14th Amendment to the U.S. Constitution, regional authorities have come to be as real and authoritative as elected officials. They became, in fact, nearly human; physically real through legislative midwifery. In general, regional authorities are created when a job is too large (read costly) for a single political entity to handle, or when what is sought is a planning window directed far enough in the future that there is no apparent harm in many different political entities banding together for discussions. Politics and planning creates the region.

There are wonderful examples of regional authorities. The Tennessee Valley Authority and the Bonneville Power Authority are two historic cases, but others are less clouded with time. The Metropolitan Water District of greater Los Angeles is prime territory; born of the successes of the Los Angeles Department of Water and Power; which preceded the Metropolitan Water District. Together, these regional entities have done the impossible, bringing reliable and unchallengeable water to 12 million in the middle of a desert. Public utilities often are blended into regional authorities, thanks in part to their being unreachable under antitrust statutes. Their boundaries are political creations: Census tract lines, county divides, the foreseeable edges of planning areas or unincorporated city limits. Other examples of these sorts of authorities include regional park districts, regional planning authorities and the occasional super-agency, like the California Coastal Commission and its allied Coastal Conservancy. They have charters buried in time, but have assumed as charge ruling on the environmental and development future of a thousand miles of California coastline. The authority of these regional entities ebbs and flows with the urgency of constituency concerns, but can be vast.

THE VERNACULAR REGION

For all the unnaturalness of some planning and political regions, there also are valiant and ongoing attempts to recognize and name places that are plainly geographically independent and coherent. The clearest attempt comes with analyzing common speech and asking the residents of different areas where they see themselves living. This leads to the bounding of "vernacular regions," areas where much of the population has little doubt about where they live and who they are. When cast in large terms, this can establish carefully documented boundaries around common places like "The Midwest," or "The Southwest," or it can lead to the recognition of sub-regions like the Panhandle, the "Oil Patch," or the German Hill Country of Texas (Jordan 1978, Shortridge 1987).

Like corporations after passage of the 14th Amendment to the U.S. Constitution, regional authorities have come to be as real and authoritative as elected officials.

A vernacular approach is the simplest regional take—people in and around a large area are asked to toss forward names, and the answers mapped. The resulting lines, or isonyms, designate areas where there is common acceptance of a regional name. The subtleties of use and meaning in this method can be telling—while residents of El Paso, Presidio, Pecos or Wink are given to consider themselves Southwesterners, the same can hardly be said of Texans who hail from Texarkana, Tyler, Pineland or Port Arthur, who hearken to the South. In matters of outlook on race or ethnicity or religion, in where people go for major shopping, or how area residents self-identify with a broad range of political, economic and social issues, these things matter.

BIOREGIONS AND WATERSHEDS

Offshoots of the physiographic regions of the 19th century, bioregions and watersheds have found a great and growing constituency among a number of contemporary essayists and poets like Gary Snyder; who press for a return to closer forms of community than anything favored by large cities (Parsons 1985). The bioregionalists hold that the good fight is best begun at home.[8] At its best, the reasoning has echoes of Pestalozzi and the reformist educators of the 1800s, who argued that learning was best conducted using the terrain, plants and animals—a local habitat—as ledger and classroom (Pestalozzi & Green 1912). Speaking (and especially writing) with passion and great literacy for attending to geographically immediate needs and understanding the physical whole of the watershed or bioregion ahead of vainly attempting to control the world's whole surface, bioregionalists pledge that community comes first. Although James Malin issued similar plaints in decades past, and Ray Dasmann placed the bioregionalist and "ecosystem" traditions in able contrast nearly 20 years ago, the rhetoric is hard to counter (Dasmann 1976; Opie 1983, Bogue 1981).

In essence, bioregionalists, many of whom also preach for a "watershed consciousness," note that too much of humanity's destructive exploitation of the Earth is driven by quick movements between dissimilar areas, which feeds growth by acquiring and exploiting colonized places, emphasizing profit over knowledge. Know a place, and you are less likely to abuse it, goes the ethos. To understand environmental history is to grapple with local needs. Citing examples from traditional peoples who have managed lands around them for centuries with but modest deterioration, bioregional advocates voice a limited respect for the ambitious architects who preach for global environmental harmony. Their resolute business, however, is to get on with saving their own nest before instructing others in how to clean up the Earth. The intelligence and influence of bioregionalists is far in excess of their numbers.[9]

CULTURAL AREAS, ETHNIC REGIONS & HOMELANDS

Interest in coherent bodies of cultural attributes goes back thousands of years; thematic mapping thrives on locating collections of traits, and early thematic maps often plotted fairly singular behaviors. Geographers have reveled in tight areas where distinctive traits are uniquely preserved, and have mapped these for generations (Gastil 1975; Rooney et al 1982, Garreau 1981, Hart 1972). The Mormon Culture Region, Amish or Cajun country, the Bible Belt, the Sun Belt, are typical tips of a vast iceberg. The traits can be religious, political, economic, racial or linguistic. That this form of region is durable goes almost without saying. In effect, residents within the region are singled out for preserving traits that can be singular or archaic. The degree of uniformity varies hugely, place to place, region to region. By and large, the areas mapped in such regions are so distinctive as to be almost beyond argument (Arreola 1993; Conzen 1993).

Mapping regions is far more than an ideal scholarly exercise. Where the overlaps between regions are pronounced, or where there is quick shrinking, conflict or the loss of distinguishing traits can occur. Where the boundaries alter little with time, the area is unlikely

soon to disappear to dilution or disturbance. And yet there are oddities. Some culture regions persist despite migration and a loss of language and economy; the Basque, if anything, have grown stronger in the last two decades, largely thanks to political liberalization. What nudges change is never entirely easy to say, but these regions can and will persist. To a point, they are self-selected and self-sustaining.

NODES IN THE GLOBAL EXCHANGE

Finally, regions are important parts of the global system. Whether the connections are those of politics, empire, economics, culture, or religion, there is no doubt that any region, in this era of mass communication, is both beholden and at times hapless before global forces, the powers that Fernand Braudel, Immanuel Wallerstein, William Appleman Williams and Donald W. Meinig have traced with rare wisdom. This bears comment, but also requires the remark, "So what?" In many a sense, this is nothing new; the links are just more obvious and better drawn than 100 years ago, and it requires more will to insist on self-reliance, to put down the cable remote, than before the World Wars. But the articulations between places are old hat, in either a historic or a geographic sense.

The existence of larger connections in no way eliminates the need or sensibility of regions. If anything, the distractions of a beckoning world act to strengthen regions. The emphasis on learning traditional languages (Welsh, Catalan, Hopi) and relearning ways of life once on the verge of extinction likely have never been so strong. Differences have become precious, and to be distinct and have a separate identity is more than faddish. It is to know and have a sense of yourself, even if the adopted identity is more fancied than honestly come by. This is the oddest part of the region as one small segment of the known world—as the boundaries really should be falling, and homogenization growing rampant, instead the ultimate luxury of 1990s society is to "discover your place."

CONCLUSION

...time is absorbed into place, and place into mind. The land becomes history, and history becomes thought as people cross space in awareness.

—Henry Glassie
Passing the Time in Ballymenone

The precision of time, whether dispensed by the clockwork grace of gnomic Swiss watchmakers or driven by quartz crystal Swatches, is not the stuff of which regions and places are made. Time is a certainty, and for all that, a subject of hate and dread. "Saving time" is no small act of desperation. But "saving a place" is geography, history and environmental preservation writ large. We live in time, but for places; they are our communities, where horses are trotted or buses colorfully "tagged" by graffiti territorialists. Here historic preservation committees solemnize over the sanctity of the past, arguing about whether "that stone house over by Fleming's" should be torn down; planning commissioners debate regional futures and decide whether a community garden ought to be fostered in the projects. Regions are among the most intelligent acts that we can work with as humans. As Buckaroo Banzai reminds us: "Remember: No matter where you go, there you are."[10] Of many stripes, places matter. And that, most of all, is why regions are relevant.

NOTES

1. Prepared with support from the S.V. Ciriacy-Wantrup Postdoctoral Fellowship in Natural Resource Economics at the University of California at Berkeley, 1993–94.
2. As good a measure as any flows from Current Contents, a vast data base for contemporary journal articles, book reviews and commentaries. Although "bioregion" appears in only one title, "culture region" is found in 44, "watershed" in 321 and "ecosystem" appears in 784 citations. Alas, a voguish term like "post-modern" is referred to in a paltry 166 items. On the other hand, "place" is cited 1,981 times, the word "region" is in 14,890 references, and when "regional" and "regionalism" are added, the count rises to 29,811 articles. Computers offer a false precision, but the bottom line is evident: Places matter.
3. The discipline of sociology had never before, and has never since, ridden so high. That the regionalist project grew moribund with economic recovery after World War II is history. However, the importance of regions (James Madison called them "sections" in his famous Federalist Number 10) is axiomatic through American history, from early days of the Republic to the Civil War. Joel Garreau's *Nine Nations of North America* suggests some of the current interest, but there is more. In California, for example, proposals regularly float through the Legislature and increasingly onto ballot measure referenda, asking for the state to be split into more "rational" divisions. So far, no joy; check in next year.
4. The globalization of information and mass communications is quixotic–as *The Economist* has noted, "And a network is more than links between places, it is itself a place" (Editors, *The Economist*, 1993). Often the changes imposed by such technology are not so direct or self-evident as the technologically-addicted might argue. William Gibson has put it nicely: "She was a courier in the city. . . . Was it significant that Skinner shared his dwelling with one who earned her living at the archaic intersection of information and technology? The offices the girl rode between were electronically conterminous–in effect, a single desktop, the map of distances obliterated by the seamless and instantaneous nature of communication. Yet this very seamlessness, which had rendered physical mail an expensive novelty, might as easily be viewed as porosity, and as such created the need for the service the girl provided." (*Virtual Light*, Bantam Books, New York, 1993): p. 93.
5. Academic debate over the intersections of place, time and space at their worst can toss even a hardened stomach. Perhaps fortunately, Patricia Nelson Limerick has dealt an elegant swat, if sadly unlikely to carry the force of a death blow, to the gamboling semi-literacy of academic fashion in her *New York Times Book Review* essay, "Dancing with Professors: The Trouble with Academic Prose," 31 October 1993, pp.3, 23–24.
6. Take, for example, the sumptuous category of "the Southland" that has been the name for Southern California for at least five decades. How can Southern California be bounded by any single term–it now reaches into the Mojave Desert, nearly to the Nevada and Arizona boundaries, and is virtually across the Techachapi Ranges, into the San Joaquin Valley, and runs south to San Diego and Tijuana. Yet the term "Southland" is a sufficiently flexible regional label to encompass it all. See Starrs 1988, Davis 1990, and *The Economist* 1994.
7. I will apologize here to John McPhee for borrowing the great phrase that he used to describe the proxemics of Bill Bradley, who was a Princeton basketball player when McPhee first used the phrase. I hope the original author will take no exception to the usurpation of titles.
8. "It is not the ecologists, engineers, economists or earth scientists who will save spaceship earth, but the poets, priests, artists and philosophers," is how Lawrence Hamilton has put it in the Introduction to a volume he edited, *Ethics, Religion, and Biodiversity: Relations between Conservation and Cultural Values.* (Knapwell, Cambridge: The White Horse Press, 1993)
9. The bioregionalists are assuredly NOT to be confused with the "biospherians" whose "space capsule" existence in Biosphere 2 near Oracle, Arizona, shows far more enthusiasm for the ecosystem model than a modest biosphere consciousness.
10. The line is Peter Weller's in "The Adventures of Buckaroo Banzai Across the 8th Dimension," Twentieth Century Fox, 1984.

SOURCES

Archer, Kevin, 1993. "Regions As Social Organism: The Lamarckian Characteristics of Vidal de la Blache's Regional Geography," *Annals of the Association of American Geographers,* September; 83(3): pp. 498–513.

Arreola, Daniel D. 1993. "The Texas-Mexican Homeland," *Journal of Cultural Geography,* Spring-Summer; 13(2): pp. 61–74.

Bogue, Allan G., 1981. "The Heirs of James C. Malin: A Grassland Historiography," *Great Plains Quarterly,* Spring, 1(2): pp. 105–131.

Campbell, Robert D., 1968. "Personality as an Element of Regional Geography," *Annals of the Association of American Geographers,* December; 58(4): pp. 748–759.

Cash, W.J. [Wilbur Joseph], 1941. *The Mind of the South;* (New York: Alfred A. Knopf); 429 pages.

Conzen, Michael. 1993. "Culture Regions, Homelands, and Ethnic Archipelagos in the United States: Methodological Considerations," *Journal of Cultural Geography,* Spring-Summer; 13(2): pp. 13–30.

Dasmann, Raymond, 1976. "Future Primitive: Ecosystem People versus Biosphere People," *The CoEvolution Quarterly,* Fall, 11: pp. 26–31.

Davis, Mike. 1990. *City of Quartz: Excavating the Future in Los Angeles* (New York & London, Verso).

Dorman, Robert L., 1993. *Revolt of the Provinces: The Regionalist Movement in America, 1920-1945;* (Chapel Hill: University of North Carolina Press); 366 pages.

The Economist, 1994. "The Point of Los Angeles," [Editorial], *The Economist* [London], 22 Jan., p. 14.

The Economist, 1993. "Make Way for Multimedia," [Lead Editorial] *The Economist* [London], 16 October: pp. 15–16.

Entrikin, J. Nicholas, 1991. *The Betweenness of Place: Towards a Geography of Modernity;* [Critical Human Geography]; (London: Macmillan).

Garreau, Joel, 1981. *The Nine Nations of North America.* (New York: Avon Books).

Gastil, Raymond, 1975. *Cultural Regions of the United States* (Seattle, University of Washington), 366 pages.

Gilbert, Anne. 1988. "The New Regional Geography in English and French-speaking Countries," *Progress in Human Geography* 12:2, June, pp. 208–228.

Goldfield, David R., 1984. "The New Regionalism [Review Essay]," *Journal of Urban History,* February, 10(2): pp. 171–186.

Hart, John Fraser; 1991. "The Perimetropolitan Bow Wave," *Geographical Review,* January , 81(1): pp. 35–51.

Hart, John Fraser [editor], 1972. *Regions of the United States;* (New York: Harper & Row).

Hough, Michael, 1990. *Out of Place: Restoring Identity to the Regional Landscape;* (New Haven, Connecticut: Yale University Press); 230 pages.

Jameson, Frederic, 1981. *The Political Unconscious: Narrative as a Socially Symbolic Work* (London, Methuen).

Jordan, Terry G., 1978. "Perceptual Regions in Texas," *Geographical Review,* July, 68(3): pp. 293–307.

3. THE REGION

Lewis, Peirce, 1979. "Defining a Sense of Place," *The Southern Quarterly: A Journal of the Arts in the South,* Spring-Summer; 27(3 & 4): pp. 24–46.

Lipietz, Alain. 1993. "The Local and the Global: Regional Individuality or Interregionalism?" *Transactions of the Institute of British Geographers, New Series;* Vol. 18, pp. 8–18.

Massey, Doreen, 1992. "A Place Called Home?" *New Formations* Number 17, pp. 3–15.

Meinig, D. W. [Donald William], 1971. *Southwest: Three Peoples in Geographical Change, 1600–1970;* (New York: Oxford University).

Nietschmann, Bernard, 1993. "Authentic, State, and Virtual Geography in Film," *Wide Angle: A Quarterly Journal of Film History, Theory, Criticism, & Practice,* October, 15(4): pp. 5–12.

Odum, Howard W., 1947. *The Way of the South; Toward the Regional Balance of America;* (New York: Macmillan;); 350 pages.

Odum, Howard W. and Katharine C. Jocher; [editors], 1973. *In Search of The Regional Balance of America;* [The University of North Carolina Sesquicentennial Publications]; (Westport, Conn.: Greenwood Press; orig. copyright 1945); 162 pages.

Opie, John, 1983. "Environmental History: Pitfalls and Opportunities," *Environmental Review,* 7(1): pp. 8–16.

Parsons, James J., 1985. "On "Bioregionalism" and "Watershed Consciousness" *The Professional Geographer,* February, 37(1): pp. 1–6.

Pestalozzi, Johann Heinrich and John Alfred Green, 1912. *Pestalozzi's Educational Writings.* New York, London: Longmans, Green & Co.; E. Arnold. 328 pages.

Pudup, Mary Beth, 1988. "Arguments Within Regional Geography," *Progress in Human Geography,* September, 12(3): pp. 369–390.

Rooney, John F., Jr., Wilbur Zelinsky, and Dean R. Louder, [General editors], 1982. *This Remarkable Continent: An Atlas of United States and Canadian Society and Cultures;* Cartographic editor John D. Viteck; (College Station, Texas: Texas A & M University Press for The Society for the North American Cultural Survey); 321 pages.

Said, Edward W., 1979. *Orientalism;* (New York: Vintage Books (Random House); 368 pages.

Shortridge, James R., 1985. "The Vernacular Middle West," *Annals of the Association of American Geographers,* March, 75(1): pp. 48–57.

Shortridge, James R., 1987. "Changing Usage of Four American Regional Labels," *Annals of the Association of American Geographers,* September 1987, 77(3): pp. 325–336.

Starrs, Paul F., 1988. "The Navel of California and Other Oranges: Images of California and the Orange Crate," *The California Geographer,* Vol. 28, pp. 1–42.

Thrift, Nigel, 1990. "For a New Regional Geography 1," in *Progress in Human Geography,* June, 14(2): pp. 272–279.

Wilson, Charles Reagan, and William Ferris, [co-editors], 1989. *The Encyclopedia of Southern Culture;* (Chapel Hill: University of North Carolina Press for the Center for the Study of Southern Culture at the University of Mississippi); 1,634 pages.

THE RISE
OF THE REGION STATE

Kenichi Ohmae

Kenichi Ohmae is Chairman of the offices of McKinsey & Company in Japan.

The Nation State Is Dysfunctional

THE NATION STATE has become an unnatural, even dysfunctional, unit for organizing human activity and managing economic endeavor in a borderless world. It represents no genuine, shared community of economic interests; it defines no meaningful flows of economic activity. In fact, it overlooks the true linkages and synergies that exist among often disparate populations by combining important measures of human activity at the wrong level of analysis.

For example, to think of Italy as a single economic entity ignores the reality of an industrial north and a rural south, each vastly different in its ability to contribute and in its need to receive. Treating Italy as a single economic unit forces one—as a private sector manager or a public sector official—to operate on the basis of false, implausible and nonexistent averages. Italy is a country with great disparities in industry and income across regions.

On the global economic map the lines that now matter are those defining what may be called "region states." The boundaries of the region state are not imposed by political fiat. They are drawn by the deft but invisible hand of the global market for goods and services. They follow, rather than precede, real flows of human activity, creating nothing new but ratifying existing patterns manifest in countless individual decisions. They represent no threat to the political borders of any nation, and they have no call on any taxpayer's money to finance military forces to defend such borders.

Region states are natural economic zones. They may or may not fall within the geographic limits of a particular nation—whether they do is an accident of history. Sometimes these distinct economic units are formed by parts of states, such as those in northern Italy, Wales, Catalonia, Alsace-Lorraine or Baden-Württemberg. At other times they may be formed by economic patterns that overlap existing national boundaries, such as those between San Diego and Tijuana, Hong Kong and southern China, or the "growth triangle" of Singapore and its neighboring Indonesian islands. In today's borderless world these are natural economic zones and what matters is that each possesses, in one or another combination, the key ingredients for successful participation in the global economy.

Look, for example, at what is happening in Southeast Asia. The Hong Kong economy has gradually extended its influence throughout the Pearl River Delta. The radiating effect of these linkages has made Hong Kong, where GNP per capita is $12,000, the driving force of economic life in Shenzhen, boosting the per capita GNP of that city's residents to $5,695, as compared to $317 for China as a whole. These links extend to Zhuhai, Amoy and Guangzhou as well. By the year 2000 this cross-border region state will have raised the living standard of more than 11 million people over the $5,000 level. Meanwhile, Guangdong province, with a population of more than 65 million and its capital at Hong Kong, will emerge as a newly industrialized economy in its own right, even though China's per capita GNP may still hover at about $1,000. Unlike in Eastern Europe, where nations try to convert entire socialist economies over to the market, the Asian model is first to convert limited economic zones—the region states—into free enterprise havens. So far the results have been reassuring.

These developments and others like them are coming just in time for Asia. As Europe perfects its single market and as the United States, Canada and Mexico begin to explore the benefits of the North American Free Trade Agreement (NAFTA), the combined economies of Asia and Japan lag behind those of the other parts of the globe's economic triad by about $2 trillion—roughly the aggregate size of some 20 additional region states. In other words, for Asia to keep pace existing regions must continue to grow at current rates throughout the next decade, giving birth to 20 additional Singapores.

Many of these new region states are already beginning to emerge. China has expanded to 14 other areas—many of them inland—the special economic zones that have worked so well for Shenzhen and Shanghai. One such project at Yunnan will become a cross-border economic zone encompassing parts of Laos and Vietnam. In Vietnam itself Ho Chi Minh City (Saigon) has launched a similar "sepzone" to attract foreign capital. Inspired in part by Singapore's "growth triangle," the governments of Indonesia, Malaysia and Thailand in 1992 unveiled a larger triangle across the Strait of Malacca to link Medan, Penang and Phuket. These developments are not, of course, limited to the developing economies in Asia. In economic terms the United States has never been a single nation. It is a collection of region states: northern and southern California, the "power corridor" along the East Coast between Boston and Washington, the Northeast, the Midwest, the Sun Belt, and so on.

From *Foreign Affairs*, Vol. 72, No. 2, Spring 1993, pp. 78-87. © 1993 by Kenichi Ohmae. Reprinted by permission.

3. THE REGION

What Makes a Region State

THE PRIMARY linkages of region states tend to be with the global economy and not with their host nations. Region states make such effective points of entry into the global economy because the very characteristics that define them are shaped by the demands of that economy. Region states tend to have between five million and 20 million people. The range is broad, but the extremes are clear: not half a million, not 50 or 100 million. A region state must be small enough for its citizens to share certain economic and consumer interests but of adequate size to justify the infrastructure—communication and transportation links and quality professional services—necessary to participate economically on a global scale.

It must, for example, have at least one international airport and, more than likely, one good harbor with international-class freight-handling facilities. A region state must also be large enough to provide an attractive market for the brand development of leading consumer products. In other words, region states are not defined by their economies of scale in production (which, after all, can be leveraged from a base of any size through exports to the rest of the world) but rather by their having reached efficient economies of scale in their consumption, infrastructure and professional services.

For example, as the reach of television networks expands, advertising becomes more efficient. Although trying to introduce a consumer brand throughout all of Japan or Indonesia may still prove prohibitively expensive, establishing it firmly in the Osaka or Jakarta region is far more affordable—and far more likely to generate handsome returns. Much the same is true with sales and service networks, customer satisfaction programs, market surveys and management information systems: efficient scale is at the regional, not national, level. This fact matters because, on balance, modern marketing techniques and technologies shape the economies of region states.

Where true economies of service exist, religious, ethnic and racial distinctions are not important—or, at least, only as important as human nature requires. Singapore is 70 percent ethnic Chinese, but its 30 percent minority is not much of a problem because commercial prosperity creates sufficient affluence for all. Nor are ethnic differences a source of concern for potential investors looking for consumers.

Indonesia—an archipelago with 500 or so different tribal groups, 18,000 islands and 170 million people—would logically seem to defy effective organization within a single mode of political government. Yet Jakarta has traditionally attempted to impose just such a central control by applying fictional averages to the entire nation. They do not work. If, however, economies of service allowed two or three Singapore-sized region states to be created within Indonesia, they could be managed. And they would ameliorate, rather than exacerbate, the country's internal social divisions. This holds as well for India and Brazil.

The New Multinational Corporation

WHEN VIEWING the globe through the lens of the region state, senior corporate managers think differently about the geographical expansion of their businesses. In the past the primary aspiration of multinational corporations was to create, in effect, clones of the parent organization in each of the dozens of countries in which they operated. The goal of this system was to stick yet another pin in the global map to mark an increasing number of subsidiaries around the world.

More recently, however, when Nestlé and Procter & Gamble wanted to expand their business in Japan from an already strong position, they did not view the effort as just another pin-sticking exercise. Nor did they treat the country as a single coherent market to be gained at once, or try as most Western companies do to establish a foothold first in the Tokyo area, Japan's most tumultuous and overcrowded market. Instead, they wisely focused on the Kansai region around Osaka and Kobe, whose 22 million residents are nearly as affluent as those in Tokyo but where competition is far less intense. Once they had on-the-ground experience on how best to reach the Japanese consumer, they branched out into other regions of the country.

Much of the difficulty Western companies face in trying to enter Japan stems directly from trying to shoulder their way in through Tokyo. This instinct often proves difficult and costly. Even if it works, it may also prove a trap; it is hard to "see" Japan once one is bottled up in the particular dynamics of the Tokyo marketplace. Moreover, entering the country through a different regional doorway has great economic appeal. Measured by aggregate GNP the Kansai region is the seventh-largest economy in the world, just behind the United Kingdom.

Given the variations among local markets and the value of learning through real-world experimentation, an incremental region-based approach to market entry makes excellent sense. And not just in Japan. Building an effective presence across a landmass the size of China is of course a daunting prospect. Serving the people in and around Nagoya City, however, is not.

If one wants a presence in Thailand, why start by building a network over the entire extended landmass? Instead focus, at least initially, on the region around Bangkok, which represents the lion's share of the total potential market. The same strategy applies to the United States. To introduce a new top-of-the-line car into the U.S. market, why replicate up front an exhaustive coast-to-coast dealership network? Of the country's 3,000 statistical metropolitan areas, 80 percent of luxury car buyers can be reached by establishing a presence in only 125 of these.

The Challenges for Government

TRADITIONAL ISSUES of foreign policy, security and defense remain the province of nation states. So, too, are macroeconomic and monetary policies—the taxation and public investment needed to provide the necessary infrastructure and incentives for region-based activities. The government will also remain responsible for the broad requirements of educating and training citizens so that they can participate fully in the global economy.

Governments are likely to resist giving up the power to intervene in the economic realm or to relinquish their impulses for protectionism. The illusion of control is soothing. Yet hard evidence proves the contrary. No manipulation of exchange rates by central bankers or political appointees has ever "corrected" the trade imbalances between the United States and Japan. Nor has any trade talk between the two governments. Whatever cosmetic actions these negotiations may have prompted, they rescued no industry and revived no economic sector. Textiles, semiconductors, autos, consumer electronics—the competitive situation in these industries did not develop according to the whims of policymakers but only in response to the deeper logic of the competitive marketplace. If U.S. market share has dwindled, it is not because government policy failed but because individual consumers decided to buy elsewhere. If U.S. capacity has migrated to Mexico or Asia, it is only because individual managers made decisions about cost and efficiency.

The implications of region states are not welcome news to established seats of political power, be they politicians or lobbyists. Nation states by definition require a domestic political focus, while region states are ensconced in the global economy. Region states that sit within the frontiers of a particular nation share its political goals and aspirations. However, region states welcome foreign investment and ownership—whatever allows them to employ people productively or to improve the quality of life. They want their people to have access to the best and cheapest products. And they want whatever surplus accrues from these activities to ratchet up the local quality of life still further and not to support distant regions or to prop up distressed industries elsewhere in the name of national interest or sovereignty.

When a region prospers, that prosperity spills over into the adjacent regions within the same political confederation. Industry in the area immediately in and around Bangkok has prompted investors to explore options elsewhere in Thailand. Much the same is true of Kuala Lumpur in Malaysia, Jakarta in Indonesia, or Singapore, which is rapidly becoming the unofficial capital of the Association of Southeast Asian Nations. São Paulo, too, could well emerge as a genuine region state, someday entering the ranks of the Organization of Economic Cooperation and Development. Yet if Brazil's central government does not allow the São Paulo region state finally to enter the global economy, the country as a whole may soon fall off the roster of the newly industrialized economies.

Unlike those at the political center, the leaders of region states—interested chief executive officers, heads of local unions, politicians at city and state levels—often welcome and encourage foreign capital investment. They do not go abroad to attract new plants and factories only to appear back home on television vowing to protect local companies at any cost. These leaders tend to possess an international outlook that can help defuse many of the usual kinds of social tensions arising over issues of "foreign" versus "domestic" inputs to production.

In the United States, for example, the Japanese have already established about 120 "transplant" auto factories throughout the Mississippi Valley. More are on the way. As their share of the U.S. auto industry's production grows, people in that region who look to these plants for their livelihoods and for the tax revenues needed to support local communities will stop caring whether the plants belong to U.S.- or Japanese-based companies. All they will care about are the regional economic benefits of having them there. In effect, as members of the Mississippi Valley region state, they will have leveraged the contribution of these plants to help their region become an active participant in the global economy.

Region states need not be the enemies of central governments. Handled gently, region states can provide the opportunity for eventual prosperity for all areas within a nation's traditional political control. When political and industrial leaders accept and act on these realities, they help build prosperity. When they do not—falling back under the spell of the nationalist economic illusion—they may actually destroy it.

Consider the fate of Silicon Valley, that great early engine of much of America's microelectronics industry. In the beginning it was an extremely open and entrepreneurial environment. Of late, however, it has become notably protectionist—creating industry associations, establishing a polished lobbying presence in Washington and turning to "competitiveness" studies as a way to get more federal funding for research and development. It has also begun to discourage, and even to bar, foreign investment, let alone foreign takeovers. The result is that Boise and Denver now prosper in electronics; Japan is developing a Silicon Island on Kyushu; Taiwan is trying to create a Silicon Island of its own; and Korea is nurturing a Silicon Peninsula. This is the worst of all possible worlds: no new money in California and a host of newly energized and well-funded competitors.

Elsewhere in California, not far from Silicon Valley, the story is quite different. When Hollywood recognized that it faced a severe capital shortage, it did not throw up protectionist barriers against foreign money. Instead, it invited Rupert Murdoch into 20th Century Fox, C. Itoh and Toshiba into Time-Warner, Sony into Columbia, and Matsushita into MCA. The result: a $10 billion infusion of new capital and, equally important, $10 billion less for Japan or anyone else to set up a new Hollywood of their own.

Political leaders, however reluctantly, must adjust to the reality of economic regional

> "Political leaders, however reluctantly, must adjust to the reality of economic regional entities if they are to nurture real economic flows."

entities if they are to nurture real economic flows. Resistant governments will be left to reign over traditional political territories as all meaningful participation in the global economy migrates beyond their well-preserved frontiers.

Canada, as an example, is wrongly focusing on Quebec and national language tensions as its core economic and even political issue. It does so to the point of still wrestling with the teaching of French and English in British Columbia, when that province's economic future is tied to Asia. Furthermore, as NAFTA takes shape the "vertical" relationships between Canadian and U.S. regions—Vancouver and Seattle (the Pacific Northwest region state); Toronto, Detroit and Cleveland (the Great Lakes region state)—will become increasingly important. How Canadian leaders deal with these new entities will be critical to the continuance of Canada as a political nation.

In developing economies, history suggests that when GNP per capita reaches about $5,000, discretionary income crosses an invisible threshold. Above that level people begin wondering whether they have reasonable access to the best and cheapest available products and whether they have an adequate quality of life. More troubling for those in political control, citizens also begin to consider whether their government is doing as well by them as it might.

Such a performance review is likely to be unpleasant. When governments control information—and in large measure they do—it is all too easy for them to believe that they "own" their people. Governments begin restricting access to certain kinds of goods or services or pricing them far higher than pure economic logic would dictate. If market-driven levels of consumption conflict with a government's pet policy or general desire for control, the obvious response is to restrict consumption. So what if the people would choose otherwise if given the opportunity? Not only does the government withhold that opportunity but it also does not even let the people know that it is being withheld.

Regimes that exercise strong central control either fall on hard times or begin to decompose. In a borderless world the deck is stacked against them. The irony, of course, is that in the name of safeguarding the integrity and identity of the center, they often prove unwilling or unable to give up the illusion of power in order to seek a better quality of life for their people. There is at the center an understandable fear of letting go and losing control. As a result, the center often ends up protecting weak and unproductive industries and then passing along the high costs to its people—precisely the opposite of what a government should do.

The Goal is to Raise Living Standards

THE CLINTON administration faces a stark choice as it organizes itself to address the country's economic issues. It can develop policy within the framework of the badly dated assumption that success in the global economy means pitting one nation's industries against another's. Or it can define policy with the awareness that the economic dynamics of a borderless world do not flow from such contrived head-to-head confrontations, but rather from the participation of specific regions in a global nexus of information, skill, trade and investment.

If the goal is to raise living standards by promoting regional participation in the borderless economy, then the less Washington constrains these regions, the better off they will be. By contrast, the more Washington intervenes, the more citizens will pay for automobiles, steel, semiconductors, white wine, textiles or consumer electronics—all in the name of "protecting" America. Aggregating economic policy at the national level—or worse, at the continent-wide level as in Europe—inevitably results in special interest groups and vote-conscious governments putting their own interests first.

The less Washington interacts with specific regions, however, the less it perceives itself as "representing" them. It does not feel right. When learning to ski, one of the toughest and most counterintuitive principles to accept is that one gains better control by leaning down toward the valley, not back against the hill. Letting go is difficult. For governments region-based participation in the borderless economy is fine,

except where it threatens current jobs, industries or interests. In Japan, a nation with plenty of farmers, food is far more expensive than in Hong Kong or Singapore, where there are no farmers. That is because Hong Kong and Singapore are open to what Australia and China can produce far more cheaply than they could themselves. They have opened themselves to the global economy, thrown their weight forward, as it were, and their people have reaped the benefits.

For the Clinton administration, the irony is that Washington today finds itself in the same relation to those region states that lie entirely or partially within its borders as was London with its North American colonies centuries ago. Neither central power could genuinely understand the shape or magnitude of the new flows of information, people and economic activity in the regions nominally under its control. Nor could it understand how counterproductive it would be to try to arrest or distort these flows in the service of nation-defined interests. Now as then, only relaxed central control can allow the flexibility needed to maintain the links to regions gripped by an inexorable drive for prosperity.

The urbanizing world
Megacities: Bane—or Boon?

■ *June's Habitat II meeting in Istanbul, the second United Nations Conference on Human Settlements, made news mainly with its stark theoretical divisions and political bickering. The delegates couldn't even agree on whether the Third World's headlong stampede to cities is good or bad for people. But it seems sure that more than half of humanity will soon live in urban areas, with at least 1,600 cities of 1 million or more inhabitants. And the conference inspired some thoughtful journalism, exploring the debate and reporting on new approaches to coping with urbanization.*

Apocalypse Postponed?

new**scientist**

I s the world plunging into an overpopulated urban sprawl, or have apocalyptic visions of "megacities" been exaggerated? Two United Nations agencies have come up with conflicting predictions for the conference on human settlements. One charts an "urban explosion" in the Third World. The other says that if there ever was an urban population bomb, it has long since been defused.

In its annual report on the state of the world's population, the United Nations Population Fund (UNPF) focused on the "unprecedented urban growth now taking place in developing countries" and the danger that cities from Bombay to Lagos to Mexico City will be "overwhelmed by the sheer numbers of the poor and the dispossessed." But the United Nations Center for Human Settlements (UNCHS), the agency that organized the Habitat II conference in Istanbul, had a very different vision. This 560-page study, "An Urbanizing World," maintains that the growth of most cities was slower in the 1980s than in any of the three previous decades. In the 1980s, it says, "for many of the world's largest cities, more people moved out than in."

The UNPF predicts that the number of megacities—those with more than 10 million inhabitants—will increase from 14 today to 27 by the year 2015, with Bombay, Karachi, and Lagos leading the rush. "The proportion of the world's population living in the largest cities is increasing," it says.

Maybe, says the UNCHS, but megacities have not grown as much as predicted a decade ago by the demographers at the UNPF. "Only 3 percent of the world's population lives in megacities," says David Satterthwaite of the International Institute for Environment and Development in London, one of the authors of the UNCHS report. And most megacities are growing little faster than the overall world population. The main growth is in smaller cities, he says. "The UNPF report talks of unprecedented urban growth, but that is rubbish," says Satterthwaite. "Manchester 200 years ago was growing as fast as any city today. And in the developing world, the biggest urban growth is in the fastest growing economies."

The conflicting interpretations go to the heart of one of the major themes of the conference: Are Third World megacities a drag on economic development, or are they the engines that drive it? In the past 20 years, says Satterthwaite, "The countries with the most successful economic performances have had the most rapid urban changes."

Even the basic proposition behind the conference—that within 10 years the majority of people will be living in urban areas—is questioned by the UNCHS study. It points out that "a significant proportion of the world's 'urban' population live in small market towns and administrative centers" rather than cities. Many areas defined as urban in India and China, the world's two most populous countries, would be described by most people as rural.

—*Fred Pearce, "New Scientist" (weekly), London, June 1, 1996.*

No, Apocalypse Now *The* **Guardian**

U rbanization is bringing about one of the most significant transformations in history. The problems are staggering," says Wally N'Dow, head of the Habitat II conference. There are now more than 600 million people officially homeless or living in life-threatening urban conditions. More than 1 billion lack sanitation. "A low-grade civil war is being fought every day in the world's urban centers," says N'Dow. "Many cities are collapsing. We risk a complete breakdown in cities. People feel alienated."

Declining resources, growing competition, food scarcity, and environmental problems will set the agenda for cities in the next 50 years, N'Dow warns. "More than 1 billion people cannot get clean drinking water. Dirty water causes 80 percent of diseases in the developing world."

The UNPF report says one of the main reasons for the decay of world cities in the past decade is economic structural adjustment programs imposed by the International Monetary Fund. These, it is said, have increased poverty, homelessness, and unemployment in more than 50 countries.

And the blame is put on the rich for much of what N'Dow calls "the emerging anarchy" in the world's cities. He criticizes the United States and other developed countries for not accepting that people have a right to adequate housing and blames liberalization of trade and the activities of multinational corporations for accelerating urbanization.

—*John Vidal, "The Guardian" (liberal), London, June 1, 1996.*

How the Prophets Goofed

M ost of the forecasts of booming megacities made in the early 1980s have failed to materialize. Calcutta should have grown from 11 million to 15 million by now. So far it has reached 11.5 million. Shanghai should have 21 million people, but has about 15 million. And so on.

How did the head-counters get it wrong? First, says David Satterthwaite, they can't count. Brazil's 1991 census revealed that São Paulo, its biggest city, had 4 million fewer people than thought. A census in Nigeria the same year revised Lagos's population from nearly 8 million to 5 million.

And what of Mexico City? In 1984, the UN held a population conference there and declared it had almost 17 million inhabitants and was overtaking Tokyo as the world's biggest city. UN statisticians say the city's population then was around 13 million, is now 15.5 million, and is unlikely to hit 17 million for another decade.

A second problem is a failure to define rules for drawing city boundaries. Witness Tokyo. The UN graphs suggest it has added 9 million people in the past decade. The real increase was about 3 million. The rest, according to Satter-thwaite, came from redrawing the city boundary to include 87 surrounding towns and cities. Depending on where you draw the boundaries, Los Angeles has 3 million, 9 million, or 14 million people; Liverpool 450,000 or 2 million; and Bangkok 6 million or 12 million.

A more fundamental mistake is to assume that lines on graphs will carry on ever upward. Most cities grow quickly before reaching a plateau. This is the point at which inhabitants feel the benefits of living in the city are outweighed by the problems—of crime, overcrowding, and pollution. From this point, many cities shrink. Milan and Liverpool have lost about 20 percent of their population in the past 20 years, and London, 10 percent. Some Third World cities are beginning to follow.

This isn't to say the world isn't becoming more urban. But the big growth is in the smaller cities and in the growing belts of suburbia—"Edge City," in the jargon.

—*Fred Pearce, "The Guardian," London, May 30, 1996.*

Cities vs. Their People GEMINI

T he frightening projections of the UN in the early 1980s proved exaggerated. By 2000, Bombay will not reach 19 million and Mexico City will not become a megacity of 25 million. This does not mean the problem has ended. Urbanization is quickening. But as the biggest centers become saturated, smaller cities have taken over as engines of urban development. Poona, Surat, and Bangalore in India are all growing faster than Calcutta or Bombay.

All over the developing world there has been conflict, between those who govern the city—and who clear out squatters to develop the urban landscape with highways, shopping malls, and corporate headquarters—and the poor people themselves, who fight for the right to remain where they had built homes and created livelihoods and the hope of a better life. Poor people are being increasingly removed from their homes—not by municipal workers and police this time, but by mysterious fires, explosions, and "accidents." This clears land for expensive apartments, shops, and offices. Meanwhile, the urban poor's ability to create homes and secure local communities has been used as a justification for the withdrawal of government services, leading to reduced subsidies for food and falling spending on health and education.

Self-help organizations are useful, but their strengths should not be overestimated. They require an enabling and positive framework that the free market can never provide. Government intervention, of a more benign and positive kind than hitherto, is vital if people are to help themselves. As it is, too often they are forced to struggle against the people elected to govern them.

—*Jeremy Seabrook, Gemini News Service (Third World-oriented), London, April 30, 1996.*

Bright Lights, Big Cities The Economist

T he doomsday scenario assumes that urban growth is both unstoppable and necessarily bad. Not so. It is a natural part of economic development. Rising populations typically go with rapid economic growth, as in Latin America in the 1960s and 1970s and in China now. When the economy falters, so do cities.

In many poor countries, towns and cities account for 70 percent or more of national output, while holding only a fraction of the population. Moving to them from the village makes good sense; they offer at least the hope of a job. And migrants tend to be intelligent about where they move to: When larger Latin cities were seeing slow or no growth in the 1980s, many smaller ones that specialized in high-value exports and tourism grew rapidly. The slums of Rio, Nairobi, or Calcutta are sad places to bring up children, yet even the poorest city families are likelier than rural ones to be able to send their children to school and to limit their number. For all the rush to China's cities, a household is less likely to face poverty there than in its countryside.

Urbanization produces mess and the chaos of what is politely known as "informal" housing. For that, though, blame not growth but the failure of city authorities to adapt to the influx. The trouble is that the occupants of many a slum could afford something better but cannot find it: A lack of property rights, outdated land-use regulations, and inept government can make cheap housing all but impossible. In fact, as some cities have shown, given economic growth and competent central and local government, the problems of urbanization can be solved—and urbanization itself can do much to create the wealth needed to solve them.

That said, real and serious problems—of public services, above all—remain. The World Bank has pledged $15 billion over the next five years to programs that bring clean water, or the occasional rubbish collector, to the hundreds of millions of people without them, and that is only a small fraction of the cost envisaged.

And the conventional, gloomy wisdom may be correct in parts of Africa and South Asia. Dacca, Karachi, Lahore, Lagos, and Kinshasa are expected to grow by 3 percent or more each year for the next 20 years. None of these is famous for splendid local government. Africa is seeing the world's fastest growth of urban population, chiefly because birth rates are high. But the continent's economic growth is low. Still, the problem is not that people are coming to cities to get a leg up the economic ladder, but that bad policies pull the ladder out from under them.

—*"The Economist" (conservative newsmagazine),*
London, June 8, 1996.

A Good Life in Bombay THE GLOBE AND MAIL

Few would envy Zahida Nadafe's urban existence. Along with her husband, daughter, son-in-law, and grandson, Nadafe lives on a sidewalk in Bombay, in a concoction of scrap wood and chicken wiring. The family's front door is a jute sack, its front yard an open sewer that carries the family's waste along with that of 30 or so other families who live in huts along the same stretch of sidewalk.

Yet Nadafe would not give up Bombay for anywhere else in India, especially not for the village she came from in the 1970s.

"You can get mutton, fish, chicken here, everything," she laughs, playing in the street with her grandchild. "In the village, you have to die without food."

Every day, an estimated 1,000 newcomers are born into

or move to Bombay, a city of 12.6 million and a metropolitan area of 15 million, already among the world's most crowded places. In 20 years, the greater city is projected to reach 27.4 million, nearly the present population of Canada.

And for all their faults, cities have become humanity's residence of choice. "If you see cities only as statistical numbers, it can be quite frightening," says Bombay's best-known architect and planner, Charles Correa. "What those figures don't take into account is that these are human places."

In big, bad Bombay, Nadafe's husband, Muhammad, selected a patch of sidewalk for his family in the 1970s because it offered a better life than they had in their village. The sidewalk was near a mosque and a railway station, offering the security of community and liberty of movement. Muhammad then found a job—a city's other great asset—as a street vendor specializing in balloons.

After losing two of their three children to diseases in the desert state of Rajasthan, the couple saw much appeal in Bombay life. A full 80 percent of the city's population is literate. With health clinics in every neighborhood and food available in abundance, Bombay's infant-mortality rate is about half the national average. Birth rates are much lower. People live much longer. And 85 percent of the homes have access to electricity and water. On Nadafe's sidewalk, each of the 30 or so huts has a television. At the end of their row, a tiny shop sells Colgate toothpaste and Lux soap.

"Urbanization is desirable. It is inevitable. It is an unstoppable phenomenon," says O. P. Mathur, an urban specialist at India's National Institute of Public Finance and Policy.

—*John Stackhouse, "Globe and Mail" (centrist),*
Toronto, June 1, 1996.

●●●

Helping Squatters Help Themselves

BUILDING HOUSES, SEWERS, AND LIVES

Tired of making do with their run-down houses, slum dwellers in India took matters into their own hands and proceeded to build the houses they have long wanted. Residents of a slum community in the city of Poona in western India designed their own small but airy brick houses, bought cheap materials, and then constructed them with residents and neighbors pitching in. In Bombay, a city with the world's biggest slum, citizens fed up with filthy, broken latrines built and maintained by the local government designed community toilet blocks that are cleaner, more functional, and cheaper to build. Residents began using these community-managed toilets much more frequently, not least because the separation of men's and women's toilets prevented harassment of the women. The new toilets were built in common areas, forcing residents to keep them clean.

Increasingly, Asia's urban poor are getting by on their own steam. "Communities are now trying to look at what was the solution they wanted for themselves, without trying to wait for the state to allot them anything," says Sheela Patel of the Bombay-based Society for the Promotion of Area Resource Centers. Maurice Leonhardt of the Asian Coalition of Housing Rights says that community efforts such as these show that the urban poor can overcome the "psychological barrier" of helplessness.

For instance, slum dwellers in Orangi, a squatter area of 1 million people in the Pakistani city of Karachi, had enough of waiting for the government to provide basic services; they laid their own network of sewage pipes and put toilets in every house.

[Behind this project is a research organization called the Orangi Pilot Project, backed by $105,000 in private funds, which operates with little government help and often refuses foreign aid. Writing in London's *New Scientist* magazine, Fred Pearce calls it "the world's most successful experiment in improving the lot of poor urban people." The 5,400 sewers and 94,000 latrines used cheap materials and simplified technology; most important, they were installed by Orangi residents, with their own labor and $1.8 million of their own money. "The lesson of Orangi has reverberated around the world," Pearce writes. "The poorest people can and will pay for services that city authorities regard as too expensive, too complicated, or simply too much trouble to provide."–WPR]

Orangi residents also put up schools, hospitals, clinics, and maternity homes in their community. "It's perfectly natural for people to have an interest in improving their own possessions." Leonhardt says.

The benefits are even greater when urban poor communities are given some form of land security or ownership rights. "Once they have got security, it just sparks them off to improve their situation," says Leonhardt. "You will find that people will plant trees, paint their houses, and take pride in their community once the threat of eviction is gone."

Unfortunately, activists say that not all national or local governments realize that evicting squatters cannot work for the long term in cities with fast-expanding urbanization. Squatting, for example, remains a crime in countries such as the Philippines. "If nine tenths of the things you do every day are illegal, then there's something wrong with the law. It's not something wrong with you. There are so many people facing this problem that they no longer feel they are criminal in doing that," says Patel.

The point is that laws have become inadequate to address such realities as informal settlements. As poor communities take more control over their destiny, government's role also needs to change. Instead of viewing itself as the provider of free housing, the government should be more of a facilitator, working with local communities, resolving conflicts, and ensuring equity, say activists.

In recent years, Bombay's government has allowed slum dwellers to upgrade their dwellings following certain rules. India's National Slum-Dwellers Federation and Manila Milan (Women Together) in Bombay have worked with

Bombay officials to design the urban poor's participation in sanitation projects and the building of toilet blocks in other slum settlements.

—Johanna Son, Inter Press Service (Third World-oriented news agency), Rome, March 20, 1996.

●●●

Discovering Voters In Brazil's 'Favelas'

HOUSING, JOBS, AND COMMUNITY ACTION

THE GLOBE AND MAIL

Lucia de Oliveira's two-bedroom house, part of a colony perched on stilts above Brazil's murky Rio Bugre, is in a medical danger zone. Besides the rats, there's a 33-foot-high ridge of garbage on the other side of the river. It is the edge of a vast dump for the city of Santos that sends foul odors and acrid smoke wafting through the neighborhood.

But relief is in sight for Oliveira, her husband, and two children. She's on the list for a new house, a concrete-block dwelling that, at the very least, should be ratproof—and unlikely to tumble into the canal during a rainstorm.

It is part of a slum-renewal scheme that illustrates the energy being invested in urban initiatives in Brazil. Officials hope at least half the 20,000 people living in the precarious stilt community known as Dique da Vila Gilda will move to more stable houses being built nearby. If it succeeds, the project will have done more than provide new housing. It will have given the residents temporary jobs and stimulated community organization among them.

The government of Santos, a city of 500,000, has invested heavily in public participation for its slum housing and other projects. Santos is spending 6.5 percent of its municipal budget—close to $15 million—on a network of residents' councils with elected neighborhood delegates, covering everything from health and education to cultural heritage.

Throughout Brazil, small and medium-sized cities are winning acclaim for such initiatives. The most famous is the program in Curitiba, capital of the southern state of Paraná, a city of about 2.5 million. There, slum dwellers are given bus tokens or food in return for turning in recyclable garbage. A fast bus system with special boarding platforms has succeeded in luring residents away from their cars. A Habitat II conference report lauds two other state capitals, Belo Horizonte and Fortaleza, for slum-housing programs that concentrate on improving dwellings rather than replacing them.

Many of the new initiatives aim to improve living conditions for residents of the *favelas*, the squatter settlements characteristic of Brazilian cities. For years, Brazilian authorities virtually ignored *favelas*. During military rule, mayors of state capitals—and of Santos, because of its strategic importance as a port—were appointed by indirectly elected state governors. Now they are elected. Besides having the same moral claim to basic municipal services as anyone else, *favelados* have masses of votes. And slum-improvement projects are springing up everywhere.

In line with municipal policy, the residents of Dique da Vila Gilda were encouraged to form an association. "It's easier to find the right way to do housing if you have all the movements together, rather than just us making the decision," says Santos Mayor David Capistrano Filho.

About 250 residents are employed building the new townhouse-style dwellings in four different designs. About 150 houses are finished, and a further 800 are planned.

—*Paul Knox, "Globe and Mail" (centrist), Toronto,
June 6, 1996.*

●●●

The UN's Struggle For Dar es Salaam

'THE CITY IS FINALLY AWAKENING'

DER SPIEGEL

A tropical storm is blowing in from the Indian Ocean to soak the city. In a few minutes, sandy paths turn into running streams, and the craterlike potholes in the paved streets into lakes. Cars get stuck and cursing pedestrians wade through the mud. It is a typical chaotic morning at six in Dar es Salaam, Tanzania's largest city.

Anna Makata is hurrying to the bus stop. In the jammed streets, her three-mile ride takes almost an hour. Her workplace consists of four wooden poles rammed into sand, with a piece of corrugated roofing on top. Two home-built tables and benches sit underneath the shelter. It is hard for her to get the damp charcoal to burn, but she makes a small cook fire. Now there is breakfast at "Mama Makata's Place"—cornmeal porridge and tea.

With what she earns from her little restaurant, she feeds an entire family: four children, her old mother, and two aunts. Her customers include a bus driver, masons from a construction site nearby, and passers-by.

> ## "We are people, not trash."

The 47 women selling food at the bus station chose Makata as chairperson when they formed a protective association. The women have only one enemy: the city government. "They are always threatening to kick us out," she says. "They don't do anything, but they get their money."

Most of the people living in Dar es Salaam share Makata's opinion of the city government. The streets are in ruins, pipes lead nowhere, buildings fall down, mounds of garbage rot in the streets, and there are constant water and electricity outages. The city is on the verge of collapse.

The United Nations Environment Program (UNEP), has been running an ambitious cleanup project here since 1992. The Sustainable Dar es Salaam Project (SDP) is a cooperative venture with international aid groups, nongovernmental organizations, and the city administration. The SDP has ambitious goals: privatizing garbage collection, cleaning up the residential areas, improving mass transit, routing traffic away from the city, fighting air pollution, putting in sewers, and improving recreation. "For each task, we have to find a foreign donor," says Paul Schuttenbelt, a Dutch aid worker, "and the whole project will take a long time. But Dar es Salaam is finally awakening."

The first results are already visible in the Hanna Nasif area of the city, where illegal settlers, now numbering 20,000, are building their own sewer. With funds from an Irish aid group, the World Bank, and the Ford Foundation, they have already dug 600 yards of trenches. The workers get about $1.50 per day, and the city wants the residents to contribute 15 to 20 percent of the cost of the project. In the Karakata district, citizens are building a walkway around the neighborhood, because the streets have been blocked for months.

City bureaucrats cannot smother the people's inventive methods of survival. In back yards and along every road, 350,000 street vendors sell old clothes and spare parts; repair cars and radios; collect trash, wastepaper, and scrap lumber; wash cars; cut hair; and fix hot food. The police are constantly rousting the street vendors from their stands because they create garbage and do not obey health laws. Last February, police with bulldozers destroyed 30,000 small stands. The vendors united under the slogan "We are people, not trash" and demanded legalization of their work.

—*"Der Spiegel" (liberal newsmagazine), Hamburg,
June 3, 1996.*

Regions and Western Europe

Regional geography is undergoing important changes in its method of study in order to achieve a greater degree of relevancy in the context of a dynamic global system. Effective knowledge of regional identities can no longer be confined to facts that establish patterns, it also demands a critical appreciation of processes and spatial interrelationships. Western Europe is taken as a case study to reflect this new approach to regional geography. Despite the complexity of this major world region, two basic models are proposed as a basis on which to develop detailed study. Essential patterns of Western Europe are established through six generalizations: location; quality of the environment; industrialization; urban development and trade; population and culture; and the European Community/European Union. Processes and interrelations are reviewed through a core-periphery model. Changing regional patterns are highlighted which suggest a movement away from a national focus for regional study to one which is more international. **Key words**: *regional geography, processes, spatial interrelationships, Western Europe, core-periphery, changing regional identities.*

Barry M. Brunt

DEPARTMENT OF GEOGRAPHY AND EUROPEAN STUDIES, UNIVERSITY COLLEGE, CORK, IRELAND[1]

Regions and Western Europe

Geography is currently facing significant challenges as the discipline tries to come to terms with both the extent and rapidity of changes that are occurring at a variety of spatial and sectoral levels. Issues such as GATT and the liberalization of world trade, the collapse of communism, and the implications of innovations in technology are only a few of many key issues that are having a critical impact on the spatial patterns of contemporary development. In this context of a rapidly changing world, a new interest in geography is emerging as people try to appreciate how the processes of change affect different parts of the world. These are, therefore, exciting times for geography and geographers as new opportunities for study present themselves and a new sense of relevance attaches itself to the discipline. The purpose of this article is to offer a new way to conceptualize the study of a region within the context of the complexity of contemporary development processes, which impact substantially on regional identities. Its focus is on the establishment of critical generalizations relating to both patterns and processes of regional expression which provide an essential basis/image for more detailed subsequent analysis of the region. Western Europe is taken as a case study to reflect this approach.

Regions and Geography

As modern technology has effectively made the world a smaller place in which to live, work, and travel, interest has grown in understanding different regions of the world. For geographers, however, the interest in regions is not confined to present trends. Since geography is involved essentially with the study of place/space and analyzing the nature of relationships that exist between spatial units over the earth's surface, the region has long been viewed as a central element for the discipline (Paddison and Morris 1988; de Blij and Muller 1994).

The traditional approach taken by geographers in the study of a region generally involved the accumulation of a large amount of facts relating to the region's physical and human characteristics. In this way, detailed regional patterns were established. This exercise, however, tended to be laborious, repetitive, and stressed the uniqueness of the region from surrounding regions. Furthermore, the established patterns were seen as static since forces of change were not central to the study.

In the present context, however, forces of change are central to any effective study of regions (e.g., Lich 1992). As regional identities or patterns change in response to new processes at work, a new relevance is given to regions, e.g., NAFTA, the European Union, the former Soviet Union, and the Third World. Regional geography must respond to the opportunities and challenges presented by this dynamic environment and, in doing so, can consolidate its pivotal position in the discipline. In addition, regional geography can assist in understanding the complex nature of today's highly interactive global system. Three key considerations are involved in establishing an effective basis for appreciating regional identities:

1. Patterns. This involves the establishment of an adequate factual base about a region's essential patterns of human and physical attributes. For example, what are the basic patterns of relief, climate, land use, and economic development that allow a region to be distinguished from surrounding regions?

2. Processes. An understanding of critical processes that are at

From *Journal of Geography*, January/February 1995, pp. 306-316. © 1995 by the National Council for Geographic Education. Reprinted by permission.

work, both within and between regions, is vital in appreciating how a particular region functions. For example, the processes of industrialization/de-industrialization, urbanization, and migration are having major implications for many regions.

3. Interrelationships. This is perhaps the most critical factor since it effectively links patterns and processes. Consideration of interrelationships establishes a greater sense of dynamism and relevancy in the study of regions. Without this linkage, patterns usually appear as static and isolated entities, while processes can be interpreted as being too abstract and lack a sense of reality by failing to be applied to the real world. Since regional boundaries are not closed to external influences, internal patterns of development generally reflect how processes originating from outside a region influence its internal development. In the European Union, therefore, patterns of agriculture in member states are not shaped simply by a region's internal attributes (e.g., relief, farm size, climate), but increasingly by how the objectives of the Common Agricultural Policy affect the region.

The effective understanding of regions demands the appreciation of all three components: patterns, processes, and especially the role of interrelationships. This can be expressed as:

Regional geography has become more complex as it attempts to reflect better the changing nature of regions, rather than concerning itself with the learning of large amounts of facts in order to create static patterns that define a region's identity. While appreciating this complexity, however, it can be suggested that an effective initial comprehension of any region can be assisted by deliberately simplifying a region's complexity, that is, by establishing a model. This approach is advanced on the premise that the region under study will possess a number of broadly based generalities that help to define the character of the region. An initial image of the region, based on generalizations, is established and can provide a context within which a more detailed and dynamic study can proceed. The key to such an approach to regional geography relates to the nature of generalization (level of simplification) required to provide an effective context for study. Western Europe can be taken as an example.

Regions and Western Europe

Western Europe is usually identified as a complex global region, exhibiting a great deal of internal differentiation (Mellor and Smith 1979; Diem 1979; Clout et al. 1994; Brunt 1991). However, at a generalized level, there are common criteria that can be used to define Europe as a whole. These common characteristics can be used to establish a general image of Western Europe which can form an effective platform for further in-depth study. Furthermore, any subsequent, detailed study of Western Europe's regional mosaic will not occur in isolation (unique regions), but rather takes place within a global context and, thereby, gains a greater sense of relevancy.

Essentially, a skeleton of knowledge of Western Europe needs to be established to cover both the patterns and processes deemed critical to define the contemporary geography of the global region. Below, six key generalizations are itemized as being suitable to establish an adequate general image of Western Europe. Using these generalizations, the detailed analysis of patterns, processes, and interrelationships can proceed as case studies to highlight the dynamics and complexities of the regional geography of Western Europe.

General Characteristics of Western Europe
Location
In terms of its global setting, Western Europe has an advantageous location (Figure 1). It forms the western extremity of the Eurasian continent, occupying an area between, approximately, 35°N to 70°N and 35°E to 10°W. As a result, it possesses a centrality within the Northern Hemisphere that provides Western Europe with important strategic advantages for trade with North America, Africa, Asia, and the Middle East. Therefore, as Europe changed from an internally oriented economy, focused essentially around the Baltic and Mediterranean Seas, to a more outward/global economy centered on the Atlantic, the Atlantic seaboard countries of

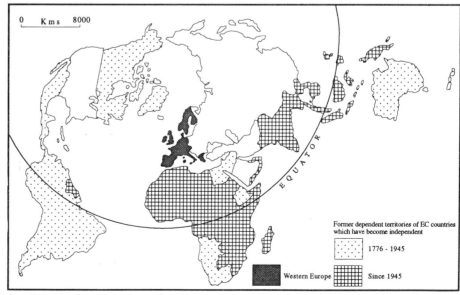

Figure 1. Western Europe, its former dependent territories and their global context.

3. THE REGION

Western Europe prospered. This has been of fundamental importance for Western Europe, and several countries along its Atlantic seaboard were able to build up major overseas colonial empires (e.g., Britain, France, the Netherlands, Spain, Portugal).

Within Western Europe, it is also important to have a knowledge of the relative location of the constituent countries (Figure 2). This has influenced their character and nature of national development. Thus, for example, the strategic location of the Netherlands allowed it to become an entrepôt for its larger and more powerful neighbors (especially Germany).

Quality of the Environment

While Western Europe has a remarkable complexity of surface relief, this can be simplified into four general patterns (Figure 3). To the north lie the Scandinavian Mountains, which extend southwestward to affect the northern and western parts of the British Isles, while to the south lie the Alpine Fold Mountains. These mountain ranges form the northern and southern margins of Western Europe and enclose the remaining two relief types. North of the Alps occur the Hercynian Fold Mountains, an east-west trending series of uplands, separated by lowland basins and river valleys, that include areas such as the Ardennes, Massif Central, and Black Forest. Finally, the North European Plain is a major lowland arc extending from southwest France through the Paris Ba-

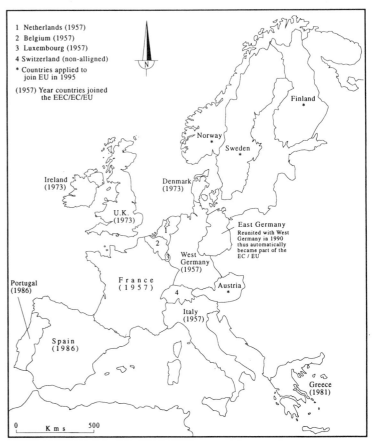

Figure 2. Countries of Western Europe and the European Union.

sin, Low Countries, and northern Germany before curving southeastward to terminate as the steppelands of the Ukraine at the shore of the Black Sea.

Apart from the Scandinavian Mountain system, the dominant relief trend throughout Western Europe is east-west. A majority of the region's major rivers, however, have a north-south orientation (e.g., Rhine and Rhône) and act as the means of integrating the different relief zones. This is perhaps best expressed by the Rhine which rises in the Swiss Alps, flows through Germany, and exits into the North Sea through the Netherlands.

The climate of Western Europe reflects a strong maritime influence which, in part, relates to the deeply penetrating seas and peninsularity that characterize the region. North of the Alps, the climatic type is "Cool Temperate Western Margins" and is dominated by southwesterly winds blowing onshore off the Atlantic. Since these onshore winds pass over the warm ocean current of the North Atlantic Drift that originates off the southeastern coast of North America as the Gulf Stream, they give rise to a relatively mild, equable temperature and precipitation that is well distributed throughout the year. The warm waters of the North Atlantic Drift also ensure that the ports of Western Europe are ice-free throughout the year, even in northern Norway, which lies within the Arctic Circle. This is a major advantage for a region heavily committed to trade. Apart from the Scandinavian Peninsula, these moderate climatic conditions extend far

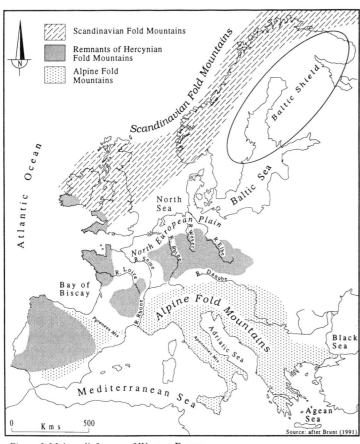

Figure 3. Major relief zones of Western Europe.

inland since the east-west trend of the relief does not limit the maritime influence to the coastal zone. This imparts another economic benefit for much of Western Europe, in that per capita energy costs tend to be lower than those experienced in other major global regions subjected to more extreme climatic influences (e.g., North America, Russia). Towards the continental interior, however, the climatic regime becomes more extreme as continentality generates cold winters and a rainfall maximum occurring in the hot summer months. South of the Alps, a distinctive "Mediterranean Climate" occurs which contrasts with conditions found over northwestern Europe. Summers are hot and dry with precipitation concentrated in the milder winter months.

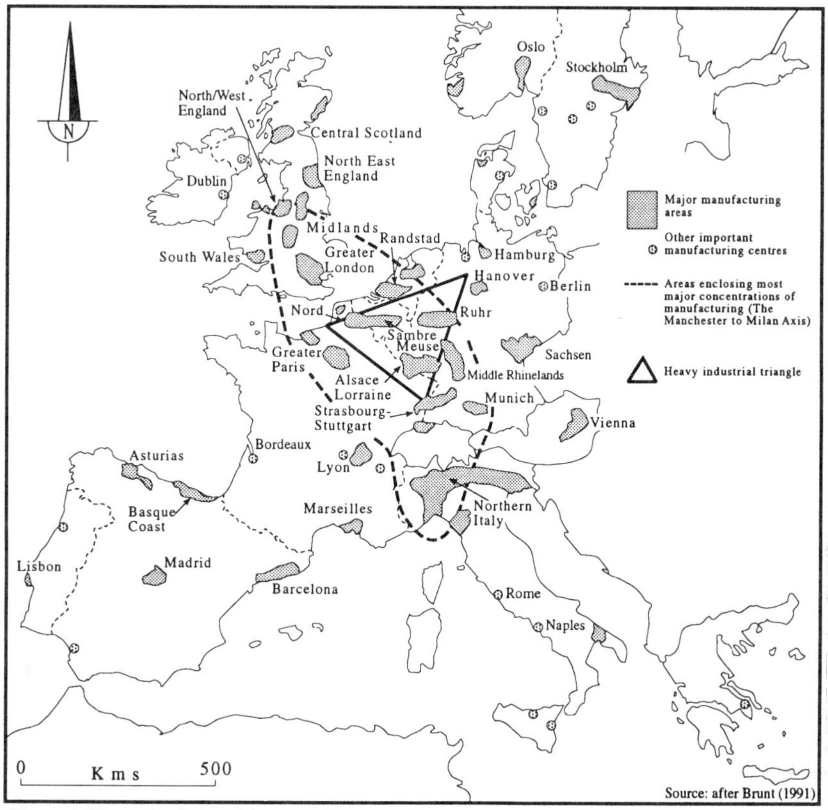

In spite of varied conditions, both the relief and climates of Western Europe do not exhibit many extremes. This provides a physical environment that is very conducive for human settlement and development (Gottman 1969; Hoffman 1990).

Figure 4. The major industrial areas of Western Europe.

Industrialization

Western Europe is the birthplace of the industrial revolution that occurred in the late 18th-early 19th centuries. It originated in northwestern Europe (especially Britain) and established the area as the "workshop of the world." Essential raw materials and energy supplies, particularly coal, were readily available in northwestern Europe and acted as the basis of a major surge in urban-industrial development. A well-integrated transport system further facilitated the flows of raw materials, energy, labor, and finished goods both within Western Europe and to the rest of the world. From these initial coalfield-dominated areas of industrialization, which can be termed the Heavy Industrial Triangle of northwest Europe, manufacturing activities have diffused into new areas (Figure 4). Following World War II, newer consumer-oriented and higher-tech industries spread the impact of industrial development over a much larger area, although the most impressive expression of growth has been along an axis that

links Manchester to Milan. This can be referred to as the Manchester-Milan axis. Outside this zone of concentrated industrialization, manufacturing regions are generally smaller in scale and are located farther apart. Despite these differences, however, much of the prosperity of Western Europe, and that of its internal regions, has depended upon the successful promotion and maintenance of a competitive industrial system (Williams 1988; Minshull 1990; Pinder 1991).

Urban Development and Trade

Western Europe is essentially an urban society. More than 80 percent of the region's population live in the large number of cities and towns that are well distributed throughout the region (Figure 5). Most urban centers in Western Europe have a long history in which the role of trade and market functions have

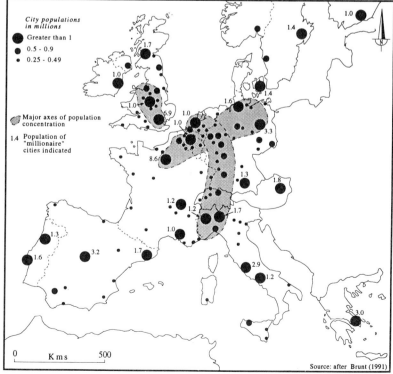

Figure 5. Urban centers of more than 250,000 inhabitants in Western Europe.

proved crucial for their development. Improvements in transportation were of particular significance because they facilitated an extension of the trading hinterlands of towns. Complex trading systems, based on the historic towns of Western Europe, therefore are essential for the definition and prosperity of this region (White 1984, Burtenshaw et al. 1991).

Trade and urban development within Western Europe have been facilitated by two major natural routes: the north-south route focused on the Rhine, and the east-west route of the North European Plain. The Rhine, and its access to Alpine passes, and the Rhône presented merchants from northern Europe with a viable, efficient route for trade with Mediterranean Europe. Similarly, the North European Plain facilitated trade and the exchange of ideas between Western and Eastern/Central Europe. The Danube also acts as a trade route from its source area in southern Germany to the Black Sea. However, its full potential as a major trade artery was reduced historically by the fact that the Danube forms a political boundary for many states in South-Central Europe. This, together with the unstable political system in this region, emphasized the Danube's role as a physical/political divide rather than a secure avenue for trade.

In addition to the overland routes, the integration of Western Europe through trade was aided by the configuration of the region's coastline. The seas that penetrate deeply into Europe (e.g., the Baltic, Mediterranean, North Sea) provide a coastline for all countries of the region, except Luxembourg, Switzerland, and Austria (Figure 3). Coastal trade routes are well established and trade promoted the growth of ports. Further, global trade networks were developed as the maritime powers of Western Europe established colonies around the world. The region became the focus of global trade and led to the growth of major port cities such as Amsterdam, Antwerp, Bordeaux, London, and Marseilles (Hoyle and Pinder 1992).

Although urbanization and trade are well developed throughout much of Western Europe, the pattern is far from uniform. Three zones of preferred urban development appear and are linked directly to the dominant trade routes of the region (Figure 5).

1. Manchester-Milan axis is the extension of the Rhine corridor across the Alps into the most urbanized part of Italy. It also incorporates Britain's major zone of urban development from the London region through the Midlands to northwestern England.
2. Paris-Hamburg axis. This axis of urban development intersects the Manchester-Milan axis in the Low Countries/North-Rhine Westphalia to establish the most intensive concentrations of major urban centers in Western Europe. Included in this concentrated zone are the major cities of the Rhine-Ruhr, based on the large-scale development of coal-related industrialization in the Ruhr coalfield and/or the opportunities for trade along the historic trading route of the Rhine. In addition, Randstad Holland (or the "Ring City") is located in this intersection zone. This is the most urbanized part of the Netherlands and is formed by two major areas of urban development that largely encircle

an important agricultural and recreational area referred to as "the Greenheart of the Netherlands." The cities of Amsterdam, Utrecht, and Haarlem form the northern arc of urbanization, with Rotterdam and The Hague forming the southern arc.
3. Cityports around the coastline of Western Europe. A majority of the region's "millionaire" cities (those with greater than 1 million population) are ports and reflect the outward-looking orientation of this region and its commitment to global trade.

Population and Culture

Within the relatively small (c. 3 million km²) and compact area of Western Europe live in excess of 350 million people (Hall 1993). Population density is 114 persons per km², which is high by global standards, and reflects the extent of urban-industrial development, the suitability of the environment for settlement, and the support of worldwide trade systems (Ilbery 1986). In addition, the population of the region enjoys relatively high standards of living, is generally well-educated, healthy, and has a long life expectancy.

Culturally, the population is essentially Caucasian, Christian, and speaks languages that are rooted in the Indo-European language family. The culture is also cosmopolitan as a great mixing of peoples, values, and ideas have occurred within Western Europe, reflecting the region's colonial empires, trade relationships, and migration patterns. While cultural traits and living standards serve to distinguish Western Europe as a whole from surrounding regions, they are best expressed in the urban-industrial heartland of northwestern Europe (Jordan 1989). Quality of life and standards of living decline to the eastern and southern margins of the region (Ilbery 1984).

The European Community/European Union

In 1957, the Treaty of Rome led to the establishment of the European Economic Community (EEC) (Parker 1981). The objective of the EEC was to facilitate economic development through a more effective integration of Western Europe's national economies. A Common Market was established to allow for free trade between EEC states while a common external tariff barrier would protect the internal market from outside competition. Policies were also developed to guide key sectors of the economy (for example, the Common Agricultural Policy). These initial economic goals were extended in the Maastricht Treaty of European Union (1992), which called for monetary and political union as well as greater economic and social cohesion between Member states (Lodge 1993; Wise and Gibb 1993).

The EEC, renamed the European Community (EC) in 1967 and European Union (EU) in 1993, has become a powerful influence in shaping the character of Western Europe (Williams 1991; Dawson 1993; Cole and Cole 1993). Not only has it increased its scope from dealing essentially with economic matters to incorporate social, environmental, and political issues, but it has also increased its membership. Originally, the EEC was composed of six states (France, West

Germany, Italy and the Benelux countries), but this had doubled by 1986 (Figure 2). Thus, Britain, Denmark, and Ireland joined the EC in 1973, Greece in 1981, and Spain and Portugal in 1986. In 1990, East Germany (GDR) was incorporated into the EC as a result of the re-unification of Germany. The former GDR is

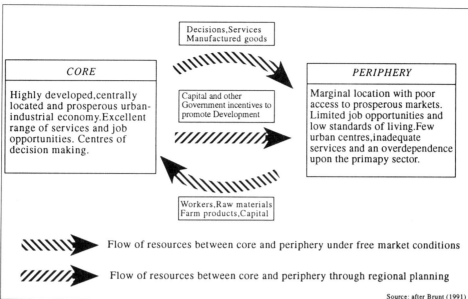

Figure 6. Characteristic patterns and interrelationships between cores and peripheries.

and Rhine-Ruhr contrast strongly with those found in regions such as the south of Italy and Ireland. Western Europe is more complex than the initial context created through the use of a number of generalizations that stress the region's similarity. Thus, an effective study of the regional geography of Western Europe

not counted as a new member state, but the absorption of East Germany has had a major impact on the German economy and thus on the EC as a whole (Harris 1991; Wild and Jones 1994). An additional four countries (Austria, Norway, Finland, and Sweden) undertook referenda in 1994 regarding their planned accession to the EU. The outcome was the addition of three new members in January, 1995, with only Norway voting to remain outside the EU. Knowledge of the membership, policies, and objectives of the EU is therefore fundamental in any attempt to appreciate the evolving character and pattern of post-war geography within Western Europe.

Through a basic knowledge of the above six generalizations, an image of Western Europe is established which acts as a platform for further study. In essence, Western Europe is well located, possesses a favorable environment within which trade and an urban-industrial society have been facilitated, the population is cosmopolitan, enjoys a high standard of living and has been strongly influenced by the operation of the EC/EU.

While this overall sense of common expression is created for the region, a critical impression of differences within Western Europe can also be identified. It is clear that some countries/regions consistently appear to have more advantage than others. For example, the favored natural environments, concentration of urban-industrial activities, and well-established trade routes of the Low Countries

must incorporate an appreciation of internal differentiation and change, associated with an evolving set of processes and spatial interrelationships. This, however, can also be achieve through the use of a simplified model.

Cores and Peripheries

At its most basic, the contrasts between favored and less-favored regions can be equated to cores and peripheries (Figure 6). In the core-periphery model, regions are distinguished not only by their internal attributes (patterns), but also by the processes acting on the regions and the nature of their linkages to other regions (interrelationships). Effectively, the different characteristic patterns found within cores and peripheries, and the biased relationships that exist between them, combine to emphasize the advantages of the core and the problems faced within the periphery.

If this model is applied to Western Europe, a core-periphery pattern of development can be observed. Seers et al. (1979), for example, illustrate the contrasts in development in Western Europe in terms of an egg-shaped pattern (Figure 7). At the core, or "yolk," are found the richest regions, which include the Paris Basin, the Low Countries, and most of West Germany. Outside the "yolk," but within the "shell," lie other regions that are comparatively well developed, e.g., southeastern England, northern Italy, southern Scandinavia, Switzerland, Austria, and most of

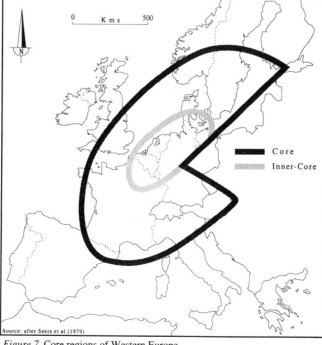

Figure 7. Core regions of Western Europe.

3. THE REGION

France. Beyond the "shell" lies the periphery, or least-developed regions of Western Europe, and includes most of the Scandinavian Peninsula, Ireland, western and northern Britain, Iberia, southern Italy, and Greece.

A more recent attempt to establish a pattern of cores and peripheries within the EC has been published by the Commission of the EC (1987a). This presents a five-fold division of the EC's regions based primarily on their characteristics of internal development (e.g., unemployment rates, GDP per capita, dependency on agricultural employment, and presence of

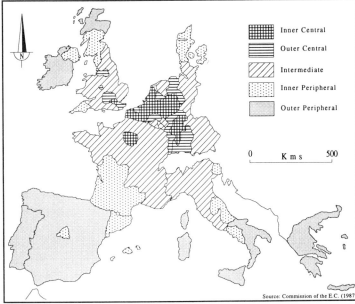

Figure 8. Central (core), intermediate, and peripheral regions in the European Community.

growth industries), together with their accessibility to markets (Figure 8, Table 1). Regions of the inner core exhibit strong development indicators, centrality within the EC, and excellent transportation linkages that give them ease of access to both internal and external markets. The inner core seems a world apart from those regions that languish in the outer periphery. In the periphery, the paucity of infrastructure, the absence of major growth industries, and problems of market access make development dependent, to a large extent, on assistance being provided by the wealthier core (e.g., regional development incentives such as capital transfers to improve transport networks).

Cores and peripheries, however, are not static entities, but are subject to change in their spatial patterns as processes that influence development change and their relationships with other regions are modified (Keeble 1989). Within Western Europe, core regions, in particular, have exhibited some dramatic changes in spatial expression.

Core Regions of Western Europe
When the EEC was established, a well-defined core area already existed in the

Heavy Industrial Triangle of northwestern Europe (Figure 4), based on the concentration of coalfields and specialized urban-industrial systems created in the 19th century. By the 1960s, however, the dominant role of coal as a location factor, and the relative importance of heavy industries such as iron and steel, began to decline. Newer, consumer-oriented industries began to lead the development process and were attracted especially to existing urban areas that were growing rapidly in population and possessed good transport linkages to a variety of markets (e.g., Stuttgart, Munich). At the same time, areas of national prosperity within Member states began to benefit from the enlarged international market created by the EC. The net result was an expansion of the West European core out of the triangle to form an axis of rapid development from Manchester to Milan. Incorporated within this axis, and oriented around the trade linkages provided by the Rhine Corridor, Alpine Passes, and ports of the English Channel/North Sea coastline, are most of the major national economic cores of Western Europe: London and southeastern England; the Paris Basin; Brussels-Antwerp; Randstad Holland; the Rhine-Ruhr and Middle Rhinelands (focused on the three cities of Frankfurt, Mannheim, and Stuttgart); and northwest Italy (centered on Milan, Turin, and Genoa).

Evolution of the economic core of the EC/EU continues, especially after the signing of the Single European Act (1987) which removed all barriers to trade within the EC by January 1993 (Commission of the EC 1987b). In particular, four poles of prosperity have emerged to take advantage of the liberalized and enhanced trading environment of the Single European Market (Drozdiak 1994). These have been termed the "four motors" of future development within the European Union and are: Baden Wurtenburg (centered on Stuttgart); Lombardy (Milan); Rhône-Alps (Lyon); and Catalonia (Barcelona) (Figure 9). Three of these "motors" point to the emergence of a new spatial expression for the international core of Western Europe. Thus, just as a sunbelt appeared in the United States as part of a national reorientation of modern industrialization, so also a sunbelt is emerging in Western Europe. This European sunbelt stretches from north-

Table 1
Disparities between Core and Peripheral Regions of the EC (1983)

Regions	GDP per capita[1]	Employment in agriculture (%)	Structural index for manufacturing[2]	Unemployment rate[3] (%)
Inner Central	129.5	2.3	1.36	16.6
Outer Central	104.6	4.6	1.36	14.0
Intermediate	105.4	7.8	1.02	18.3
Inner Peripheral	89.3	10.7	0.70	30.2
Outer Peripheral	63.7	23.8	0.50	32.4
Entire EC(12)	**100.0**	**8.9**	**1.05**	**21.7**

[1]in purchasing power parities.
[2]ratio of employment in modern industries (e.g., electronics) to that in traditional industries (e.g., textiles).
[3]unemployment rate per persons aged under 25 years.
(Commission of the European Communities 1987)

west Italy (Lombardy) through southern France (Rhône-Alps) and into northeastern Spain (Catalonia). However, while the southern extremity of the Manchester-Milan axis has expanded, the northern extremity (northwest England and Midlands) has experienced problems of industrial restructuring. The result has been the emergence of a new spatial configuration to Western Europe's international core, taking the form of a "dogleg" stretching from London to Milan and then westward to Barcelona.

The spatial pattern of the international core of Western Europe has changed from a "triangle" to an "axis" and currently forms a "dogleg". This reflects the vital elements of change and complexity to the regional geography of Western Europe. However, it is important to note that while there are differences between the various regions that constitute the international core, there are also similarities which contribute to their success. An understanding of these generalizations should act as a starting point to appreciate the nature of core regions, e.g., the existence of a large, dynamic, urban center as the focus of development, the presence of high quality transport and communication systems, availability of investment capital, and an educated and skilled labor force. Subsequently, case studies can be undertaken to emphasize specific conditions in regions such as Lombardy, Paris, and Randstad Holland.

Figure 9. The "four motors" of the European Union and the "dogleg" of development.

Peripheries of Western Europe

In contrast to cores, peripheries tend to cover much larger areas, show less evidence of change, and display an array of problems (Ilbery 1984; Clout 1987). Given the scale and variety of regional problems in its periphery, the EC has attempted to classify problematic regions according to specific symptoms of underdevelopment. Thus, the EC's Regional Policy and Structural Funds, which are available to help finance development initiatives, are now focused on a series of common objectives (Commission of the EC 1991). Five priority objectives have been advanced for support from Structural Funds in an attempt to achieve a greater sense of economic and social cohesion between the constituent regions of the EC/EU. Three of the objectives (1, 2, 5b) are specifically regional in nature and involve measures restricted to certain eligible regions (Figure 10). The remaining objectives (3, 4, and 5a) apply to the whole EC and are therefore not confined to problematic regions.

The spatially specific objectives and criteria for aid under Structural Funds are:

Objective 1: The development and structural adjustment of regions where development is lagging. Objective 1 regions are defined on the basis of a per capita income of 75 percent of the Community's average. These regions incorporate 27 percent of the Community's total population. Approximately three quarters of all Structural Funds are allocated to these problematic regions.

Objective 2: Converting the regions or parts of regions affected seriously by industrial decline. For eligibility, areas must have an unemployment rate greater than the Community average, a higher percentage of industrial employment than Community average, and a decline in this category of employment. Approximately 15 percent of the Community's population is covered by this objective.

Objective 5b: To facilitate the development and structural adjustment of rural areas. In order to qualify for Community support, regions must

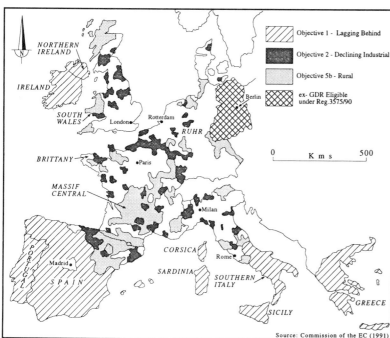

Figure 10. Regions of the European Community eligible for financial support from Structural Funds.

3. THE REGION

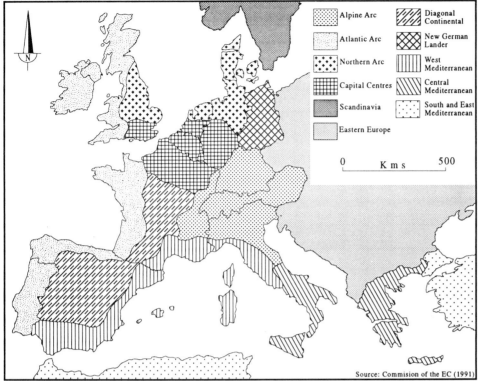

Figure 11. Euro-regions based on international groupings of regions that possess similar basic qualities.

Legend:
- Alpine Arc
- Atlantic Arc
- Northern Arc
- Capital Centres
- Scandinavia
- Eastern Europe
- Diagonal Continental
- New German Lander
- West Mediterranean
- Central Mediterranean
- South and East Mediterranean

0   K m s   500

Source: Commision of the EC (1991)

Treaty on European Union (1992), was opposed by strong political elements in Denmark, the United Kingdom, and France. These countries, in particular, were concerned over their perceived loss of sovereignty and national identity to an over-centralized bureaucracy based in Brussels.

Given the historic importance of the nation state in Europe, most studies of the geography of this major world region were centered on individual countries. Consequently, the distinctiveness of an individual country was stressed rather than its relationships or similarities with other countries. Furthermore, in order to establish a better in-depth knowledge of the countries of Europe, teachers emphasized their internal subdivision. Through a detailed description of a country's subregions, it was believed that students would acquire a more effective knowledge and understanding of a particular country. Thus, a student would come to understand France through a detailed knowledge of its subregions e.g., Paris Basin, Brittany, Massif Central. In a similar manner, knowledge of the geography of Western Europe could best be effected by teaching the detailed geography of each country of this world region. Although this approach built up an adequate factual basis on Western Europe, it paid little attention to the changing spatial relationships that operated within and between countries, and which are crucial to the appreciation of this dynamic region.

Since the 1970s, however, the focus of study of regional geography has undergone some important changes within Western Europe. A growing concern has emerged in many regions over the degree to which their regional identities are being lost within the nation state and within the EU. This is particularly apparent in those regions that possess a strong cultural heritage. The result has been a growing demand for the devolution of power from central governments to the regions. This is perhaps best expressed in Britain (Scotland and Wales), France (Corsica), and Spain (Catalonia and Basques).

With the strength of regionalism growing within many countries of Western Europe, the study of regional geography within an exclusive national framework becomes open to questions of relevancy. Thus, as regions gain, or strive to gain, greater control over their cultural integrity and development trends, they seek to interact more effectively with regions in other countries that are experiencing the same types of problems or opportunities. In this way, the context for the geographical study of regions within Western Europe is shifting from the national to the international level. As a result, the

exhibit a low level of economic development and, at least, two of the following: a high share of agricultural employment; a low level of agricultural income; and a low population density, and/or a significant depopulation trend.

Through an appreciation of the generalizations that define, for example, Objective 1 regions, a basis is established to understand the problems of regions as far removed as Ireland and southern Italy. Similarly, problems of industrial decline have common roots whether the focus of study is South Wales or the Sambre Meuse Valley. Case studies reveal differences between problem regions in a general context. The study of a particular problem region and the buildup of a factual base (pattern/trends) are not seen, therefore, as being unique nor as an end in themselves; rather, they serve to illustrate the extent to which the region conforms to or deviates from general patterns of development. In this way, patterns, processes, and spatial interrelationships are all involved in establishing the characteristics of peripheral or problematic regions.

A New Regionalization of Western Europe

In Western Europe, much of its distinctiveness has been built up around the complexity of its internal national and regional characteristics. At the national level, major differences are clearly apparent between countries such as Ireland and Germany, the Netherlands and Italy. Furthermore, the powerful force of nationalism ensured that these differences would be both promoted and protected to emphasize the sense of distinctiveness for Europe's nation states (Mead 1982). Attempts to reduce this distinctiveness and impose a greater degree of uniformity on the countries of Western Europe have been met with resistance. Thus, for example, the Maastricht teaching of Western Europe has to change its focus from stressing detailed factual patterns that are specific to individual regions, to one which identifies generalities and processes of spatial interrelationships. This is the simple recognition of the fact that regions, cores, and peripheries are all interacting more effectively through space as national boundaries become more open to processes and spatial interrelationships (Dunford and Kufkalas 1992).

Within the EC, the Commission (1991) has recognized the international dimension of regionalism within Western Europe by proposing a new set of regional groupings (Figure 11), based on the geographic ideals of proximity, internal similarities (patterns), processes of development, and spatial interrelationships.

Although differences exist within these new Euro-regions, the essential theme is to recognize that similarities (generalizations) establish a particular regional grouping. Thus, while differing in detail, diverse regions of the Atlantic Arc, such as Ireland, Galicia (a province in northwest Spain), and Brittany (the western peninsula of France), show many similarities including overdependency on the primary sector, a restricted urban base, and dependence on external core regions for transfers of resources and job creation. In the same manner, the major metropolitan growth regions of the Capitals Center show similarities. While London, Paris, Brussels, Randstad Holland, and the Rhine-Ruhr are distinctive in their own right, they nevertheless all exhibit highly developed economic systems and advanced transport and communication infrastructures, and are the centers of decision making for much political and economic activity. They also possess common problems of congestion, environmental degradation, and difficulties of urban renewal.

Dynamic forces of change are at work in Europe causing new regional patterns to emerge, and any effective study of its regional geography has to recognize this fact. Thus, while a study of an international grouping of regions such as the Atlantic Arc and Capitals Center may seem unfamiliar, it nevertheless reflects the significance of new patterns, processes, and spatial interrelationships. Already, the "four motors" of the European Union have signed a cooperation pact (1988) which transcends national loyalties. Business people in Milan and Barcelona, for example, are recognizing that they have more in common with colleagues in Lyon and Stuttgart than with fellow citizens in Rome or Madrid. In a similar fashion, in the weaker peripheral regions, a small-scale Breton dairy farmer may recognize more in common with a counterpart in the west of Ireland than with a Parisian. Furthermore, the collapse of the Iron Curtain and the erosion of barriers to integration between Western and East/Central Europe will also encourage the emergence of new regional patterns and alignments (Murphy 1991; Cole and Cole 1993).

Western Europe is, therefore, both a complex and evolving global region. However, these newly forming regional patterns, just as more familiar traditional regional identities, can be studied initially by identifying the broad similarities that tie the diverse regions together rather than focusing on

differences. Critical differences and the further complexities of regions can emerge subsequently through the case study.

Conclusion

These are exciting times for geography, and the discipline has the opportunity of being identified as possessing increasing relevancy for contemporary study. This demands that geography be presented and promoted in a modern curriculum as providing something that will better equip society to understand the changing nature of the world in which we live. In particular, with the marked reduction in the frictional effect of distance, and the increased ease of interrelationships in the late 20th century, the study of regions has grown in both relevancy and complexity.

Regional geography finds itself in a central role in the renewed interest in geography. The context of the study of regional geography has to reflect, however, the dynamics of the modern global system. Regions cannot be studied in isolation. The focus cannot be only on internal patterns that stress the uniqueness of a region. Instead, regions have to be studied in a broader context that expresses processes of change and interrelationships between regions. For a region like Western Europe, contemporary patterns are showing important changes from those identified in the past. We need to study Europe as an integrating community which finds expression in the changing nature of its internal regional geography as well as through the strengthening of its global linkage.

References

Brunt, B. 1991. *Western Europe: A social and economic geography.* Dublin: Gill and Macmillan.

Burtenshaw, D., M. Bateman, and G. J. Ashworth. 1991. *The European city: A western perspective.* New York: Wiley.

Clout, H. D., ed. 1987. *Regional development in western Europe.* 3d rev. ed. New York: Wiley.

Clout, H. D., M. Blacksell, R. King, and D. Pinder. 1994. *Western Europe: Geographical perspectives.* 3rd rev. ed. London: Longman.

Cole, J. P., and F. J. Cole. 1993. *The geography of the European community.* London: Routledge.

Commission of the European Communities. 1987a. *Third periodic report from the Commission on the Social and Economic Situation and Development of the Regions of the Community* (COM 87-230). Brussels: CEC.

_____. 1987b. *Europe without frontiers towards a large internal market.* European File 13/87.

_____. 1991. *Europe 2000-outlook for the development of the community territory.* Brussels-Luxembourg: Directorate General for Regional Policy.

Dawson, A. H. 1993. *The geography of European integration: A common European home.* New York: Wiley/Belhaven.

de Blij, H. J., and O. Muller. 1994. *Geography: Realms, regions, and concepts.* 7th rev. ed. New York: Wiley.

Diem, A. 1979. *Western Europe: A geographical analysis.* New York: Wiley.

Drozdiak, W. 1994. Revving up Europe's four motors. *Washington Post* 27 March, c-3.

Dunford, M., and G. Kufkalas, eds. 1992. *Cities and regions in the new Europe: The global-local interplay and spatial development strategy.* New York: Wiley.

Gottman, J. A. 1969. *A geography of Europe.* 4th rev. ed. New York: Holt, Rinehart & Winston.

Hall, R. 1993. Europe's changing population. *Geography* 78(1):3-15.

3. THE REGION

Harris, C. D. 1991. Unification of Germany in 1990. *Geographical Review* 81(2):170-182.

Hoffman, G. W., ed. 1990. *Europe in the 1990s: A geographical analysis.* 6th rev. ed. New York: Wiley.

Hoyle, B. S., and D. A. Pinder, eds. 1992. *European port cities in transition.* London: Belhaven.

Ilbery, B. W. 1984. Core-periphery contrasts in European social well-being. *Geography* 69:289-302.

_____. 1986. *Western Europe: A systematic human geography.* 2d rev. ed. Oxford: Oxford University Press.

Jordan, T. G. 1989. *The European culture area: A systematic geography.* 2nd rev. ed. New York: Harper & Row.

Keeble, D. 1989. Core-periphery disparities, recession and new regional dynamism in the E.C. *Geography* 74(1):1-11.

Lich, G. E., ed. 1992. *The interplay of land and people.* College Station: Texas A&M University Press.

Lodge, J., ed. 1993. *European community and the challenge of the future.* 2d rev. ed. New York: St. Martin's Press.

Mead, W. R. 1982. The discovery of Europe. *Geography* 67:193-202.

Mellor, R.E.H., and E. A. Smith. 1979. *Europe: A geographical survey of the continent.* New York: St. Martin's Press.

Minshull, G. N. 1990. *The new Europe: An economic geography of the EEC.* 4th rev. ed. London: Hodder & Stoughton.

Paddison, R., and A. S. Morris. 1988. *Regionalism and the regional question.* New York: Blackwell.

Parker, G. 1981. *The logic of unity: A geography of the EEC.* 3d rev. ed. New York: Longman.

Pinder, D., ed. 1991. *Western Europe: Challenge and change.* New York: Guilford.

Seers, D., B. Schaeffer, and M. L. Kiljunen, eds. 1979. *Underdeveloped Europe: Studies in core-periphery relations.* Hassock, Sussex: Harvester Press.

White, P. 1984. *The West European city: A social geography.* London: Longman.

Wild, T., and P. N. Jones. 1994. Spatial impacts of German unification. *Geographical Journal* 160(1):1-16.

Williams, A. M. 1988. *The West European economy: A geography of postwar development.* Savage, MD: Rowan & Littlefield.

_____. 1991. *The European community: The contradictions of integration.* Cambridge, MA: Blackwell.

Wise, M., and R. Gibb. 1993. *Single market to social Europe: The European Community in the 1990s.* Harlow: Longman Scientific and Technical.

Note

[1]An earlier version of this paper was delivered to the Geography for Life conference, organized by the Virginia Geographic Alliance, in Williamsburg, Virginia, April 15-17, 1994. Dr. Brunt was jointly a visiting professor at Old Dominion University and The College of William and Mary.

Two-Way Corridor Through History

Once one of the busiest trade routes in North America, the Camino Real is now the focus of preservation and research efforts in both Mexico and the U.S.

Bjørn Sletto

Bjørn Sletto is a writer and photographer based in Bonham, Texas, and a previous contributor to Américas. *The author wishes to acknowledge the generous assistance of the Las Cruces Convention and Visitors Bureau, as well as Casa Blanca Guesthouse, San Antonio; Le Baron Inn & Suites, Albuquerque; and Inn on the Paseo, Santa Fe, New Mexico.*

Don Juan de Oñate might have stood like this, perched on the crest of a juniper-studded butte, watching the setting sun wash across a parched desert plain and the great, shimmering peaks of the San Andres Mountains beyond. Maybe he was out of breath from climbing the gravelly hill, slipping in his rush for the top. Maybe his hands were scratched by mesquite, his coat peppered with saltbush seeds, his fine leather boots caked with red desert dust from the arroyo below. But he must have felt a triumphant surge that made it all worthwhile, for he knew he was blazing a trail for his king, Philip II, and for Spain.

Oñate, impatient, wealthy son of a Mexican conquistador, had already traveled far when he saw his great vista in present-day southern New Mexico, just north of Las Cruces. He had started in Santa Bárbara, near present-day Chihuahua, in January 1598. After a grueling passage through the merciless Chihuahuan desert, the ragged group of 129 soldiers—many of whom had brought their families along with eighty-four wooden ox-drawn carts and more than

seven thousand farm animals—finally reached the Rio Grande four months later, on April 20. From there, they traveled across the dry mountain pass Oñate had seen from his hilltop vantage point, the dreaded Jornada del Muerto, or Journey of Death, so named later for all the travelers who would die there.

After making it safely through the Jornada, the first Spanish colonizers continued north along the *bosque*—the cool cottonwoods lining the Rio Grande—and through a strange mountain pass later known as El Contadero, only making prolonged stops in the many, dusty adobe pueblos clustered along the river. On July 27 Oñate finally ended his seven-month, 750-mile journey in the now-abandoned Indian pueblo of Ceypa, about thirty-five miles north of present-day Albuquerque. A few years later, other explorers would extend Oñate's trail a few miles further north, across a plain dotted with piñon trees and a hilly landscape cluttered with creosote bushes and ocotillo—the *bajadas*. Around 1610 they would found the terminus of the new trail, Santa Fe.

Oñate had succeeded where others before him had·failed—to blaze a route to the most remote, northern realm of the Spanish empire in the Americas. His trail would be known by future Spanish travelers as the Camino Real de Tierra Adentro—the royal road to the interior—and by nineteenth-century Americans as the Chihuahua Trail. Along this trail would travel thousands of Franciscan missionaries and Spanish colonizers, centuries before the arrival of settlers from the east.

For these early pioneers in northern Mexico and current-day Texas and New Mexico, the Camino Real would be their material and cultural lifeline to Western civilization, as they knew it.

"The Camino Real is probably the most significant trail in the country," says Santa Fe-based historian Gabrielle Palmer, director of the Camino Real Project, a nonprofit organization dedicated to preserving and promoting the Camino Real. "It changes the way we think about the history of the Southwest. Settling the West was not the east-to-west movement that most people think. The West was settled from Mexico."

In 1993, to preserve the few existing remnants of the Camino Real, the National Park Service and the Spanish Colonial Research Center at the University of New Mexico began to compile historic information and prepare a historic dictionary of sites and structures along the trail. The study is conducted under national legislation passed in November of that year, in which Congress directed the Park Service to evaluate the Camino Real as a possible candidate for the National Trail System. The first binational accord occurred in January 1994 when the University of New Mexico and Mexico's Instituto Nacional de Antropología e Historia (INAH) agreed to cooperate regarding technical, academic, and cultural projects related to the Camino Real. Then, in June 1995 the First International Conference on the Camino Real was held in Valle de Allende, Chihuahua, Mexico, funded by INAH, the Universidad de Ciudad Juárez, the U.S. National Park Service, and Bureau of Land

From *Américas*, May/June 1996, pp. 8-17. Reprinted with permission from *Américas*, bimonthly magazine published by the General Secretariat of the Organization of American States in English and Spanish.

3. THE REGION

Management. The convening Mexican and U.S. participants discussed current binational projects, such as archaeological research into cave painting art in New Mexico and Chihuahua, historical sites of the Camino Real in both areas, and pre-Columbian agricultural systems.

In late 1996 the Park Service is expected to recommend that the U.S. portion of the Camino Real be designated a National Trail, which would grant official protection to remnants of the trail located on government property. Meanwhile, the New Mexico Bureau of Land Management, the Museum of New Mexico, and the Camino Real Project are developing an interpretive plan for an El Camino International Heritage Center, to be built along Interstate 25 just south of Socorro by the end of 1998, funding permitting.

As for the Mexican portion of the Camino Real, anthropologist José Luis Perea, director of INAH in Chihuahua, says: "Some portions of the road have already been declared zones of historic monuments, such as Querétaro, San Miguel de Allende, Zacatecas, Guanajuato, and Durango. INAH has concluded studies to declare the cities of Hidalgo del Parral and Valle de Allende in Chihuahua as zones of historic monuments this year. We hope that these two historic cities, which are a part of the Camino Real, will become protected through a special presidential declaration."

As they wade through dusty travelogues and fading, yellowing maps, historians reconstructing the route of the Camino Real face problems unique to historic trail research. First of all, the Camino Real was not a clearly defined road, as we know it.

©HELIA MARIA DURAN (4)

The Camino Real was not a clearly defined road. Early travelers were pioneers, in the true sense of the word, and were loathe to follow in the footsteps of travelers before them

The amount of products shipped on the Camino Real was only restricted by what settlers in New Mexico were willing to pay and by how much the wagons could carry

Early travelers were pioneers, in the true sense of the word, and were loathe to follow in the footsteps of travelers before them. Also, rutted and muddy wheel tracks could be treacherous, even deadly, in such remote areas as the Jornada del Muerto.

During the early decades following Oñate's expedition, caravans from Mexico City would arrive in the isolated settlements in New Mexico only once every three years. The caravans were subsidized by the government and organized by the Franciscan order, which had early on established missions in the Indian pueblos.

"The Camino Real was a corridor," explains Bruce Erickson, historian at the Spanish Colonial Research Center in Albuquerque. "The exact path of the route changed slightly within the corridor as new towns, haciendas, pueblos, and *parajes*—rest stops—were developed or abandoned. In some areas, the route passed on either side of the river, depending on the flooding." Only a few landmarks along the route remained unchanged, such as major river crossings, mission churches, watering holes in the Jornada del Muerto, the Palace of the Governors in Santa Fe, and El Contadero—so named because cattle or sheep drivers would force their animals to walk in a line through the narrow pass, the better to count them accurately.

Also, the trail served different purposes, as New Mexico matured from a rugged frontier to a regional Spanish province in its own right. In fact, it is easiest to think of the Camino Real in three, distinct historic periods. During the first century after Oñate's journey, the Camino Real was mainly a missionary trail, until the Franciscan priests were forced to flee the area when the Pueblo Indians united and rose up against Spanish domination in 1680. After the Spanish reconquest of their territory in 1692 and until Mexican independence in 1821, the Camino Real was a route for Spanish trade and cultural exchange between new Mexico and old Mexico. In the last period—from Mexican independence, through the U.S.–Mexican War of 1846-48 and the early years of New Mexican statehood—the Camino Real was one of the busiest international trading routes in North America.

©BJØRN SLETTO

The Cathedral of Chihuahua, opposite top, and the Parish of San Bartolomé in the Valley of Allende, Chihuahua, opposite bottom, were both built in the eighteenth century after the Franciscans fled the region during an Indian revolt against the Spanish. This area was once home to Indian groups known as the Conchos, San Pedro, and Florido, who lived in small agricultural settlements. Petroglyphs in the Cueva de las Monas preserve images of their native traditions, such as the peyote ritual, top, alongside the Christian icons of the cross and rosary, right. San Pedro, New Mexico, center, once a bustling stop along the Camino, is one of many ghost towns that have been lost to history

©BJØRN SLETTO (3)

For the missionaries in their remote outposts, the triennial caravans were a matter of life and death, for they provided practically everything the Franciscans needed: livestock, spices, sugar, grindstones, cooking utensils, clothes, bedding, medicines, razors, and church supplies such as tabernacles, crosses, paintings, statues, silver items, and vestments. In keeping with Spanish colonial practices everywhere, the caravans were strictly regulated, usually consisting of thirty-two mule-drawn wagons divided into two sections—*cuadrillas*—of sixteen wagons each. Each section was supervised by a wagonmaster—*mayordomo*—who himself answered to the Franciscan procurator-general, the leader of the wagon train. There were two

The Dunes of Samalayuca   by Joseph Leach

Thirty miles south of El Paso, Texas, beyond a green ribbon of cotton farms along the Rio Grande, lies a cluster of pink and gold dunes. Towering five hundred feet above the dry plains, the Médanos de Samalayuca are not only hauntingly beautiful, but over the centuries as the constantly shifting sands posed a treacherous obstacle to travelers heading north and south, they have also become a storehouse, indeed an archive of items that prehistoric Indians, Europeans, and their descendants dropped as they struggled to survive and pass on. Today, after a wind storm, the slopes are often peppered with potsherds, arrow points, corn-grinding stones, broken majolica dishes, brass bullet casings, harness buckles, rusted canteens, beer cans, and Coke bottle caps—as well as bleached-white human skulls.

More fortunate travelers—like Spanish colonist Don Juan de Oñate, who trekked through the area in 1598— lived to write down their memoirs. And, during the next three centuries as the Camino Real trade route from Veracruz through Mexico City and Chihuahua to El Paso and Santa Fe became Mexico's busiest highway, travelers related their woes of passing through the dreaded dunes.

In 1766 the Spanish explorer Nicolás de Lafora found the dunes "very troublesome" and that approaching the only water near them required moving cautiously, for the Apache Indians "are wont to surprise and kill passers-by."

Plodding south with his wagon train in 1839, the American merchant Josiah Gregg found that Apaches "continue to lay waste the ranches in the vicinity, and to depredate at will." Two year later George W. Kendall and a group of political prisoners of the Mexican army were trudging south when they arrived at "large mountains of loose sand" over which it was impossible to drag the wooden *carretas* without doubling their teams. In that "dreary Sahara," the horses sank below their fetlocks, and the men and animals were exhausted before they could pass the sandy "pyramids which raised their heads high in air."

One night, Kendall and his companions invented a welcome diversion. Directly in their path lay a stone weighing some two hundred pounds. Years before, they were told, a band of muleteers had commenced lifting it for sport, and sets of eight mules per wagon, one team pulling the wagon, while the other rested. A caravan would also bring thirty-two spare mules to replace those who inevitably died on the six-month journey from Mexico City to Santa Fe, for a total of 544. In addition to the mules, the train would bring seventy-two head of cattle as food during the trip.

Needless to say, the wagon train was a rare highlight in a quiet, drab existence. Life at the missions consisted mostly of continual building projects, as the adobe mission churches were expanded and repaired, storehouses and hospitals were constructed, and roadways and plazas were laid. Today, some of these mission churches are still standing, mute testimony to a life in an isolation deeper and more profound than most of us today can begin to fathom. "The Spanish knew there was no gold in New Mexico," comments Ruben Flores, program manager of the El Paso Mission Trail Association. "They were driven to come here, looking for converts."

St. Augustine, located in the Pueblo of Isleta, just south of Albuquerque, is one of the oldest of these mission churches. It was built as early as 1613 and rebuilt in 1692, after the Pueblo revolt had left all of it except the nave in ruins. Today, the church and the village surrounding it look much the same as they must have centuries ago when the weary caravans trundled into the echoing plaza. The streets are still dusty dirt roads, the low-slung adobe buildings still huddle cheek-by-

jowl beneath the desert sun. In the hushed silence, stocky men chop firewood and sun-wrinkled women sweep leaves in cluttered front yards. Smoke rises slowly from dome-shaped clay ovens. Dogs yawn and stretch languidly, before settling back down in the dappled shade of the dogwood trees.

Pueblo artist Benjamin Jojola carves gypsum figures in Isleta Pueblo, south of Albuquerque, site of one of the oldest mission churches in New Mexico, opposite. *Spanish-style adobe homes still dot the streets of La Mesilla, New Mexico,* top, *a historic town settled by pioneers who braved the desolate terrain. This old dirt road,* above, *follows the path of the Camino Real near San Antonio*

After the reconquest of New Mexico, the nature of the caravans changed. Instead of solely serving the needs of the Franciscan missions, the caravans became regular, annual wagon trains—*conductas*, or convoys—run by private contractors. In the seventeenth century, the hauling was

one or two had managed to vault it a few feet in the direction of Mexico City. In time, other muleteers had come to "superstitiously regard it their duty" to help the stone along. After many decades, says one report, it had advanced about fourteen miles.

In August 1846 a German scientist, Adolph Wislizenus, faced "the much-dreaded sand hills" that resembled "a piece of Arabian desert transplanted into the plain." During the night, lightning illuminated "our wagons moving along as slow and solemn as a funeral procession; ghostly riders on horseback, wrapped in blan-

kets; some tired travelers stretched out on the sand, others walking ahead, and tracing the road with the fire of their *cigarritos.*"

Later that same year George Ruxton, a young English soldier-of-fortune, reported: "Road there is none, but a track across is marked by the skeletons and dead bodies of oxen, and of mules and horses, which everywhere meet the eye. On one ridge the upper half of a human skeleton protruded from the sand. The sand is knee-deep, and constantly shifting, and pack-animals have great difficulty in passing."

During the U.S.-Mexican War, Colonel Alexander Doniphan and a thousand American foot soldiers were escorting a wagon train loaded with merchandise for Chihuahua when they headed into the sand. Their mules sank to their knees, leaving the wagon wheels buried almost to their hubs. With their animals dying of thirst and their own tongues swollen and dry, the men tossed aside eight thousand pounds of flour and several barrels of salt to lighten their loads. To move the wagons forward, the soldiers and teamsters pushed them along with their shoulders.

Today, travelers down Mexico's CN 45 Highway can imagine such stories as they glimpse the great dunes just east of the road. Though unprotected as yet by any government designation, the artifacts that emerge as the dunes constantly shift speak now, in their own fashion, of the human procession that once passed that way.

Joseph Leach is a freelance writer based in El Paso, Texas.

still done by ox cart or mule train—*hatajo*—but the convoys were no longer strictly regulated. Anyone could travel on a *conducta,* provided that he had money to pay for the passage. And the amount of products shipped on the Camino Real was only restricted by what settlers in New Mexico were willing to pay and by how much the wagons could carry.

Santa Fe had long been the only town in New Mexico, but now the population along the Camino Real began to increase, and several smaller settlements grew into towns in their own right: El Paso del Norte (today the twin cities of Juárez, Mexico, and El Paso, Texas) in 1659; Albuquerque in 1706; and Chihuahua in 1709. But in addition to these four major centers of trade and population, dozens of smaller settlements also blossomed. By the late eighteenth century, farming villages represented the very heart of a new, New Mexican culture.

Settlers in these villages imitated the Spanish culture they had left behind, including the clothing, music, and art, but eventually developed their own regional forms. For example, because New Mexican artisans lacked the fine hardwoods and tools available in Mexico, they created a new carving style—evident in their figures of saints, or *santos*—cruder and less refined than that of Mexico but nevertheless imbued with a remarkable power. Those settlers who could afford it even bought luxury items in Mexico City—mirrors, silk dresses, Venetian glass earrings, silver cutlery—and tried to maintain a refined, cultured life-style reminiscent of Mexico or Spain.

"The settlers in New Mexico still felt connected to Spain," says Palmer, "and they wanted to sustain their vision of what they had left behind. They prided themselves on being Spanish."

In some of the old villages along the Camino Real in northern New Mexico, people still take pride in their Spanish past. Just off the Camino Real, north of Santa Fe, is Truchas, a cluster of earth-colored buildings sprinkled helter-skelter on a rocky hillside in the Sangre de Cristo Mountains. Life in the village still revolves around the Mission of the Holy Rosary, which has gazed sternly over the village since 1754. Taciturn men still speak Spanish on the streets and in the cramped *tiendas,* children pick blood-red chilies growing along flaking plaster walls, and bent women tend the beanfields behind the village.

But not all Spanish towns have fared so well. The village of San Pedro, once a bustling stop along the Camino Real just south of Socorro, is now a ghost town. In the hush of the early morning, snow geese fly noisily overhead, heading for the nearby Bosque del Apache National Wildlife Refuge. A sea of mesquite, fringe sage, and snakeweed have swallowed the remaining adobe ruins, allowing only the tops of the crumbling buildings to reach for the first rays of the sun. At the very edge of the cottonwoods stands the tottering remnant of a wooden church, its tower a bleak skeleton, black willows piercing the nave. On the other side of the dirt road looms a giant, abandoned 1960s post office building, a hapless result of poor regional planning or perhaps just undue optimism for the future.

San Pedro's heyday was the nineteenth century, when the Camino Real became one of the busiest trade routes in North America. Before Mexican independence, trade on the Camino Real had been restricted to Mexican and Spanish traders. Merchants in the city of Chihuahua, in particular, wanted to maintain their trade monopoly, which earned them outlandish profits and kept the population in New Mexico in perpetual debt. But the Louisiana

Purchase in 1803 had netted the United States all the territory east of New Mexico, and Anglo-American traders were eager to break into the lucrative New Mexican market with their cheaper—and often better—American and European goods.

For the next half-century, Santa Fe was a bustling port of entry for trade caravans from St. Louis, Missouri, destined for Chihuahua and beyond. Some particularly enterprising traders traveled from Missouri to Europe in the winter, purchased their goods, assembled their caravans in St.

Towns such as Truchas, left, *and La Mesilla are living witnesses of the rich cultural exchange that was promoted by the Camino Real. Longtime residents of La Mesilla include Robert Hill,* top right, *potter Bill Cook,* bottom right, *vegetable vendor María Ines Contreras,* opposite bottom, *and New Mexico state representative Paul Taylor,* opposite top, *shown here reading from a historic family bible in the chapel of his mid-nineteenth-century home. Today's conservation efforts will preserve the pathway that facilitated complex patterns of commerce and cross-cultural communication*

"*The cultural legacy of our villages and regions is like a mirror of a thousand images of a thousand faces who live side by side*"

at the close of the Mexican-American War in 1848. New Mexicans had already developed their own, regional Hispanic culture, and the young Mexican government—beset by problems closer to Mexico City—could expend little effort to retain its remote, northern province. Meanwhile, thanks to the Santa Fe Trail, the American West seemed closer than ever. Eventually, by the mid-nineteenth century, the influx of Anglo settlers in New Mexico had forged a new regional mix, an Anglo-Hispanic culture unique in North America.

This cross-cultural society still lives on in La Mesilla, a historic village just minutes south of Las Cruces. Founded by Mexican settlers in 1849, when this verdant strip of land just north of the Rio Grande was part of Mexico, the village became part of the United States only four years later, with the Gadsden Purchase. Given the choice of moving back to Mexico, most of the settlers decided to remain. By the late 1880s, the railroad had arrived in Las Cruces, bringing with it Anglo settlers and signaling the end of the Camino Real.

Today, many Hispanics in La Mesilla reside in the century-old adobe houses their ancestors built, appointed in traditional Spanish style with dark wood furniture, somber family portraits in ornate frames, and colorful *santos* perched on plaster shelves. Their Anglo-American neighbors, meanwhile, speak a Spanish-accented English and run cluttered souvenir shops and pottery shacks in the brick buildings fronting on the tree-shaded square.

For the researchers involved with mapping the Camino Real, the cultural exchange witnessed in La Mesilla typifies the best and most noble aspects of the vanishing trail. For it was the trail that helped the Spanish and Anglo settlers bridge ideological, linguistic, and religious differences, and in the end, allowed them to merge into a greater whole. By resurrecting the memory and ideals of the Camino Real, perhaps their descendants again will recapture the spirit of the royal road.

"The cultural legacy of our villages and regions is like a mirror of a thousand images of a thousand faces who live side by side expressing themselves in the different economic, social, and cultural aspects of daily life," says INAH's Perea. "The Camino Real is an international challenge worth fighting for."

"Maybe the trail will help us reestablish the old cultural links between New Mexico and 'old' Mexico," muses David Gaines of the National Park Service. "After all, we're all residents of the same street."

Louis in the spring, and lumbered all the way to Mexico City via Santa Fe in the summer. From 1825 to 1846—the year the U.S. army invaded New Mexico—the annual number of wagons arriving in Santa Fe on the Santa Fe Trail from Missouri increased from twenty-five to three hundred. In fact, the impact of the trade with Mexico was so great that for a few decades, people in the American West preferred the more stable and valuable Mexican peso to the American dollar.

"The trade on the Chihuahua Trail led to a great exchange of language, cultural elements, and music," says Joseph Sánchez, director of the Spanish Colonial Research Center. "It became a two-way street, both an emigrant route and an immigrant route."

In the end, this cultural exchange paved the way for U.S. annexation of New Mexico

©BJØRN SLETTO (5)

Indigenous Cultural and Biological Diversity:

Overlapping Values of Latin American Ecoregions

Bruce A. Wilcox and Kristin N. Duin

Bruce Wilcox is Director of the Institute for Sustainable Development based in Menlo Park, California. Kristin Duin is a biologist from Stanford University and an intern at the Institute.

It is well known that the number of culturally distinct indigenous populations tends to be high in tropical rain forests, the most biologically rich and ecologically significant ecosystems in the world. Yet the overall correspondence of cultural diversity with globally significant biological values within and between ecosystems generally is less well known. We had the opportunity to measure this correspondence on the basis of two recently completed map-based data sets. A pioneering project backed by The World Bank and implemented by David Olson and Eric Dinerstein at World Wildlife Fund-US (the results of which are to be published early in '95) has produced a preliminary set of 218 ecoregions in Latin America. Meanwhile, a decade-long project to map indigenous groups in South America has been recently completed by Manual Lizarralde of the Department of Anthropology at U.C. Berkeley, complementing Mac Chapin's Central American map (*CSQ*, Fall, 1992).

In parallel with the above developments, our group has been working on an operational framework for applying valuation concepts based on ecological economics to the measurement of sustainability, in collaboration with The 2050 Project at the World Resources Institute in Washington, D.C. This work involves employing the notion of "biological utility," or the beneficial role of ecosystem function and biodiversity in the sense of the "goods and services" provided by different kinds of natural ecosystems; forest and woodland, savanna/grassland, wetland, shrubland, scrubland and desert, and the many sub-types of these and other terrestrial ecosystems. Different ecosystems in general, and in different locations in particular, vary greatly in their biodiversity and ecological properties of utility to humans. For example, forest and woodland tend to support large numbers of species, especially trees, of enormous value as harvestable resources, along with genetic resources for the improvement of domesticated species. Wetlands, on the other hand, which generally have much lower levels of species and genetic diversity, are of higher value for the storage and cleansing of water resources and regulation of water flows. Yet both are the most important terrestrial ecosystems for the storage or accumulation of carbon, thus for the amelioration of global climate change.

Because an ecoregion is effectively an area delineated on the basis of biotic features including the dominant ecosystem type, various measures of utility value can be attributed to a single ecoregion unit or a collective set constituting a larger biogeographic or geopolitical area, or major ecosystem category (e.g., all of the tropical moist forest in Latin America). So, along with the measurement of indigenous cultural significance, utility value in terms of the con-tribution to globally significant functions, like maintenance of genetic resources or amelioration of global climate change, is mappable. The result can be an "accounting," which theoretically can be made at different aggregate geographic scales, of the value of different regions in terms of their contribution to at least these aspects of global sustainability.

BIOLOGICAL UTILITY AND CULTURAL DIVERSITY

The linkage between indigenous cultural diversity and biological diversity has been shown to be as complex as it is inextricable by Madhav Gadgil of the Indian Institute of Science in Bangalore and his collaborators. They have found, for example, that traditional endogamous groups in India, including tribal peoples, partition the biological resource base, exploiting different niches in a manner of speaking. Some groups specialize as honey gatherers, others as shifting cultivators (traditional cultivators who clear forest plots, cultivate them for several years, then leave them fallow to be reclaimed by the forest while moving on to clear and cultivate a new plot), and so on. This obviously results in a greater efficiency of biological resource use than is possible when the economic production system is "industrialized," which basically involves "homogenizing" the resource base, reducing both cultural and

 From *Cultural Survival Quarterly*, Winter 1995, pp. 49-53.

Comparative Utility Rank Values for Major Ecosystems

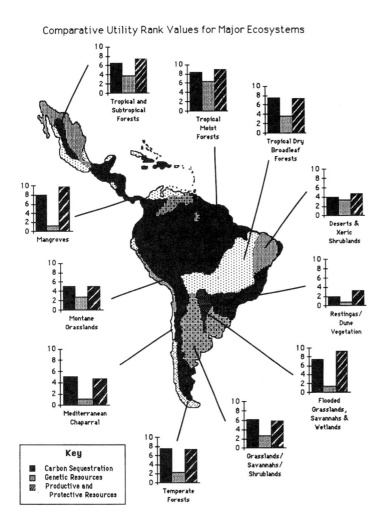

biological diversity. Industrial development generally results in the transformation of environmentally heterogeneous landscapes into ones dominated by large blocks of state or privately controlled lands used for intensive agriculture, plantation forestry, parks, industrial activity, and urban settlements.

There presumably is much to be learned by societies engaged in industrial modes of production from cultures whose production systems are compatible with or may even enhance intrinsic levels of biodiversity. By "intrinsic levels" we mean amounts of habitat, species, and genetic diversity comparable to that which would exist in the absence of human activity. It has become a more or less accepted principle among ecologists that moderate levels of physical disturbance, such as often imposed by traditional forms of resource exploitation, enhances ecological complexity, landscape heterogeneity, and species

diversity, thus promoting overall biodiversity. Also, empirical evidence exists showing indigenous cultivators' plantings of perennial species, for example, increases overall species diversity at a site. This has been shown by Dominique Irvine in her research on the Runa people of the Ecuadorian Amazon. Based on these two lines of evidence and population biology and ecological theory in general, a strong argument can be made that traditional use of biological resources, even with a cautious mix of conventional land and resource use, could maintain and even enhance biodiversity. Yet despite this possibility, excessive rates of population growth in the South and consumption in the North are overwhelming the land and biological resource base globally. Gadgil provides an interesting slant on the distinction between indigenous and industrial cultural perspectives of biodiversity which has important consequences to global

sustainability. He points out that a convenient, although not always exclusive, dichotomy can be drawn between "ecosystem people" and "biosphere people." Ecosystem people derive their sustenance from biological resources in their vicinity, while biosphere people (most of us reading this article), base their sustenance on biological and non-renewable resources from distant sources, often including the ecosystems in which indigenous people live. The distinction is not simply academic. People physically distant from the biological resources they consume tend to undervalue them, indirectly facilitating their over-exploitation and the degradation of the ecosystems producing them. By contrast, those with a direct stake in the biotic integrity of an ecosystem supplying their needs, tend to be conscious of their dependency. This is precisely the consciousness required by society at large for global sustainability.

The concept of biological utility may be one way to help build this consciousness. "Utility" is simply the notion that humans value things that provide them with some use or instrumental benefit. This contrasts with intrinsic value which we attach to things we believe have value in their own right. It is often argued as dangerously anthropocentric to ascribe utility or economic value to things like biological or cultural diversity which clearly are inherently valuable regardless of any monetary or other quantitative measures. However, the measurement of utility value provides a more objective means of identifying which components of nature or culture are considered more important than others. The alternative, which is to insist everything be valued equally, results in little value being ascribed to anything. In fact, as Brent Berlin of U.C. Berkeley (now at the University of Georgia) and others have shown, indigenous people classify biological diversity based on utility value. This contrasts the system of biological classification used in Western science.

In indigenous cultures, rational stewardship (conservation) of biological resources is effectively based on a knowledge of functional utility and institutionalized in the form of taboos. For example, in many tropical forest ecosystems figs (Ficus spp.) act as keystone species, and this recognition by tribal cultures in India is the basis of the reverence held for *Ficus religiosa* and the taboos against the cutting of such trees. Unfortunately, such rational connections based on biological utility are less well developed among non-traditional and non-indigenous societies. Recognizing attributes of biodiversity that represent utility benefits is an obvious first step toward the institutionalization (formal or informal) of modes or methods of sustainable resource use.

BIOLOGICAL UTILITY OF LATIN AMERICAN ECOREGIONS

A thorough accounting of functional connections between human welfare, in terms of global sustainability and ecosystems, is both impossible and impractical. Not only is the number of scientifically demonstrated connections a small fraction of the total that may possibly exist, but the perception of utility is "user-dependent." The "direct output benefits" of ecosystems–tangible commodities represented by plants and animals consumed directly or marketed as food, fiber, forage, or chemically active compounds–generally overlap very little among traditional users of biological resources and industrial society. The

other major class of utility values, represented by the so-called "indirect functional benefits" of ecosystems, tend to overlap more, and particularly so if "function" is considered on a larger scale–spatially and temporally. For example, the role of forests in the maintenance of global and regional climate benefits indigenous, and non-indigenous "biosphere" people alike.

Unfortunately, despite such overlapping dependencies, the response to ecological degradation in many biodiversity rich areas tends toward the designation of natural areas as parks and protected enclaves from which indigenous control of resources is minimized or excluded. More than this, however, the focus on biodiversity by non-indigenous and non-ecosystem people has been on popular, charismatic and mythological elements, such as "endangered species" and "rain forests." Important utility benefits of ecosystems, essential to all people as well as the survival of charismatic elements of biodiversity, are often overlooked. These indirect functional benefits derive from *ecological* functions or processes, or other attributes related to physical structure in ecosystems, that do not necessarily correspond to high levels of globally unique biodiversity.

Some kinds of ecosystems like rain forests apparently do have higher bio-

logical utility value, as well as high element diversity, measured in terms of the benefits for society at large, including indigenous people. However, it is important to know how these broader utility values vary among different types of ecosystems as a means of assessing the social and economic impacts of deforestation and other pressures on ecosystems. Part of our research was conducted within USAID's Biodiversity Support Program (BSP), and was directed toward contributing a valuation framework for setting conservation investment priorities on a country basis. This effort, particularly the development of ecoregion maps by Olson and Dinerstein afforded an opportunity to attach utility value to specific terrestrial ecosystems in Latin America and the Caribbean.

The mapping of ecoregions and indigenous populations provided a unique opportunity to determine the extent to which measures of biological utility value, as perceived by society at large, and cultural diversity correspond. A high correspondence would demonstrate, for example, that the ecosystems most important to maintaining indigenous cultural diversity are also the most important to maintaining global ecosystem functions such as the amelioration of global climate change, the maintenance of genetic resources, and

Figure 1

Indicators of Biological Utility, Cultural Diversity and Biodiversity in Latin America

Habitat Type	Biomass Carbon Content[1]	Forest Tree Genetic Resources[2]	Centers of Plant Diversity[3]	Origins of Important Crop Species[3]	Domesticated Animal Origins[3]	Net Primary Productivity[4]	Indigenous Populations	Base Ecoregions
Tropical Moist Forests	16	95	40	18	14	1800	334	54
Tropical Dry Broadleaf Forests	7	70	12	12	11	800	89	32
Tropical and Subtropical Forests	7	48	9	1	0	1300	56	15
Temperate Forests	17	1	2	0	1	1300	2	4
Grasslands/Savannahs/Shrublands	3.3	17	3	4	5	850	46	16
Flooded Grasslands, Savannahs and Wetlands	3	5	0	2	3	2000	21	13
Montane Grasslands	1	7	9	1	6	600	13	13
Mediterranean Chaparral	1	3	0	0	0	250	2	2
Deserts and Xeric Shrublands	0.5	39	9	9	7	250	31	27
Restingas/Dune Vegetation	0	1	0	0	0	0	0	3
Mangroves	7	2	2	0	2	2000	10	39

[1] Units are in kg/m². Data source is J. S. Olson, J. A. Watts, L. J. Allison, "Carbon in Live Vegetation of Major World Ecosystems," Oak Ridge National Laboratory, 1983.

[2] Food and Agriculture Organization of the United Nations, "Appendix 7: Forest Genetic Resources Priorities, in the Report on the 8th Session of FAO Panel of Experts on Forest Gene Resources," Rome, 1994.

[3] Updated from original data in WCMC, "Global Biodiversity; Status of the Earth's Living Resources," Chapman and Hall, 1992.

[4] Units are in g/m²/yr. Data Source is H. Likens and R. Whittaker, "Primary Productivity of the Biosphere," Springer-Verlag, 1975.

protective and productive functions of ecosystems. This would have implications beyond development agency investment priorities, by suggesting a reexamination of the perception of values and benefits held by those of us in industrial society vis à vis those of indigenous people.

In our preliminary analysis reported here, 57 aggregated ecoregion units comprising the eleven Major Habitat Types in Latin America were scored and ranked according to the number of distinct linguistic/ethnic indigenous populations that occurred within their boundaries as well as their utility value. (In all, 218 base ecoregions currently are identified in the Olson and Dinerstein ecoregion scheme.) As indicators of utility value we used measures of carbon sequestration, genetic resources, and protective and productive benefits collectively associated with the ecoregions that constituted a Major Habitat Type. The scores were based on measured values drawn from the scientific literature, such as rates of biomass storage or accumulation. Where quantitative measures were unavailable, but clear qualitative differences exist, ecoregions were simply given scores based on their relative rank for a particular function. The first two

utility values are global in the sense of the scale on which they benefit humans: The amelioration of global climate change through the sequestering of carbon in plant matter and the accumulation of carbon in the form of soil organic matter; and the maintenance and continued evolution of gene pools necessary for the improvement of the World's economically most valuable crops and livestock. The third category captures an ecosystem's utility or functional value in two senses, its protective and productive capacity. The former refers to an ecosystem's buffering capacity against regional or local environmental change: drought, storms, floods, etc. Productive capacity refers to the rate of biomass production, which ecologists measure as "net primary production," and the "export" of nutrients or provision of fishery habitat upon which other (particularly aquatic and marine) ecosystems depend. The Vareza flood forests of the lower Amazon for example, and the mangroves that occur throughout coastal zones in the tropics are the ecological foundation for traditional and commercial fisheries. In a parallel sense, the Amazon Basin "exports" precipitation to surrounding regions, making possible rainfed crop and

livestock production, as well as providing water resources for domestic and industrial use.

GEOGRAPHICALLY COINCIDING VALUES AND BENEFITS

The biological utility, biodiversity, and cultural diversity indicator measures for Major Habitat Types are shown in the Table. The relative rankings of each Major Habitat Type for each of the three utility value categories are shown in Figure 1. A more detailed study presenting analysis at a higher level of resolution (i.e., the aggregate ecoregion and base ecoregion levels) is planned. Although not shown here, measures of biological utility value are generally correlated with those of element biodiversity, including estimates of species richness and endemism, which were made preliminarily by expert groups at the BSP biodiversity priority setting workshop in Miami in October. The data in the table allow further comparison of variables representing the three utility value categories, indigenous cultural diversity (number of distinct indigenous populations), and biodiversity in terms of habitat diversity within Major

Figure 2

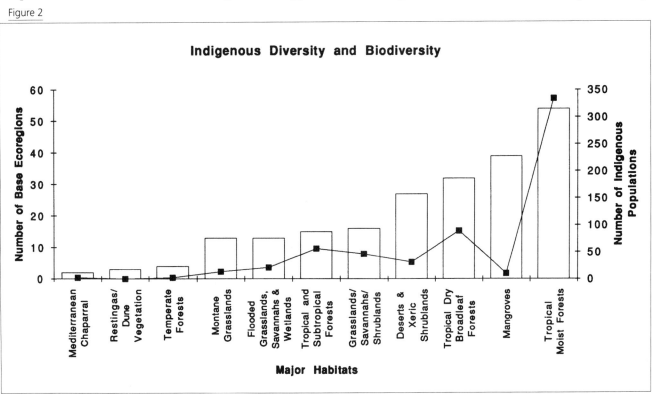

3. THE REGION

Habitat Types (Number of Base Ecoregions). The comparisons of most interest to us here, the relationships between the types of diversity–biological and cultural–and between cultural diversity and biological utility, show strong positive correlation (Figure 2). Mangroves are the only habitat type diverging markedly from this pattern by having far fewer indigenous populations than expected. This perhaps should not be surprising since the coastal location and inhabitability of mangroves makes their mapped distributions least likely to overlap with those of indigenous populations.

Behind these data, there are a number of interesting patterns for various smaller scale ecoregion units. For example, it is apparent that among ecoregions consisting of tropical moist forest, those of the Amazon Basin, in addition to being the most species rich, score highest in biological utility value while supporting the largest number of indigenous populations (with 334, or over two-thirds of the total diversity recorded for all of Latin America). Yet Tropical Dry Forests, which often are overlooked for their conservation value, are hardly lacking in cultural and biological diversity overall, or in interesting ecoregional patterns. In total, 89 indigenous groups were recorded for tropical dry forests in Latin America. While not having nearly as high value on the basis of indicators affected primarily by rainfall, such as carbon storage and net primary production, dry forests are nonetheless relatively rich in genetic resources. The aggregate ecoregion unit encompassed by Mexican dry forests is particularly noteworthy in this regard. This "ecosystem" not only supports a relatively high indigenous cultural diversity (about 30 distinct groups), albeit much of it assimilated or displaced, it also represents one of the world's most important repositories of genetic resources. Its forest tree genetic resources rival that of any tropical moist forest region. Even more significantly, its crop plant genetic resources, which include wild relatives of maize (*Zea maize*), cotton (*Gossypium* spp.), peppers (*Capsicum* spp.), and squash (*Cucurbita* spp.), are the basis of some of the world's most valuable commercial crops. Thus our results show that even within a major habitat type such as dry forests, biological diversity, both of utility and non-utility, and indigenous cultural diversity seem to be highly correlated. In this instance, protecting the integrity of ecosystems containing the biological diversity most important to the food security of present and future generations, could simultaneously maximize the protection of indigenous cultural diversity.

We were frankly surprised to find such a strong correlation between biological diversity utility value and cultural diversity, especially since our utility indicators are based on value from a global or regional, but not local use perspective. We will be continuing our research to see how these patterns hold up at a higher level of ecogeographic resolution. Certainly the occurrence of a large number of indigenous groups, whose use of biological diversity is probably as proportionately diverse, is an automatic expression of high utility value for an ecosystem. However, why should such ecosystems also rank high in utility measures based on an industrial society perspective?

Considering some basic ecological and co-evolutionary principles, the correspondence may not be so surprising. For cultures dependent entirely on biological resources the possibilities for diversification and coexistence should, in theory, be greatest where the resource base is richest. Biotic richness in this regard has two major components, productivity, such as that measured by net primary production (essentially the rate of accumulation of plant biomass), and diversity, primarily in the form of the variety of biological resources to exploit. Thus as ecologists have found in studying the distribution and abundance of plants and animals, species diversity tends to increase with habitat diversity and increasing productivity or energy flow through an ecosystem. The theoretical explanation is that there are lower limits to population size and upper limits to niche overlap for species persistence. Therefore the higher the productivity and diversity of a habitat, the greater the opportunity for biological diversification; and the same may hold for indigenous cultures.

However, there is an additional explanation for these patterns. Stanford anthropologist William Durham, an expert on historical land use conflicts involving indigenous people, leans toward a cultural competitive exclusion explanation: Colonizing European populations are likely to have displaced indigenous populations disproportionately from preferred "European-like" habitats (such as scrubland and savannah-woodland)-leaving rainforests to the last! Whatever the causative agent, the results of our analysis show that contemporary industrial society and indigenous societies may be more interdependent than is often appreciated. If the results of this analysis hold up after further study, they will help confirm scientifically what perhaps most know intuitively: all societies are mutually interdependent with each other and on natural ecosystems, and this interdependency crosses all spatial and temporal scales.

Does it matter where you are?

The cliché of the information age is that instantaneous global telecommunications, television and computer networks will soon overthrow the ancient tyrannies of time and space. Companies will need no headquarters, workers will toil as effectively from home, car or beach as they could in the offices that need no longer exist, and events half a world away will be seen, heard and felt with the same immediacy as events across the street—if indeed streets still have any point.

There is something in this. Software for American companies is already written by Indians in Bangalore and transmitted to Silicon Valley by satellite. Foreign-exchange markets have long been running 24 hours a day. At least one Californian company literally has no headquarters: its officers live where they like, its salesmen are always on the road, and everybody keeps in touch via modems and e-mail.

Yet such developments have made hardly a dent in the way people think and feel about things. Look, for example, at newspapers or news broadcasts anywhere on earth, and you find them overwhelmingly dominated by stories about what is going on in the vicinity of their place of publication. Much has been made of the impact on western public opinion of televised scenes of suffering in such places as Ethiopia, Bosnia and Somalia. Impact, maybe, but a featherweight's worth.

World television graphically displayed first the slaughter of hundreds of thousands of people in Rwanda and then the flight of more than a million Rwandans to Zaire. Not until France belatedly, and for mixed motives, sent in a couple of thousand soldiers did anyone in the West lift so much as a finger to stop the killing; nor, once the refugees had suddenly poured out, did western governments do more than sluggishly bestir themselves to try to contain a catastrophe.

Rwanda, of course, is small (population maybe 8m before the killings began). More important, it is far away. Had it been Flemings killing Walloons in Belgium (population 10m) instead of Hutus slaying Tutsi in Rwanda, European news companies would have vastly increased their coverage, and European governments would have intervened in force. Likewise, the only reason the Clinton administration is even thinking about invading Haiti is that it lies a few hundred miles from American shores. What your neighbours (or your kith and kin) do affects you. The rest is voyeurism.

The conceit that advanced technology can erase the contingencies of place and time ranges widely. Many armchair strategists predicted during the Gulf war that ballistic missiles and smart weapons would make the task of capturing and holding territory irrelevant. They were as wrong as the earlier seers who predicted America could win the Vietnam war from the air.

In business, too, the efforts to break free of space and time have had qualified success at best. American multinationals going global have discovered that—for all their world products, world advertising, and world communications and control—an office in, say, New York cannot except in the most general sense manage the company's Asian operations. Global strengths must be matched by a local feel—and a jet-lagged visit of a few days every so often does not provide one.

Most telling of all, even the newest industries are obeying an old rule of geographical concentration. From the start of the industrial age, the companies in a fast-growing new field have tended to cluster in a small region. Thus, in examples given by Paul Krugman, an American economist, all but one of the top 20 American carpet-makers are located in or near the town of Dalton, Georgia; and, before 1930, the American tire industry consisted almost entirely of the 100 or so firms carrying on that business in Akron, Ohio. Modern technology has not changed the pattern. This is why the world got Silicon Valley in California in the 1960s. It is also why tradable services stay surprisingly concentrated—futures trading (in Chicago), insurance (Hartford, Connecticut), movies (Los Angeles) and currency trading (London).

HISTORY'S HEAVY HAND

This offends not just techno-enthusiasts but also neo-classical economics: for both, the world should tend towards a smooth dispersion of people, skills and economic competence, not towards their concentration. Save for transport costs, it should not matter where a tradable good or service is produced.

The reality is otherwise. Some economists have explained this by pointing to increasing returns to scale (in labour as well as capital markets), geographically uneven patterns of demand and transport costs. The main reason is that history counts: where you are depends very much on where you started from.

The new technologies will overturn some of this, but not much. The most advanced use so far of the Internet, the greatest of the world's computer networks, has not been to found a global village but to strengthen the local business and social ties among people and companies in the heart of Silicon Valley. As computer and communications power grows and its cost falls, people will create different sorts of space and communities from those that exist in nature. But

these modern creations will supplement, not displace, the original creation; and they may even reinforce it. Companies that have gone furthest towards linking their global operations electronically report an increase, not a decline in the face-to-face contact needed to keep the firms running well: with old methods of command in ruins, the social glue of personal relations matters more than ever.

The reason lies in the same fact of life that makes it impossible really to understand from statistics alone how exciting,

say, China's economic growth is unless you have physically been there to feel it. People are not thinking machines (they absorb at least as much information from sight, smell and emotion as they do from abstract symbols), and the world is not immaterial: "virtual" reality is no reality at all; cyberspace is a pretence at circumventing true space, not a genuine replacement for it. The weight on mankind of time and space, of physical surroundings and history—in short, of geography—is bigger than any earthbound technology is ever likely to lift.

Low Water in the American High Plains

David E. Kromm

David E. Kromm, professor of geography at Kansas State University, has authored and coauthored numerous articles and one book on water management issues.

Depletion of the Ogallala Aquifer once threatened to return the region to a Dust Bowl, but much is being done to conserve groundwater today.

Water defines many regions. It determines their character and sustains their well-being. Ironically, this is especially true of areas with an inherent water scarcity. What would Southern California and central Arizona be like without water imported from distant sources? The green fields and golf courses would give way to dry plains and hills, populated more by grazing animals than by people.

A huge dry area in the middle of the United States depends no less on water to transform a dusty outback into a productive garden. This is the High Plains overlying the Ogallala Aquifer.

There exists widespread concern that America's largest underground water reserve is drying up. The vast Ogallala Aquifer that underlies 174,000 square miles of the High Plains from west Texas northward into South Dakota has been partially depleted as more than 150,000 wells pump water for irrigation, municipal supply, and industry. In some areas the wells no longer yield enough water to make irrigation possible. In others there remains sufficient water, but it lies 300 or more feet below the surface. The cost of lifting water from such depths makes it uneconomical for many uses.

Touching base with some key words in the groundwater vocabulary helps tell the Ogallala story more precisely. One is *aquifer*. An aquifer is a zone of water-saturated sands and gravels beneath the earth's surface. It is not an underground lake or river. It is the porous rock structure that contains the water that we tap with wells. Some aquifers release water to wells readily, whereas others hold the water tightly. This affects the rate at which water can be withdrawn and is called the *specific yield* of a well. *Depth to water* describes the vertical distance from ground level to the aquifer. Together with the volume and quality of water, the depth and specific yield define the economic limit of water withdrawal. The fresh water in an aquifer is called *groundwater*, in contrast to surface waters such as rivers and lakes. Over half the nation's population depends on groundwater for its drinking water. Although there are several aquifers, the Ogallala ranks as the main formation in the High Plains aquifer system. Most people in the region refer to the entire system as the Ogallala.

The unconsolidated sand and gravel that form the Ogallala aquifer were laid down by fluvial deposition from the Rocky Mountains about 10 million years ago. More recent, near-surface deposits

3. THE REGION

of the late Tertiary and Quaternary ages compose the High Plains aquifer.

The volume of available water varies from place to place. Nebraska has about two-thirds (65 percent) of the High Plains groundwater, followed by Texas (12 percent), and Kansas (10 percent). The total water in storage is enough to fill Lake Huron or to cover the state of Colorado to a depth of 45 feet. Physical characteristics of the aquifer result in one farmer in a county having little or no access to water while another has substantial reserves. Ogallala water moves gradually from west to east, following the general slope of the land surface. This movement does not affect use or depletion, as it takes nearly a century and a half to flow a mere 10 miles.

Changing views

When Stephen Long explored the region in the early nineteenth century, he discovered a sea of grass that contrasted with the trees that dominated landscapes to the east. Few lakes or rivers can be found. These signs of aridity led Long to name the area "The Great American Desert." Settlers on their way to rainy Oregon viewed the plains as worthless territory that had to be crossed in order to reach a land more promising. Even those few who attempted to break the prairie sod found it tough to plow. The native Americans and buffalo herds were initially displaced by cattle ranching, not by cultivation.

A whole new perception of the plains burst forth in the middle of the nineteenth century as railroads penetrated the region and touted its virtues. The promoters encouraged the development of farming communities that would depend on the rails for goods and the delivery of grain to eastern markets. New steel plows cracked the soil and many boost-

The Ogallala Aquifer

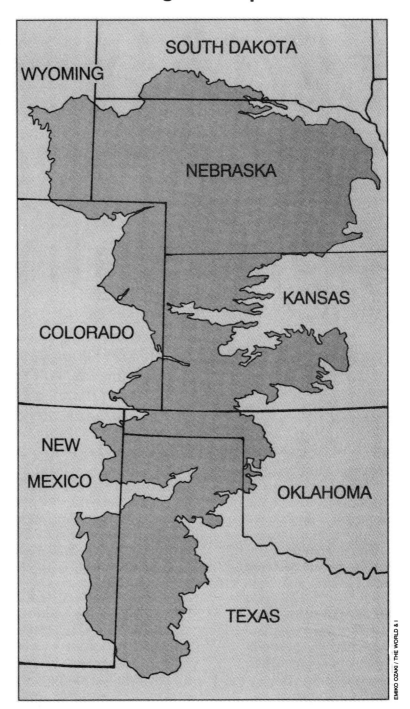

EMIKO OZAKI / THE WORLD & I

ers came to believe that "the rain follows the plow." Once the ground was broken and crops planted, the aridity would end. Hopeful farmers took up homesteads from the government or bought lands directly from the railroad companies.

There ensued frequent dry years and just enough wet ones

to allow many of the farmers to hang on. The rosy view of the High Plains as a garden was soon tarnished but never wholly abandoned. This changed with the 1930s. Everything went wrong. Depression weakened markets and reduced capital availability and drought destroyed the crops. A new name was coined for the

■ The promotional railroad poster, 1887: the advantages of settling the High Plains.

High Plains—the Dust Bowl. Out-migration swelled and the popular image was that of skies darkened by blowing dirt, desolate farmsteads surrounded by drifting soil, and impoverished families attempting to leave with whatever they could carry in their dilapidated vehicles. John Steinbeck chronicled the depth of misery in *The Grapes of Wrath*.

Emergence of a new Corn Belt

Even as the last settlers were taking up land in the 1890s, irrigation was beginning. It occupied small patches dependent on surface sources such as the Arkansas River or shallow wells. The Dust Bowl brought renewed interest in soil and water conservation and encouraged irrigation to create a stable moisture supply. Farmers suffered greatly from climatic variability in the High Plains. In a given year it might be a land of bountiful rain or a sun-drenched and parched desert.

Irrigation expanded in the 1930s and even more so in the dry years of the 1950s, as new technologies made possible large-scale tapping of the Ogallala aquifer. Pump engines came on the market that could lift large quantities of water from sources deep underground. New watering methods, such as center-pivot sprinklers, allowed irrigation of sandy and hilly areas. The green circles seen from aircraft flying more than 30,000 feet above the surface became the most prominent feature in the High Plains. The perception of the 1960s and 1970s was of a new Corn Belt flourishing in the land of the underground rain. Thanks to the Ogallala, stability had at last come to the High Plains.

Or had it? For the most part the Ogallala is a fossil water aquifer. It was formed millions of years ago and has been minimally recharged since. Only in a few areas such as the Nebraska Sandhills and the sand-sage prairie of southwestern Kansas

was new water being added. Elsewhere, whatever was pumped out was forever gone. Wells sunk into zones with limited saturation thickness dried up early. Many were in west Texas, where large-scale irrigation began. By the late 1970s the whole High Plains region seemed threatened again, no less than it had been in the dirty thirties. Between 1978 and 1987, the irrigated area harvested in the High Plains sharply fell from nearly 13 million acres to 10.4 million acres.

Depletion ranks as such a serious problem that quality and streamflow issues are easily overlooked. In its natural state, the High Plains aquifer is generally of high quality. It is suitable for a wide array of uses without filtration. Where soils are sandy, however, precipitation can reach the water table, bringing with it nitrates from fertilizers and other surface contaminants. Abandoned water wells directly link pollutants and the aquifer. Where irrigation development is intense, decline in stream flows often follows. In Kansas, more than 700 miles of once permanently flowing rivers are now dry. The blue band on maps representing the Arkansas River in western Kansas hides the reality of a dry streambed.

An integrated agribusiness economy

Fears of impending disaster were real as the regional economy had expanded and grown relatively prosperous on the basis of irrigated agriculture. Except for the Platte River valley in Nebraska and Colorado, and minor surface sources in other places, groundwater sustained irrigation. In the southern reaches of the High Plains, irrigated cotton supports gins, oil mills, and a denim factory. Throughout most of the region farmers cultivate forage crops to

■ Center-pivot irrigation has permitted the short-term cultivation of sandy, sloping land. Such areas are suitable only for grazing in the long term.

feed cattle. Much of the cattle industry centers on huge feeder lots that collectively consume many tons of grain daily. The cattle in turn supply large meat processing plants, some of which are among the largest in the world.

Through the multiplier effect, irrigated agriculture affects all aspects of the regional economy. Where irrigation prevails, most rural towns seem vital, alive, and healthy. Where irrigation is absent, much less economic activity occurs, far fewer people are employed in commerce, and a decreasing volume and array of goods and services are available. Boarded-up storefronts provide visual evidence of the decline. One measure of civic progress in these communities is the tearing down of no longer needed buildings. Another is keeping the weeds under control in empty lots where structures once stood.

Observing this depopulation and decay, Deborah and Frank Popper of Rutgers University have recommended that the entire area be turned over to native grasses and animals. They

call for a buffalo commons. The Poppers see a natural process of people moving away, with the population becoming so small and scattered that basic educational, medical, and commercial services could no longer be provided. To be fair, it should be noted that extensive cultivation and cattle ranching would continue to occupy the land, leaving little space for buffalo. Nonetheless, the reduction in the number of towns and farmsteads would approximate the appearance of the High Plains of more than a century ago. This general contraction of people and services occurs where dryland farming prevails. It could become the norm for irrigated areas, where scarcity results from high pumping costs as water is lifted from ever-greater depths, reduction in specific yield, or lack of water as wells are physically depleted.

The High Plains has exemplified what Wes Jackson, director of the Land Institute in Kansas, calls "the failure of success." The success of irrigation was sowing the seeds of its own destruction through depletion. Relying on a single water source

also creates vulnerability. Take away the aquifer and the High Plains is without sufficient precipitation or surface water to sustain intensive agriculture or most other activities.

Responding to water scarcity

Few residents in the High Plains are standing idly by, merely watching a drama of decline being played out as irrigation becomes less and less a part of the regional economy. Water conservation has become more prevalent and is seen as the answer to sustaining irrigation and the integrated agribusiness economy it supports. Municipalities, factories, and other water users have lessened water use, but the major concern remains irrigation. More than 90 percent of the water consumed in the High Plains goes to irrigation. If irrigators are able to significantly reduce water consumption, for most there should be adequate and accessible water for many decades to come.

What are irrigators doing to conserve water? In 1988–90, with support from the Ford Foundation, the author and fellow geographer Stephen E. White looked into this question. A questionnaire was mailed to 1,750 irrigators in Texas, Oklahoma, Kansas, and Nebraska, asking them what water-saving practices they had adopted. Over 40 percent (709) returned a completed survey. Those who responded cited over 21 conservation practices now in wide use throughout the High Plains. Some of these techniques are: periodically checking pumping plant efficiency, planting drought-tolerant crops, replacing open ditches with underground pipes, and recovering runoff from fields. On the center-pivot sprinkler system, low-pressure heads are being installed on drop tubes to reduce overwatering and wind drift.

Several of the widely used practices are sophisticated, information-based techniques that can be highly effective. Scheduling irrigation based on moisture need serves as an example. The goal is to ensure that just enough water is in the root zone of a plant to accomplish the management objectives of the farmer. Soil water levels and plant stress are monitored so that the farmer can determine how much water to apply and when. The days of large amounts of water draining off the fields into ditches or leaching downward beyond the root zone are largely gone.

Institutions play a major role in how the Ogallala and other aquifers are used and who controls the decisions affecting water use. Water law provides an example. Two general forms of water rights exist in the United States, and both function in the High Plains. In Texas, *riparian water rights* prevail, wherein the owner of land overlying an aquifer has the right to use the groundwater beneath. In the remaining states in the region differing forms of the *appropriation doctrine* exist. Under appropriation, the first party to establish the right to use a specified amount of groundwater (or surface water such as a river) has priority of use in times of scarcity. Junior rights may be reduced or even curtailed when they endanger senior rights. The doctrine may be summarized as "first in time, first in right." It has served the western states well, in that insufficient water is available to provide enough for all landowners, as is necessary to apply the riparian doctrine. Most states have developed a priority in water use, with domestic and livestock consumption usually ranking first.

These water rights are administered by various levels of organizations and agencies. Water largely falls under state control, but substate or local districts are often permitted by law. These authorities are formed usually to ensure that existing rights, often for irrigation, are protected. The authority of the local district varies from largely educational, establishing programs to advocate water conservation, to requiring a land-use plan or metering of water flow for all irrigators with water rights. Local districts frequently have enforcement authority. As a rule, a main goal of both state and local groups is to protect existing water rights, most of which are held by irrigators. Increasingly, water markets are being introduced that allow rights to be sold to other users. A farmer, for example, may sell a water right to a municipality or to a developer converting land from agricultural to residential use.

Much remains to be done, but the institutions and technologies of the High Plains show that the region is responding effectively. Most of the states now have water or resource management districts that are responsible for ensuring wise use of the Ogallala. A variety of policies have emerged. In various areas, wells are spaced so as not to interfere with each other, flow meters are required to measure water use, and drilling of new irrigation wells is prohibited. Although planned and orderly depletion constitutes the primary goal, one groundwater management district in western Kansas is considering a zero-depletion policy.

Innovation in irrigation technology has been striking. Many of the water-saving practices and devices used by farmers in the region and elsewhere were developed or first applied in the High Plains. Most are manufactured in the area. Land-grant universities throughout the region lead the way in developing techniques to conserve water. Nonprofit groups such as the Nebraska Groundwater Foundation support public education efforts. The High Plains ranks as a global center of technology and institutions for improving efficiency in irrigation.

What next?

Although numerous writers continue to cite the High Plains as a region where significant groundwater depletion occurs and where irrigation is doomed by its own excesses, current practices and conditions no longer support these views. Because of institutional and technical innovation, educational campaigns, and the land and water stewardship of most farmers, sustainable irrigation appears likely in the High Plains. The Great American Desert will not reappear as the Buffalo Commons.

China's Three Gorges Dam will soon transform the Yangtze.

The Long River's Journey Ends

Erling Hoh
Photographs by Greg Girard; Contact Press Images

Erling Hoh decided to travel the upper Yangtze, knowing that in a matter of years, the Three Gorges Dam reservoir will transform the region. He anticipates that the current flurry of scientific research in the area will help throw new light on the development of Chinese culture. **Greg Girard,** who was born in Vancouver, Canada, has traveled and worked extensively in Asia, first as a sound recordist for BBC TV News and for the past decade as a photographer.

China, with its diverse river systems, extreme fluctuations in rainfall, and wet-rice agriculture, has long looked to hydraulic works to solve problems of transportation, irrigation, and flood prevention. The classical Chinese term for hydraulic engineering, *shuili,* means "benefit of water," and the question of how to harness water resources has been crucial throughout the country's history. Taoist engineers argued that rivers should be managed by dredging and channeling; while Confucians favored reliance on dikes, either low and far apart, or high and near one another. The modern Chinese government has followed in this latter tradition by building some 86,000 dams and reservoirs during the past forty-seven years.

Now the biggest hydroelectric dam in the world—606 feet high and 7,640 feet wide—will tame the Yangtze (Chang Jiang, or Long River) in the Three Gorges, a 125-mile-long string of canyons. Construction is well under way, with the river scheduled to be partly cut off by September 1997. At its completion in 2009, the dam will raise the water level about 330 feet higher than the current normal level, impounding 31 million acre-feet of water in a snakelike lake stretching 370 miles upstream to Chongqing. The reservoir will not only diminish a scenic treasure but also submerge sites of historical, archeological, paleontological, and biological interest. On a recent trip on the Yangtze, I embarked at Chongqing, well upstream of the Three Gorges, and traveled down past the dam site. Along the way, I sampled the region's rich heritage, meeting people who are working to preserve it before the impending changes.

My first stop was Fuling, a gray, bustling city renowned for spicy, crisp pickled cabbage cores. Situated on the terraced banks of the Yangtze, 300 miles upstream from the dam site, the city will be partly inundated when the reservoir is full. There I met Huang Dejian, head of Fuling's Cultural Relics Office and one of the many scientists taking part in the biggest salvage operation since the one that preceded the building of Egypt's Aswan Dam.

On the wall in Huang's spartan office was a map showing the scores of known archeological sites around the city. Too many Han Dynasty (206 B.C.–A.D. 220) graves for them even to be remarkable, he said. More notably, Fuling was a burial ground for the kings of Ba, a people who controlled salt production in the Three Gorges during the Xia Dynasty (ca. twenty-first to sixteenth centuries B.C.) and who slowly migrated upstream along the Yangtze. In 316 B.C. they were subjugated by the Qin, who went on to unify China in 221 B.C.

Huang was also eager to talk about his latest project, a book about White Crane Ridge, a mile-long sandstone formation that only appears when the water recedes to its lowest level, in February and March. "At Fuling there are stone fish, engraved beneath the waves," wrote the prefect Xiao Xinggong in the late seventeenth century. "Their appearance portends a good harvest." Numerous inscriptions on White Crane Ridge mark low-water levels. The oldest entry is a fish, carved no later than 763. Its belly line corresponds to the river's present average low-water level. Although the dam will render these historic records irrelevant, they will be kept on view in an underwater museum.

Thirty miles downriver from Fuling lies Fengdu, the first capital of Ba, where, according to Chinese folklore, departed souls go to await their transition to heaven or hell. There are several Buddhist and Taoist temples in the "ghost city" above the town, as well as a somewhat gaudy exhibition of the tortures awaiting those who are sent to hell. People come on certain days of the lunar calendar and burn paper money, paper boats, and joss sticks to expedite their ancestors' transition to the afterlife.

One morning, as I stood outside the gates of the temple precincts above the city, I spotted a sign that read 175M (175 meters, or 575 feet), one of many that are preparing people for the coming flood. When the residents of Fengdu are resettled on higher ground across the river, their abandoned buildings will become an underwater ghost town, mirroring the ghost city above it.

Not far from Fengdu, in the little town of Gaojia, Professor Wei Qi, of the Institute of Vertebrate Paleontology and Paleoanthropology at the Academia Sinica in Beijing, was supervising the excavation of one of the most bounteous paleolithic sites in south China. By the time I paid a visit, the thirty young archeologists in Wei's training class, working their way down through the three layers of the 645-square-foot locale, had unearthed more than 1,000 stone tools made from cobbles and boulders. According to Wei, the artifacts are the remains of a tool workshop, situated on the banks of the Yangtze 100,000 years ago. The tools were probably used to collect roots, unlike the smaller tools of northern China, which paleontologists believe were used for hunting.

After returning to Fengdu, I boarded a passenger boat headed downstream toward the Three Gorges. In the evening we arrived in the city of Wanxian, where the muddy river makes a sharp turn and heads due east. The steep hillsides were largely planted with rows of pine trees to prevent landslides and erosion—major worries for the dam builders. Geologists have identified 263 historic landslides in the Three

Passengers and goods pass through Chongqing.

Gorges reservoir area. One, in 1030, cut off river navigation for twenty-one years; another, in 1542, for eighty-two. On June 12, 1985, the town of Xintan, fifteen miles upstream from the dam site, was obliterated when more than 70 million cubic feet of earth came sliding down a nearby hill, creating a 128-foot-high surge wave on the river. Fortunately, the town had been evacuated a few days earlier.

One of the difficulties with reforestation is that soil degradation is already so severe that only coniferous trees can be introduced easily. These trees acidify the soil, reduce its fertility, and increase the risk for plant diseases and insect pests, thereby knocking out the surviving indigenous broad-leafed forest. Another problem is that the hundreds of thousands of farmers displaced by the rising reservoir will need new land for cultivation.

Despite the concentration of agriculture, the Three Gorges reservoir area actually boasts a diverse flora. Little affected by the Pleistocene glaciations and enjoying a varied topography, mild climate, and abundant rainfall, the region is home to many ancient species of plants and trees, such as dawn redwood, dove tree, magnolia, and gingko. The Chinese Academy of Sciences lists forty-seven species as rare

and endangered. One that is threatened by the dam is lotus leaf maidenhair, a fern found near the river's banks. It is used in Chinese herbal medicine to treat kidney stones. Botanists have succeeded in propagating it artificially by cultivating the spores in test tubes before planting them.

My next stop along the river was Yunyang. Approaching it and the Three Gorges also meant stepping into an era, the Three Kingdoms, treasured by both teahouse storytellers and television producers. After the dissolution of the Han Dynasty in A.D. 220, three separate kingdoms became established—Shu in the west; Wu, east of the gorges; and Wei in the north. They fought a series of wars that immortalized such heroes as the Shu general Zhang Fei, whose temple stands on a hill opposite Yunyang. At 460 feet, the temple falls well below the new water level and will be moved farther up the hill. To find out more about what had befallen Zhang Fei, I paid half a yuan for the river crossing and climbed the steep slope.

It all started when Sun Quan, the ruler of Wu, beheaded the Shu proconsul Guanyu, the sworn brother of both Zhang Fei and the Shu king Liu Bei. The impetuous Zhang Fei obtained Liu Bei's permission to exact immediate revenge. As

3. THE REGION

Of the Three Gorges, Qutang is the farthest upstream.

recounted in *The Romance of the Three Kingdoms,* a popular fictional account of the events, Zhang gave his two commanders only three days to equip the army with white flags and whitened arms in mourning for Guanyu. Faced with this impossible task, the two commanders decapitated their general and set off to present his head to Sun Quan.

Legend has it that while traveling down the Yangtze past Yunyang, the two commanders, haunted by their hideous act of treason, threw their general's head into the water, where it became caught in a whirlpool around an old fisherman's boat. At night, the old man dreamed that the head belonged to Zhang Fei, and that he was asked to save it and bury it. He did, and that is where the temple now stands.

Following the deaths of his two sworn brothers, Liu Bei himself set out with an army of 25,000 men to wreak vengeance on Wu. He was routed, however, and retreated to Baidi Cheng (White Emperor City), where he died in A.D. 223. Baidi Cheng stands on a hilltop at the entrance to Qutang Gorge, the most upstream of the Three Gorges. When the dam is completed, the hilltop will become a small island and an important villa on the side of the hill—the Western Pavilion—will be moved to higher ground.

In the eighth century, the Western Pavilion witnessed what American sinologist D. R. McCraw calls the "greatest lyrical outpouring in Chinese literary history." Having traveled down the Yangtze with his family, the poet Du Fu arrived in Baidi Cheng in the spring of 766. The local warlord, an old aquaintance, set him up with a house, a fruit garden, a rice paddy, and a few servants. For perhaps the first time in his peripatetic life, the fifty-five-year-old Du Fu did not have to worry about the basic necessities.

Although debilitated by malaria, tuberculosis, diabetes, and arthritis, Du Fu had a burst of creativity. During his twenty-one months in the area, he wrote a third of his life's work, 429 poems, many of them in the highly demanding five- or seven-character regulated octaves called *lushi*. One is "From the Highest Building in White Emperor City" (translation by Paul Rouzer of Columbia University):

> *The walls are sharp, the paths steep—the*
> *banners droop in grief.*
> *Alone I stand in the misty void, here in this*
> *lofty hall.*
> *Through cloven gorges, the clouds shadow*
> *the tigers and dragons in their sleep;*
> *On the bright river, the sunlight enfolds the*
> *water lizards at play.*
> *Western limbs of the Tree of Dawn face*
> *these broken crags;*
> *Eastern sparkle of the Sunset River follows*
> *the Yangtze's flow.*
> *Leaning on staff, lamenting the times—who*
> *am I, after all?*
> *As bloody tears splash the sky, I turn my*
> *gray head home.*

In this poem, "cloven gorges" evokes the legendary Yu, founder of China's first hereditary dynasty, who supposedly opened the cliffs at Qutang to let the Yangtze through. How these 3,000-foot-high, vertical, thick-bedded limestone gates were formed, along with the gorges that lead eastward to the lake-studded Hubei plains, has since been investigated by modern-day geologists. According to the British scientist G. B. Barbour, who surveyed the region in the 1930s, the Yangtze formerly flowed on an extensive eroded surface (a peneplain) that developed after the main folding of the underlying rock. Subsequently, the land was uplifted and the river carved through it to create the gorges. J. S. Lee, the founder of modern geology in China, offered another theory: What is now the middle Yangtze was once two rivers flowing in opposite directions, eastward and westward, divided by an anticline (an arched fold of rock). Erosion of this divider allowed the east-flowing river to capture the west-flowing one, unifying them in an eastward flow.

Walking on the path along the north side of Qutang Gorge, which is five miles long and at most 500 feet wide, I saw the heavily folded rock up close—towering slabs of limestone tilted at sharp angles. About halfway through, I passed Wind Box Gorge, where the path cut into the cliff's vertical wall. Until a few decades ago, this was a "tracker's gallery," used by gangs of up to 300 men whose job it was to tow junks, sampans, and other boats through rapids flowing against them with a speed of up to ten knots.

The innumerable crevices, caves, and shelters in this rugged limestone region led archeologist N. C. Nelson, of the American Museum of Natural History, to speculate that they contained "perhaps the whole story of the Old Man of Asia." In 1925, as part of the Museum's Central Asiatic Expedition, he traveled to the Three Gorges, "trying to see the entire environmental setting from the point of view of an imaginary primitive man; to guess which of the caves and shelters he would most likely have occupied." Instead, he found many of them inhabited by modern humans. "In the end," he wrote, "after scanning more than two hundred miles of the Yangtze trough proper and traversing in more hasty fashion a similar distance in the back

In Fengjie, above and right, China's economy still relies on hard human labor.

country, mainly to the south of the river, we were in possession of only the faintest suggestions that prehistoric man had ever been near the caves!"

Although Nelson failed to find the "Old Man of Asia," his intuition seems to have been correct. Ten years ago, paleoanthropologists found a fragment of a mandible and a single tooth at Dragon Hill Cave, about fifteen miles south of Qutang Gorge. These are now being hailed as evidence of the earliest Asians yet (see *Natural History,* December 1995).

In Wushan, a city situated just before the entrance of the next gorge, I met Zhuang Kongshao and Liu Mingxin, two anthropologists from the Central University for Nationalities in Beijing. Traveling upstream from Yichang, they had been meeting with local writers, archeologists, and historians, pursuing several projects—among them a study of the Tujia minority, who claim descent from the Ba people. Zhuang and Liu invited me along to their next destination, Wuxi, a little town fifty miles up the Daning River, a northern tributary of the Yangtze.

The Daning, with its Three Little Gorges, offers a popular side excursion for tourists. We left early in the morning with a motorized sampan whose shady operator soon abandoned us in favor of something

more profitable—a stranded tourist group. Despite our protests, we were transferred to a wooden cargo sampan to continue our journey. I sat beside a case of goods imprinted with the characters for "amusement tiles," a common euphemism for mah-jongg, which, despite being frowned upon officially, is played everywhere. As the sampan sputtered peacefully along, we saw plentiful birdlife along the banks, and once even spotted a group of golden monkeys. The clear, shallow water and narrow passage made the perpendicular limestone cliffs along the pristine Daning even more dramatic than those of the monumental Yangtze gorges. High up all along the

3. THE REGION

western wall, spaced four to six feet apart, ran a single row of square holes. These were what remained of the bamboo pipeline for brine and the plank road that once served as an important military, commercial, and cultural conduit between northern and central China. During the Tang Dynasty (A.D. 618–906) the concubine Yang Guifei had her favorite lichees sent fresh from Fuling along this route. We stopped to eat lunch in Dachang, and reached Wuxi, above the Three Little Gorges, late in the evening.

The ultimate goal of our excursion was the cliff graves at Jingzhu Gorge. Li Ming, from Wuxi's Cultural Relics Office, took us there the next morning. With binoculars, we spotted twenty-four wooden coffins wedged into horizontal crevices in the cliff wall, about 1,000 feet above the river. According to archeologists from Sichuan University, who "excavated" one coffin in 1980 and another in 1988, they date from as far back as the Warring States period (403–321 B.C.) and were a burial form used by a people called Pu. Exactly how they got there remains a mystery, as is the reason for this peculiar manner of burial—although Li Ming suggests it may simply have been a way to display wealth.

On our way back to Wuxi we passed by the desolate salt-producing town of Ning Chang and saw some pensioners playing mah-jongg in the sun. An old lady greeted us. "This used to be a very good place," she said with tears in her eyes. A year or so before, the salt factory had finally been shut down after some 2,000 years. In times gone by, Ning Chang had flourished as the center of the region's economy, teeming with inhabitants from every province in China. Produced in only a limited number of places, salt held a position in the country's economic life commensurate with its indispensibility to humans. Merchants accumulated fortunes trading the commodity, while the taxes levied upon it provided the imperial government with a major source of revenue.

East of the Three Gorges, the whole Yangtze Valley received its supplies from factories in Jiangsu Province. Because of the distance and the difficulty of navigating up the river, however, Sichuan produced its own salt from brine wells drilled

The city of Wushan, above, stretches out before Wu Gorge.

as much as 3,000 feet deep. Ning Chang's prosperity arose from the fluke that it possessed a saltwater spring. Furnaces were used to extract the salt, and since wood fuel produced the best salt, the forest around Ning Chang had been chopped down until no trees remained; then coal, which made the salt blackish and slightly bitter, had to be used instead.

Back in Wushan, on a chilly morning I boarded the *Double Dragon,* one of the hundreds of passenger boats that ply the Yangtze from Chongqing to Shanghai. The rising sun cast shafts of light across the deep, shadowed ravine. In a few hours, the boat passed through the twenty-five miles of Wu Gorge and down the next thirty miles of river, making stops along the way. At the entrance to the last and longest gorge, forty-seven-mile-long Xiling Gorge, I went for a walk uphill. I met a lucky orange farmer whose house and groves were situated just above the coming high-water level. "We're going to buy a boat," he told me.

The trip down Xiling Gorge the following day took about eight hours. As the boat neared the end of the Three Gorges, I viewed the immense earth-moving activity at the dam site, which has been transformed into a lunarlike dust bowl. On the

northern bank, the bedrock was being blasted to accommodate the five shiplocks that will raise and lower vessels 330 feet.

Treacherous rapids in the Xiling Gorge have already been tamed by dredging and by the low-level Gezhouba Dam, twenty-seven miles downstream from the Three Gorges Dam site. Completed in 1989, Gezhouba is a hydroelectric dam that will also serve as a regulating dam when the new project is complete.

In the fast-flowing waters below the Gezhouba Dam, the Chinese sturgeon—whose fossil record extends back at least 140 million years—is trying to adapt to the new obstacle. The sturgeon's old spawning grounds were more than 600 miles farther upstream. Mature fish returned there as often as every three years from the China and Yellow Seas. Efforts have been made to capture fish below the dam and get them to release their eggs by treating them with hormones. The artificially raised hatchlings can then be returned to the river. Research also shows that some fish are now spawning at sites below Gezhouba Dam. If the sturgeon is adjusting to its new situation, one reason could be that it is not so new. Since the sturgeon is probably older than the gorges, this part of the river just might have been the place where it spawned before Yu clove the gorge.

Russia and Japan: Drifting in Opposite Directions

While the dispute over the Kuril Islands has sparked heated exchanges between and within Russia and Japan, the real obstacle to improved relations is Russian domestic instability

SERGEI V. CHUGROV

THE PART OF RUSSIA THAT FACES JAPAN IS called in Russian *dalnii vostok,* which means "far east." A stretch of Japanese coast on the opposite side of the Sea of Japan traditionally bears the Japanese name *omote-no Nihon,* which means "Japan's backyard." Whether both countries can turn around and finally face each other is an open question.

The conventional view holds that, in order to promote mutually beneficial relations, Moscow and Tokyo must resolve the conflict over four disputed islands in the Kurils, a conflict that has left Moscow without internationally recognized sovereignty over the other, undisputed islands in the Kuril chain or over the territory of southern Sakhalin.[1] Analysis of the economic and political developments of the 1990s demonstrates, however, that the territorial conflict is not the main cause of poor relations but is an intermediate factor in a downward spiral originating in Russian domestic problems and resulting in markedly strained relations. Moscow and Tokyo have not tried to solve the territorial issue because, for reasons of their own, neither is sufficiently interested in improving relations. In the future, after Russia's domestic situation improves, Russia and Japan will be in a position to resolve the conflicts that currently divide them.

Russian domestic developments concerning security issues appear to be more influential than international variables in shaping the political climate in the region. The source of new trends is not so much the international environment in general or Japan in particular but rather the exploitation of those international factors by domestic forces in Russia. Some members of the Russian military establishment, discouraged by recent military cuts, have used the exacerbation of international tensions to their advantage in their struggle to restore the military's former prestige and place in the social hierarchy. Because of its highly centralized organization and specialized expertise, the military holds an influence in Russia disproportionate to its size. Military officials focus on the risk of losing the islands in order to underscore the security threat that Russia faces and to try to maintain their budgets. There are also political entrepreneurs who could benefit from coupling national sentiments with the military's vested interests by pressuring the government over the island issue.

LOST CHANCES?

Students of comparative politics divide countries into "strong states" and "weak states" — those that have a strong capacity for autonomous action and those that lack such ability.[2] Traditionally, Russia was a "strong state" ruling over a "weak society," since civic society was never truly developed and social groups had little ability to influence state policy. However, with the breakup of the Soviet

The author is grateful to James Mayall and Margot Light of the London School of Economics Centre for International Studies and to Susan Pharr of Harvard University's Program on U.S.-Japanese Relations, who created a constructive atmosphere for this research.

[1] For details on the political, economic, and legal implications of the Kurils problem for Russia, see Graham Allison, Hiroshi Kimura, and Konstantin Sarkisov, *Beyond Cold War to Trilateral Cooperation in the Asia-Pacific Region: Scenarios for a New Relationship Between Japan, Russia, and the United States* (Cambridge, Massachusetts: The Kennedy School of Government, 1994).

[2] Peter Gourevitch, "The Second Image Reversed," *International Organization,* no. 4, August 1978, p. 901.

Union, Russia has passed through a period of upheaval and turmoil that has left it with both a weak state and a weak society. A country needs either a strong state (democratic or authoritarian) or a strong society (consensus among powerful groups) in order to solve issues of great importance, including questions of territory. The absence of resolute state or social actors on the Russian domestic political scene prevents the country from arriving at a solution to the conflict with Japan.

Could former Soviet leader Mikhail Gorbachev or current Russian President Boris Yeltsin have solved the Kurils problem? Because governmental structures are weak and public institutions are fragmented, the role of individual leaders assumes crucial importance. That enhanced role enabled Gorbachev to pursue a decisive course in foreign policy. However, the democratization of Russia has led to a complex and unstable foreign-policy-making process. The West's personification of the democratic changes in Russia in one single figure was repeatedly used against first Gorbachev and then Yeltsin by their domestic foes. One of both leaders' main goals was to evade the "puppet of the West" tag that the opposition pinned on them. The dispute with Japan came to be seen as a symbolic test of a Russian leader's ability to stand up for Russian national interests.

Gorbachev showed an active interest in improving relations with Japan: in 1990, he declared he would make "drastic concessions."[3] However, signs of contention were apparent. In January 1991, some three months before Gorbachev visited Tokyo, his spokesman found it necessary to deny a report that the Soviet Union and Japan had reached a secret agreement providing for the disputed islands to be given back to Japan in return for Japanese investments in the stumbling Soviet economy.

Progress did not hinge on Gorbachev's actions alone. During the six years that he was in power, four different Japanese prime ministers held office, which partly explains why Gorbachev failed to produce a major breakthrough in relations. In addition, while Gorbachev was focused on crucial domestic problems, the Japanese leadership was not sufficiently insistent on exploring channels for improving relations, and — in sharp contrast to developments in Central Europe — the opportunity to solve the problems inherited from the past was lost. In the mid-1980s, when Gorbachev came to power, Japanese Prime Minister Yasuhiro Nakasone appeared to be a leader capable of bold compromises who enjoyed substantial backing from both the elite and the general population. The Soviet media, however, attacked him more bitterly than they had any other Japanese leader, calling him militarist and chauvinist.[4] Despite Nakasone's strong diplomatic style, his role in shaping policy toward

Moscow diminished over time.[5] In 1991, Gorbachev lost his control over foreign policy and new, nationalist-minded social actors with better-articulated interests emerged.

There is considerable evidence to suggest that Yeltsin could have improved relations with Japan in 1991, immediately after he emerged victorious in the wake of the abortive putsch in Moscow. Late that year, Russia semiofficially confirmed the validity of a 1956 declaration that contained a commitment to return two of the Kuril islands to Japan. Some researchers, among them Tsuyoshi Hasegawa, emphasize Yeltsin's personal motivations and ambitions: "Riding on the crest of his popularity after the collapse of the coup, Yeltsin was eager to seize the Japan issue in order to undercut Gorbachev's authority further by intruding in bilateral negotiations with Japan."[6]

The failure of Yeltsin's policy in 1991–1992 represents a lost opportunity to heal relations with Japan. 1992 was clearly a watershed year. The ability of different pressure groups to mobilize public opinion was especially evident that summer as Yeltsin prepared for an official visit to Japan. On 10 August 1992, the Kurils Defense Committee was formed as part of the president's administration. At that time, Yeltsin was fully engaged in pressing ahead with economic reform in order to secure multibillion-dollar credits from the West. The real or perceived domestic risks for the Russian president exceeded the possible benefits of unblocking relations with Japan. The result was the postponement of Yeltsin's October 1992 visit with only four days' notice. Russian officials close to the president used every possible occasion to emphasize Russia's independence in order to avoid accusations of any intention to sell the country out.

Yeltsin's rescheduled trip to Japan was considered a success. On 13 October 1993, Yeltsin and Prime Minister Morihiro Hosokawa signed two important documents — the Tokyo Declaration on Japanese-Russian Relations and the Declaration on the Future Outlook of Relations

Japanese observers point to some discrepancies between the Russian president's and prime minister's foreign policies.

Between Japan and the Russian Federation in the Areas of Trade, Economy, and Science and Technology. The first agreement contains two noteworthy statements that could provide good opportunities for unblocking relations. According to the document, the two sides "share the recognition that the democratic and economic reforms under way in the Russian Federation are of tremendous signifi-

---

[3]TASS, 27 July 1990.

[4]Dmitrii Petrov, "Rossiya i Yaponiya: stereotipy vospriyatiya" [Russia and Japan: Stereotypes of Perception], *Znakomtes — Yaponiya*, no. 6, October 1994, p. 49.

[5]Gilbert Rozman, *Japan's Response to the Gorbachev Era, 1985–1991: A Rising Superpower Views a Declining One* (Princeton: Princeton University Press, 1992), pp. 20–21.

[6]Tsuyoshi Hasegawa, "Russo-Japanese Relations in the New Environment — Implications of Continuing Stalemate," in Tsuyoshi Hasegawa, Jonathan Haslam, and Andrew Kuchins, eds., *Russia and Japan: An Unresolved Dilemma Between Distant Neighbors* (Berkeley, California: University of California, 1993), p. 420.

cance not only for the people of Russia but also for the entire world." In addition, "all treaties and other international agreements between Japan and the Soviet Union continue to apply between Japan and the Russian Federation." Tokyo expected that Moscow would recognize the need to resolve the Kurils dispute in order to sign a peace treaty. Moscow, in turn, could count on Tokyo's support for the democratic process in Russia.

However, all did not proceed so smoothly. Within Yeltsin's entourage, there were differences of interpretation over the meaning of Russia's commitment to stick to "all treaties and other international agreements." And an embarrassingly timed dumping of liquid nuclear waste into the Sea of Japan by Russian naval vessels took place only days after Yeltsin's return. Planned long before the visit, the dumping was not a show of bad faith but rather a symptom of poor control over foreign policy and lack of coordination among Russian agencies.

NATIONALISM AND INTRIGUE

Talks on resolving the territorial dispute, originally scheduled for January 1994, were postponed because of the confusion that followed the Russian elections of December 1993. The window of opportunity almost closed after Yeltsin declared on 11 January 1994 that Russia was still a "great power," thus providing convincing evidence of a nationalist shift in the Russian establishment.[7] A planned visit to Russia by Japan's then-foreign minister, Tsutomo Hata, was canceled because newly empowered Russian nationalists had taken a hard line on the territorial issue. Russian First Deputy Prime Minister Oleg Soskovets's visit to Tokyo in fall 1994 brought no breakthrough. The lethargy in bilateral relations was interrupted only by Russian border guards' periodic use of force against Japanese fishermen in Russian waters. Those incidents served as grounds for further mutual accusations. Furthermore, on 31 May 1995, Yeltsin sniped at Japan over its offers of relief following the Sakhalin earthquake. He accused Japan of intending to use the aid to strengthen its hand in the territorial dispute. It seemed apparent that the president, with an eye to the upcoming elections, intended his uncharitable remarks for the ears of Russia's powerful nationalist lobby.[8]

Nationalist tendencies in Russia have deep roots and threaten the chances for reaching a better understanding with Japan. With the disintegration of the Soviet state, Russia has suffered an intense crisis of national integrity. Of all the newly independent states it has arguably had the most difficulty creating a modern national identify. The voluntary relinquishing of even a small part of its territory would mean great national humiliation. As a result, the territorial dispute with Japan has become both a target for the nationalistic passions of the general population and a trump card in political games. The idea of striking a bargain with Japan (economic aid in exchange for the return of the is-

lands) only feeds critics' fears of an anti-Russian conspiracy. The opposition claims that financial assistance is in fact designed to render Russia submissive to external dictates[9] and emphasizes that Japan will make Russia pay a very high political price for economic help by insisting on territorial concessions.[10] The hardliners managed to make the Kuril problem a litmus test to weigh the willingness of the leaders and the general population to stand up for Russia's "national interests," playing upon the emotions of a people humiliated by the striking events of recent years.

The impact of this nationalist campaign on the young generation has been especially strong.[11] In a May survey of the general population of Moscow, 6.7 percent of all respondents considered Japan an enemy (after the United States, Iraq, Iran and Libya), whereas among young people, that figure was about 18 percent[12] Another poll, a survey of the future foreign policy elite—graduate students of the Moscow Institute of International Relations and of the humanities departments of Moscow State University—had interesting results. Japan was cited by the second-largest number of respondents as a potential enemy of Russia. The United States was named by 11 percent, Japan by 7 percent, the Baltic states by 7 percent, Iran and Turkey by 5 percent each, and Poland and China by 1 percent each.

Table 1 shows the attitudes of the future foreign policy elite toward the territorial issue. None of the students surveyed favored the return either of all four disputed islands or of only Shikotan and Habomai, which Moscow had been ready to return to Japan under the 1956 Soviet-Japanese Declaration. This suggests that there is little reason to expect Russia's position to change when these young foreign policy specialists move up into positions of authority.

DOMESTIC SQUABBLES

The Kurils issue notwithstanding, the main reason for the poor state of Russian-Japanese relations is the constant instability and unpredictability of Russian domestic politics. On the Japanese side, Tokyo is extremely sensitive about political instability in other countries and is therefore hesitant to invest in or donate funds to Russia. The Japanese are using the issue of the islands as a convenient excuse for their unwillingness to pursue deeper economic involvement with Russia. According to various experts, the Japanese are far more concerned about political stability in Russia than are the Americans or the Europeans, who emphasize democratization.[13] Authoritarian trends in Russia have provoked less dismay in Tokyo than in Washington or European capitals, since Japan, which is not as

---

[7]*Rossiiskaya gazeta,* 12 January 1994.
[8]Richard Balmforth, "Yeltsin Snubs Japan Over Offer for Aid," *The Moscow Tribune,* 1 June 1995, p. 2.

---

[9]Vladimir Zhirinovsky, *O sudbakh Rossii, Chast 2: Poslednii brosok na yug* [About Russia's Destinies, Part 2: The Last Surge to the South] (Moscow: Agentstvo Rait, 1993), pp. 62, 91.
[10]Interview with Sergei Baburin, leader of the All-Russian People's Union, 30 August 1993.
[11]See Georgi Arbatov, "Eurasia Letter: A New Cold War?" *Foreign Policy,* no. 95, Summer 1994, p. 92.
[12]*Segodnya,* 9 June 1995, p. 9.
[13]Interview with Kyoji Komachi, former head of the Japanese Foreign Ministry's Russian division and current consul general in London, 5 May 1995.

3. THE REGION

Westernized as is commonly asserted, is more tolerant than the West of an authoritarian pattern of rule.[14]

On the Russian side, foreign policy has become the battlefield in a bitter struggle between the opposition and the government. Competition among branches of government for control over the decision-making process has rendered Russia's foreign policy priorities ambiguous and its political behavior simultaneously unpredictable and inflexible.[15] The struggle over foreign policy is part of the broader problem of the lack of a clear-cut division of powers among the president, cabinet, and parliament. Different branches of power continue to make conflicting statements and moves regarding foreign policy, as no clear division of responsibility exists among them. This summer's confrontation between Yeltsin and the State Duma in the wake of the Budennovsk raid has demonstrated that even though the constitution grants Yeltsin considerable authority (for example, the power to dissolve the Federal Assembly), in practice, he is wary of exerting that authority when the result could be a new, more conservative legislature. Political instability will be fueled throughout the year by campaigns for the upcoming elections to the Federal Assembly and, next year, to the presidency. In this atmosphere of bitter struggle, any changes in Russian foreign policy that could be favorable to the resolution of the territorial dispute with Japan are unlikely. The problem of the Kurils is one of the most contentious issues between the executive and legislative branches.

Another major domestic constraint on Russian leadership is the poor institutional performance of foreign policy decision-making mechanisms. The short record of Russian-Japanese relations in 1991–1995 provides many examples of clear and well-articulated statements on the Kurils by the president, prime minister, foreign minister, presidential press secretary, and others. But all those statements directly contradict each other.[16] There is some evidence that the struggle over strategy in Russian-Japanese relations has resulted in intrigues and provocations in the highest echelons of executive power. Yeltsin, for example, announced his plan to visit Japan at a Kremlin awards ceremony on 12 April 1993, as he decorated Rokuro Saito, president of the All-Japan World War II Internees Association, with the Order of Friendship of Peoples. This ceremony was supposed to have taken place a month earlier, during then-Vice President Aleksandr Rutskoi's visit to Tokyo. But in February, Rutskoi had been accused in the Russian press of planning to go to Japan at the invitation of a small organization that was far from "big politics."[17] Those accusations, which caused Yeltsin to cancel Rutskoi's visit, looked very much like a deliberate leak.

Another shocking leak was an unsigned governmental document containing a proposal to make territorial concessions to Japan. A commentary on the document, published in May 1993 by the liberal daily *Komsomolskaya pravda,* said the information had been provided by Sergei Baburin, one of the most active opposition leaders in the parliament.[18] On 18 May, Russia's Foreign Ministry denied that there had been any change in its policy toward Japan. The published document, the ministry said, was neither a fake nor a top-secret document, but rather a working paper analyzing one of the alternative scenarios on resolving the territorial issue. However, this document was used by the opposition to stir public passions.

Japanese observers point to some discrepancies between the president and the prime minister in the foreign policy sphere. On an August 1993 visit to Khabarovsk and the Kurils during his first term in office, Russian Prime Minister Viktor Chernomyrdin said that Russia would never transfer the four disputed islands to Japan and that discussion of their fate was a nonissue.[19] Remarks by Yeltsin himself did little to clarify the problem; he said that Chernomyrdin's statements reflected only one of a number of options that were being considered by the Russian government. After founding the political bloc Our Home Is Russia last April — and especially after mediating in the Chechen hostage crisis in June — Chernomyrdin emerged as a more powerful and independent figure who repeatedly tried to amend the Foreign Ministry's positions.

Table 1: Attitudes of the Future Foreign Policy Elite Toward Territorial Dispute with Japan

Q: "What should the Russian leadership do with the Kuril Islands?"

	MGIMO*	MGU**	Avg.
not return a single island	69	62	63
proclaim joint sovereignty over them	21	23	23
lease the islands to Japan	4	2	3
return only two of the islands	0	0	0

*Moscow Institute of International Relations   **Moscow State University

Source: G.A. Drobot (Moscow State University, Department of Sociology), "Budushchee vneshnei politiki Rossii" [Russia's Future Foreign Policy], Mirovaya Ekonomika i Mezhdunarodnye Otnosheniya [The World Economy and International Relation] November 1995 (forthcoming)

Russian Foreign Minister Andrei Kozyrev has become a target of open attacks from extreme nationalists and ex-communists as well as a new group of national-democrats — and, probably as a result, he kept silent on his initial plans for settlement with Japan.[20] Among the negative factors that eventually surfaced as major impediments to Russian-Japanese rapprochement was the discrepancy between Yeltsin's position and the discredited "Kunadze option." Deputy Foreign Minister Georgii Kunadze had proposed giving two islands (Shikotan and Habomai) to Japan in return for negotiation over the status of the other two.[21] But his abrupt transfer to the post of ambassador to South Korea in the early fall of 1993 — obvi-

[14]Edwin O. Reischauer, *The Japanese Today: Change and Continuity* (Cambridge, Massachusetts: Harvard University Press, 1988), p. 172.
[15]Heinz Timmermann, *Profil und Prioritaeten der Aussenpolitik Russlands unter Jelzin* [Profile and Priorities of Russian Foreign Policy under Yeltsin] (Cologne: Bundesinstitut fuer ostwissenschaftliche und internationale Studien, Bericht 21, 1992).
[16]Yevgenii Bazhanov, "Diplomata vsyakii mozhet obidet" [Anyone Can Offend a Diplomat], *Segodnya,* 23 June 1995, p. 9.
[17]*Izvestiya* and *Komsomolskaya pravda,* 9 February 1993.

[18]*Komsomolskaya pravda,* 16 May 1993.
[19]See *Izvestiya,* 18, 20, and 21 August 1993.
[20]See, for example, Sergei Stankevich, "Derzhava v poiskakh sebya" [A Power in Search of Itself], *Nezavisimaya gazeta,* 28 March 1992; and Nina Petrova, "Vneshnyaya politika Rossii dolzhna byt prezidentskoi" [Russia's Foreign Policy Must Be Presidential], ibid., 17 and 18 May 1995.
[21]For details see Hasegawa, "Russo-Japanese Relations ... ," pp. 420–421.

ously a demotion or a deliberate sacrifice — signified that nationalist forces had gained the upper hand.

Disputes between the Foreign Ministry and the Security Council have created one more line of rivalry over definition of foreign policy priorities and play a prominent role in Russian-Japanese relations. The Security Council's general foreign policy concept, adopted in April 1993, contained two controversial points related to Japan: that the integrity of Russia's territory is considered relevant to the national interests of the country and that Russia attaches great significance to the normalization of its relations with Japan and to continuing the search for a territorial settlement, as long as that settlement does not harm Russian interests. The definition of territorial integrity as a national interest combined with the refusal to reach a settlement that goes against those interests would seem to rule out any Foreign Ministry compromise that involved relinquishing some of the islands.

LACK OF STABILITY

As long as Russian domestic politics and foreign policy remain volatile, no progress in relations with Japan is possible. Russian political instability fosters caution in the Japanese government. Japanese leaders see no reason to deal with a country with shifting positions, changing laws, no clear allies, and changeable political rules. Constraints for Japanese assistance to Russia lie not so much in the sphere of bilateral diplomatic relations as in the chaotic state of Russia's economy and politics. That also explains the government's unwillingness to guarantee private investments in Russia. The Japanese business community generally avoids insecure contracts and risky investments that have no government guarantees.

The Japanese react primarily to economic indicators, whereas Americans and other Westerners are more attracted by hopes for democratic change in Russia. According to many Japanese researchers, the Russian economy is a nightmare and is not currently of interest to Japanese business. Even if the current production slump is halted in 1995–1996, stabilization will occur at only about 40 percent of 1989 production levels.[22] Ambiguous or unstable government regulations and policies are among the top-priority problems.[23] The present abnormal situation — in which criminal groups enjoy control over much of wholesale and retail trade, investment capital is frozen in bank accounts, and trade payments are often not honored — hinders investment and trade negotiations. It is not, however, so much the corruption and "mafiaization" of Russia that makes Japanese entrepreneurs suffer: they would be ready to follow any rules, if only they were clearly defined. But as it is, investors are intimidated by the individualist entrepreneurial business culture that has sprung up in Russia — it seems to have no rules at all and oscillates between sheer anarchy and bouts of political interference. As a result, Japanese private

investments in the Russian economy stand at next to nothing — less than 0.1 percent of Japan's total overseas investment.[24] The attitudes of Japanese business toward the prospects in this field are marked by growing pessimism. The dominant point of view in Japan is that there is little to be gained from further economic contact with Russia. Therefore, top Japanese officials are not under any domestic pressure to find a way out of the political deadlock.

RUSSIAN DISINTEREST

As a result of economic decay and political instability, there is a lack of domestic groups that could pressure the Russian leadership to improve relations. Those groups that are willing to pay a price — the surrender of the islands — in order to improve Russian-Japanese relations do not enjoy much political influence. Yegor Gaidar, for example, still adheres to the principle that Russia must "restore justice and keep the Soviet Union's promise of 40 years" in regard to Japan.[25] His Russia's Democratic Choice party, however, is steadily losing political influence, especially since breaking with Yeltsin over the Chechen war.

The "new wave" Russian entrepreneurs, who are generally interested in opening up their country, are potential advocates of normalizing relations with Japan. Tokyo is focusing its nominal assistance on this category of entrepreneurs because of their ability to think logically yet unconventionally and their relative freedom from communist blinkers. For the moment, however, horizontal links between those entrepreneurs within Russia are rare. Lobbies and pressure groups that could support them in governmental circles as well as in parliament are still in their infancy and cannot yet defend entrepreneurs' interests. Lobbying today often simply means bribing politicians. Although they often engage in behind-the-scenes lobbying of this sort, most business people are reluctant to become directly involved in politics.

The majority of Russian industries have little interest in bettering relations with Japan. One might think that Russian industrialists would exert pressure upon their government to attract more foreign investment, lowering the cost of capital in Russia. But in a poll of 312 top industrial directors, only 12 percent considered direct foreign investments to be a likely answer to their problems. Presumably they either dismissed the option as unrealistic or were wary of the strings they assume foreign investors would attach.[26] But those business groups that want to

---

[22]Otto Latsis, "On the Verge of Success," *The Moscow Times*, 9 June 1995, p. 8.

[23]K. Naito, "Posto-Eritzin-no Daitoryo wa Dare ka?" [Who Will Be President After Yeltsin?], *Sekai Shuho*, 1 February 1994, pp. 14–15.

[24]Ministry of Finance, *Direct Overseas Investment Recorded in Fiscal Year 1994* (Tokyo: Foreign Press Center, 1995), p. 3.

[25]Yegor Gaidar, *Rossiya XXI veka: Ne mirovoi zhandarm, a forpost demokratii v Evrazii* [21st-Century Russia: Not a World Policeman, but a Stronghold of Democracy in Eurasia], *Izvestiya*, May 1995, p. 4.

[26]Leonid Kosals, VCIOM and Tsentr Economicheskoi Informatsii, *Ekspress-analiz rezultatov oprosa direktorov krupnykh predpriyatii Rossii* [Express Analysis of the Survey of Large-Industry Directors], 24 February 1994, p. 14. See also Peter Rutland, *The Economic Foundation of Foreign Policy in the States of the Former Soviet Union*, paper presented at the Harvard University Russian Research Center Seminar, November 1993, p. 21.

keep the islands in Russian hands are organized around shared values and appear to form cohesive, clanlike networks of trust and affiliation.[27]

Oil and especially gas lobbies in Russia generally favor maintaining an open economy. At the same time, however, they want to protect the domestic market from competition from world oil giants. The electronics industry favors protectionism because it cannot survive competition with Japanese products (with the exception of a few firms affiliated with the aircraft-construction industry). Machine-building industries are split: space programs are doing well and support open competition, but other engineering is underdeveloped and protectionist. A vociferous agrarian lobby with well-articulated protectionist interests is strongly repre-

sented in parliament and has a proponent in Deputy Prime Minister Anatolii Zaveryukha, who exerts constant pressure on the president and the government, with some success. For example, Japanese observers were shocked in July when Yeltsin yielded to the agrarian lobby's demands to increase import tariffs on foreign foodstuffs.[28]

The Russian military-industrial complex is the most spectacular lobby. Military industries have become more protectionist since Western countries showed resistance to the idea of sharing their arms markets with Russia. While in late 1980, the Soviet Union controlled 38 percent of world arms markets and the United States controlled 20 percent, by 2000, Russia is expected to control no more than 5 to 6 percent and the United States about 60 percent of global

---

[27]See David Stark, "The Great Transformation? Social Change in Eastern Europe," *Contemporary Sociology,* May 1992, no. 3, pp. 300–303.

[28]Svetlana Lyuboshits, "Ostanovite prezidenta" [Stop the President], *Moskovskii komsomolets,* 9 June 1995, pp.1–2.

Struggle Over the Kuril Islands

The Kuril Islands have been a bone of contention between Russia and Japan for more than a century.[1] The 56-island chain stretches south from the Kamchatka peninsula to just a few miles off the northern Japanese island of Hokkaido. The 1855 Treaty of Shimoda recognized Japanese sovereignty over the four southernmost islands but granted the northern islands to Russia. In the 1875 Treaty of St. Petersburg, Russia ceded the northern islands to Japan in return for Russian control over the large island of Sakhalin. In 1905, after the Russo-Japanese War, the Japanese regained control over the southern half of Sakhalin. At the end of World War II, under the Potsdam Declarations, Japan handed Sakhalin and the whole Kuril chain over to the Soviet Union. Repossession of at least the southern Kurils became an important factor in Japanese politics, but Cold War pressures dashed hopes of a compromise deal. A peace declaration signed in 1956 promised the return of the two southernmost islands to Japan upon conclusion of a comprehensive peace treaty between Russia and Japan — which has yet to be concluded.

TREASURED ISLANDS — *The Russian military claims the Kurils are vital to Russian security and has lobbied the government strongly to retain all four of the disputed islands.*

The islands are important to Russia for economic reasons, such as fishing, as well as for military purposes: they provide a forward air-defense screen and guarantee ice-free access for Russian submarines from the Sea of Okhotsk to the Pacific Ocean.[2] There are also the islands' 25,000 Russian inhabitants to consider. Above all, Soviet intransigence was rooted in a symbolic desire not to hand over even an inch of territory, which would have meant opening the Pandora's box of border revisions that were put into place after World War II. During the Gorbachev era, various compromise proposals were floated for resolving the Kurils issue, but the essential Soviet position remained unchanged.[3] Moscow blamed Japan for the impasse, arguing that domestic politics had turned the issue into a "sacred cow" that prevented Japan from seeking a pragmatic solution.[4] The Japanese cannot help but feel exasperated by the fact that perestroika and the Soviet Union's collapse brought about a revision of the postwar settlement in Europe — in the form of the unification of Germany — while Japan, which did not fight the Soviet Union directly until the closing weeks of the war, is denied the return of its northern territories.

— Peter Rutland

---

[1]Stephen Foye, "The Struggle Over Russia's Kuril Islands Policy," *RFE/RL Research Report,* no. 36, 11 September 1992, pp. 34–40.
[2]Andrei Krivtsov, "Russia and the Far East," *International Affairs* (Moscow), January 1993, pp. 77–84.
[3]Stephen Foye, "Russo-Japanese Relations," *RFE-RL Research Report,* no. 25, 24 June 1994, pp. 26–36.
[4]Krivtsov, "Russia … ," p. 81.

weapons trade.[29] Therefore, the military-industrial lobby has accused the West of uncooperativeness and has nurtured Russia's recent wave of nationalism. The territorial issue has become a trump card for the military and a focal point of tension.

There were, however, military grounds for objecting to the return of the islands. The Russian military argues that the active presence of the U.S. Navy in the Far East poses a threat to Russia and that Russia therefore needs the Kuril Islands for strategic purposes. However, Tokyo will not jeopardize relations with the United States for the sake of better relations with Russia. Military alliance with Washington is far more important to Japan than is striking a deal with Russia to win control of the islands. So, in the spring of 1992, Russia's military leadership seized the perceived opportunity and began what appeared to be a campaign to undermine Yeltsin's initiatives on the islands: the military consistently protested the downsizing of far eastern bases and the cuts in the military budget. The campaign culminated at the end of July with the publication by the General Staff and the Naval Main Staff of harshly worded strategic evaluations. Admiral Georgii Gurinov, who was appointed commander of the Pacific Fleet in 1993, opposed making territorial concessions to Japan that, he argued, could undermine Russian strategic interests in the region. Both docu-ments warned of dire consequences if Russia were to make concessions to Tokyo.[30]

In the international context, the territorial issue is not such a serious problem, and resolving it would not drastically improve the political and economic relations between Russia and Japan. Politicians in each country have used the issue to stir nationalist fervor, but it is only one component in a complex set of factors discouraging closer ties with Tokyo. Domestic factors in both countries overshadow the territorial issue: in fact, the territorial conflict is less the cause than a symptom of bad relations. Only the stabilization of the political and economic situation in Russia is likely to lead to improved relations.

The return of the disputed islands to Japan would not in itself destabilize Russian domestic politics. However, one cannot rule out the possibility that it could trigger an unpredictable chain reaction inside Russia that could eventually destroy all chances for democracy and market reform. Japan is aware of this possibility and is reluctant to risk such an outcome. Still, Moscow and Tokyo cannot shelve the problem indefinitely. The continuation of bilateral talks is crucial to overcoming a new wave of distrust between the two countries.

IN95013 25 AUGUST 1991

---

[29]EKO-TASS, *Finansovye izvestiya,* 1 June 1995, p. 1. See also Lyudmila Pertsevaya, "Oboronka vykhodit iz shtopora" [Defense Industry Gets out of Crisis], *Moskovskie novosti,* 4–11 June 1995, p. 29.

[30]The texts of the two documents were published in *Nezavisimaya gazeta,* 30 July 1992.

Spatial Interaction and Mapping

Geography is the study not only of places in their own right but also of the ways in which places interact. Places are connected by highways, airline routes, telecommunication systems, and even thoughts. These forms of spatial interaction are an important part of the work of geographers.

In "Transportation and Urban Growth: The Shaping of the American Metropolis," Peter Muller considers transportation systems, analyzing their impact on the growth of American cities. Next are featured the latest developments in high-speed rail transportation in Europe and Japan. Then Peter Bogucki traces the diffusion of agriculture from the Near East to Europe. "Raising the Dead Sea" covers a planned canal linking the Red Sea and the Dead Sea. The next two selections address aspects of Caucasian and Hispanic migration and population redistribution in the United States.

It is essential that geographers be able to describe the detailed spatial patterns of the world. Neither photographs nor words could do the job adequately, because they literally capture too much of the detail of a place. There is no better way to present many of the topics analyzed in geography than with maps. Maps and geography go hand in hand. Although maps are used in other disciplines, their association with geography is the most highly developed.

A map is a graphic that presents a generalized and scaled-down view of particular occurrences or themes in an area. If a picture is worth a thousand words, then a map is worth a thousand (or more!) pictures. There is simply no better way to "view" a portion of Earth's surface or an associated pattern than with a map. How else could we see the entirety of South America, for example, in one glance? In the last article of this section, Mark Monmonier reviews the basics of geographic information systems (GIS) and its relationship to cartography.

Looking Ahead: Challenge Questions

Describe the spatial form of the place in which you live. Do you live in a rural area, a town, or a city, and why was that particular location chosen?

How does your hometown interact with its surrounding region? With other places in the state? With other states? With other places in the world?

How are places "brought closer together" when transportation systems are improved?

What problems occur when transportation systems are overloaded?

How will public transportation be different in the future? Will there be more or fewer private autos in the next 25 years? Defend your answer.

How good a map reader are you? Why are maps useful in studying a place?

UNIT 4

Transportation and Urban Growth

The shaping of the American metropolis

Peter O. Muller

In his monumental new work on the historical geography of transportation, James Vance states that geographic mobility is crucial to the successful functioning of any population cluster, and that "shifts in the availability of mobility provide, in all likelihood, the most powerful single process at work in transforming and evolving the human half of geography." Any adult urbanite who has watched the American metropolis turn inside-out over the past quarter-century can readily appreciate the significance of that maxim. In truth, the nation's largest single urban concentration today is not represented by the seven-plus million who agglomerate in New York City but rather by the 14 million who have settled in Gotham's vast, curvilinear outer city—a 50-mile-wide suburban band that stretches across Long Island, southwestern Connecticut, the Hudson Valley as far north as West Point, and most of New Jersey north of a line drawn from Trenton to Asbury Park. This latest episode of intrametropolitan deconcentration was fueled by the modern automobile and the interstate expressway. It is, however, merely the most recent of a series of evolutionary stages dating back to colonial times, wherein breakthroughs in transport technology unleashed forces that produced significant restructuring of the urban spatial form.

The emerging form and structure of the American metropolis has been traced within a framework of

Horse-drawn trolleys in downtown Boston, circa 1885. (Library of the Boston Athenaeum)

four transportation-related eras. Each successive growth stage is dominated by a particular movement technology and transport-network expansion process that shaped a distinctive pattern of intraurban spatial organization. The stages are the Walking/Horsecar Era (pre-1800–1890), the Electric Streetcar Era (1890–1920), the Recreational Automobile Era (1920–1945), and the Freeway Era (1945–present). As with all generalized models of this kind, there is a risk of oversimplification because the building processes of several simultaneously developing cities do not always fall into neat time-space compartments. Chicago's growth over the past 150 years,

for example, reveals numerous irregularities, suggesting that the overall metropolitan growth pattern is more complex than a simple, continuous outward thrust. Yet even after developmental ebb and flow, leapfrogging, backfilling, and other departures from the idealized scheme are considered, there still remains an acceptable correspondence between the model and reality.

Before 1850 the American city was a highly compact settlement in which the dominant means of getting about was on foot, requiring people and activities to

tightly agglomerate in close proximity to one another. This usually meant less than a 30-minute walk from the center of town to any given urban point—an accessibility radius later extended to 45 minutes when the pressures of industrial growth intensified after 1830. Within this pedestrian city, recognizable activity concentrations materialized as well as the beginnings of income-based residential congregations. The latter was particularly characteristic of the wealthy, who not only walled themselves off in their large homes near the city center but also took to the privacy of horse-drawn carriages for moving about town. Those of means also sought to escape the city's noise

Electric streetcar lines radiated outward from central cities, giving rise to star-shaped metropolises. Boston, circa 1915. (Library of the Boston Athenaeum)

and frequent epidemics resulting from the lack of sanitary conditions. Horse-and-carriage transportation enabled the wealthy to reside in the nearby countryside for the disease-prone summer months. The arrival of the railroad in the 1830s provided the opportunity for year-round daily commuting, and by 1840 hundreds of affluent businessmen in Boston, New York, and Philadelphia were making round trips from exclusive new trackside suburbs every weekday.

As industrialization and its teeming concentrations of working-class housing increasingly engulfed the mid-nineteenth century city, the deteriorating physical and social environment reinforced the desires of middle-income residents to suburbanize as well. They were unable, however, to afford the cost and time of commuting by steam train, and with the walking city now stretched to its morphological limit, their aspirations intensified the pressures to improve intraurban transport technology. Early attempts involving stagecoach-like omnibuses, cable-car systems, and steam railroads proved impractical, but by 1852 the

first meaningful transit break-through was finally introduced in Manhattan in the form of the horse-drawn trolley. Light street rails were easy to install, overcame the problems of muddy, unpaved roadways,

---

Before 1850 the American city was a highly compact settlement in which the dominant means of getting about was on foot, requiring people and activities to tightly agglomerate in close proximity to one another.

---

and enabled horsecars to be hauled along them at speeds slightly (about five mph) faster than those of pedestrians. This modest improvement in mobility permitted the opening of a narrow belt of land at the city's edge for new home construction. Middle-income urbanites flocked to

these "horsecar suburbs," which multiplied rapidly after the Civil War. Radial routes were the first to spawn such peripheral development, but the relentless demand for housing necessitated the building of crosstown horsecar lines, thereby filling in the interstices and preserving the generally circular shape of the city.

The less affluent majority of the urban population, however, was confined to the old pedestrian city and its bleak, high-density industrial appendages. With the massive immigration of unskilled laborers, (mostly of European origin after 1870) huge blue-collar communities sprang up around the factories. Because these newcomers to the city settled in the order in which they arrived—thereby denying them the small luxury of living in the immediate company of their fellow ethnics—social stress and conflict were repeatedly generated. With the immigrant tide continuing to pour into the nearly bursting industrial city throughout the late nineteenth century, pressures redoubled to further improve intraurban transit and open up more of the adjacent countryside. By the late 1880s that urgently needed mobility revolution was at last in the making, and when it came it swiftly transformed the compact city and its suburban periphery into the modern metropolis.

The key to this urban transport revolution was the invention by Frank Sprague of the electric traction motor, an often overlooked innovation that surely ranks among the most important in American history. The first electrified trolley line opened in Richmond in 1888, was adopted by two dozen other big cities within a year, and by the early 1890s swept across the nation to become the dominant mode of intraurban transit. The rapidity of this innovation's diffusion was enhanced by the immediate recognition of its ability to resolve the urban transportation problem of the day: motors could be attached to existing horsecars, converting them into self-propelled vehicles powered by easily constructed overhead wires. The tripling of average speeds (to over 15 mph) that resulted from this invention brought a large band of open land beyond the city's perimeter into trolley-commuting range.

The most dramatic geographic change of the Electric Streetcar Era was the swift residential development of those urban fringes, which transformed the emerging metropolis into a decidedly star-shaped spatial entity. This pattern was produced by radial streetcar corridors extending several miles beyond the compact city's limits. With so much new space available for homebuilding within walking distance of the trolley lines, there was no need to extend trackage laterally, and so the interstices remained undeveloped. The typical streetcar suburb of the turn of this century was a continuous axial corridor whose backbone was the road carrying the trolley line (usually lined with stores and other local commercial facilities), from which gridded residential streets fanned out for several blocks on both sides of the tracks. In general, the quality of housing and prosperity of streetcar subdivisions increased with distance from the edge of the central city. These suburban corridors were populated by the emerging, highly mobile middle class, which was already stratifying itself according to a plethora of mi-

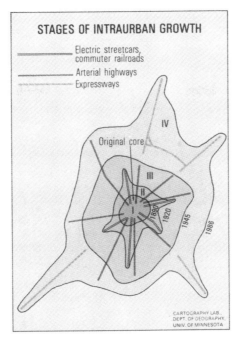

nor income and status differences. With frequent upward (and local geographic) mobility the norm, community formation became an elusive goal, a process further retarded by the grid-settlement morphology and the reliance on the distant downtown for employment and most shopping.

The ready availability and low fare of the electric trolley now provided every resident with access to the intracity circulatory system, thereby introducing truly "mass" transit to urban America.

Within the city, too, the streetcar sparked a spatial transformation. The ready availability and low fare of the electric trolley now provided every resident with access to the intracity circulatory system, thereby introducing truly "mass" transit to urban America in the final years of the nineteenth century. For nonresidential activities this new ease of movement among the city's various parts quickly triggered the emergence of specialized land-use dis-

tricts for commerce, manufacturing, and transportation, as well as the continued growth of the multipurpose central business district (CBD) that had formed after mid-century. But the greatest impact of the streetcar was on the central city's social geography, because it made possible the congregation of ethnic groups in their own neighborhoods. No longer were these moderate-income masses forced to reside in the heterogeneous jumble of rowhouses and tenements that ringed the factories. The trolley brought them the opportunity to "live with their own kind," allowing the sorting of discrete groups into their own inner-city social territories within convenient and inexpensive traveling distance of the workplace.

By World War I, the electric trolleys had transformed the tracked city into a full-fledged metropolis whose streetcar suburbs, in the larger cases, spread out more than 20 miles from the metropolitan center. It was at this point in time that intrametropolitan transportation achieved its greatest level of efficiency—that the bustling industrial city really "worked." How much closer the American metropolis might have approached optimal workability for all its residents, however, will never be known because the next urban transport revolution was already beginning to assert itself through the increasingly popular automobile. Americans took to cars as wholeheartedly as anything in the nation's long cultural history. Although Lewis Mumford and other scholars vilified the car as the destroyer of the city, more balanced assessments of the role of the automobile recognize its overwhelming acceptance for what it was—the long-awaited attainment of private mass transportation that offered users the freedom to travel whenever and wherever they chose. As cars came to the metropolis in ever greater numbers throughout the interwar decades, their major influence was twofold: to accelerate the deconcentration of population through the development of interstices bypassed during the streetcar era, and to push the suburban frontier farther into the countryside, again producing a compact, regular-shaped urban entity.

Afternoon commuters converge at the tunnel leading out of central Boston, 1948. (Boston Public Library)

While it certainly produced a dramatic impact on the urban fabric by the eve of World War II, the introduction of the automobile into the American metropolis during the 1920s and 1930s came at a leisurely pace. The earliest flurry of auto adoptions had been in rural areas, where farmers badly needed better access to local service centers. In the cities, cars were initially used for weekend outings—hence the term *"Recreational* Auto Era"—and some of the earliest paved roadways were landscaped parkways along scenic water routes, such as New York's pioneering Bronx River Parkway and Chicago's Lake Shore Drive. But it was into the suburbs, where growth rates were now for the first time overtaking those of the central cities, that cars made a decisive penetration throughout the prosperous 1920s. In fact, the rapid expansion of automobile suburbia by 1930 so adversely affected the metropolitan public transportation system that, through significant diversions of streetcar and commuter-rail passengers, the large cities began to feel the negative effects of the car years before the auto's actual arrival in the urban center. By facilitat-

> **Americans took to cars as wholeheartedly as anything in the nation's long cultural history.**

ing the opening of unbuilt areas lying between suburban rail axes, the automobile effectively lured residential developers away from densely populated traction-line corridors into the suddenly accessible interstices. Thus, the suburban homebuilding industry no longer found it necessary to subsidize privately-owned streetcar companies to provide low-fare access to trolley-line housing tracts. Without this financial underpinning, the modern urban transit crisis quickly began to surface.

The new recreational motorways also helped to intensify the decentralization of the population. Most were radial highways that penetrated deeply into the suburban ring and provided weekend motorists with easy access to this urban countryside. There they obviously were impressed by what they saw, and they soon responded in massive numbers to the sales pitches of suburban subdivision developers. The residential development of automobile suburbia followed a simple formula that was devised in the prewar years and greatly magnified in scale after 1945. The leading motivation was developer profit from the quick turnover of land, which was acquired in large parcels, subdivided and auctioned off. Understandably

Central City-Focused Rail Transit

The widely dispersed distribution of people and activities in today's metropolis makes rail transit that focuses in the central business district (CBD) an obsolete solution to the urban transportation problem. To be successful, any rail line must link places where travel origins and destinations are highly clustered. Even more important is the need to connect places where people really want to go, which in the metropolitan America of the late twentieth century means suburban shopping centers, freeway-oriented office complexes, and the airport. Yet a brief look at the rail systems that have been built in the last 20 years shows that transit planners cannot—or will not—recognize those travel demands, and insist on designing CBD-oriented systems as if we all still lived in the 1920s.

One of the newest urban transit systems is Metrorail in Miami and surrounding Dade County, Florida.

It has been a resounding failure since its opening in 1984. The northern leg of this line connects downtown Miami to a number of low- and moderate-income black and Hispanic neighborhoods, yet it carries only about the same number of passengers that used to ride on parallel bus lines. The reason is that the high-skill, service economy of Miami's CBD is about as mismatched as it could possibly be to the modest employment skills and training levels possessed by residents of that Metrorail corridor. To the south, the prospects seemed far brighter because of the possibility of connecting the system to Coral Gables and Dadeland, two leading suburban activity centers. However, both central Coral Gables and the nearby International Airport complex were bypassed in favor of a cheaply available, abandoned railroad corridor alongside U.S. 1. Station locations were poorly planned, particularly at the University of Miami and at Dadeland—where terminal location necessitates a dangerous walk across a six-lane highway from the region's largest shopping mall. Not surprisingly, ridership levels have been shockingly below projections, averaging only about 21,000 trips per day in early 1986. While Dade County's worried officials will soon be called upon to decide the future of the system, the federal government is using the Miami experience as an excuse to withdraw from financially supporting all construction of new urban heavy-rail systems. Unfortunately, we will not be able to discover if a well-planned, high-speed rail system that is congruent with the travel demands of today's polycentric metropolis is capable of solving traffic congestion problems. Hopefully, transportation policymakers across the nation will heed the lessons of Miami's textbook example of how not to plan a hub-and-spoke public transportation network in an urban era dominated by the multi-centered city.

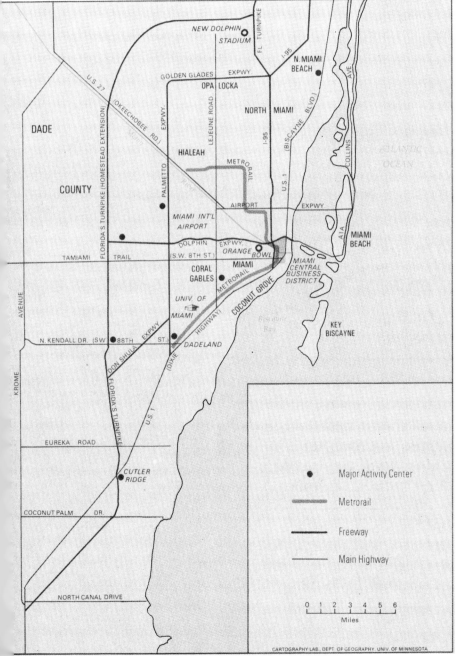

developers much preferred open areas at the metropolitan fringe, where large packages of cheap land could readily be assembled. Silently approving and underwriting this uncontrolled spread of residential suburbia were public policies at all levels of government: financing road construction, obligating lending institutions to invest in new home-building, insuring individual mortgages, and providing low-interest loans to FHA and VA clients.

Because automobility removed most of the pre-existing movement constraints, suburban social geography now became dominated by locally homogeneous income-group clusters that isolated themselves from dissimilar neighbors. Gone was the highly localized stratification of streetcar suburbia. In its place arose a far more dispersed, increasingly fragmented residential mosaic to which builders were only too eager to cater, helping shape a kaleidoscopic settlement pattern by shrewdly constructing the most expensive houses that could be sold in each locality. The continued partitioning of suburban society was further legitimized by the widespread adoption of zoning (legalized in 1916), which gave municipalities control over lot and building standards that, in turn, assured dwelling prices that would only attract newcomers whose incomes at least equaled those of the existing local population. Among the middle class, particularly, these exclusionary economic practices were enthusiastically supported, because such devices extended to them the ability of upper-income groups to maintain their social distance from people of lower socioeconomic status.

Nonresidential activities were also suburbanizing at an increasing rate during the Recreational Auto Era. Indeed, many large-scale manufacturers had decentralized during the streetcar era, choosing locations in suburban freight-rail corridors. These corridors rapidly spawned surrounding working-class towns that became important satellites of the central city in the emerging metropolitan constellation. During the interwar period, industrial employers accelerated their intraurban deconcentration, as more efficient horizontal fabrication methods replaced

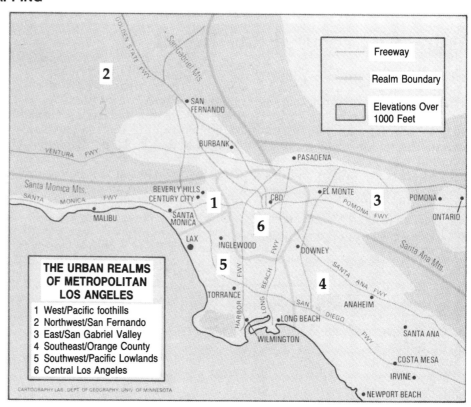

THE URBAN REALMS OF METROPOLITAN LOS ANGELES

1 West/Pacific foothills
2 Northwest/San Fernando
3 East/San Gabriel Valley
4 Southeast/Orange County
5 Southwest/Pacific Lowlands
6 Central Los Angeles

older techniques requiring multistoried plants—thereby generating greater space needs that were too expensive to satisfy in the high-density central city. Newly suburbanizing manufacturers, however, continued their affiliation with intercity freight-rail corridors, because motor trucks were not yet able to operate with their present-day efficiencies and because the highway network of the outer ring remained inadequate until the 1950s.

Retail activities were featured in dozens of planned automobile suburbs that sprang up after World War I—most notably in Kansas City's Country Club District, where the nation's first complete shopping center was opened in 1922.

The other major nonresidential activity of interwar suburbia was re-

tailing. Clusters of automobile-oriented stores had first appeared in the urban fringes before World War I. By the early 1920s the roadside commercial strip had become a common sight in many southern California suburbs. Retail activities were also featured in dozens of planned automobile suburbs that sprang up after World War I—most notably in Kansas City's Country Club District, where the nation's first complete shopping center was opened in 1922. But these diversified retail centers spread slowly before the suburban highway improvements of the 1950s.

U nlike the two preceding eras, the postwar Freeway Era was not sparked by a revolution in urban transportation. Rather, it represented the coming of age of the now pervasive automobile culture, which coincided with the emergence of the U.S. from 15 years of economic depression and war. Suddenly the automobile was no longer a luxury or a recreational diversion: overnight it had become a necessity for commuting, shopping, and socializing, essential to the successful realization of personal opportunities for a rapidly expanding majority of the metropolitan population. People snapped up cars as fast as the reviving peacetime automobile industry could roll them off the assembly lines, and a prodigious highway-building effort was launched, spearheaded by high-speed, limited-access expressways. Given impetus by the 1956 Interstate Highway Act, these new freeways would soon reshape every corner of urban America, as the more distant suburbs they engendered represented nothing less than the turning inside-out of the historic metropolitan city.

The snowballing effect of these changes is expressed geographically in the sprawling metropolis of the postwar era. Most striking is the enormous band of growth that was added between 1945 and the 1980s, with freeway sectors pushing the metropolitan frontier deeply into the urban-rural fringe. By the late 1960s, the maturing expressway system began to underwrite a new suburban co-equality with the central city, because it was eliminating the metropolitanwide centrality advantage of the CBD. Now *any* location on the freeway network could easily be reached by motor vehicle, and intraurban accessibility had become a ubiquitous spatial good. Ironically, large cities had encouraged the construction of radial expressways in the 1950s and 1960s because they appeared to enable the downtown to remain accessible to the swiftly dispersing suburban population. However, as one economic activity after another discovered its new locational flexibility within the freeway metropolis, nonresidential deconcentration sharply accelerated in the 1970s and 1980s. Moreover, as expressways expanded the radius of commuting to encompass the entire dispersed metropolis, residential location constraints relaxed as well. No longer were most urbanites required to live within a short distance of their job: the workplace had now become a locus of opportunity offering access to the best possible residence that an individual could afford anywhere in the urbanized area. Thus, the overall pattern of locally uniform, income-based clusters that had emerged in prewar automobile suburbia was greatly magnified in the Freeway Era, and such new social variables as age and life-style produced an ever more balkanized population mosaic.

The revolutionary changes in movement and accessibility introduced during the four decades of the Freeway Era have resulted in nothing less than the complete geographic restructuring of the metropolis. The single-center urban structure of the past has been transformed into a polycentric metropolitan form in which several outlying activity concentrations rival the CBD. These new "suburban downtowns," consisting of vast orchestrations of retailing, office-based business, and light industry, have become common features near the highway interchanges that now encircle every large central city. As these emerging metropolitan-level cores achieve economic and geographic parity with each other, as well as with the CBD of the nearby central city, they provide the totality of urban goods and services to their surrounding populations. Thus each metropolitan sector becomes a self-sufficient functional entity, or *realm*. The application of this model to the Los Angeles region reveals six broad

---

The new freeways would soon reshape every corner of urban America, as the more distant suburbs they engendered represented nothing less than the turning inside-out of the historic metropolitan city.

---

realms. Competition among several new suburban downtowns for dominance in the five outer realms is still occurring. In wealthy Orange County, for example, this rivalry is especially fierce, but Costa Mesa's burgeoning South Coast Metro is winning out as of early 1986.

The legacy of more than two centuries of intraurban transportation innovations, and the development patterns they helped stamp on the landscape of metropolitan America, is suburbanization—the growth of the edges of the urbanized area at a rate faster than in the already-developed interior. Since the geographic extent of the built-up urban areas has, throughout history, exhibited a remarkably constant radius of about 45 minutes of travel from the center, each breakthrough in higher-speed transport technology extended that radius into a new outer zone of suburban residential opportunity. In the nineteenth century, commuter railroads, horse-drawn trolleys, and electric streetcars each created their own suburbs—and thereby also created the large industrial city, which could not have been formed without incorporating these new suburbs into the pre-existing compact urban center. But the suburbs that materialized in the early twentieth century began to assert their independence from the central cities, which were ever more perceived as undesirable. As the automobile greatly reinforced the dispersal trend of the metropolitan population, the distinction between central city and suburban ring grew as well. And as freeways eventually eliminated the friction effects of intrametropolitan distance for most urban functions, nonresidential activities deconcentrated to such an extent that by 1980 the emerging outer suburban city had become co-equal with the central city that spawned it.

As the transition to an information-dominated, postindustrial economy is completed, today's intraurban movement problems may be mitigated by the increasing substitution of communication for the physical movement of people. Thus, the city of the future is likely to be the "wired metropolis." Such a development would portend further deconcentration because activity centers would potentially be able to locate at any site offering access to global computer and satellite networks.

Further Reading

Jackson, Kenneth T. 1985. *Crabgrass Frontier: The Suburbanization of the United States.* New York: Oxford University Press.

Muller, Peter O. 1981. *Contemporary Suburban America.* Englewood Cliffs, N.J.: Prentice-Hall.

Schaeffer, K. H. and Sclar, Elliot. 1975. *Access for All: Transportation and Urban Growth.* Baltimore: Penguin Books.

High-Speed Rail: Another Golden Age?

*Neglected in North America but nurtured
in Europe and Japan, high-speed rail systems
are a critical complement to jets and cars*

Tony R. Eastham

*Tony R. Eastham is a professor in the
department of electrical and computer
engineering at Queen's University in
Kingston, Ontario. His research interests include advanced ground transportation, electric drives and the design of
machines and electromagnetic devices.
This year he is visiting professor of
transportation systems engineering at
the University of Tokyo.*

I looked at her with the uncompre-
hending adoration one feels for locomo-
tives.... Against the fan of light her
great bulk looms monstrous, a raving
meteor of sound and mass.

That trains were once routinely
described so breathlessly may
come as a surprise. But the gold-
en age of rail travel was arguably at its
zenith when in 1935 columnist Chris-
topher Morley wrote those words for
the *Saturday Review of Literature.* Dozens of trains left New York City's Grand
Central Station every day, bound for
Chicago, Montreal, St. Louis and the
like. Extensive networks of lines per-
vaded the continent and moved people, food stocks, primary resources and
industrial products. Passenger trains
such as the *Golden Arrow* in the U.K.,
the *Orient-Express* in Europe and the
Zephyr in the U.S. came to exemplify
not just speed, power and comfort but
technological progress itself.

Of course, the six decades since that
time have encompassed the advent of
commercial air travel, as well as of interstate and international highway systems all over the world. Both these
transportation modes have continued
to develop and even now seem poised
for further advances. Such developments prompt the question: What will
be the role of rail travel in a world of
large, subsonic transport aircraft and
advanced automobiles running on
"smart" highways?

The answer, in many advanced countries, is that trains will play a very im-

portant role indeed. In these regions,
rail services have been dramatically enhanced through an evolution of systems
and technologies in societies that have
never relied on the automobile in quite
the same way most in North America
have. In many parts of Europe and Asia,
trains, rather than airplanes, are now
the preferred means of travel on routes
of about 200 to 600 kilometers. Their
use of fast and technologically advanced
train systems began decades ago and
may be supplemented in coming years
by even more advanced magnetic-levi-
tation (maglev) trains. Steel-wheel-on-
steel-rail trains are now operating at
speeds of up to 300 kilometers per
hour, and maglev trains are being developed and tested for introduction at
speeds of 400 to 500 kilometers per
hour, perhaps within 10 years.

In North America, the implementation of high-speed rail has been frus-
tratingly slow. Interurban and commuter rail services now account for less
than 2 percent of passenger miles per
year. Rail still moves substantial freight,
but even here trucks have become the
dominant carrier.

Nevertheless, there is growing recognition that mobility on the continent is
being threatened by clogged freeways
in metropolitan areas and by "wing-
lock," the analogous condition at hub
airports at peak times. Sustaining mobility and economic development will
demand a more balanced combination
of rail, air and road travel. Thus, a rail
renaissance is being proposed. Millions
of dollars have been spent on evaluations, systems design studies, route surveys and ridership assessments for
heavily traveled corridors between cities several hundred kilometers apart.

Such studies have benefited from long
records of experience in other places. In
1964 in Japan, for example, the famed
Shinkansen (bullet train) opened between Tokyo and Osaka. Over the years,
speeds have climbed from 210 to 270

kilometers per hour, decreasing the trip
time on the 553-kilometer Tokyo-to-
Osaka run from four to 2.5 hours. Japan's Shinkansen network now covers
2,045 kilometers, from Morioka in
northern Honshu to Hakata in Kyushu,
and carries 275 million passengers every year. At the same time, technology
development continues, led by Japan
Railways Central, one of the country's
regional railway companies. Among the
projects under way is a Super Train for
the Advanced Railway of the 21st century (STAR 21), whose prototype has
achieved 425 kilometers per hour.

It is France, however, that has the
fastest commercial train system in the
world, the Train à Grande Vitesse (TGV).
The TGV Atlantique has a maximum
speed of 300 kilometers per hour. Paris
forms the hub of a network that extends north to Lille and the Channel
Tunnel, west to Tours and Le Mans, and
south to Lyons. TGV trains also operate
into Switzerland. In 1992 they began
running in Spain between Madrid and
Seville, and by 1998 they are to travel
between Seoul and Pusan in Korea.

Germany also has a high-speed train,
the InterCity Express (ICE), which now
zips along at 250 kilometers per hour
between Hannover and Würzburg and
also between Mannheim and Stuttgart.
Like those in Japan and France, this system operates on a dedicated right-of-
way, maximizing passenger and public
safety by eliminating road crossings
and by using advanced control.

Sweden has adopted a somewhat different approach in its X2000, which
achieves a top speed of 220 kilometers
per hour on the 456-kilometer line from
Stockholm to Göteborg and gets the
most out of existing railroad infrastructure by actively tilting the passenger
compartment relative to its wheeled un-
dercarriage. The scheme avoids subject-
ing passengers to uncomfortable lateral
forces while rounding curves at high
speed. In Italy the ETR-450 tilt-body

Rolling or Floating at 300 Kilometers per Hour

Advanced ground transportation has three categories: high speed, very high speed and magnetic levitation (maglev). High-speed systems, such as Amtrak's Northeast Corridor in the U.S., use the traditional steel-wheel-on-rail technology and can operate at top speeds ranging from 200 to 240 kilometers per hour (125 to 150) miles per hour). Very high speed systems are considered capable of reaching 350 kilometers per hour (218 mph), using enhanced wheel-on-rail technology. They are always electrically powered and require relatively straight route alignments to accommodate the higher speeds. The French Train à Grande Vitesse (TGV), Germany's InterCity Express (ICE) and Japan's Shinkansen (bullet train) are all examples of very high speed rail.

Maglev systems are quite different from traditional trains. They use electromagnetic forces to levitate, guide and propel train cars along a guideway at projected speeds of 320 to 500 kilometers per hour (200 to 310 mph). The German Transrapid on the elevated guideway, and Japan's MLU—both noncommercial prototypes—are the only full-scale examples of high-speed maglev technology. A feature unique to maglev is the use of a synchronous motor that provides linear rather than rotational motion, with power supplied to magnet windings in the guideway.

—John A. Harrison, Parsons Brinckerhoff Quade & Douglas, Inc.

train provides similar service between Rome and Florence.

In North America, experience with high-speed rail has been limited for the most part to paper studies and demonstrations of European technology to stimulate public interest. Many reports have evaluated the suitability of high-speed rail for such corridors as Pittsburgh-Philadelphia, Las Vegas-Los Angeles, San Francisco-Los Angeles-San Diego, Dallas-Houston-San Antonio, Miami-Orlando-Tampa and Toronto-Ottawa-Montreal. Nothing has been built, however, because the economics are projected to be marginal and because federal and state governments are reluctant to commit substantial funds.

Amtrak, the U.S. rail passenger carrier, does plan significant upgrades on its flagship Northeast Corridor routes, however. Part of this network, between Washington, D.C., and New York City, already runs at speeds of up to 200 kilometers per hour and carries more passengers than either of the competing air shuttles. In the immediate future, Amtrak plans to award a $700-million contract to purchase and maintain up to 26 high-speed train sets for use in the corridor; depending on budget negotiations in the U.S. Congress, the contract could be awarded later this autumn. The new trains will link Boston, New York City and Washington, D.C., with service of up to 225 kilometers per hour, once upgrading of the railroad infrastructure is finished, possibly in 1999. The trains are to be manufactured in the U.S., most likely as a joint venture with an offshore developer. Companies competing for the Amtrak contract are offering TGV, X2000 and ICE/Fiat technologies.

Flying Low

Many of these promising applications for high-speed rail stem from the technology's evolutionary nature—most projects will keep costs down by making use of existing infrastructure. This is an advantage not shared by high-speed rail's revolutionary counterpart—maglev trains. Maglev is the generic term for a family of technologies in which a vehicle is suspended, guided and propelled by means of magnetic forces. With its need for an entirely new infrastructure, maglev is likely to find application primarily in a few heavily traveled corridors, where the potential revenue could justify the cost of building guideways from the ground up.

Mainly because of this obstacle, maglev has had a prolonged adolescence. The first conceptual outlines were published some 30 years ago by two physicists at Brookhaven National Laboratory on Long Island, N.Y. James R. Powell and Gordon Danby envisioned a 480-kilometer-per-hour (300-mile-per-hour) train suspended by superconducting magnet coils. Within a decade, however, virtually all the research and development shifted to Germany and Japan, which pursued different technical variations with substantial government and private funding.

With maglev, alternating-current electricity is fed to windings distributed along the guideway, creating a magnetic wave into which the vehicle's magnets are locked. Speed is controlled by varying the frequency of the electrical energy applied to the guideway windings. In effect, the vehicle's magnets and the

windings in the guideway constitute a single synchronous electric motor, which provides linear rather than rotational motion.

There are two variations on this theme. The so-called repulsion-mode electrodynamic system, proposed by Powell and Danby and pursued in Japan, uses superconductive magnets on board the vehicle to induce currents in conductive coils in the guideway. This interaction levitates the vehicle about 15 centimeters, as though it were a low-flying, guideway-based aircraft. Indeed, the Japanese vehicle achieves magnetic liftoff at about 100 kilometers per hour; at lower speeds, it rolls on wheels.

The other type, which has been developed in Germany, is the attraction-mode electromagnetic system. Conventional (nonsuperconducting) iron-core electromagnets carried by the vehicle are attracted upward toward ferromagnetic components attached to the underside of the guideway structure. This type of magnetic suspension is inherently unstable and needs precise control to maintain a clearance of about 1.5 centimeters between the vehicle's magnets and the guideway. One advantage, however, is that the vehicle remains levitated even when motionless and thus could be used for urban and commuter transit as well as for longer, high-speed routes. Indeed, the first operational maglev system was a low-speed shuttle installed in 1984 between the airport terminal and nearby railway station in Birmingham, England.

Japan's repulsion-mode system is being developed by the country's Railway Technical Research Institute in collaboration with a number of large engineering companies. A series of test vehicles included the ML-500R, which in 1979 achieved a speed of 517 kilometers per hour—a record for maglev—on a seven-kilometer test track near Miyazaki, on the island of Kyushu. Its successor, a prototype vehicle, will start test runs in 1997 on a 42.7-kilometer precommercial test and demonstration facility in Yamanashi prefecture near Tokyo. This double-track guideway will allow essentially all aspects of an operational system to be tested, including full-size vehicles going through a tunnel at 500 kilometers per hour. Backers of the project are hopeful that a commercial version could be ready for deployment between Tokyo and Osaka by 2005.

In Germany the attraction-mode electromagnetic "Transrapid" maglev system has been under development by Magnetbahn GmbH since the late 1960s. Again, test vehicles led to the construction of a demonstration facility, at Emsland in the early 1980s. Its 31-kilometer, figure-eight-shaped guideway allows full-scale vehicles to run under conditions similar to operational ones. The preproduction vehicle TR-07 has been under evaluation for almost five years, regularly achieving speeds of from 400 to 450 kilometers per hour. The German government recently chose the technology for a new line linking Berlin and Hamburg. The route, to be built by about 2005, will be the centerpiece of a program to enhance east-west travel in the reunified Germany.

U.S. Maglev: Suspended Animation

In the U.S., maglev development was abandoned after a brief period of research from the late 1960s to the mid-1970s at Ford Motor Company, the Stanford Research Institute and the Massachusetts Institute of Technology. The concept was rejuvenated in the late 1980s, however, and a government-sponsored National Maglev Initiative was launched in an attempt to apply some relevant technologies—cryogenics, power electronics, aerodynamics, control and vehicle dynamics—from the aerospace and related industries. The goal was a second-generation maglev system to meet the needs and conditions of North America.

In 1994 government funding ran out without spurring any sustained private-sector commitment. Four innovative maglev systems were designed. None were built, but the exercise generated several interesting ideas, including novel concepts for synchronous propulsion and a superconducting version of electromagnetic suspension with a large air gap between vehicle and track. By 1994 maglev R&D in North America had returned to its previous minimal state.

To some extent, maglev finds itself a victim of changing circumstances. Twenty or 25 years ago the technology was thought to be ideal for connecting densely populated areas up to 600 kilometers apart. Speeds of 450 to 500 kilometers per hour would make maglev competitive with air travel, it was reasoned, amid concerns about the cost and availability of oil-based fuels.

This argument largely depends on the maximum speed of steel-wheel-on-rail trains being significantly less than the speed of maglev; otherwise these conventional trains could in many cases fill the bill more economically. Two or three decades ago the practical speed limit for steel-wheel-on-rail was generally thought to be about 250 kilometers per hour. Yet, as noted, high-speed rail

has developed to the point that operating speeds have reached 300 kilometers per hour. The achievement has followed from a better understanding of wheel-rail dynamics, aerodynamics and the transferring of high levels of electric power to a moving train from an overhead line. Even more impressively, wheeled trains have been tested at speeds of up to 520 kilometers per hour—three kilometers per hour faster than the maglev record. Although no one claims it would be feasible to run a passenger train at this speed, 350 kilometers per hour is now considered to be operationally workable.

Thus, maglev's speed and total-trip-time advantage is not what it once was; realistically, it would seem to be about 20 or 30 percent, in comparison with the best wheel-on-rail systems. It remains to be seen how many governments will find this margin compelling enough to commit to a fundamentally new transportation technology, for those few medium-range, heavily traveled routes where market share might be won from the airlines.

Of course, higher speeds would make maglev more attractive, and 500 kilometers per hour is not the final, upper limit by any means. But one of the main limiting factors at such speeds is aerodynamics. The power needed to overcome aerodynamic drag increases as the cube of speed; noise from aerodynamic sources increases as the sixth power.

And the dynamic perturbations caused by trains passing one another or entering and exiting tunnels become increasingly severe at high speed. Such factors have led to proposals to run maglev trains in a fully or partially evacuated tube.

Years ago a study suggested that such a tunnel could link New York City, Los Angeles and perhaps other international cities as well through transoceanic links to provide the ultimate in global transportation. Top speed could be as high as 2,000 kilometers per hour, and a dipping and rising profile between stations would let gravity assist in propulsion and braking. Engineering considerations, such as the cost of building and maintaining such a tunnel, make the idea fanciful, to say the least.

Although it may be many decades before it will be possible to make reservations for the two-hour trip from New York to Los Angeles, important milestones are ahead for both maglev and more conventional, wheel-on-rail trains. The next decade should see the inauguration of the first moderately long-distance commercial maglev routes. High-speed rail, meanwhile, will be steadily enhanced in speed, comfort and passenger amenities. European services will become increasingly networked. At the same time, many more lines will be built in Asia, including the completion of a national network in Japan and new routes in Korea, Taiwan and China.

High-Speed Rail versus Maglev	
HIGH-SPEED RAIL	**MAGLEV**
Speeds of 330 kilometers per hour planned for the near future	Likely top speeds in commercial service of 400 kilometers per hour
New rights-of-way and tracks needed for high speed, but existing tracks might be used for urban operations at lower speed; construction costs are lower	Totally new infrastructure required; higher construction costs; maintenance costs may be lower
At speeds of 260 kilometers per hour, noise level reaches 85 to 90 decibels at a distance of 25 meters from the track	Noise level equal to or lower than that of high-speed rail at identical speeds; quieter at low speeds because of lack of friction
31-year history of revenue-generating lines	No high-speed, commercial lines in operation
Energy use, per seat-mile, projected to be similar to maglev's at top speeds	Less energy use in general
	Faster acceleration than high-speed rail; can climb steeper grades
Source: Office of Technology Assessment, U.S. Congress	

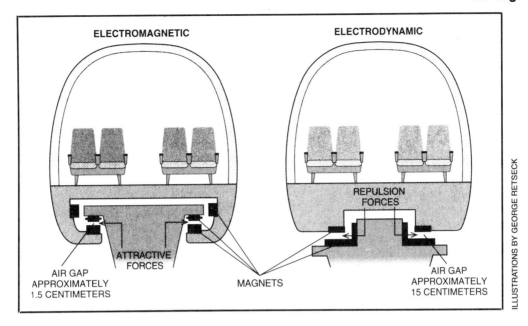

High-speed maglev vehicles employ one of two kinds of suspension: electromagnetic (EMS) or electrodynamic (EDS). Used on the German Transrapid system, EMS relies on attraction between vehicle-mounted electromagnets and others on the underside of the guideway. In contrast, the electrodynamic system (shown above) pushes the vehicle up above the guideway using repulsing magnets. As implemented in the Japanese MLU prototypes, EDS is based on superconducting magnets, creating a gap about 10 times greater than EMS is capable of producing. The greater gap allows for less precision in guideway construction tolerances. At present, however, the ride quality of EDS vehicles is poorer than for EMS ones and therefore requires more development.

The U.S. is clearly a follower rather than a leader in the new high-speed rail technologies. But the country will find it necessary to rejuvenate its rail passenger routes, starting with the Northeast Corridor. Probably, some additional motivation will be needed, such as another oil crisis, or road and air congestion so bad that it interferes with economic growth. True, videoconferencing and other forms of telecommunications will lessen the need to travel and will save time and money. Nevertheless, there is no hard evidence yet that such communications facilities are slowing the growth of business travel. High-tech trains will come to North America—it is just a matter of time, need and a more favorable economic environment. Telecommunications may be the next best thing, but being there is best of all.

Further Reading

SUPERTRAINS: SOLUTIONS TO AMERICA'S TRANSPORTATION GRIDLOCK. Joseph Vranich. St. Martin's Press, 1993.

THE 21ST CENTURY LIMITED: CELEBRATING A DECADE OF PROGRESS. High Speed Rail/Maglev Association, Alexandria, Va. Reichman Frankle, Englewood Cliffs, N.J., 1994.

HIGH-SPEED GROUND TRANSPORTATION IS COMING TO AMERICA—SLOWLY. J. A. Harrison in *Journal of Transportation Engineering*, Vol. 121, No. 2, pages 117–123; March–April 1995.

HIGH-SPEED GROUND TRANSPORTATION DEVELOPMENT OUTSIDE THE UNITED STATES. Tony R. Eastham in *Journal of Transportation Engineering*, Vol. 121, No. 5, pages 411–416; September–October 1995.

The Spread of Early Farming in Europe

The "Neolithic revolution" is best thought of as a gradual transition as farming crossed Europe haltingly over the course of 3,000 years

Peter Bogucki

Peter Bogucki is the assistant dean for undergraduate affairs of the School of Engineering and Applied Science at Princeton University. He has conducted research on early European farmers in Poland since 1976. He received his Ph.D. in anthropology from Harvard University in 1981. Address: Engineering Quadrangle, Princeton University, Princeton, NJ 08544-5263. Internet: bogucki@pucc.princeton.edu.

The shift from a mobile life of hunting and gathering to a sedentary one based on domesticated plants and animals was a remarkable transformation in human history. Although this change took place independently in at least seven distinct parts of the world over the past 10,000 years, it would have remained a local curiosity except for the fact that agricultural techniques, and often the people who used them, spread quickly throughout much of the globe. One of the most successful agricultural movements occurred between 9,000 and 6,000 years ago when a suite of domesticated plants and animals spread from the Levant and Zagros mountains of the Near East to Egypt, the Iranian Plateau and Europe.

Archaeologists call this period the Neolithic (or New Stone Age), a term coined by Sir John Lubbock in 1865 to differentiate it from the Palaeolithic (or Old Stone Age). In the 1920s the British prehistorian V. Gordon Childe, perhaps the first person to focus systematically on the historical transition to agriculture, described the change from mobile foraging to sedentary farming as the "Neolithic revolution." In recent years archaeologists have tended to play down the revolutionary character of the Neolithic and to emphasize instead the processes by which agriculture developed and spread.

The movement of agriculture into Europe is particularly interesting because of the remarkable variability across the continent. From the Aegean Sea to the Orkney Islands off the coast of Scotland, the transition to agriculture occurred many times in very different ways. We now recognize that there was no single mode by which Europe made the shift from foraging to farming. Instead, sedentary farming communities were established through one of two fundamental processes. In some instances agricultural peoples moved into an area, bringing their crops and livestock with them. Although archaeologists are now reluctant to ascribe prehistoric change to movements of peoples (an explanation applied uncritically in the early days of archaeology), it is clear that in some areas colonization indeed took place. In other cases the indigenous hunters and gatherers of a region gradually adopted elements of Neolithic subsistence and technology and eventually became fully sedentary communities. Although the primary crops and some of the livestock were clearly of southwestern Asiatic stock, the domesticates were integrated into the existing forager-subsistence patterns.

Both types of transitions raise questions in the mind of the archaeologist. Where agricultural colonization occurred, the issue is to determine the routes taken by the people and perhaps get some idea of *why* they moved. Where hunters and gatherers adopted agriculture, archaeologists wonder why the people relinquished a comfortable lifestyle in favor of the risks and the work associated with an agricultural economy.

Some of this variability can be attributed to regional differences in climate, or to the quality of the soils or the drainage of the land. In many instances, however, the regional variation is probably due to the size and organization of the pre-existing foraging populations and the choices made by the farming peoples about their crops and livestock. The resulting mosaic of agricultural communities across Europe persisted for many centuries. Here I review what we understand about the distribution of early farming and the development of Neolithic technology as well as what we know about the people themselves. (Recent refinements in radiocarbon-dating techniques have allowed archaeologists to recalibrate the chronology of these events. All dates in this paper are based on revised carbon-14 age determinations.)

The European Habitats

More than 40 years ago, the British prehistorian Grahame Clark recognized two broad divisions of Europe, which he termed *Mediterranean* and *Temperate:* Mediterranean Europe consists of the lands bordering the sea and extending west to include the Iberian Peninsula. It corresponds to the zone whose natural vegetation would consist of Mediterranean evergreen forest, the result of summer drought and winter rains. Temperate Europe, by contrast, is the region whose natural vegetation, before being transformed by farming and industry, consisted of deciduous forest. It reaches from the Atlantic coast and the British Isles, across central Europe and southern Scandinavia, into European Russia. This zone experiences marked seasonal differences. (One of the remarkable aspects of the transition to agriculture in Europe is the rapid adaptation of plants and animals that had originated in semi-arid regions to temperate conditions.)

Although Mediterranean Europe presents relatively similar climate, soil variety, topography and natural vegetation from Greece to Spain, temperate Europe has several environmental zones. In southeastern Europe, the plains of Bul-

From *American Scientist*, May/June 1996, pp. 242-253. © 1996 by Sigma Xi, The Scientific Research Society, Inc. Reprinted by permission.

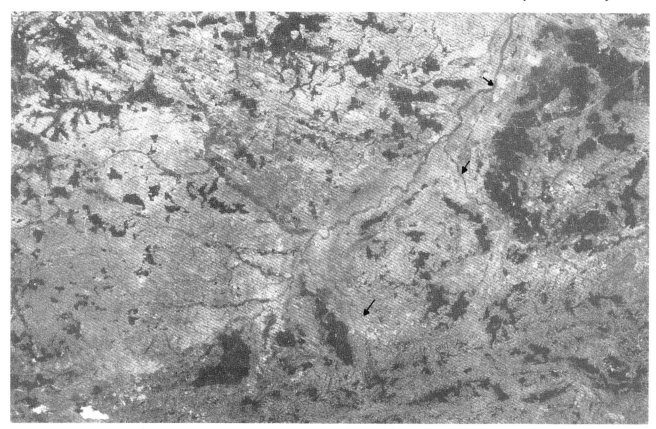

Figure 1. Fertile regions along rivers and streams of the upper Vistula basin in southern Poland supported the first farmers in the region. The moist valleys of these waterways (arrows) appear in this satellite image against the drier watersheds (dark grey areas). Post-glacial windblown sediments, or loess (left and center), provided rich soils for the colonizing farmers who entered the area in about 5400 B.C. The city of Kraków is visible as the white area in the lower left of the image. (Image courtesy of NASA Landsat.)

garia and Romania are separated from the rolling uplands of Serbia and Croatia by the Balkan mountains. River valleys such as those of the Maritsa and Morava were filled with fertile alluvium and upland basins such as the Ovče Polje in Macedonia were also important for early farmers. Further north lies the Hungarian Plain, which is broken in parts by marshes and river levees.

From Ukraine to Belgium stretches a very important region for early farming in central Europe. I have termed this area the loess belt, so named for the pockets of fertile soil called *loess*, a wind-blown sediment deposited under periglacial conditions during the ice age that ended 12,000 years ago. In some areas, where the sediment was trapped by hills and basins, the loess blankets the landscape dozens of meters thick. Small rivers and creeks cut through the loess to form a dendritic drainage pattern. Loess is very fertile but also very dry. The moister zones are the floodplains of the streams rather than the watersheds that separate them. This is evident even today in LANDSAT images of central Europe.

In contrast, the North European Plain, stretching from the Netherlands to Belarus and the Baltic States, was largely covered by ice during the last glaciation. The ebb and flow of the ice altered the landforms and soils considerably, producing a richly varied—but flat—landscape. Soils vary from sandy glacial outwash to clay from glacial moraines. Lakes dot the landscape, including finger lakes scraped out by the ice and kettle lakes formed by melting blocks of ice left behind in the glacial retreat. Slow, meandering streams fill valleys left by glacial meltwaters. Along the Baltic and North Seas, shorelines have changed significantly in the last ten millennia as sea levels rose and land rebounded from the weight of the ice, then settled back down.

On the south side of the loess belt, the foreland of the Alps has many features in common with the North European Plain. It is also characterized by glacial soils, outwash fans and lake basins. The key difference is that the topography has much more variation in elevation. Moreover, the nearby mountains introduced another vertical element of variety in the local environment, while Alpine streams fed by melting snow provided ample moisture.

Finally, the broad region of western Europe to the west of the loess belt, North European Plain, and Alpine foreland can be termed the *Atlantic façade*. Unlike that of the inland regions, the climate here is maritime and moist, and the soils relatively thin. Chalk and limestone underlie much of the region; wetlands such as bogs and fens formed in areas of poor drainage. Postglacial sea-level changes were important in the formation of the coastal landscapes, although the English Channel already separated Britain from the continent during the Neolithic.

The differences among the regions of temperate Europe had considerable relevance to the first farmers. Terrain, drainage, natural vegetation and soils all conditioned the geographic patterns that characterize early farming communities. Coasts and estuaries supported large populations of indigenous hunters and fishers, whereas the dry loess basins were sparsely populated prior to the arrival of farming. Most importantly, the spread of farming did not occur

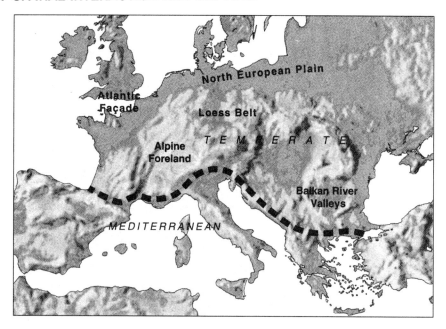

Figure 2. European habitats today and about 8,000 years ago—when the first farmers came to Europe—can be divided into a temperate zone and a Mediterranean zone *(above and below the dashed line)*. The Mediterranean zone (consisting of lands bordering the sea) comprises a more or less homogeneous habitat with respect to climate, soil variety, topography and natural vegetation (an evergreen forest). In contrast, the temperate zone consists of several environmental regions (such as the Alpine foreland, North European Plain, loess belt and the Atlantic façade) that had profound effects on the distribution and nature of the early farming economies.

at a uniform pace. There were spurts and halts at different points in its advance across the continent.

Farming Enters Europe

The initial toehold of farming in Europe took place in Greece as crops, livestock and farmers crossed the Aegean Sea. Indeed, the earliest agricultural settlements along the Aegean coast and in Thessaly have much in common with their immediate precursors in Anatolia. Many scholars of the European Neolithic begin tracing the spread of farming from settlements such as Çatal Hüyük in south-central Turkey and Hacilar in southwestern Turkey. These two sites from the seventh and sixth millennia B.C. represent large, fully agricultural communities, outside the core area of domestication in the Levant. Mud-brick houses, each with an area of about 25 square meters, were built one against another to form a dense architectural complex. Domestic cattle and pigs were added to the basic Near Eastern suite of emmer and einkorn wheat, sheep and goats. Cattle also played a key role in the symbolic life of Çatal Hüyük, for in many of the houses cattle skulls were plastered into the walls. Obsidian (volcanic glass) from nearby sources was a valuable trading commodity.

The Anatolian sites of the early seventh millennium B.C. were the launching pad for agricultural dispersal to Europe. Early Neolithic sites in Greece show distinct similarities to the Anatolian settlements in their suite of domesticates and their ceramics and other artifacts. Rather than being impoverished cousins of their Anatolian precursors, the first farming sites of Greece indicate a robust agricultural economy. The domestication of cattle and pigs in Anatolia had provided the final key elements in the complex of crops and livestock that formed the basis for agricultural dispersals into Europe.

Neolithic settlements appeared suddenly on the alluvial plains of Thessaly and Macedonia, suggesting that they were established by colonists from points to the east and that indigenous peoples' involvement in the establishment of these communities was minimal. The route of the colonization is unclear. Although the Bosporus strait between southwestern Asia and Europe provides the narrowest water barrier, a lack of early farming sites on either side suggests that this may not have been the route taken by the early farmers. Tjeerd van Andel of the University of Cambridge and Curtis Runnels of Boston University propose an island-

hopping route across the Aegean, with some groups perhaps making a detour to Crete, which was settled by farmers about this time.

Van Andel and Runnels have recently emphasized the preference of the earliest Greek farming communities for alluvial and floodplain habitats. The fact that these areas have virtually no evidence of indigenous habitation strengthens the colonization hypothesis. Research by van Andel and Runnels on early farming sites in the Peneios drainage in Thessaly indicates that the choice of these locations was dictated by the presence of perennially wet floodplains whose fertility was recharged by spring flooding.

Several hundred early Neolithic sites have been found in Greek Macedonia and Thessaly, but one of the best-known remains Nea Nikomedia (more than 30 years after it was excavated by the British archaeologist Robert Rodden). By the middle of the seventh millennium B.C., Nea Nikomedia was a farming village with several small rectangular houses. The houses, although densely packed, are freestanding. Unlike the mud-brick houses at Çatal Hüyük and Hacilar, they were built using light timber frames onto which thick walls of mud plaster were applied. Thus from the very beginning, early European farming settlements had a distinct character. The diet, however, was similar to that of the Anatolian sites, with most of the faunal remains consisting of sheep and goats (with some cattle and pigs), and botanical remains yielding the southwestern Asiatic complex of emmer and einkorn wheat, barley and legumes. Pottery was present from the earliest levels.

A contrasting picture emerges in southern Greece, where the moist floodplains are absent. At Franchthi Cave, a continuous record of human habitation for 15 millennia begins about 20,000 years ago. Early in the seventh millennium B.C., the people of Franchthi Cave began to keep sheep and goats and to grow emmer wheat and barley. Continuities in the stone-tool technology indicate connections with the earlier foragers. It is unclear whether this represents the adoption of elements of the farming economy by indigenous foragers or the incorporation of local hunter-gatherers into a group of intrusive agriculturalists. At the moment, however, it appears that there were two processes at work in the Greek peninsula: the occupation of unpopulated alluvial zones by colonists from outside the area, and some form of interaction between foragers and farmers in southern and western Greece, where pockets of indigenous peoples could be found.

After Greece, two grand currents of farming dispersal can be identified: westward along the Mediterranean littoral and northwest into temperate Europe along major rivers. The dispersal along the Mediterranean coast provides ample evidence that watercraft were in use by the seventh millennium B.C.—the locations of the earliest domesticated plants, animals and pottery are widely separated at both mainland and island sites. Inland, the mountainous and forested terrain posed obstacles. Communication routes presumably existed along the major rivers, and animals and

indigenous foragers had already made paths and trails along which people could move and interact.

Transition in the Balkans

About a millennium after their appearance in Greece, agricultural communities were established in the southern Balkans, first in the valleys of the Vardar, Morava, Struma and Maritsa rivers and later in the Danube valley itself. Although the settlements vary in their architecture and in the composition of the animal remains, the domestic plants and animals consisted of the now-familiar southwestern Asiatic complex of emmer and einkorn wheat and barley, as well as sheep, goats, cattle and pigs. As in Greece, the presence of alluvial soils on river and lake floodplains was a critical determinant of settlement location.

In the early agricultural settlements

of the Balkans, there are clear signs of an adaptation to temperate conditions. At most sites, cattle and pigs become more important than sheep and goats, while wheat and barley became summer (rather than winter) crops. Just as Anatolia provided the springboard for agricultural dispersal into Greece, the Balkans were the scene of important transitions in Neolithic subsistence and settlement that enabled the spread of agriculture further into central and northern Europe.

Studies of the transition to agriculture in southeastern Europe are hampered by an almost complete ignorance of the local hunter-gatherer populations. The sites of early foragers are almost invariably found where the early farmers did not settle, such as in the western Balkan mountains of Montenegro and Bosnia or the Iron Gates gorges between Serbia and Romania. Because of this it has

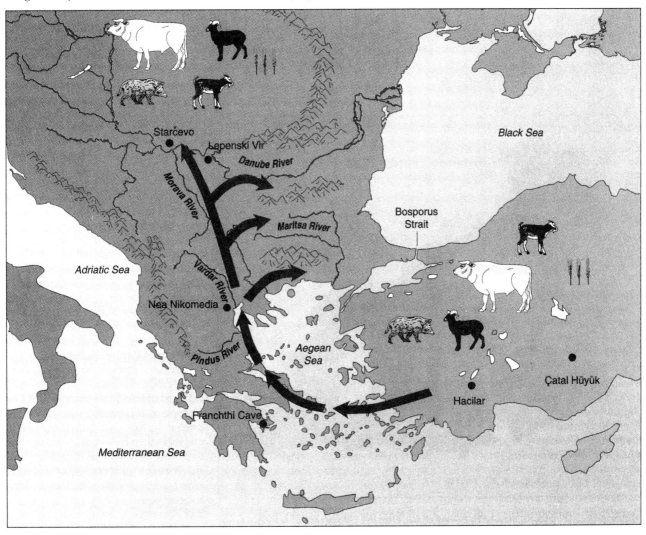

Figure 3. First farmers in Europe probably came from the centuries-old agricultural economies of southwestern Asia by island-hopping across the Aegean Sea. Archaeological remains reveal that these colonists brought their livestock (cattle, sheep, goats and pigs) and crops (emmer and einkorn wheat and barley) with them as they entered Greece. Several hundred early Neolithic sites are now known in Greek Macedonia and Thessaly.

been argued that colonization was the primary mechanism of the initial agricultural dispersal into temperate Europe. For example, van Andel and Runnels see the dispersal of agriculture to the southeastern Balkans as an extension of agricultural settlement in Thessaly. An alternative view is possible, however. Haskel Greenfield of the University of Manitoba has recently pointed out variations in the proportions of bones from wild and domestic animals at Balkan sites of this period. He suggests that such a pattern might be expected as indigenous foraging groups integrate domesticated plants and animals into their economy, each in its own fashion. Although the evidence is equivocal, it will be important to subject the colonization hypothesis to critical scrutiny and perhaps to amend it as new observations warrant.

One broad geographical division seen in the Balkan Neolithic is between the eastern Balkans (generally, Bulgaria and Romania) and the western Balkans (in the region of the former Yugoslavia). In the eastern Balkans, as in Greece, Neolithic sites generally occur as mounds,

or *tells*, formed by the accumulation of baked-clay construction. The classic Bulgarian tell is Karanovo, where 12 meters of debris accumulated between the beginning of the Neolithic and the early Bronze Age three thousand years later. The layers from the early part of the sixth millennium B.C. reveal a settlement of several dozen freestanding one-room houses, built by daubing mud plaster onto upright wooden posts. Each was apparently occupied by a family or household. The nearby sites of Chevdar, Azmak and Kazanluk have yielded important information on subsistence and crop processing.

In the central and western Balkans between about 6100 and 5100 B.C., the sites of the Starčevo culture were established along the Vardar, Morava and Danube rivers. Unlike the tells of the eastern Balkans, Starčevo sites generally have relatively little vertical accumulation of debris. Instead, they consist of complexes of subterranean features, some of which have been interpreted as pit-houses, whereas others may have been borrow pits for clay plaster for surface structures. The pit complexes con-

tain dense concentrations of broken pottery, animal bones and other rubbish, indicating a secondary use as disposal areas. Blagotin in central Serbia and Foeni in Romania are two such Starčevo settlements excavated recently by Haskel Greenfield and his collaborators.

Variable as this patchwork of new agricultural settlements was, one area stands out as unique: the Iron Gates gorge on the border between Serbia and Romania. Here the site of Lepenski Vir has puzzled archaeologists since its discovery in the late 1960s. Situated next to a whirlpool at a bend in the Danube, Lepenski Vir is a multi-period settlement with numerous trapezoid-shaped huts, each with a stone hearth and often with enigmatic piscine stone sculptures. For most of its existence the economy of Lepenski Vir appears to have been based on fishing and hunting, with domestic plants and animals and Starčevo pottery appearing only towards the end of the settlement. The dating of Lepenski Vir is controversial, but there is some overlap with neighboring farming cultures.

Two interpretations of Lepenski Vir are possible. One is that it was a settlement of hunters and fishers who resisted the adoption of agriculture through their successful foraging adaptation and only belatedly incorporated domestic plants, livestock and pottery into their economy. Another is of a foraging community that had already adopted a sedentary lifestyle prior to the appearance of agriculture and that very quickly adopted food production once it became available nearby. Unfortunately, a hydroelectric project has inundated this part of the Danube Valley. It is unlikely that it will ever be possible to find new evidence that bears on this problem.

Farming in Central Europe

In central Europe early farmers encountered soils and terrain markedly different from those of southeastern Europe, and domestic plants were expected to flourish in a climate with considerably more rainfall and with even sharper seasonal differences than the Near East. Moreover, this terrain was heavily forested with well-established species such as linden, elm and oak. Beneath these forests, however, were basins of fertile loess and moist stream valleys, which were very attractive to farming communities.

Agriculture appears to have been introduced into central Europe by farm-

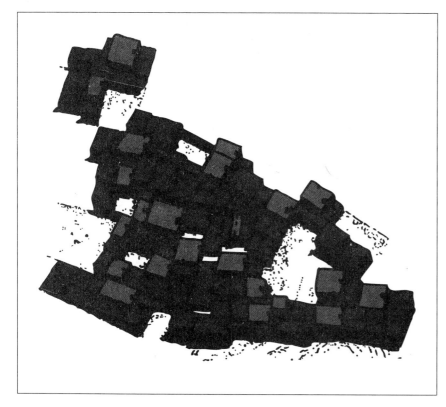

Figure 4. Densely packed, mud-brick houses characterize the homesteads of the early farmers in Near Eastern sites such as Çatal Hüyük in the seventh millennium B.C. As the mud-brick buildings collapsed through decades of use, new buildings were built on top of the old remains, eventually forming large mounds, or *tells*. Archaeological excavations of the mound at Çatal Hüyük reveal that the city (one section of which is tentatively reconstructed here) was continuously inhabited for at least eight centuries. (Adapted from Mellaart 1975.)

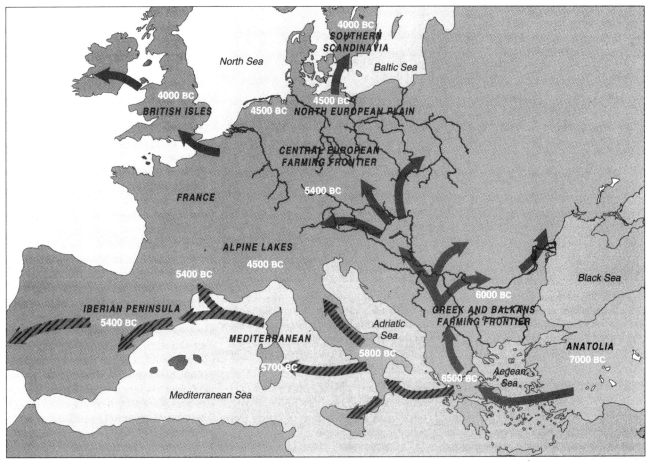

Figure 5. Two major currents of movement characterize the spread of European agriculture after the first farmers entered Greece from southwestern Asia. One progression corresponds to the Mediterranean habitat zone in which agriculture spread along the coast and across the sea to the major islands, (*striped arrows*). Another current of early farmers followed the fertile river valleys of the Balkans and into central, northern and western Europe (*black arrows*).

ing peoples who colonized the loess basins. From Slovakia to the Netherlands, the similarity of pottery, house forms, crops, settlement locations and stone tools strongly suggests that the indigenous peoples did not participate in bringing agriculture to the region. These early farmers of central Europe are known as the Linear Pottery Culture (or *Linearbandkeramik*, LBK) because of the distinct ceramics they decorated with incised lines. The Linear Pottery Culture has its roots on the Hungarian Plain about 5600 B.C. and spread within a matter of centuries across central Europe westward to France and northward to Poland and Germany.

The loess basins were attractive to the Linear Pottery Culture for several reasons. First, these areas appear to have had few settlements of indigenous foragers, although recent work has revealed that some hunter-gatherers were present. Any foragers living on the loess were rapidly absorbed or displaced into outlying areas such as

the glacial outwash plains of central Poland. Second, the natural fertility of the loess was especially suited to wheat and barley. A third reason was the nature of the terrain and drainage in the loess basins. The spring flooding and groundwater from the watersheds would have recharged the soil nutrients in the narrow floodplains of the small central European streams. As a result, the fertility of these regions was sustained for years despite continuous cultivation.

The crops grown by the Linear Pottery farmers were the familiar domesticates of Near Eastern origin, emmer and einkorn wheat and barley, as well as lentils and peas. Adaptation of these crops to the soils and climate of central Europe indicates the genetic malleability of these plants. It also suggests that the climate of central Europe was somewhat warmer than it is at present, providing a gentler transition from the Balkan and Near Eastern temperatures. Mixed among the carbonized plant re-

mains found on Linear Pottery sites are seeds of shade-loving weeds, which appear to have grown among the crops. Palaeobotanists have concluded from this that Linear Pottery fields were relatively small forest clearings, where the edges were shaded by adjacent trees.

The animal bones found on Linear Pottery sites are characterized by a large proportion of cattle, with relatively few sheep and goats and almost no pigs. These proportions are notable for a number of reasons. In a largely forested environment it would make good sense to minimize the number of sheep, although goats as browsers would still have found adequate food. The numbers of cattle that could be supported in such a habitat also would have been relatively low, yet this species dominates the faunal collections. Pigs, which are ideally suited for forested conditions, are remarkably scarce in Linear Pottery faunal assemblages.

To raise cattle only for meat in the forests and small meadows of central

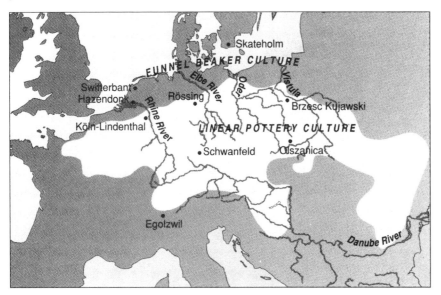

Figure 6. Distribution of the Linear Pottery Culture of the early Neolithic from western Ukraine to France approximates the extent of the fertile loess belt deposited during the last ice age (which ended about 10,000 B.C.) Early farmers probably entered central Europe from the Balkan Peninsula about 5400 B.C. by following the rich soils along the major rivers, such as the Danube. These farmers relied on the Near Eastern staple crops of emmer, einkorn, barley, lentils and peas. The livestock included cattle, sheep, goats and pigs.

Europe would have been inefficient and risky. The dominance of the faunal assemblages by cattle makes economic sense only if the cattle are seen as multipurpose livestock whose males yielded meat and females were kept primarily for dairy products. Use of dairy products is further documented by the presence on many Linear Pottery sites of ceramic sieves whose only function could have been the straining of curds from whey to make cheese.

The settlements of the Linear Pottery farmers consist of houses that are clustered along the valleys of creeks that drain into the larger central European rivers. They are not on the banks of the streams but rather are set back near the border between the floodplain and the rising edge of the watersheds. These clusters may extend for several kilometers and then be separated from additional clusters by several more kilometers. Archaeologists apply the term *settlement cells* to such units. The locations of the houses presumably bore a relation to the locations of the fields and pastures of the inhabitants, most of which were probably on the floodplain or in vales in the rolling hills back from the stream.

The distinctive houses of the Linear Pottery farmers are markedly different from those found in the Balkans. They are long timber-framed structures, about 6 meters wide and up to 40 meters long. These houses were the largest freestanding buildings in the world at this time, but the only traces that remain of them are the dark stains that the posts left in the loess. Clusters of these houses have often been called villages, implying a certain structure and settlement organization. Recently, many archaeologists have come to view Linear Pottery settlements as collections of farmsteads, with each house separated from its neighbors by some physical and social distance. The shifting of house locations over time produced a palimpsest of postholes and

Figure 7. Distinctive patterns of incised lines on clay pottery made by the early farmers of central Europe are the basis for the name of the Linear Pottery Culture. Although similar ceramic forms and decoration suggest that the Linear Pottery culture was relatively homogeneous, some regional and temporal variation does exist.

pits, which makes settlement on Linear Pottery sites appear denser than was really the case.

Until the 1970s archaeologists believed that the Linear Pottery sites were occupied for only short periods of time. Unlike a Balkan tell, the timber architecture and dispersed layout of a Linear Pottery site did not lead to a large accumulation of debris in one spot—giving the impression of short-term occupation. The apparent brevity of the occupation at these sites was believed to be a consequence of the farmers' agricultural system. Since many subsistence farmers around the world today practice slash-and-burn agriculture (sometimes called shifting agriculture or swidden), Linear Pottery farmers were presumed to have done likewise. Since slash-and-burn depletes soil nutrients quickly (hence requiring the shifting of fields and settlements), the Linear Pottery farmers were thought to have relocated their settlements every few years because they depleted the fertility of the loess.

Recently, however, several lines of research have converged to displace this argument. First was the realization that loess, particularly in the rich habitats favored by the early farmers, is capable of sustaining high crop yields almost indefinitely. It differs significantly in this regard from the thin nutrient-poor soils of the tropics where slash-and-burn is practiced today. Second, a careful study of Linear Pottery settlements indicates that they were in fact long-term habitations. Settlement cells were occupied for several centuries, although houses may have been rebuilt in slightly different locations or abandoned as their inhabitants died. Most archaeologists today do not believe that Linear Pottery farmers routinely "shifted bag and baggage to a new site on fresh virgin soil," as Childe once wrote.

If soil depletion was not the cause of Linear Pottery dispersal, then what was? Settlement cells were not overpopulated—there was ample room in areas that were subsequently occupied by later peoples. Its more likely that community fissioning was the result of local factors. It is possible to envision the occupants of a longhouse as a single social unit (a household), which was the primary unit of social organization and decision making. A household could decide to relocate for many reasons, including conflicts with adjacent households and perceived opportunities for economic and social improvement.

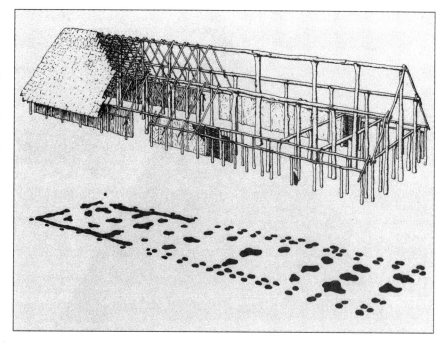

Figure 8. Free-standing timber-framed houses—as large as 40 meters long and 6 meters wide—characterize the farmsteads of the Linear Pottery Culture. Each building is believed to have housed an extended family, and several would make up a settlement site not far from a river or a creek. The dramatic change in architectural design from the densely packed houses of Çatal Hüyük reflects the use of a modular house type suitable for pioneer settlement and made from abundant local materials. The separated dwellings also suggests a greater social distance among the household units that colonized central Europe. Here a reconstruction from a settlement site in Rössing in Germany is positioned over the remains of the wood-frame building left in the soil. (Reproduced from *Ausgrabungen in Niedersachsen*, ed. K. Wilhelmi, 1985.)

Moreover, desire for suitable mates and rules of postmarital residence may also have caused moves that eventually resulted in the establishment of a new household cycle. In any event, it is likely that the reasons for the dispersal of farming across central Europe lie more in the motivations and aspirations of individual households than in single-factor explanations such as soil depletion or population pressure.

Farming along the Mediterranean

As agriculture spread along the Danube basin into central Europe, it was also spreading along the Mediterranean coast westward to Spain. For many years archaeologists believed that there was a Mediterranean "Neolithic package" similar to that found in central Europe—pottery, domesticates and sedentary settlements—that was dispersed through colonization. Recent research, however, has shown that the picture is much more complex, and there is no consensus about the nature of the process. It is a difficult question to answer partly because the coastal and estuarine areas are now submerged after the rising sea levels in post-Neolithic

times. As a result most of the research has focused on caves and rock shelters.

One hypothesis holds that the indigenous foraging communities around the Mediterranean selectively adopted some of the characteristics of a food-producing economy as much as a millennium before they became sedentary farmers. In Tuscany, for example, pottery is found in levels dating to the late seventh millennium B.C. even though there is no evidence for an agricultural economy. Evidence from the Grotta dell'Uzzo in Sicily indicates that crops and livestock had moved west by the early sixth millennium B.C., yet the local diet consisted primarily of wild plants and animals. Domesticates also appeared in southern France, Sardinia, Corsica and eastern Spain around this time. Of particular note is the discovery of domestic sheep at several sites, which may have been acquired through trade (or poaching) between foragers and herders.

The Portuguese archaeologist João Zilhão takes a dissenting view, arguing that the beginning of the Neolithic in the western Mediterranean occurred when small groups of settlers brought domesticated plants, animals and pot-

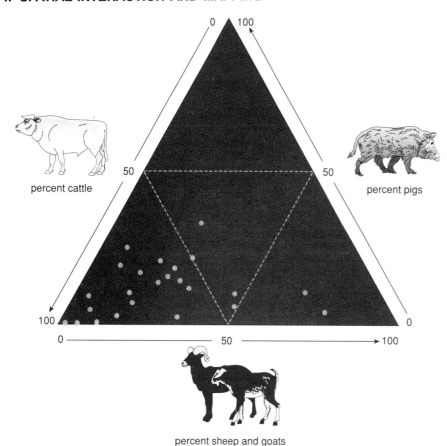

percent cattle

percent pigs

percent sheep and goats

Figure 9. Representation of different livestock types among the remains at farming sites of the Linear Pottery Culture suggests that domesticated cattle were very important to the agricultural economy of Neolithic Europeans. The bones of cattle almost always outnumber the remains of sheep, goats and pigs. The recovery of ceramic sieves—which may have been used for straining curds from whey to make cheese—suggests that the cattle may have been used for dairy production. The bones of wild mammals are usually rare, suggesting that hunting was a small part of the farmers' subsistence strategy. Here the percentages of the domesticated species are estimated from the relative number of bones found at 24 sites in central Europe. (Adapted from Bogucki and Grygiel 1993.)

tery and eventually interacted with the indigenous foragers. Zilhão bases his position on critical analysis of the stratigraphy at many early sites and claims that the mixing of deposits gives the impression that Neolithic technology and domesticates appeared piecemeal earlier than they actually did.

By the late sixth millennium B.C. fully agricultural villages are found in several areas. On the Tavoliere Plain in southern Italy at sites like Passo di Corvo, household complexes, each surrounded by a ditch, contained a complete range of domesticates—sheep, goats, cattle, pigs, emmer and einkorn, barley and lentils. In central Italy, sedentary pottery-using agricultural communities lived at sites like San Marco. The key question here is to determine what happened during the millennium between the acquisition of pottery, crops and

livestock by foragers and the development of fully agricultural settlements. Did the foragers settle down and begin to farm in earnest, or was there an influx of farmers from elsewhere?

Critical to understanding the adoption of agriculture in the Mediterranean is the analysis of trade in various materials and products to examine patterns of regional interaction. William Barnett of the American Museum of Natural History has traced the circulation of Neolithic pottery in southern France, and Albert Ammerman of Colgate University and Robert Tykot of Harvard University have both studied the distribution patterns of obsidian. In the absence of evidence for large-scale movements of people, there is a good possibility that the dispersal of agricultural techniques and domesticated plants and animals followed patterns

of exchange that were established by the indigenous foragers.

North and South of the Loess
Areas north and south of the loess belt (on the North European Plain and in the alpine foreland) were populated by more hunter-gatherers than was the loess during the sixth and fifth millennia B.C. Forager bands appear to have confined their movements to increasingly smaller areas during this period, particularly the meltwater valleys, marshes, estuaries and coastal regions on the North European Plain and the glacial lakes in the alpine foothills. In some parts of the North European Plain (in central Poland and along the lower Oder river) outlying settlements of the Linear Pottery Culture and its descendants formed "islands" of sedentary agriculturalists.

My Polish colleague Ryszard Grygiel of the Museum of Archaeology and Ethnography in Lódź and I have focused our research on one such "island" in north-central Poland, where we have investigated a series of early farming settlements of the Linear Pottery Culture and its successor, the Lengyel Culture, which spans the period between 5400 and 4000 B.C. These sites are located in glacial meltwater channels, which are analogous to the moist stream basins of the loess. Lengyel settlements in northern Poland represent long-term commitments to particular settlement locations. Here the inhabitants built trapezoidal-plan longhouses among which they buried their dead. The full suite of domesticated plants and animals is found on these sites along with extensive evidence that they relied on local wildlife, including waterfowl, turtles and fish.

Domestic plants and animals became a part of the forager subsistence pattern about a millennium after the appearance of farming communities on the southern edge of the North European Plain. The basis for agriculture was available during this period, but the foragers resisted adopting it until about 4000 B.C. As T. Douglas Price and Anne Birgitte Gebauer of the University of Wisconsin point out, the most reasonable explanation for the delay is that the success of their foraging adaptation meant that the hunter-gatherers saw little immediate use for domestic plants and animals. The answer to the question of *why* they eventually adopted agriculture remains elusive.

We can be reasonably confident that agriculture came to the North European Plain through a complex and poorly understood interaction between the indigenous foragers and the inhabitants of the neighboring farming settlements. Beyond that general characterization, however, only hypotheses can be generated. Feral livestock were probably the first elements of food production to pass through the frontier between foragers and farmers. Mutually beneficial relationships may have formed between hunter-gatherers and agriculturalists, possibly involving the exchange of forest products for surplus crops. Perhaps the sedentary farming life appealed to some foragers, who became drawn to agricultural communities and eventually intermarried with the farmers. Another possibility is that the farmers adopted some aspects of the dispersed foraging settlement pattern while keeping their domestic plants and animals.

At this time the foragers of the Ertebølle culture flourished along the estuaries of the western Baltic coast. The food remains found on Ertebølle sites reflect a maritime focus, which is confirmed by carbon-isotope ratios in human bones. Elaborate cemeteries are known from sites such as Skateholm in southern Sweden. There is some evidence for exchange with farming communities to the south, but despite the local innovation of pottery there is no conclusive evidence of domestic plants or animals. All indications point to Ertebølle as having been a sedentary foraging society based on the intensive use of rich marine resources.

Around 3900 B.C., however, there is a shift to an agricultural economy in the western Baltic littoral. Although these Neolithic farmers are given a different name—the Funnel Beaker Culture—it is clear that they are a continuation of the foraging communities that have added agriculture, livestock and Neolithic technology. As Price and Gebauer put it, the last hunters in this area were also the first farmers. Funnel Beaker sites are found over a wide area, from Poland to the Netherlands and north into Denmark and Sweden. The key change from their foraging predecessors is a shift away from a maritime economy to inland farming, a transition also documented with carbon-isotope samples of collagen from human bones.

In the delta of the Rhine and Maas Rivers and on tidal creeks along the IJsselmeer near Amsterdam, several sites have been found that reveal a different type of adaptation. Hazendonk, Bergschenhoek and Swifterbant are locations that are unattractive for agriculture and have restricted arable land. Nonetheless, there is evidence of agriculture, including crops in the form of charred grain and chaff and the bones of domestic animals. These sites appear to have served different functions. Hazendonk, where 90 percent of the bones are those of wild animals, appears to have been a hunting station. The Swifterbant sites to the north were probably longer-term habitations. Bergschenhoek, which was on a floating peat island, was a short-term winter fishing and fowling station. Some remarkably-preserved fish traps have been uncovered here.

Leendart Louwe Kooijmans of Leiden University has called this type of subsistence "semi-agrarian," because hunting, fowling and fishing were supplemented with animal husbandry and the consumption of cereals. It may be that these sites are the wetland part of a larger settlement system, but sites in drier areas nearby have yet to be discovered. It seems clear, however, that these sites are an example of indigenous foragers who gradually adopted elements of a food-producing economy, probably from farmers not far to the south. This semi-agrarian pattern continued for almost a millennium, until about 3000 B.C., when it was finally superseded by a full farming economy.

A process similar to that seen on the North European Plain appears to have taken place in the foothills of the Alps. The earliest traces of farmers in the late sixth millennium B.C. are found in the form of pioneering communities from the loess to the north and from the Mediterranean basin to the south. Outlying Linear Pottery sites are found in northern Switzerland at Gächlingen and Bottmingen. In southern Switzerland, traces of early farmers with connections to northern Italy have been found at Sion-Planta and Castel Grande-Bellinzona.

As on the North European Plain, there was a delay of almost a millennium before further developments occurred. Around the glacial lake basins in north-central Switzerland, several forager communities had already settled for some time. For example, around the Wauwilersee, a series of hunter-gatherer sites mark the preagricultural shoreline. Around 4400 B.C., agricultural settlements were established on the banks of a number of similar lake basins. At the Wauwilersee, the complex of sites at Egolzwil has yielded

Figure 10. A cave in southern France (Cova de l'Esperit) contains evidence of early farming dating to the late sixth millennium B.C. The cave is located at the edge of the coastal plain, near upland valleys, ideally situated to take advantage of resources offered by both locales. (Photograph courtesy of William K. Barnett.)

Figure 11. Ceramics of the Ertebølle culture—such as this pointed-base pot and a small animal-blubber lamp—are found along the northern coast of Europe and the southern parts of Scandanavia. The people of the Ertebølle culture were sedentary hunters and gatherers who relied on the rich marine life in the region. Around 3900 B.C. the Ertebølle foragers adopted crops, livestock and Neolithic technology. Archaeologists recognize this transition to farming by giving the farmers a different name, the Funnel Beaker Culture. (Photograph courtesy of the National Museum of Denmark).

considerable data on diet and settlement plans, whereas at the Zürichsee an early settlement is found at the Kleiner Hafner.

Although there is evidence of interaction with the communities that succeeded the Linear Pottery Culture to the north, the lake-shore settlements of the Alpine Foreland are best regarded as a local development. They are found in areas of prior forager settlement and in similar lakeside locations. The remarkable preservation of organic material has provided an unusually complete picture of their subsistence economy. Although there was a primary reliance on domesticated plants and animals, a wide spectrum of wild resources was also used, including red deer, wild cattle and many different types of plants. The inhabitants of these sites lived in small rectangular houses (about 4 meters by 8 meters) in rows along the lake shore. Contrary to popular depictions of the "Swiss Lake Dwellings," these structures were not built on pilings over the water, but rather had numerous posts driven into the soft lake shore to support the house.

Farming Reaches the Atlantic
The arrival of agriculture on the Atlantic façade of Europe is still poorly under-stood, partly because archaeologists have been preoccupied with megalithic chambered tombs and other stone monuments (which were built somewhat later). Few settlements have been excavated, and there is little systematic information on subsistence. Western France is particularly lacking in evidence of the first agriculture. The sites of Téviec and Hoëdic suggest the presence of substantial foraging populations in Brittany. There are indications that domestic animals reached these communities, perhaps the feral livestock from farmers to the east. The little evidence we have suggests that the Neolithic of western France was a local development of the indigenous foragers.

The introduction of agriculture to the British Isles presents a particularly interesting archaeological problem. By 5000 B.C. the English Channel and the Irish Sea had attained their present-day width, so it is clear that contact with the continent required the use of watercraft large enough to carry not only seed grain but also livestock. Beyond the fact that someone had to bring grain and livestock from the European continent, the colonization-versus-adoption debate in the British Isles is lively. The evidence can usually be interpreted to support either position, largely because it is highly variable. I suggest that this variability is consistent with a gradual adoption of food production by native communities rather than a large influx of people from the continent. In contrast to the situation in Greece and on the loess, the British Isles provide ample evidence for pre-agricultural groups, who may have been part of a larger exchange network that spanned the water barriers.

The transition from foraging to farming has received particularly close scrutiny in Ireland recently, and much evidence indicates continuity from hunter-gatherers to agriculturalists. For example, in the Bally Lough area of southern Ireland, Stanton Green of Clarion University of Pennsylvania and Marek Zvelebil of the University of Scheffield have documented that the land-use patterns of foragers and farmers were not particularly different, suggesting continuity in population, resource use and social organization. As in southern Scandinavia and elsewhere in Atlantic Europe, a case can be made that the last Irish hunters were the first Irish farmers. Yet somehow the livestock and grain had to be brought across the Irish Sea. Gabriel Cooney and Eoin Grogan of the University College of Dublin have recently urged that the traditional colonization model not be discarded completely, suggesting that small-scale intrusions of farmers brought a way of life that presented an attractive alternative to foraging.

Conclusion
The introduction of agriculture to Europe does not appear to have been a uniform process in which a "Neolithic package" of domestic plants and animals, pottery and long-term settlements spread steadily across the continent. Instead, there was considerable geographic and temporal variability. In some regions, such as Greece and central Europe, colonization by farming populations from elsewhere appears to have taken place. In other areas, as in northern and western Europe, indigenous foragers adopted agriculture and pottery. In many places, controversy still exists over whether colonization or indigenous adoption was the prime mechanism of agricultural dispersal; reasonable arguments have been voiced for both positions.

Refinement of chronology through radiocarbon dating has made it possible to examine the punctuated nature of the agricultural dispersal across Europe.

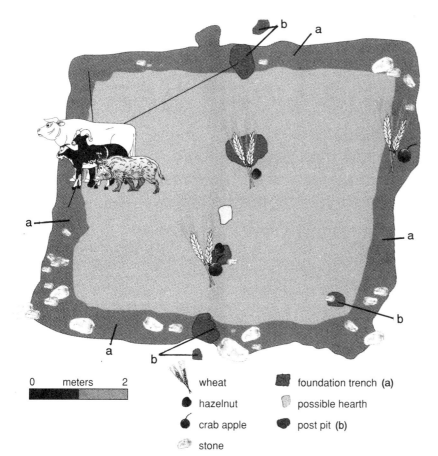

wheat

hazelnut

crab apple

stone

foundation trench (a)

possible hearth

post pit (b)

0 meters 2

Figure 12. Remains of crops and livestock scattered about the site of a Neolithic house date the arrival of agriculture in Ireland to the early fourth millennium B.C. It appears that crops and livestock were brought to Ireland by small groups of farmers who integrated their economy with the hunting-and-gathering lifestyle. Here the location of livestock and crop remains are shown from a site in Tankardstown South, County Limerick. (Adapted from Cooney and Grogan 1994.)

household. Such questions ensure that the study of early European farmers will be an important research topic for years to come.

Acknowledgments

Curtis Runnels, William Barnett, and Haskel Greenfield made helpful comments on an earlier draft of this paper.

Bibliography

Barker, G. 1985. *Prehistoric Farming in Europe.* Cambridge: Cambridge University Press.

Barnett, W. K. 1995. Putting the pot before the horse: Earliest ceramics and the Neolithic transition in the western Mediterranean. In *The Emergence of Pottery: Technology and Innovation in Ancient Societies,* ed. W. K. Barnett and J. W. Hoopes. Washington: Smithsonian Institution Press, pp. 79–88.

Bogucki, P. 1988. *Forest Farmers and Stockherders. Early Agriculture and Its Consequences in North-Central Europe.* Cambridge: Cambridge University Press.

Bogucki, P., and R. Grygiel. 1993. The first farmers of north-central Europe. *Journal of Field Archaeology* 20(3):399–426.

Cooney, G., and E. Grogan. 1994. *Irish Prehistory: A Social Perspective.* Dublin: Wordwell.

Green, S. W., and M. Zvelebil. 1993. Interpreting Ireland's prehistoric landscape: The Bally Lough Archaeological Project. In *Case Studies in European Prehistory,* ed. P. Bogucki. Boca Raton: CRC Press, pp. 1–29

Greenfield, H. 1993. Zooarchaeology, taphonomy, and the origin of food production in the central Balkans. In *Culture and Environment: a Fragile Coexistence,* ed. R.W. Jamieson, S. Abonyi, and N.A. Mirau. Calgary: University of Calgary Archaeological Association, pp. 111–117.

Hodder, I. 1990. *The Domestication of Europe.* Oxford: Basil Blackwell.

Louwe Kooijmans, L. P. 1993. The Mesolithic/Neolithic transformation in the lower Rhine basin. In *Case Studies in European Prehistory,* ed. P. Bogucki. Boca Raton: CRC Press, pp. 95–145.

Mellaart, James. 1975. *The Neolithic of the Near East.* New York: Charles Scribner's Sons.

Perlès, C. 1994. Les débuts du Néolithique en Grèce. *La Recherche* 266:642–649.

Price, T. D., A. B. Gebauer, and L. H. Keeley. 1995. The spread of farming into Europe north of the Alps. In *Last Hunters—First Farmers. New Perspectives on the Prehistoric Transition to Agriculture,* ed. T. D. Price and A. B. Gebauer. Santa Fe: School of American Research Press, pp. 95–126.

Scarre, C. (ed.). 1983. *Ancient France.* Edinburgh: Edinburgh University Press.

van Andel, T. H., and C. Runnels. 1995. The earliest farmers in Europe. *Antiquity* 69:481–500.

Whittle, A. 1996. *Europe in the Neolithic.* Cambridge: Cambridge University Press.

Wilhelmi, K. 1985. *Ausgrabungen in Niedersachsen.* Stuttgart: Konrad Theiss.

Zilhão, J. 1993. The spread of agro-pastoral economies across Mediterranean Europe: a view from the far west. *Journal of Mediterranean Archaeology* 6:5–63.

For example, farming communities existed in Greece for nearly a millennium before penetrating north into the Balkans. Similarly, along the southern part of the North European Plain, a frontier between foragers and farmers persisted until nearly 4000 B.C. From a global perspective the spread of agriculture in Europe took place very quickly, but when studied in detail the spurts and halts become more apparent.

As many investigators have emphasized, soil moisture was a primary determinant of early agricultural settlement in Anatolia, the Balkans and central Europe. In these cases colonization remains the most viable hypothesis. Perhaps eventually the generalization can be made that a clear preference for floodplain and alluvial habitats is a hallmark of agricultural colonization. In contrast, where hunter-gatherers adopted agriculture, the early farming settlements continue in the same locations as their foraging predecessors. This would suggest that domesticates

were integrated into an existing subsistence system.

A question that has perplexed archaeologists is why foragers who have successful, and apparently stable, hunting-and-gathering lifestyles adopt agriculture with all its risks and hard work. Perhaps the "stability" of these forager adaptations is illusory and only appears that way through the prism of the archaeological record. It is probably more realistic to assume that foragers, particularly in temperate seasonal latitudes, were *not* in equilibrium with their environment over time. Rather, they were prone to fluctuations in resource availability on both seasonal and annual time scales and on various spatial scales. Even the Ertebølle foragers with their abundant maritime resources may have experienced short-term shortages. One promising hypothesis is that it is precisely during these unstable periods that agriculture took root among foragers in certain regions at the social level of the band or

Raising the Dead Sea

A canal linking the Red Sea and the Dead Sea could be a concrete symbol of the peace between two old enemies, Israel and Jordan. But, as Fred Pearce discovers, it may not be the best way to solve a water crisis

The River Jordan has watered civilisation for ten thousand years. Now, for much of the year, only a slow, salty trickle leaves the Sea of Galilee and meanders south to the Dead Sea. As a result the Dead Sea is shrivelling and Jordan is suffering unprecedented water shortages.

King Hussein has hit on a plan to refill the Dead Sea from the south and revive his country. He wants to link the Red Sea to the Dead Sea with a 240-kilometre canal. The king hopes that as the Red Sea's waters flow inland, they will transform one of the hottest desert valleys on

---

Human interaction with the Dead Sea has caused the level to fall significantly over the years. Unless something is done to reverse the trend, the Dead Sea will dry up in 50 years.

Earth into a green oasis, and fuel industrial development. And since signing the peace treaty with Israel last October, Hussein has been dreaming of a "peace dividend" in the form of international backing for his project. But will this peace dividend become a well of prosperity for Jordan—or a billion-dollar mirage in the desert?

Jordan is one of the driest countries on Earth. It has less water per head of population than its neighbour Israel, less than

Saudi Arabia and most of the Gulf states, which spend a large portion of their oil revenues desalinating seawater, and much less than any of the states of the Sahara.

The causes of Jordan's hydrological poverty are part geographical and part political. It is an almost totally landlocked desert kingdom, with few rivers. Until thirty years ago, the River Jordan was the country's lifeblood. But in 1964, Israel started diverting most of the river's annual flow of 1200 million cubic metres into the National Water Carrier, to irrigate its own fields. As hostilities between the two countries continued, international donors refused to lend money to allow Jordan to build dams on its few remaining rivers and the "wadis", the watercourses that are dry apart from during the rainy season.

To supply its taps and irrigate its fields, Jordan has had to pump water from natural underground reserves. Much of this water percolated underground centuries ago in wetter times, and is not being replaced. Within a generation, say hydrologists, most of it will be gone.

LOWERING THE DEAD

Meanwhile, the level of the Dead Sea is failing. For hundreds of years it remained around 392 metres below sea level, but since Israel diverted the waters of the River Jordan, the level has been sinking by half a metre a year, says Muhammad Shatanawi, director of the water and environment research centre at the University of Jordan, Amman. It is now down to 409 metres below sea level and the surface area has shrunk by almost 300 square kilometres, or 30 per cent of its former area. And as the coastline has retreated, factories that extract potash and other salts from the water have found themselves stranded several kilometres from the sea.

Unless something is done, says Shatanawi, the Dead Sea is doomed. "Within a few years, the Israelis, Jordanians and Palestinians will be using all the wadis, as well as all the flow from the River Jordan. There will be no water at all going into the Dead Sea, and in 50 years it will have dried up altogether."

The plight of the Dead Sea was one of the reasons why Hussein agreed to peace terms with Israel, ending almost fifty years of conflict, and opening the way for international aid. He also secured Israel's agreement to work on a development programme along the border between the two countries in the Rift Valley south of the Dead Sea. And now the World Bank and the US government's Overseas Private Investment Corporation are offering to promote the programme in a

 From *New Scientist*, July 22, 1995, pp. 32-37.

bid to attract international and private funds.

At the heart of the development programme is Hussein's proposal for a "Red-Dead" canal. Weaving back and forth across the Jordan-Israeli border, the canal would not only link the two seas, it would also irrevocably link the two countries. The canal would exploit the 400-metre height difference between the two seas to generate hydroelectricity. This, in turn, would power desalination works serving both countries.

In the week that Israel and Jordan signed their peace accord, the World Bank published the results of its feasibility study on the Red-Dead canal. It suggested that such a canal could carry 1900 million cubic metres of water a year, enough to raise the Dead Sea to its former level within a decade. Thereafter, flow would be reduced to around 1200 million cubic metres, similar to the former flow of the River Jordan.

The canal, the World Bank said, could provide a hydroelectric generating capacity of around 600 megawatts, similar to a medium-sized power station. There was one drawback. The route from the Red Sea to the Dead Sea is not downhill all the way. The first stretch involves a 220-metre climb. The World Bank calculated that about two-thirds of the power generated by the canal on its downward journey would be needed to pump the water up the initial climb. Even so, there would still be enough power left to desalinate around 800 million cubic metres of water annually from the canal and local saline groundwaters.

The Bank estimates that the canal would cost between $3 billion and $4 billion, roughly half as much as the Channel Tunnel, and take ten years to build. But, once built, it "could become the backbone of an intensive development strategy" for the barren, empty and stifling valley between the two seas, one of the hottest deserts in the world. The canal could provide water for fish farms, industry, agriculture and recreational lakes along the canal, as well as for "solar ponds" to generate further electricity.

In April, Jordan and Israel agreed to set up a joint authority to oversee development in the Rift Valley. At the top of their agenda will be tourism. Since the peace deal unlocked the border, tourists have flooded into the valley to visit the ancient city of Petra, the beaches and coral reefs of the Red Sea, and desert attractions such as the annual bird migrations through the Rift Valley.

Israel plans "the Lowest Park on Earth", comprising a mix of nature reserves and health spas on the Dead Sea. Not to be outdone, Abdul Kader, development officer at the Jordan Valley Authority, has announced Jordanian plans for "a recreation area of some 325 square kilometres on the eastern shore of the Dead Sea". It would, he said, include a "Disneyland-style theme park" and cable cars to a hot spring resort at the hill town of Ma'in overlooking the sea.

Already, Jordan and Israel are finding that American industrialists and construction companies are queuing up to invest American aid grants in funfairs and fish farms, electricity pylons and potash. But without more water to prime the pumps, most of the industrial, tourist and agricultural projects will come to nothing. Which is why Hussein wants to build a Red-Dead canal.

OTHER OPTIONS

But is the project viable, or is there a cheaper, less grandiose way to achieve the same objective? The need to do something about Jordan's water supplies is evident wherever you go in the country. For the fifth summer running, water rationing has been introduced in urban areas, with supplies cut off for many hours at a time. And while other Middle East countries grow two or three crops a year on their irrigated fields, Jordan manages only one.

fed by rainwater percolating into rocks across a wide area of desert, much of it from the Druz Mountains in neighbouring Syria. But in the mid-1960s, European engineers recommended the exploitation of the Azraq groundwaters, first for irrigation and later to supply water to Amman.

Hydrologists estimate that, after evaporation losses, the aquifer refills at a rate of around 20 million cubic metres a year. But pumping far exceeds that figure. "The current rate of pumping is 45 to 50 million cubic metres a year," says Shatanawi. "This is more than twice the safe yield." Jane Dottridge of University College London estimates that the pumps have already "mined" 200 million cubic metres, some of it "fossil water" more than 10 000 years old. Nobody knows how much is left.

The damage to the oasis has been catastrophic, says Shatanawi. In the 1950s, 3000 cubic metres of water an hour gushed into the oasis. By 1980, the springs supplied just 10 cubic metres an hour. By 1992, the last of the springs had expired. Now the only water reaching the oasis comes from local flash floods. "Even with this year's good rains," says Shatanawi, "the water cover at the oasis is only a fifth what it used to be."

RANSACKED RESERVES

In 1989, the Jordanian environment department agreed that pumping should be reduced to 20 million cubic metres per

Water reserves shared by Jordan and Israel have been badly mismanaged over the years, and when the Palestinian state emerges the strains on water resources will increase even more.

Below ground, the crisis is less apparent—except at the Azraq oasis in the east of the country. The oasis was once the largest expanse of freshwater in the Middle East, an ancient magnet for Bedouin camel and goat herders and desert wildlife. Its water bubbled up from springs,

year. But local farmers have continued to dig new wells. And the amount of water being pumped to Amman continues to increase, with the Azraq oasis now providing about a quarter of the capital's water—more than 20 million cubic metres in most years.

The same story of ransacked reserves holds throughout the country. Water was first piped from Azraq to Amman because the aquifer beneath the capital itself was being overexploited. It still is. Currently around 70 million cubic metres is removed annually, and only 40 million cubic metres refill naturally. A government study says that the aquifer will be empty within 25 years.

In desperation, Jordan has looked at ways to supply water to Amman from another "fossil water" resource in the far south of the country, the Disi aquifer, which extends across the border into Saudi Arabia. According to Britain's Overseas Development Administration, Disi could yield up to 100 million cubic metres a year. The cost, including the 350-kilometre pipeline to Amman, would be about $450 million.

The peace agreement, however, opens up new possibilities, especially for developing surface waters. Until last year, Jordan received an average of 120 million cubic metres annually from the Jordan River basin—a sixth as much as Israel. Most of its share came from wadis. Jordan's largest dam, the King Talal dam 30 kilometres north of the capital, holds back the water in such a wadi. Following the settlement last October, Israel agreed to allow an extra 200 million cubic metres to flow down the River Jordan from the Sea of Galilee. And it has agreed to Jordan building two dams to capture this water.

Jordan also wants to build a dam on the River Yarmuk, a tributary of the River Jordan that rises in Syria and flows through Jordan. The Yarmuk flows for only a few months each year, but contributes 40 per cent of the surface water in Jordan. It could yield up to 80 million cubic metres a year, but the country has never been able to dam it. Construction was halted in 1967 by Israeli troops who invaded and destroyed the partially built dam in the final hours of the Six Day War. But peacemakers hope that the dam may soon be built.

There are also schemes afoot to share other waters in the region. Israeli engineers, for example, are keen to divert part of the flow of the Litani River in southern Lebanon through a tunnel into the headwaters of the River Jordan. According to Hillel Shuval of the Hebrew University of Jerusalem, two-thirds of the Litani's flow currently "runs to the sea unused". The water, he says, should go to a Middle East "water bank", run jointly by the governments of the region, which would be responsible for brokering such arrangements. The first takers would probably be the Palestinians. Everybody in the region is painfully aware that the new Palestinian state, when it finally emerges, is likely to be even shorter of water than Jordan.

Shuval, however, is convinced that the key to the sensible use of water in the eastern Mediterranean lies in increasing the efficiency with which existing water reserves are used, rather than in developing new resources and juggling old ones. Modern methods of "micro-irrigation", for example, can halve the water needed to grow a crop by delivering it in small quantities close to the roots. Saul Arlosoroff, also of the Hebrew University of Jerusalem, notes that during the past 30 years Israel has increased fivefold the value of crops it can grow with a given amount of water.

Jordan has tried to follow the example of its neighbour. In the Jordan valley, most farms use drip irrigation and grow vegetables under plastic to conserve water. But on the desert margins, where investment in agriculture is lower, more water is wasted. John Waddington of the University of Newcastle upon Tyne has surveyed every farm in the Azraq basin and found widespread overwatering of crops and frequent leaks from water mains. Waddington estimates that 4.1 million cubic metres is wasted each year, or around 30 per cent of the total used.

But losses are probably at their worst in the urban areas around Amman. According to Munther Haddadin, head of water negotiations for the Jordanian government, "56 per cent of the water put into urban supply is unaccounted for, at least half of which is through leakage". Despite Jordan's shortages, the prices that farmers and householders pay for their water are a fraction of those in Israel. Farmers pay nothing towards the capital cost of water-supply projects, and only half of their operating costs. This, he says, means that "the public has no incentive to conserve water".

WASTED RESOURCE

Haddadin says his country must follow Israel's example and recycle urban sewage to irrigate crops. Eventually, he claims, 60 per cent of sewage could be used in this way. The country's largest reservoir, behind the King Talal dam, is already topped up with effluent from a large sewage works. But failures in sewage treatment left the water in the reservoir so dirty, says Haddadin, that "some irrigated vegetables and citrus crops have been lost in the past four years". In 1991, polluted water destroyed vegetables worth $90 million.

Here is the crux: should Jordan be investing in recycling its sewage, plugging its leaks and improving its irrigation techniques, or should it be investing in water-supply "megaprojects", such as the Red-Dead canal?

Arlosoroff says there is no contest. Water from the canal would cost between 50 and 100 cents per cubic metre, whereas the price of recycled sewage is 25 to 35 cents. And most methods of demand management, such as advanced irrigation systems, could save water at even less expense. Shuval agrees. He says desalinated canal water would cost "at least three times more than is economic for agricultural use. Its customers would certainly not be farmers. Only the urban population, or tourist projects, could afford it." Even Shatanawi, an enthusiastic sup-

One positive ramification of going forward with the building of a Dead Sea canal will be a more peaceful relationship between Israel and Jordan as they mandatorily share in the success of such a project.

porter of the canal, says that it will never "green" the Rift Valley desert: "It won't be economic to use the water for irrigation."

There are environmental objections to the scheme, too. While the canal could certainly refill the Dead Sea, Shatanawi admits that the resulting mix of waters would be chemically very different, with unpredictable consequences for the lucrative salt-extracting factories. And the World Bank warns that the saltwater in the canal could leak into underground water reserves beneath the Rift Valley. It would be absurd if, as the canal project expensively desalinated sea water, it polluted existing freshwater reserves.

The prognoses for the Red-Dead canal are not encouraging. And yet, the project is likely to live for its geopolitical symbolism. Does this mean the project is likely to become a costly white elephant? Not necessarily, says Shuval. "We scientists have to recognise that sometimes very big projects have a life of their own. I don't think the Red-Dead project is very attractive economically. But it is a grand, heroic scheme." And if it can cement a peaceful relationship between two countries that have gone to war twice in a generation, "then even at $4 billion it may be worth it".

The New White Flight

SUMMARY Migration flows are widening the demographic differences among states. In six states, minority immigration from other countries may be driving poor whites away, but not the college-educated. Florida and five other states that attract interstate migrants are magnets for the nation's most talented and skills workers. And states with heavy out-migration are especially likely to lose their best and brightest.

William H. Frey

William H. Frey is research scientist and associate director for training at the Population Studies Center, the University of Michigan.

Immigrants exert a powerful influence on the U.S., but only in a handful of states. During the 1980s, newcomers from Mexico, China, and other countries flooded into Los Angeles, New York, and other major cities. As they moved in, large numbers of whites moved away from these areas. Minority-dominated in-migration combined with interstate "white flight" is leading to sharp differences in the racial and socio-demographic characteristics of different states. [†]

The effect of migration on a state's population depends on three things: the size of the migration stream, its direction, and its source. A migration stream can be comprised of immigrants from abroad or of internal migrants from other states. In the U.S., the geographic patterns of international migrants and state-to-state migrants generally do not overlap. States with large immigrant streams, like California and New York, tend to have large existing settlements of earlier immigrants from Latin America and Asia. A somewhat different group of states, most of which are located in the South Atlantic, Pacific, and Mountain regions, are magnets for internal migrants.

Conventional wisdom says that people who move from state to state tend to be America's better-educated and affluent citizens. In the past, states with high out-migration have lost a disproportionately large share of their most educated and talented residents to states with high in-migration. But this rule does not apply to states with high rates of international immigration. In these states, low- and middle-income whites appear to be most likely to move away. Increased competition for low-skilled jobs, the indirect social cost of a growing population of immigrants (rising taxes, overcrowded schools, and language barriers), and simple fear of unfamiliar people may drive these migrants away. At the same time, the high-skilled jobs clustered in many high-immigration states also attract highly educated whites.

The race-migration dynamics associated with different migration streams can also be linked to trends in poverty status, educational attainment, and even the age distribution of different states. These trends are different in high-immigration states than in states that attract large numbers of interstate migrants, or in states that lose people to other states.

WIDENING DIFFERENCES

The internal migration flows of white Americans* are similar to the patterns of the nation as a whole. In the late 1980s, net white migrant gains were largely in the South Atlantic, Pacific, and Mountain regions of the country, and net losses were concentrated in states with high international immigration or declining economies. The broad pattern suggests an "emptying out" of whites from the upper Midwest region of the country. It also shows that whites left several Mountain

The term "white" in this article refers to non-Hispanic whites. Minorities refer to all other population segments combined. The time period for net migration (the number of in-migrants minus the number of out-migrants) in this article is between 1985 and 1990. See "Behind the Numbers" at end of article.

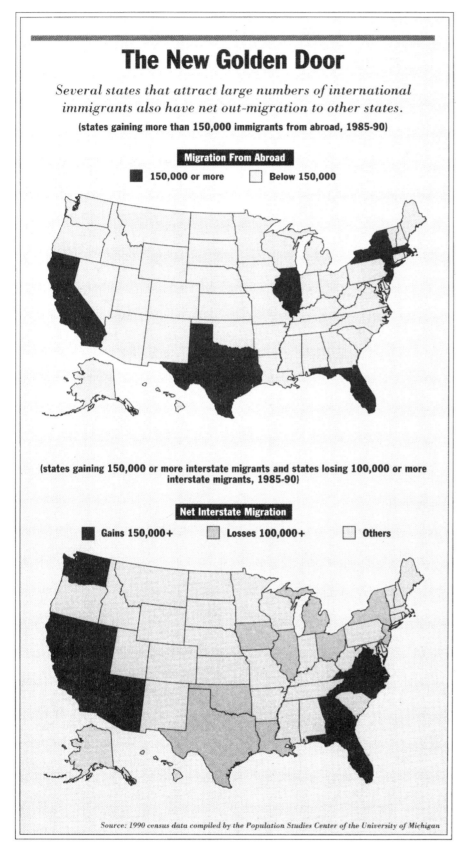

The New Golden Door

Several states that attract large numbers of international immigrants also have net out-migration to other states.

(states gaining more than 150,000 immigrants from abroad, 1985-90)

Migration From Abroad

150,000 or more   Below 150,000

(states gaining 150,000 or more interstate migrants and states losing 100,000 or more interstate migrants, 1985-90)

Net Interstate Migration

Gains 150,000+   Losses 100,000+   Others

Source: 1990 census data compiled by the Population Studies Center of the University of Michigan

Between 1985 and 1990, a significant number of whites made the leap from Texas to California.

Minorities followed this pattern to some degree. Their gains in South Atlantic states are heavily concentrated in Florida and Georgia, and to a lesser extent in Virginia and Maryland. In the Pacific region, minority net gains are dominated by California, where Asians contributed substantially to interstate migration. Minorities and whites alike are moving away from New York, Illinois, Texas, and other states with declining or slow-growing economies. Unlike whites, minorities

> **Florida continues to be a magnet for whites from many northern states, especially New York.**

are moving away from Mississippi, Alabama, and Arkansas and filtering into Minnesota, Wisconsin, and Kansas. All six states in New England, including Massachusetts, experienced a net gain of minorities from other states.

Among minorities, five of the ten greatest migration streams flow outward from New York state. As with whites, the largest stream flows between New York and Florida. But New York also has a net loss of minorities to New Jersey, North Carolina, Virginia, and California.

Another important minority migration stream flows from Washington, D.C. to Maryland, as successful minorities seek new suburban homes. Minority migration streams are most likely to begin in states that are already home to large numbers of blacks, Hispanics, and Asians. They typically flow toward faster-growing, more economically vibrant areas of the South and West.

Minority patterns of migration differ subtly from those of whites. But the differences between low-income and higher-income whites are far more pronounced. Like internal migrants of all races, poor

states that sustained economic downturns during the second half of the 1980s.

Florida continues to be a magnet for whites from many northern states, espe-cially New York. A strong "spillover" of whites also occurred as New Yorkers moved into New Jersey. And whites in Massachusetts moved to New Hampshire.

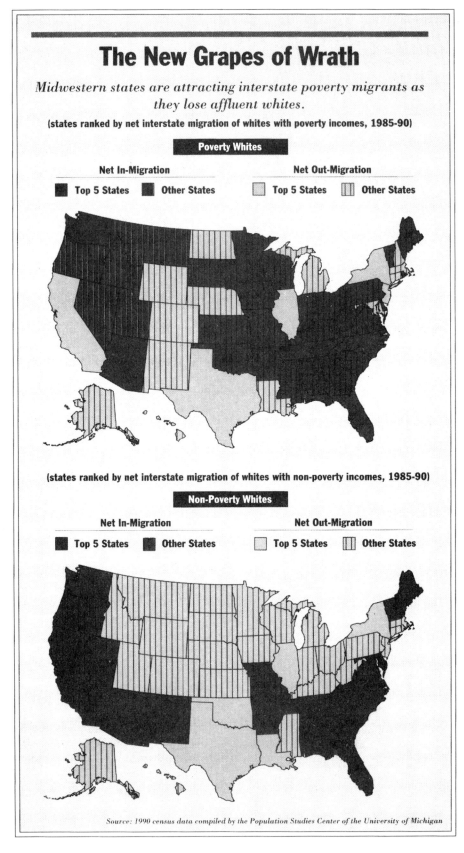

The New Grapes of Wrath

Midwestern states are attracting interstate poverty migrants as they lose affluent whites.

(states ranked by net interstate migration of whites with poverty incomes, 1985-90)

Poverty Whites

Net In-Migration | Net Out-Migration
■ Top 5 States ■ Other States | □ Top 5 States ▥ Other States

(states ranked by net interstate migration of whites with non-poverty incomes, 1985-90)

Non-Poverty Whites

Net In-Migration | Net Out-Migration
■ Top 5 States ■ Other States | □ Top 5 States ▥ Other States

Source: 1990 census data compiled by the Population Studies Center of the University of Michigan

nearby states of Washington, Arizona, Oregon, Utah, and Arkansas. A large number of midwestern states are gaining poor whites even as they experience a net loss of all whites. In general, the white poverty population is spreading away from states with high levels of immigration. Still, Florida has had the greatest increase in poverty migrants, as it does for most other population groups.

Florida also leads the nation in the number of white college graduates it receives. California ranks ninth in attracting all whites and registers losses among poor white migrants, but it ranks number two in its ability to attract white college graduates. This pattern is more evidence of the "dual economy" found in many high-immigration states. Cities with large financial centers and other information-economy jobs often employ high-wage and low-wage service workers, with few posts available for mid-wage manufacturing workers.

The flow of white college graduates is particularly heavy from northern industrial and midwestern states such as Ohio, Pennsylvania, and Wisconsin. Strong one-sided exchanges appear to be directing college-educated whites away from these states toward Florida and California. More than other whites, college graduates are attracted to America's coasts.

> **Ohio, Pennsylvania, and Wisconsin are suffering heavy losses of college graduates.**

The elderly population is another important contributor to white internal migration. While education and skills migrate from the interior states to the coast, elderly migration is more likely to flow from the Snowbelt to the Sunbelt. With the notable exceptions of California and Louisiana, a solid block of southern and western states receive a net gain of white elderly residents. Florida and Arizona top the list of gainers, while the losers are dominated by large northern states.

whites are leaving New York faster than they move in. But New York is not the leading exporter of poverty migrants, as it is for all other population segments. The outflows of poor whites are even greater from Texas, New Jersey, and California.

As poor whites migrate away from California and Texas, they move into the

HIGH-IMMIGRATION STATES

Between 1985 and 1990, six states—California, New York, Texas, New Jersey, Illinois, and Massachusetts—experienced high immigration from abroad, but did not attract large numbers of internal migrants. In fact, California was the only one of this group that attracted more interstate migrants than it lost during the time period. Although California ranked seventh in attracting internal migrants, its population growth is clearly dominated by immigration from abroad.

Among the six high-immigration states, California best embodies the migration patterns of a dual economy. Its economy is attracting educated white workers but is losing unskilled whites perhaps because of increased competition for low-skilled jobs. Between 1985 and 1990, California gained over 100,000 white college graduates and a significant number of minority college graduates. It lost less-educated migrants.

Another truism in migration studies is that college graduates are more mobile than people with less education. After all, older Americans are less likely to migrate than younger adults, and they are also the group with the lowest educational attainment. But in five of the six high-immigration states, college graduates were less likely than high school graduates to move away between 1985 and 1990. The exception is New York, a state with high net losses for all whites and especially high losses for whites with college degrees. In all six states, immigration boosted population at both extremes of the education scale. But people with no college experience form the majority of immigrants from abroad and provide competition for less-skilled native-born whites. College graduates are more attuned to job markets and are more likely to respond to economic pushes and pulls.

California stands out because its net migration is positive for higher-income whites and negative for lower-income whites. New Jersey is noteworthy as well for its exceptionally high losses of lower-income whites. In California, New Jersey, and Illinois, minority out-migration is higher for minority poverty populations than for other minorities. In Massachusetts, poor minorities register significantly higher net migration gains than do minorities with higher incomes. Still, immigration rates in each state are higher among poverty than nonpoverty immigrants.

In all the high-immigration states except Texas, net out-migration rates of elderly whites are greater than those for younger whites. The strong pull of the Sunbelt for retirees accounts for the gains in Texas as well as the losses from northern states. But the loss of elderly migrants in sunny California comes as a surprise.

Once a strong magnet for the elderly, California is now the third biggest loser of elderly migrants. The state's higher cost of living makes it a less desirable destination for elderly whites, who are increasingly likely to choose Oregon and nearby states. Between 1985 and 1990, the net loss of elderly whites in California was 37,000.

For almost all groups studied—whites,

Moveable States

Seventeen U.S. states are intensely affected by migration: six because they attract immigrants from abroad, six because they are magnets for internal migrants, and five because they are losing population to other states.

(total migration from abroad and net interstate migration in thousands for states with high immigration, high internal migration, and high out-migration, 1985-90)

rank	state	migration from abroad	net interstate migration
HIGH FOREIGN IMMIGRATION STATES			
1	California	1,499	174
2	New York	614	−821
3	Texas	368	−331
4	New Jersey	211	−194
5	Illinois	203	−342
6	Massachusetts	156	−97
HIGH INTERNAL MIGRATION STATES			
1	Florida	390	1,072
2	Georgia	92	303
3	North Carolina	66	281
4	Virginia	149	228
5	Washington	102	216
6	Arizona	80	216
HIGH OUT-MIGRATION STATES			
1	Louisiana	30	−251
2	Ohio	69	−141
3	Michigan	74	−133
4	Oklahoma	32	−128
5	Iowa	17	−94

Note: Net interstate migration equals in-migration minus out-migration between 1985 and 1990. High immigration states are those where immigration from abroad exceeded net interstate migration. High internal migration states are those where net interstate migration exceeded immigration from abroad, and high out-migration states experienced negative interstate migration and were also not recipients of large numbers of immigrants from abroad.

Source: 1990 census data compiled by the Population Studies Center of the University of Michigan minorities, poor whites, higher-income whites, white college graduates, and elderly whites—California lost in its exchanges with Washington, Oregon, Nevada, and Arizona. This "spreading out" of American-born whites and minorities to nearby areas is a departure from traditional migration patterns. For decades, the nation's most talented and mobile citizens leaped across the interior states to reach California's economic promised land. The new pattern may be a response to demographic, economic, and social pressures exerted by the continuing large waves of immigrants into California.

A large influx of minority immigrants, coupled with substantial outflows of American-born whites, is the new pattern of white flight from high-immigration states. Minority immigrant flows dominate demographic change in all of these states. And in most cases, these immigrant in-flows are roughly equal to their interstate losses.

INTERSTATE MIGRANTS

The six states with the greatest net increases from interstate migration between 1985 and 1990 are Florida, Georgia, North Carolina, Virginia, Washington, and Arizona. With the exception of Miami and Seattle, cities in these states do not attract large waves of immigrants through traditional ports of entry. In every state, including Florida, the net in-migration of people from other states far exceeds immigration from abroad. A warm climate or other amenities help these states attract elderly retirees, new employers, and others.

The migration rates of higher-income whites into Florida, Georgia, and Virginia are greater than those of poor whites. In North Carolina and Arizona, the total numbers of migrants in these economic groups are roughly equal. But in Washington, poor white migrants outnumber the affluent. White immigration to Washington and Arizona is highly influenced by outflows from California. North Carolina's pattern is influenced by the return of migrants to the North whose

efforts to find work were unsuccessful; it also attracts those in quest of economic opportunity in newly emerging southern job centers like Charlotte and Raleigh.

> **Once a strong magnet for the elderly, California is now the third biggest loser of elderly migrants.**

Minority migration exhibits similar economic patterns. Both Washington and North Carolina have greater rates of gain for poor minorities than for those with higher incomes.

White in-migration by educational attainment follows the traditional rules in these states; all six are attracting the most educated interstate migrants. For five of the six states with high internal migration, rates of net migration for whites with college degrees are highest. Only in Arizona is it less apparent—and here the difference by education between the two groups is slight.

Clearly, the six high internal migration states are more than just magnets for snowbirds. In fact, significantly high net in-migration rates for elderly migrants are evident only in Florida, Arizona, and North Carolina. Florida's rates are high for both the elderly and younger movers. In North Carolina, younger migrants are increasing faster than those aged 65 and older. And in the other five states with high internal migration, substantially more younger than older whites are arriving. These trends are not surprising considering the strong economic gains in all of these states during the second half of the 1980s.

Florida draws more migrants than it exports in virtually every demographic category measured here, and it has a positive balance with most states. Yet Florida is losing elderly migrants to the western retirement magnets of Arizona and Nevada. And it is losing migrants in all categories to Georgia, North Carolina,

and Oregon. As a result, Georgia and North Carolina are challenging Florida's dominance in the South Atlantic.

Like Florida, Georgia gains migrants from a majority of states in every demographic segment. Net in-migration to Georgia is particularly strong from the populous northern states of New York, Illinois, and Ohio. Georgia is also a regional draw for migrants from Florida

> **Georgia and North Carolina are challenging Florida's dominance in the South Atlantic.**

and Texas. In fact, no state draws more migrants from Georgia than it supplies.

The migration dynamics of the states with high internal migration contrast sharply with those of the high-immigration states. In the domestic-migration states, the influx of whites dominated population growth between 1985 and 1990. White interstate migration is particularly strong into Florida, Washington, and Arizona. American-born minorities—especially blacks—make up a sizeable proportion of the net in-migration flows to Georgia, Virginia, and North Carolina. Both Florida and Virginia attract significant numbers of immigrants from abroad, but white internal migration dominates their demographic outlook.

HEAVY OUTMIGRATION

A third class of states, including Louisiana, Ohio, Michigan, Oklahoma, and Iowa, have high out-migration. Among the states that did not receive large numbers of immigrants from abroad, these five experienced the greatest out-migration between 1985 and 1990. The out-migration from these states stems from the declining economies of the "oil patch," "rust belt," and "farm belt" regions in the late 1980s.

On most socio-demographic dimensions, Michigan is a loser in its migration exchanges. Elderly out-migration is more severe in Michigan than in the other states in this category. But Michigan's northerly location could be more responsible than its struggling economy for its losses. College graduates are more likely to leave Michigan than to move there, and the state's inflow of poor whites is slightly greater than its outflow.

Michigan's population gains in the late 1980s came from interior states, especially those in the "oil patch." Some of this gain was the return migration of former Michigan residents who moved out when jobs were plentiful in Texas and Oklahoma. People who leave Michigan frequently wind up in the fast-growing South Atlantic states.

In the other high out-migration states, the rate of elderly net out-migration is less than that of younger immigrants. This pattern will speed up aging in these states.

The race-migration dynamics in high out-migration states are the reverse of states with high internal migration. Out-migration of whites dominates demo-

graphic change in these states. In fact, with the exception of Louisiana, the heavy out-migration states are not losing minorities. Rather, they are losing large numbers of whites without replacing them

> **Michigan's population gains in the late 1980s came from interior states, especially those in the "oil patch."**

with immigrants from abroad. And the whites who are leaving tend to be well-educated.

Migration drives demographic change in all three types of states. In states with heavy overall losses, migration speeds up the aging of the population and robs employers of their most valuable labor resources. Educated whites and minorities are relocating to states with the most

internal migration. These states are frequently magnets for elderly retirees, but younger people in search of greater employment opportunities are drawn to them even faster. States that attract many immigrants from abroad lose lower-income whites, even though they may still be attracting educated whites. Migration patterns are increasing the gaps between rich, poor, minority, and white.

Behind the Numbers The full report on this study (*Research Report No: 93-297, Interstate Migration and Immigration for Whites and Minorities, 1985-90: The Emergence of Multi-ethnic States*) is available from the University of Michigan Population Studies Center; telephone (313) 998-7141. The data were drawn from the 1990 census 5-percent Public Use Microsample (PUMS) files. The question about "residence five years ago" identified immigrants from abroad and net interstate migration (in-migration from other states minus out-migration to other states) between 1985 and 1990. White selectivity in migration and its potential implications for states is emphasized in this article. The term "whites" in this paper refers to non-Hispanic whites. Minorities include blacks, Asians, Hispanics, and all others.

HISPANIC MIGRATION
AND POPULATION REDISTRIBUTION
IN THE UNITED STATES

The US Hispanic population has grown rapidly over the last two decades and remains geographically concentrated in nine states. Redistribution away from core states through internal migration has been largely offset by heavy immigration to traditional areas of Hispanic concentration. Geographical patterns of Hispanic migration show broad similarities to overall patterns of population redistribution in the United States. New York and California serve as key spatial redistributors or pivots in the Hispanic migration system. **Key Words: Hispanic concentration, Hispanic migration, population gateway, spatial redistributor.**

Kevin E. McHugh

KEVIN E. McHUGH (Ph.D., University of Illinois) is Assistant Professor of Geography at Arizona State University, Tempe, AZ 85287. His primary research interests are in migration and residential mobility.

The Hispanic population in the United States has grown rapidly over the last two decades, increasing from 9.1 million in 1970 to an estimated 18.8 million in 1987 (US Bureau of the Census 1988). Hispanics now represent the fastest growing minority in the nation. Between 1980 and 1987, the Hispanic population increased 30% while the non-Hispanic population grew less than 6%. Projections of the Hispanic population for the year 2000 range from 23 to 31 million (US Bureau of the Census 1986). According to the middle series projections, Hispanics will account for one-fourth of total US population growth between 1983 and 2000.

"Hispanic" is an umbrella term that refers to US residents whose cultural heritage traces back to a Spanish-speaking country (Valdivieso and Davis 1988). Other than having common ancestral ties to Latin America or Spain, peoples of Spanish origin in the US are highly diverse (Bean and Tienda 1988). Mexican-Americans, the largest group, account for 63% of US Hispanics in 1987; Puerto Ricans account for 12% and Cuban-Americans 5%. Hispanics with origins in Central Amer-

ica (excluding Mexico) and South America comprise 11%, and the residual category "other Hispanics" makeup the remaining 8% of US Hispanics (US Bureau of the Census 1988).

Hispanic immigration has received considerable scholarly attention, but Hispanic migration and population redistribution *within* the United States is seldom investigated (Garcia 1981). Some recent studies examine the geographical distribution of particular Hispanic groups, such as Boswell's (1984, 1985a, 1985b) work on Cuban-Americans and Puerto Ricans, Arreola's (1985) examination of Mexican-Americans, and Portes and Bach's (1985) longitudinal study of Cuban and Mexican immigrants in the United States. Bean et al. (1988) recently reviewed the geographical distribution and interregional migration of Hispanic groups. There has not been a comprehensive examination of place-to-place migration flows of Hispanics in the United States, partly due to the historical lack of information on Hispanic migration within the United States. Hispanic interstate migration for the period 1975–80 are the first place-to-place Hispanic migration data published by the Bureau of the Census (1985).

The purpose of this paper is to identify patterns of Hispanic migration and population redistribution within the United States. The paper focuses on whether Hispanics are becoming more or less geographically concentrated in the United States and on identifying recent migration patterns that are contributing to Hispanic population redistribution.

Hispanic population redistribution is examined in two ways. First, changes in the geographical distribution of Hispanics over recent decades are examined through state percentage shares of the total Hispanic population and state percentage shares of four major Hispanic groups: Mexican-Americans, Puerto Ricans, Cuban-Americans, and Central/South Americans. Shifts in the state shares over time indicate trends in the geographical concentration and deconcentration of Hispanic groups in the United States.

Second, I examine the role of immigration from abroad and internal migration within the United States in contributing to Hispanic population redistribution. These analyses provide insights into the relative importance of immigration versus internal migration in contributing to Hispanic population change at the state level. I also identify large net interstate migration streams within the US and compute the effectiveness of these streams in redistributing the Hispanic population. This shows the interstate connections most instrumental in redistributing Hispanics within the United States.

The paper draws upon the concept of spatial redistributors in contributing to a geographical understanding of the US Hispanic migration system. Spatial redistributors are places that exhibit asymmetry between patterns of in- and out-migration and thus serve as pivots in systems of population redistribution (Roseman 1977; Morrison 1977; Roseman and McHugh 1982). Key states should

* This research was supported by a Faculty Grant-in-Aid, Office of the Vice President for Research, Arizona State University. I thank Barbara Trapido for drafting the map.

TABLE 1
TOP NINE STATES IN HISPANIC POPULATION

State	1970 Population	% Dist.	1980 Population	% Dist.	1987[a] Population	% Dist.
California	2,369,292	26.1	4,544,331	31.1	6,249,000	33.3
Texas	1,840,648	20.3	2,985,824	20.4	4,207,000	22.4
New York	1,351,982	14.9	1,659,300	11.4	2,182,000	11.6
Florida	405,036	4.5	858,158	5.9	1,256,000	6.7
New Jersey	288,488	3.2	491,883	3.4	737,000	3.9
Illinois	393,204	4.3	635,602	4.4	692,000	3.7
Arizona	264,770	2.9	440,701	3.0	664,000	3.5
New Mexico	308,340	3.4	477,222	3.3	535,000	2.9
Colorado	225,506	2.5	339,717	2.3	347,000	1.9
Total for nine states	7,447,266	82.1	12,432,738	85.1	16,869,000	89.9
United States	9,072,602	100.0	14,608,673	100.0	18,790,000	100.0

[a] 1987 figures are estimates of the civilian, noninstitutional Hispanic population from the March Current Population Survey. They are not directly comparable to the 1970 and 1980 census populations.
Sources: US Bureau of the Census, 1982; US Bureau of the Census, Current Population Survey, March 1987, Public Use File.

serve as Hispanic spatial redistributors at the international and national scales. International redistributors are states that attract large numbers of Hispanics from abroad and redistribute Hispanics within the United States, thus serving as population gateways. Key states should also serve as internal redistributors of Hispanics, as indicated by large net interstate migration streams. The redistributor concept is particularly relevant to the geographic concentration and deconcentration of Hispanics in the United States.

I first summarize shifts in the geographical distribution of Hispanic groups in the United States. The second section examines Hispanic immigration from abroad and internal migration within the United States, emphasizing the role of key states as Hispanic population gateways. Geographical patterns of migration that contribute to Hispanic population redistribution within the United States are identified in the third section. The final section is a discussion of three key issues: (1) whether Hispanic groups are becoming more or less geographically concentrated, (2) determinants of Hispanic migration within the United States, and (3) linkages between Hispanic immigration from abroad and internal migration within the United States.

Geographical Distribution of Hispanics

The US Hispanic population is concentrated geographically. Nine states accounted for 82% of the total Hispanic population in 1970 (Table 1). This percentage rose to 85% in 1980 and an estimated 90% in 1987. The following states had 1987 Hispanic populations greater than 300,000: New York and New Jersey in the Northeast, Illinois in the Midwest, Florida in the Southeast, and California, Texas, Arizona, New Mexico, and Colorado in the Southwest.

There has been some redistribution between these nine states as measured by

their share of the total US Hispanic population, most notably a seven-point rise in California's share, so that California now accounts for one-third of all Hispanics in the country. Texas, Florida, and Arizona have also increased their share of the Hispanic population over the last two decades. New York's declining share between 1970 and 1980 is noteworthy. Illinois, New Mexico, and Colorado also posted small declines in their share of the Hispanic population.

The US Hispanic population is diverse in nationality and cultural heritage. Disaggregating Hispanics by national origin and showing state percentage shares in 1960 and 1980 indicate trends in the geographic concentration and deconcentration of individual Hispanic groups (Table 2).

Hispanics of Mexican origin dominate in the southwestern states of California, Texas, Arizona, New Mexico, and Colorado, and also in Illinois. California and Texas in 1980 accounted for three-fourths of the Mexican-origin population in the United States. The most important shifts in the distribution of Mexican-Americans are the increase in California's share coupled with a declining share for Texas. This long-term trend began early in the twentieth century. In 1910, 60% of persons of Mexican stock in the United States resided in Texas, and California accounted for only 13% (Grebler et al. 1970). At that time, Texas had greater employment opportunities for the Mexican population, particularly in agriculture. Throughout the twentieth century, California's share of the Mexican-origin population steadily increased as job opportunities shifted to California, initially in agriculture and later through urban expansion (Jaffee et al. 1980).

Illinois is the only state outside the southwest with a large Mexican-American population. The Mexican-origin population in Illinois grew from less than 2% of the national total in 1960 to nearly 5%

in 1980. The development of the Mexican-origin population in Illinois resulted from their "settling out" from midwestern migratory labor streams as well as from direct migration to Chicago in response to employment opportunities in railroad maintenance, steelmaking, meatpacking, and other manufacturing sectors (Grebler et al. 1970). In 1980, Chicago ranked third among metropolitan areas in Mexican origin population, behind Los Angeles and Houston (Bean et al. 1988).

Puerto Ricans are the largest Hispanic group in New York and New Jersey. The most important redistribution of Puerto Ricans has been away from New York to nearby states in the Northeast, in addition to Florida and California. New York's share of the Puerto Rican population dropped from 72% in 1960 to 49% in 1980. Conversely, New Jersey, Massachusetts, Connecticut, Pennsylvania, Illinois, Florida, and California increased their share of Puerto Ricans. The deconcentration of Puerto Ricans away from New York resulted from declining employment opportunities, poor housing, and crime problems in New York City (Boswell 1984).

Cuban-Americans represent the largest Hispanic group in Florida, where they have become increasingly concentrated in south Florida, partly in response to the Cuban Refugee Resettlement Program (Boswell and Curtis 1984). Cuban-Americans resettled outside south Florida under this government-sponsored program began returning to Miami in the late 1960s. By the mid-1970s this return flow increased to a major migration stream. A survey commissioned by *The Miami Herald* in 1978 found that 40% of the population of Cuban origin in Dade County were returnees to Miami from elsewhere in the United States (Boswell and Curtis 1984).

The increased concentration of the Cuban-origin population in south Florida continues in the 1980s. The 1980 census figures do not include the estimated 125,000 Cuban "Marielito" refugees who arrived in Miami shortly after the 1980 enumeration. In addition, Cuban return movement to south Florida has continued in the 1980s. Boswell and Curtis (1984) cite estimates prepared by the Cuban National Planning Council that between 65 and 70% of Cuban-Americans reside in Florida.

Outside Florida, sizable numbers of Cuban-Americans reside in New York, New Jersey, and California. Before the Castro revolution in 1959, New York City was the primary destination of Cuban immigrants. New York's share of Cuban-Americans declined from 45% in 1950 to 10% in 1980. Cuban-Americans in New Jersey are highly concentrated in the area of Union City–West New York, across the

Hudson River from New York City. This concentration of Cuban-Americans is the largest outside Miami. California accounts for 8% of the 1980 Cuban-origin population. Los Angeles ranks fourth among urban areas in Cuban-American population (Boswell and Curtis 1984).

Hispanics with origins in Central America (excluding Mexico) and South America are concentrated in New York and California, with smaller concentrations in Florida and New Jersey. New York has a greater number of Hispanics with origins in South America and the Dominican Republic, while California has larger numbers of Central Americans (Allen and Turner 1988). Although fewer in number than Hispanics of Mexican and Puerto Rican origin, persons with origins in Central and South America represent the fastest growing Hispanic group in the United States, increasing an estimated 40% between 1980 and 1987 (US Bureau of the Census 1988). Much of the recent influx of Central Americans is a response to political turmoil in El Salvador, Nicaragua, and Guatemala (Allen and Turner 1988).

Hispanics are a highly urban population. In 1980, 81% of Mexican-Americans resided in metropolitan areas. Other Hispanic groups show greater levels of metropolitan concentration: 96% for Puerto Ricans, 94% for Cuban-Americans, and 96% for Central/South Americans. In comparison, 73% of non-Hispanic whites resided in metropolitan areas in 1980 (Bean et al. 1988). Twenty-nine metropolitan areas in 1980 had more than 100,000 Hispanics. Los Angeles and New York alone accounted for nearly one-quarter of the US Hispanic population (Davis et al. 1983).

Hispanics also show a propensity to concentrate in central cities within metropolitan areas. In 1980, 65% of Mexican-Americans, 81% of Puerto Ricans, 45% of Cuban-Americans, and 67% of Central/South Americans living in metropolitan areas were in central cities. The comparable figure for non-Hispanic whites is only 35%. Cuban-Americans have shown the greatest suburbanization, indicating their higher socioeconomic status relative to other Hispanic groups (Bean et al. 1988).

Hispanic Population Gateways

Immigration from abroad has contributed greatly to Hispanic population growth in the United States. Data on Hispanic immigration from abroad coupled with internal migration within the United States show that key states serve as Hispanic population gateways (Table 3). These data include immigration from abroad and internal migration within the United States, 1975–80, for 15 states with Hispanic populations over 100,000 in 1980. These migration data are not available for

Hispanic groups defined by national origin and are based on Hispanics enumerated in the 1980 Census of Population. The actual number of Hispanic migrants, particularly from abroad, is greater because a significant share of undocumented immigrants were not enumerated in the 1980 census (Warren and Passel 1987; Bean and Tienda 1988). Migrants from abroad refer to persons of Hispanic origin residing outside the United States in 1975 and in the designated state in 1980. This calculation includes foreign immigrants as well as US citizens returning from abroad. The vast majority of Hispanic movers from abroad are immigrants.

As expected, California, Texas, and New York attract very large numbers of Hispanics from abroad; Florida, Illinois, and New Jersey also receive sizable numbers

of Hispanic immigrants. These six states are the primary Hispanic gateways to the United States. Immigration from abroad more than offsets internal net migration losses for four of these states: New York, New Jersey, Illinois, and California. Despite internal migration away from these core states, they maintain or strengthen their Hispanic population concentrations through immigration. Florida and Texas, on the other hand, experienced both substantial immigration as well as net gains from elsewhere in the United States for the period 1975–80.

Geographical Patterns of Hispanic Migration

Geographical patterns of Hispanic migration within the United States can be seen by mapping the 25 largest net inter-

TABLE 2
GEOGRAPHICAL DISTRIBUTION OF HISPANICS BY NATIONAL ORIGIN, 1960 AND 1980[a]

State	Percent of US total							
	Mexican		Puerto Rican		Cuban		Central/South American	
	1960	1980	1960	1980	1960	1980	1960	1980
Massachusetts	—	0.1	0.3	3.8	0.7	0.8	1.6	1.8
Connecticut	—	—	1.6	4.5	2.1	0.7	1.9	1.1
New York	0.1	0.4	72.2	49.2	31.9	10.1	29.5	34.9
New Jersey	0.1	0.1	6.5	12.2	6.9	10.7	5.1	8.4
Pennyslvania	0.1	0.2	2.1	4.4	1.5	0.6	1.9	0.8
Ohio	0.2	0.5	1.3	1.7	0.8	0.4	1.7	0.5
Illinois	1.7	4.7	3.9	6.7	1.9	2.3	3.7	3.2
Michigan	0.6	1.2	0.3	0.5	0.2	0.4	1.7	0.6
Florida	0.1	0.7	2.1	4.8	43.0	58.4	5.2	9.1
Texas	38.7	32.4	0.7	1.0	1.1	1.7	3.3	2.8
Colorado	4.2	2.4	0.1	0.2	0.1	0.2	0.7	0.4
New Mexico	7.1	2.7	—	0.1	0.1	0.1	0.1	0.2
Arizona	5.7	4.7	0.2	0.2	—	0.1	0.6	0.3
Washington	0.4	0.9	0.1	0.2	0.7	0.2	0.8	0.4
California	38.7	42.1	3.1	4.4	3.2	8.0	24.9	25.4
Total for 15 states	97.7	93.1	94.5	93.9	94.2	94.7	82.7	89.9

[a] States listed have 100,000 or more persons of Hispanic origin, 1980.
Source: Bean et al. 1988.

TABLE 3
INTERNAL HISPANIC MIGRATION AND HISPANIC MOVERS FROM ABROAD, 1975–80[a]

State	Internal migration			Number from abroad
	Inmigration	Outmigration	Net migration	
Massachusetts	13,848	12,619	1229	20,118
Connecticut	11,148	10,005	1179	15,937
New York	27,552	133,061	−105,509	139,961
New Jersey	41,478	43,917	−2439	51,198
Pennyslvania	14,118	13,739	379	16,279
Ohio	9928	14,571	−4643	6355
Illinois	25,882	48,105	−22,133	66,124
Michigan	10,595	15,582	−4987	5958
Florida[b]	106,042	40,406	65,636	96,273
Texas	120,749	97,702	23,047	155,851
Colorado	28,578	27,137	1441	8596
New Mexico	32,485	31,036	1449	7535
Arizona	30,567	29,440	1127	15,229
Washington	24,051	11,826	12,225	8890
California	132,948	139,357	−6409	412,958

[a] States listed are those with 100,000 or more persons of Hispanic origin, 1980.
[b] Number of Hispanic movers to Florida from abroad, 1975–80, does not include the estimated 125,000 Cuban "Marielito" refugees who arrived shortly after the 1980 census enumeration.
Source: U.S. Bureau of the Census, 1985.

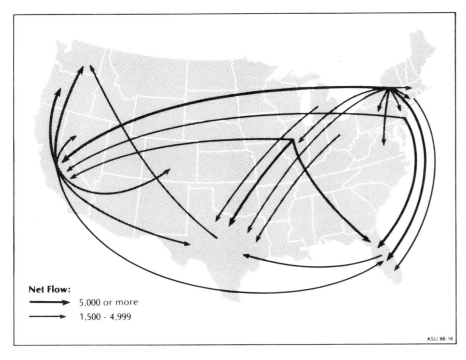

Net Flow:

→ 5,000 or more

→ 1,500 - 4,999

ASU 88-16

Figure 1. Large hispanic net interstate migration streams, 1975–80.

state migration streams for 1975–80, the most recent internal Hispanic migration data available (Fig. 1). In addition to the 25 net migration streams, the underlying gross migration flows and a percent effectiveness value for each interstate connection are reported (Table 4).

Percent effectiveness (E_{ij}) indicates the level of net migration exchange between a pair of states relative to the size of the underlying gross migration flows. It is computed by dividing net migration by the sum of the gross migration flows in both directions, and multiplying the resulting ratio by 100:

$$E_{ij} = [N_{ij}/M_{ij} + M_{ji}] \times 100 \quad (1)$$

where

E_{ij} = percent effectiveness of migration from state i to state j.

N_{ij} = net migration exchange between state i and state j ($M_{ij} - M_{ji}$)

M_{ij} = gross migration flow from state i to state j.

M_{ji} = gross migration flow from state j to state i.

In absolute terms, E_{ij} varies from 0 to 100%. A 0% effectiveness indicates that equal numbers of migrants are moving in both directions resulting in no population redistribution between the pair of states. Conversely, an effectiveness value of 100% would mean that *all* movement is unidirectional (either M_{ij} or M_{ji} = 0). Thus, effectiveness values indicate strong currents in a migration system (Plane 1984).

Several patterns of Hispanic migration are evident (Fig. 1). Net movement from northeastern and midwestern states to the three large Sunbelt states—Florida, Texas, and California—is conspicuous. Northeastern states are linked most strongly with Florida. Net flows from New York and New Jersey to Florida are very large and highly effective in redistributing Hispanics (E_{ij} = 83.6% and 75.6%).

New York stands out for registering highly effective Hispanic migration losses to Florida, Texas, and California (Table 4). This result parallels the overall trend of large migration losses for New York during the 1970s. In fact, currents of migration from New York to Florida and California, as measured by percent effectiveness values, were stronger among Hispanics than non-Hispanics.

Bean et al's. (1988) breakdown of Hispanic migration by national origin between New York and Florida, 1975–80, indicates why this stream is highly effective. Cuban-Americans constitute the greatest number of Hispanics in the New York-to-Florida stream. More than ten times as many Cuban-Americans migrated from New York to Florida as moved in the opposite direction. Many Cuban immigrants had been resettled from Miami to New York in the Cuban Refugee Resettlement Program (Boswell and Curtis 1984), so it is very likely that a substantial share of Florida-bound Cuban-Americans were returning to south Florida. Most Cuban-Americans returning to Dade County from outside Florida cite climate and a desire to be near family

and friends as reasons for their return (Boswell and Curtis 1984). Net movement of people of Puerto Rican and Central/South American origin from New York to Florida is also significant, although these streams are not as effective as Cuban-origin movement to Florida (Bean et al. 1988).

The midwestern states of Illinois, Michigan, and Ohio are linked most strongly with Texas (Fig. 1). These Hispanic migration streams are overwhelmingly Mexican-American, and are moderately effective in redistributing Mexican-Americans from the Midwest to Texas, with effectiveness values of 38.8% for Illinois, 25.2% for Michigan, and 39.1% for Ohio (Table 4). Significant numbers of Hispanics from Illinois move to Texas, Florida, and California, although the connection to Florida is most effective.

New York and California serve as spatial redistributors of the Hispanic population within the United States (Fig. 1). In addition to sending large numbers of Hispanics to Florida and California, New York is a redistributor of Hispanics within the Northeast. Large numbers of Hispanics move from New York to nearby states, including New Jersey, Pennsylvania, Connecticut, and Massachusetts. These four net migration streams from New York have moderately high effectiveness values (Table 4). Puerto Ricans are the dominant group in these streams, although Cuban-Americans and Central/South Americans are also likely to be present, especially in the stream to New Jersey. Puerto Rican migration away from New York relates to declining manufacturing employment, particularly in the textile and garment industries (Bean and Tienda 1988). Boswell (1984) also cites poor housing and crime as additional push factors in Puerto Rican migration from New York.

California is also a spatial redistributor of the Hispanic population. California gains Hispanics from New York, New Jersey, and Illinois, but loses Hispanics to western states, including Washington, Oregon, Nevada, and Colorado (Fig. 1). Thus, California is emerging as an interregional Hispanic redistributor, just as it has served as an interregional redistributor among Anglos since the late 1960s (US Bureau of the Census 1973). Overall, California recorded modest net out-migration of Hispanics within the United States, 1975–80, as losses to western states more than offset gains from northeastern and midwestern states.

Examining place of birth for Hispanics in western states also provides evidence that California is a Hispanic redistributor. In 1980, 50% of Hispanics in California were native to the state and 40% were foreign born. Only 12% of California Hispanics were born elsewhere in the United States. On the other hand, 40 to 50% of Hispanics in Washington, Oregon, and Nevada were born elsewhere in the United States, most likely California (US Bureau of the Census 1985).

For 1975–80, Texas gained Hispanics from northern states as well as from Florida and California (Fig. 1). Net flows to Texas from California and Florida, however, are small relative to large gross migration exchanges. Effectiveness values for the net streams to Texas are only 7.9% for California, and 18.0% for Florida (Table 4). In fact, Texas may be losing Hispanics to Florida and California since the recent decline in the energy-based Texas economy.

Discussion

Are Hispanics becoming more or less geographically concentrated in the United States? There has been some redistribution of the Hispanic population through internal migration as a result of (1) movement from northeastern and midwestern states to Florida, Texas, and California; (2) net movement from New York to nearby states in the Northeast; and (3) net migration from California to other western states. Immigration from abroad, however, continues to traditional areas of Hispanic concentration. For several states, heavy immigration among Hispanics has more than offset migration losses to other places within the country. A complete understanding of Hispanic population redistribution will require examination of both immigration and internal migration, as well as consideration of differentials in natural population increase among Hispanic groups.

The Hispanic population remains geographically concentrated in nine states, but this overall view masks differences among individual Hispanic groups. Cuban-Americans and Hispanics of Central/South American origin are becoming more concentrated, the former in Florida and the latter in California and New York. The increasing concentration of Cuban-Americans in south Florida is partly attributable to return migration following the Cuban Refugee Resettlement Program and to the strength of the Cuban-American community in Dade County. It is not surprising that most Central/South Americans concentrate in California and New York, given their recent arrival in the United States.

Hispanics of Mexican origin show some deconcentration away from core states. Bean et al. (1988) reached similar conclusions through their analysis of dissimilarity indexes that compared the geographic distribution of Hispanic groups and the overall US population. They found that the concentration of the Mexican-or-

igin population has become less pronounced from 1960 to 1980. Bean et al. (1988) also found that Puerto Ricans exhibit some deconcentration away from core states, especially New York, over the 20-year period. Recent interstate migration has played the dominant role in the deconcentration of Puerto Ricans away from their New York core.

Hispanic migration patterns are broadly similar to overall patterns of migration within the United States. Hispanic migration from northern states to Florida, California, and Texas is part of the larger population redistribution to the Sunbelt (Biggar 1979; Long 1988). Currents of migration to Florida, California, and Texas tend to be stronger among Hispanics than non-Hispanics, perhaps because of the greater concentration of the Hispanic population and opportunities in the three large Sunbelt states. Social networks defined on the basis of ethnicity probably serve to channelize Hispanic migration flows to Florida, California, and Texas.

New York and California have emerged as spatial redistributors of Hispanics, just as they have redistributed the Anglo population. California's emergence as an interregional redistributor in the late 1970s—attracting Hispanics from states in the Northeast/Midwest and losing Hispanics to states in the West—follows a similar trend among Anglos. New York and California are likely to continue as central pivots in the Hispanic migration system: both have large Hispanic populations and serve as gateways for large

numbers of new immigrants to the United States.

Comparisons of immigration from abroad and internal migration of Hispanics within the United States should show that Hispanics born in the United States, or those residing in the United States for a number of years, are more likely to migrate than are recent immigrants. Recent immigrants are typically less familiar with the United States, know less English, and tend to be of lower socioeconomic status than longer-term residents. Recent immigrants tend to concentrate in ethnic enclaves for social and economic support. Grebler et al. (1970) found that Hispanics of Mexican origin showed greater rates of intercounty migration, 1955–60, the further they were removed from the immigrant generation.

Portes and Bach (1985) studied the link between immigration and internal migration through a six-year residential history of a sample of Mexican and Cuban immigrants who entered the United States in 1973. They found that Mexican immigrants were more likely to change residences after living in the United States for three years, and that less than 25% remained at the same residence over the six-year period, 1973–79. Slightly more than one-half of the Mexican immigrants remained in Texas (state of entry), one-fourth moved to other states in the Southwest, and 16% moved northward to Chicago. Return immigrants (those who had been to the United States previously) were more likely to move and showed a more

TABLE 4
LARGE HISPANIC NET INTERSTATE MIGRATION STREAMS
AND PERCENT EFFECTIVENESS OF STREAMS, 1975–80

State i	State j	Gross flow i to j	Gross flow j to i	Net gain state j	Percent effect.
New York	Florida	38,398	3431	34,967	83.6
New York	New Jersey	28,080	7098	20,982	59.7
New Jersey	Florida	18,071	2515	15,556	75.6
New York	California	16,960	3369	13,591	66.9
Illinois	Texas	12,949	5710	7239	38.8
Illinois	Florida	7806	1754	6052	63.3
California	Oregon	8344	2459	5885	54.5
California	Washington	10,005	4178	5827	41.1
California	Texas	32,234	27,494	4740	7.9
California	Nevada	6916	2234	4682	51.2
New York	Texas	5702	1187	4515	65.5
New York	Pennsylvania	5626	1141	4485	66.3
New York	Connecticut	5644	1617	4027	55.5
New York	Massachusetts	5701	1833	3868	51.3
Illinois	California	9387	5707	3680	24.4
Florida	Texas	8499	5910	2589	18.0
California	Colorado	7888	5476	2412	18.0
New Jersey	California	3906	1510	2396	44.2
Michigan	Texas	4925	2942	1983	25.2
Ohio	Texas	3411	1492	1919	39.1
Connecticut	Florida	2385	635	1750	57.9
New York	Virginia	2288	539	1749	61.9
New York	Illinois	2664	1009	1655	45.1
California	Florida	7160	5531	1629	12.8
Texas	Washington	3037	1512	1525	33.5

Source: U.S. Bureau of the Census, 1985.

dispersed pattern of settlement than first-time Mexican immigrants. This study demonstrates that experience in the United States as well as social and economic ties can be developed through circular migration between Mexico and the United States (Massey 1985). In contrast to the rather dispersed settlement pattern of Mexican immigrants, Portes and Bach (1985) found that the Cubans concentrated in Miami and remained there over the six-year period.

As the US Hispanic population grows, questions and issues relating to migration and population redistribution will be of increasing concern to social scientists and policy-makers at local, state, and federal levels. At the microlevel, there is a need for household level research that examines linkages between migration and socioeconomic and demographic status of Hispanics. Relationships between immigrant generation/length of residence in the United States, internal migration, and socioeconomic and demographic status will contribute to a broader theory of migration, adjustment, and assimilation.

At the aggregate level, Hispanic migration and population redistribution impacts labor markets and has important implications for the provision of educational and social services. The issue of geographic impacts is particularly important given the growth of the Hispanic population and uncertainties surrounding consequences of the Immigration Reform and Control Act of 1986.

Literature Cited

Allen, J. P., and E. J. Turner. 1988. *We the People: An Atlas of America's Ethnic Diversity.* New York: Macmillan Publishing.

Arreola, D. D. 1985. Mexican Americans. In *Ethnicity in Contemporary America: A Geographical Appraisal*, ed. J. O. McKee, 77–94. Dubuque, IA: Kendall/Hunt Publishing.

Bean, F. D., and M. Tienda. 1988. *The Hispanic Population of the United States.* New York: Russell Sage Foundation.

Bean, F. D., M. Tienda, and D. S. Massey. 1988. Geographical distribution, internal migration, and residential segregation. In *The Hispanic Population of the United States*, ed. F. D. Bean and M. Tienda, 137–77. New York: Russell Sage Foundation.

Biggar, J. C. 1979. The sunning of America: Migration to the Sunbelt. *Population Bulletin* 34:1–42.

Boswell, T. D. 1984. The migration and distribution of Cubans and Puerto Ricans living in the United States. *Journal of Geography* 83:65–72.

Boswell, T. D. 1985a. The Cuban-Americans. In *Ethnicity in Contemporary America: A Geographical Appraisal*, ed. J. O. McKee, 95–116. Dubuque, IA: Kendall/Hunt Publishing.

Boswell, T. D. 1985b. Puerto Ricans living in the United States. In *Ethnicity in Contemporary America: A Geographical Appraisal*, ed. J. O. McKee, 117–144. Dubuque, IA: Kendall/Hunt Publishing.

Boswell, T. D., and J. R. Curtis. 1984. *The Cuban-American Experience.* Totowa, NJ: Rowman and Allanheld Publishers.

Davis, C., C. Haub, and J. Willette. 1983. U.S. Hispanics: Changing the face of America. *Population Bulletin* 38:1–44.

Garcia, J. A. 1981. Hispanic migration: Where they are moving and why. *Agenda: A Journal of Hispanic Issues* 2:14–17.

Grebler, L., J. W. Moore, and R. C. Guzman. 1970. *The Mexican-American People.* New York: The Free Press.

Jaffee, A. J., R. M. Cullen, and T. D. Boswell. 1980. *The Changing Demography of Spanish Americans.* New York: Academic Press.

Long, L. 1988. *Migration and Residential Mobility in the United States.* New York: Russell Sage Foundation.

Massey, D. S. 1985. The settlement process among Mexican migrants to the United States: New methods and findings. In *Immigration Statistics: A Story of Neglect*, ed. D. B. Levine, K. Hill, and R. Warren, 255–92. Washington, DC: National Academy Press.

Morrison, P. A. 1977. Urban growth and decline in the United States: A study of migration's effect in two cities. In *Internal Migration: A Comparative Perspective*, ed. A. A. Brown and E. Neuberger, 235–54. New York: Academic Press.

Plane, D. A. 1984. A systematic demographic efficiency analysis of US interstate population exchange, 1935–80. *Economic Geography* 60:294–312.

Portes, A., and R. L. Bach. 1985. *Latin Journey: Cuban and Mexican Immigrants in the United States.* Berkeley, CA: University of California Press.

Roseman, C. C. 1977. *Changing Migration Patterns within the United States*, Resource Paper No. 77-2. Washington, DC: Association of American Geographers.

Roseman, C. C., and K. E. McHugh. 1982. Metropolitan areas as redistributors of population. *Urban Geography* 3:22–33.

US Bureau of the Census. 1973. Census of population: 1970. *Mobility for States and the Nation*, Final Report PC(2)-2B. Washington, DC: Government Printing Office.

US Bureau of the Census. 1982. Census of population: 1980. *Persons of Spanish Origin by State: 1980*, Supplementary Report PC80-S1-7. Washington, DC: Government Printing Office.

US Bureau of the Census. 1985. Census of population: 1980. *Geographical Mobility for States and the Nation*, PC80-2-2A. Washington, DC: Government Printing Office.

US Bureau of the Census. 1986. Projections of the Hispanic population: 1983 to 2080. *Current Population Reports*, Series P-25, No. 995. Washington, DC: Government Printing Office.

US Bureau of the Census. 1988. The Hispanic population in the United States: March 1986 and 1987. *Current Population Reports*, Series P-20, No. 434. Washington, DC: Government Printing Office.

Valdivieso, R., and C. Davis. 1988. US Hispanics: Challenging issues for the 1990s. *Population Trends and Public Policy* 17:1–16.

Warren, R., and J. S. Passel. 1987. A count of the uncountable: Estimates of undocumented aliens counted in the 1980 United States census. *Demography* 24:375–93.

Raster Data for the Layman

Just What Is GIS?

MARK MONMONIER

Mark Monmonier *is professor of geography in the Maxwell School of Citizenship and Public Affairs at Syracuse University. He holds a Ph.D in geography from The Pennsylvania State University and has served as editor of* The American Cartographer *and president of the American Cartographic Association.*

In today's tight job market, college courses on geographic information systems (GIS) are on the "What's hot?" list of many undergraduates. Offered in civil engineering, environmental studies, forestry and landscape architecture as well as in geography departments, training in GIS has proved a foot in the door at cartographic contractors, environmental consulting firms, public utilities, energy companies, planning agencies, and numerous government agencies at the federal, state, and local levels. This job niche is hardly surprising—location is a key element in many public and commercial enterprises, and software for geographic analysis demands far more expertise than word processors or spreadsheets.

Although GIS is often called an electronic map, its focus is data, not maps.

Although GIS is often called an electronic map, its focus is data, not maps. As instructors and textbook authors take pains pointing out, the typical geographic information system must cope with the storage, retrieval, manipulation, analysis and display of geographic data. Their use of "display" is deliberately vague, because the final product might be tax bills or address labels, maps are not essential. In many instances visual maps are used only to check the accuracy of an electronic map read by a computer, not by humans. Carefully structured data let the computer "see" geographic relationships. However, with grid data, touch is a more appropriate analogy than sight. Superimposing a grid over a map partitions land into cells, arranged in rows and columns, as in Figure 1. Each cell has a unique pair of row and column addresses, which

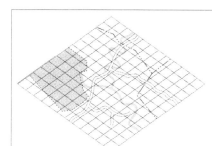

Figure 1. Raster data superimpose a grid on the landscape.

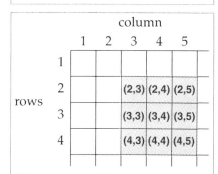

Figure 2. A cell's neighbors have row and column numbers that differ by no more than 1.

allow the computer to store and retrieve a number representing elevation, land use or soil type. Because row and column numbers are integers (1, 2, 3, . . .), the computer can compare a cell with its neighbors, as in Figure 2, by examining all cells with a row or column number that differs by 1. Because the cells are arranged in rows like the "raster" pattern on a television screen, gridded data are commonly called raster data.

Readily displayed on a computer monitor, raster data are especially useful for environmental phenomena like land cover and elevation, which occur throughout a region and can, with patience and money, be measured anywhere, at any level of precision. To raise the level of detail, the GIS user need only decrease the cell size and add more rows and columns. Less readily accommodated by the raster format are linear features like roads, streams and curved boundaries, which might require a massive grid of tiny cells, most of which are empty.

Geographic information systems typically represent linear features as lists of points, with pairs of rectangular (X,Y) coordinates recorded sequentially along the feature's length, as in Figure 3. Because the line segment between each consecutive pair of points is, in mathematical parlance, a "vector," GIS pioneers awarded these lines, points and lists the collective label vector data. Although a highly detailed map of contorted roads and boundaries requires long lists of points, vector data are more efficient than raster data for measuring lengths and areas as well as for generating aesthetically pleasing conventional maps. Map projection software can readily transform coastlines and political boundaries to a new perspective, and vehicle navigation systems can quickly rotate features so that "ahead" remains at the top of the display when the road curves or the car turns a corner.

To help the computer detect patterns and spatial relationships with vector data, GIS designers treat the map as a network of lines, points and areas. The first step involves disconnecting all lines that cross other lines, thereby creating arcs that run between consecutive nodes (intersections). The next steps, "build-

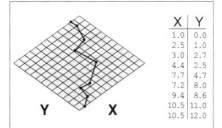

Figure 3. Vector data represent linear features with lists of point coordinates.

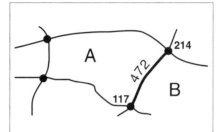

Figure 4. Arc 471 is bounded by nodes 117 and 214 and co-bounded by polygons A and B.

ing the topology" in GIS-speak, require many lists. Lists of arcs representing roads describe specific streets and highways, and lists of arcs representing boundaries describe the perimeters of counties, towns, census tracts and other polygons.

Topological structure is thorough and detailed. As Figure 4 illustrates, an arc is "bounded" by two nodes and "co-bounded" by two polygons. Each arc is assigned a specific direction, which yields another list designating each co-bounding polygon as either left-hand or right-hand. Like raster data, which have the implicit structure of the grid, this arc-polygon list gives the computer a crude set of "eyes." As Figure 5 describes, finding an area's neighbors is a straightforward process of identifying the arcs that are bounded by the polygon in question and recording all polygons on the opposite side of a bounded arc.

Address information makes a rich geographic data base even richer. In addition to giving street arcs an orientation (from the low-address end of the block to the high-address end), address ranges let the com-

puter estimate relative position between intersections and determine whether a residence or business lies on the left or right side of the street.

This information helps computers guide taxi drivers, pizza couriers and emergency vehicles. After finding the quickest, most direct route, a GIS can print a detailed itinerary so that drivers need not hunt for missing, hidden or illegible street signs.

Odd-even information is especially important to the Bureau of the Census, which uses automated address-matching to count the number of residents in each block. As Figure 6 shows, the computer that identifies a household's street segment and matches its numerical address with the odd or even address range can then increment the running total for the appropriate block. Once census-takers have tabulated data at the block level, they compile counts for census tracts, cities and larger units. In addition to the decennial head count mandated by the Constitution, the Census Bureau enumerates demographic, social and economic characteristics. Data on age, income, race and employment help direct-mail advertisers refine their mailing lists. Address-matching allows marketing consultants to differentiate blue-collar neighborhoods interested in beer and bowling from upscale suburbs attuned to imported wines and health clubs. Special tabulations by zip code area or voting precinct are especially valuable for targeting households for charitable solicitations or political pitches. Census data in GIS also helps real-estate

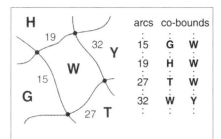

Figure 5. To find a polygon's neighbors, identify the other polygons co-bounding its arcs.

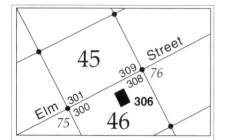

Figure 6. 306 Elm Street, located on the even-numbered side of the arc between nodes 75 and 76, belongs to block 46.

Figure 7. Buffers describe impact zones around points, lines and areas.

firms answer clients' questions about neighborhoods and housing values. And after politicians readjust legislative districts to reflect population shifts since the previous census, the Justice Department uses data on race and ethnicity to verify compliance with the Voting Rights Act.

Lists of one-way streets, intersections with traffic lights, and the streets that meet at each node complete the electronic street map. This information helps computers guide taxi drivers, pizza couriers and emergency vehicles. After finding the quickest, most direct route, a GIS can print a detailed itinerary so that drivers need not hunt for missing, hidden or illegible street signs. Given a list of several addresses, the computer can generate minimum-distance routes for parcel-delivery and express-courier drivers. Letting the GIS read the map and the driver watch traffic can increase safety as well as cut costs.

Vehicle navigation requires a highly specialized GIS that tracks the driver's progress across the electronic map. Sensors measure forward movement as well as change in direction. A small screen to the right of the steering wheel shows nearby streets, and a flashing dot in the center marks the vehicle's position. As the car or truck moves forward, new streets come into view at the top of the screen. When the vehicle turns a corner, the map flips so that the forward direction is always at the top of the screen. A turn also requires a complete regeneration of the map's street names, which must be horizontal for legibility. The system must continually reconcile the vehicle's position with the electronic map, and warn the driver who takes a ferry or an off-the-road route to reset the map's location.

Because an accurate, up-to-date description of street geometry is essential, keeping the map current has become the primary business of one manufacturer of in-car navigation systems. The firm's most important customers are GIS users for whom the Census Bureau's electronic street map, which is updated once every ten years, is inadequate. Users who don't buy their data from a specialist vendor can be overwhelmed by data capture, as well as entry and editing of electronic maps. Eventually, of course, all geographic data will be captured electronically in a format suited for computerized analysis.

Land information systems and environmental modeling are the most prominent part of the GIS industry. In addition to selecting sites for fast-food restaurants, discount stores and land-fills, geographic data systems guide the preparation of environmental impact statements and help local governments register deeds, assess property, collect taxes and enforce zoning regulations.

The two most basic operations in site selection are buffer construction and map overlay. As shown in Figure 7, a buffer encompasses all locations within a given distance of a point, line or area. Locational analysts use buffers to represent zones of service or impact. Circular buffers around fire hydrants, for instance, identify areas reached by a hose of a given length, stretched to its full extent, whereas circular buffers around schools and churches show where zoning ordinances prohibit bars and liquor stores. Similarly, a linear buffer along a pipeline delineates a safety zone, where construction is prohibited, and a buffer around a proposed hazardous-waste landfill describes an impact zone within which the operator must buy out or compensate property owners.

Viewsheds also help land developers and real-estate assessors estimate the scenic value of home sites.

Not all buffers have a simple geometry. Planners concerned about visual blight near a proposed landfill or power line might use an electronic elevation map to delineate an irregularly shaped viewshed comprising areas from which the offending facility is visible. Viewsheds also help land developers and real-estate assessors estimate the scenic value of home sites.

Map overlay is a common technique for assessing the suitability of a site or route. The example in Figure 8 shows how overlaying a buffer and building inventory can identify incompatible structures along a proposed gasoline pipeline. Site selection can involve a dozen or more map layers called coverages. A landfill study, for instance, might call for coverages representing slope, soil permeability, land use, zoning, surface drainage, ground water, and even proximity to local airports. Because garbage attracts birds, which pose a hazard to aviation, siting regulations might prohibit landfill within 10 miles of any runway used by jet aircraft.

Emergency managers have begun to rely heavily on GIS to simulate the effects of catastrophes ranging from natural disasters like earthquakes and floods to technological disasters such as chemical releases and ground water contamination. For example, a plume model identifying affected areas downwind from a leaking chlorine tank, as in Figure 9, is a tool for both emergency response and emergency planning. Police and fire fighters, who query the GIS before setting up road blocks and evacuating residents during a real emergency, can also use the system in training for the evacuation of schools, nursing homes and other "special needs" populations. Moreover, because maps are an effective propaganda tool, local officials might use the GIS to persuade a hazardous facility to either relocate or reduce its stockpile of lethal material.

The geographic information system is part of a cartographic revolution as momentous as those inspired by printing and photography. Computers and telecommunication are radically altering how we use and value maps. Most notably, the paper map is no longer the principal medium for storing geographic information. Yet because of easy electronic customization, paper maps are more numerous, more timely and generally more appropriate to users' needs. In computerese, paper can be very user-friendly. Even so, the ease with which users can interrogate data makes interactive maps eminently more valuable than their paper cousins for data analysis, if not for communication and propaganda. And as with earlier technological catalysts, the computer brings new problems and exacerbates old ones: technology will never repeal the GIGO principle (garbage in, garbage out), for instance, and cartographic historians and archivists have yet to deal with electronic maps. Policy makers seem equally perplexed by issues of public access, copyright protection, liability and privacy. For map enthusiasts as well as students of GIS, these are exciting times, with challenges as complex as those that confronted Mercator.

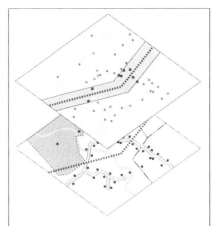

Figure 8. Map overlay and linear buffer identify incompatible structures along a pipeline route.

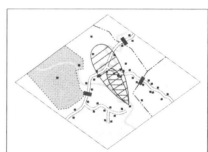

Figure 9. Model plume delineates an evacuation zone downwind of a chemical accident.

Population, Resources, and Socioeconomic Development

The final unit of this anthology includes discussions of several important problems facing humankind. Geographers are keenly aware of regional and global difficulties. It is hoped that their work with researchers from other academic disciplines and representatives of business and government will help bring about solutions to these serious problems.

Probably no single phenomenon has received as much attention in recent years as the so-called population explosion. World population continues to increase at unacceptably high rates. The problem is most severe in the less-developed countries, where in some cases, populations are doubling in less than 20 years.

The first three articles in this section deal with the related issues of population growth, poverty, overuse of the land, and resource shortages. The human population of the world will pass the 6 billion mark in 1999. And it is anticipated that population increase will continue well into the twenty-first century, despite a slowing in the rate of population growth globally since the 1960s. "Russia's Population Sink" reports on the dilemma of death rates exceeding birth rates in this postcommunist country.

The next article warns of the widespread degradation of agricultural soils from erosion and overuse. Then

Martha Farnsworth Riche discusses the radically changing ethnic composition of the U.S. population. Lastly, "Preventive Medicine: A Broader Approach to the AIDS Crisis," provides a sobering account of a global plague that will only worsen.

Looking Ahead: Challenge Questions

How are you personally affected by the population explosion?

Give examples of how economic development adversely affects the environment. How can such adverse effects be prevented?

How do you feel about the occurrence of starvation in developing world regions?

What might it be like to be a refugee?

In what forms is colonialism present today?

How is Earth a system?

For how long are world systems sustainable?

What is your scenario of the world in the year 2010?

UNIT 5

Population, Poverty and the Local Environment

*As forests and rivers recede, a child's labor
can become more valuable to parents, spurring
a vicious cycle that traps families in poverty*

Partha S. Dasgupta

PARTHA S. DASGUPTA, who was educated in Varanasi, Delhi and Cambridge, is Frank Ramsey Professor of Economics at the University of Cambridge and Fellow of St. John's College. He is also chairman of the Beijer International Institute of Ecological Economics of the Royal Swedish Academy of Sciences in Stockholm and Fellow of the British Academy. Dasgupta's research has ranged over various aspects of environmental, resource and population economics, most recently poverty and malnutrition.

As with politics, we all have widely differing opinions about population. Some would point to population growth as the cause of poverty and environmental degradation. Others would permute the elements of this causal chain, arguing, for example, that poverty is the cause rather than the consequence of increasing numbers. Yet even when studying the semiarid regions of sub-Saharan Africa and the Indian subcontinent, economists have typically not regarded poverty, population growth and the local environment as interconnected. Inquiry into each factor has in large measure gone along its own narrow route, with discussion of their interactions dominated by popular writings—which, although often illuminating, are in the main descriptive and not analytical.

Over the past several years, though, a few investigators have studied the relations between these ingredients more closely. Our approach fuses theoretical modeling with empirical findings drawn from a number of disciplines, such as anthropology, demography, ecology, economics, nutrition and political science. Focusing on the vast numbers of small, rural communities in the poorest regions of the world, the work has identified circumstances in which population growth, poverty and degradation of local resources often fuel one another. The collected research has shown that none of the three elements directly causes the other two; rather each influences, and is in turn influenced by, the others. This new perspective has significant implications for policies aimed at improving life for some of the world's most impoverished inhabitants.

In contrast with this new perspective, with its focus on local experience, popular tracts on the environment and population growth have usually taken a global view. They have emphasized the deleterious effects that a large population would have on our planet in the distant future. Although that slant has its uses, it has drawn attention away from the economic misery endemic today. Disaster is not something the poorest have to wait for: it is occurring even now. Besides, in developing countries, decisions on whether to have a child and on how to share education, food, work, health care and local resources are in large measure made within small entities such as households. So it makes sense to study the link between poverty, population growth and the environment from a myriad of local, even individual, viewpoints.

The household assumes various guises in different parts of the world. Some years ago Gary S. Becker of the University of Chicago was the first investigator to grapple with this difficulty. He used an idealized version of the concept to explore how choices made within a household would respond to changes in the outside world, such as employment opportunities and availability of credit, insurance, health care and education.

One problem with his method, as I saw it when I began my own work some five years ago, was that it studied households in isolation; it did not investigate the dynamics between interacting units. In addition to understanding the forces that encouraged couples to favor large families, I wanted to understand the ways in which a reasoned decision to have children, made by each household, could end up being detrimental to all households.

In studying how such choices are made, I found a second problem with the early approach: by assuming that decision making was shared equally by adults, investigators had taken an altogether too benign view of the process. Control over a family's choices is, after all, often held unequally. If I wanted to understand how decisions were made, I would have to know who was doing the deciding.

Power and Gender

Those who enjoy the greatest power within a family can often be identified by the way the household's resources are divided. Judith Bruce of the Population Council, Mayra Buvinic of the International Center for Research on

Women, Lincoln C. Chen and Amartya Sen of Harvard University and others have observed that the sharing of resources within a household is often unequal even when differences in needs are taken into account. In poor households in the Indian subcontinent, for example, men and boys usually get more sustenance than do women and girls, and the elderly get less than the young.

Such inequities prevail over fertility choices as well. Here also men wield more influence, even though women typically bear the greater cost. To grasp how great the burden can be, consider the number of live babies a woman would normally have if she managed to survive through her childbearing years. This number, called the total fertility rate, is between six and eight in sub-Saharan Africa. Each successful birth there involves at least a year and a half of pregnancy and breast-feeding. So in a society where female life expectancy at birth is 50 years and the fertility rate is, say, seven, nearly half of a woman's adult life is spent either carrying a child in her womb or breast-feeding it. And this calculation does not allow for unsuccessful pregnancies.

Another indicator of the price that women pay is maternal mortality. In most poor countries, complications related to pregnancy constitute the largest single cause of death of women in their reproductive years. In some parts of sub-Saharan Africa as many as one woman dies for every 50 live births. (The rate in Scandinavia today is one per 20,000.) At a total fertility rate of seven or more, the chance that a woman entering her reproductive years will not live through them is about one in six. Producing children therefore involves playing a kind of Russian roulette.

Given such a high cost of procreation, one expects that women, given a choice, would opt for fewer children. But are birth rates in fact highest in societies where women have the least power within the family? Data on the status of women from 79 so-called Third World countries display an unmistakable pattern: high fertility, high rates of illiteracy, low share of paid employment and a high percentage working at home for no pay—they all hang together. From the statistics alone it is difficult to discern which of these factors are causing, and which are merely correlated with, high fertility. But the findings are consistent with the possibility that lack of paid employment and education limits a woman's ability to make decisions and therefore promotes population growth.

There is also good reason to think that lack of income-generating employ-

ment reduces women's power more directly than does lack of education. Such an insight has implications for policy. It is all well and good, for example, to urge governments in poor countries to invest in literacy programs. But the results could be disappointing. Many factors militate against poor households' taking advantage of subsidized education. If children are needed to work inside and outside the home, then keeping them in school (even a cheap one) is costly. In patrilineal societies, educated girls can also be perceived as less pliable and harder to marry off. Indeed, the benefits of subsidies to even primary education are reaped disproportionately by families that are better off.

In contrast, policies aimed at increasing women's productivity at home and improving their earnings in the marketplace would directly empower them, especially within the family. Greater earning power for women would also raise for men the implicit costs of procreation (which keeps women from bringing in cash income). This is not to deny the value of public investment in primary and secondary education in developing countries. It is only to say we should be wary of claims that such investment is a panacea for the population problem.

The importance of gender inequality to overpopulation in poor nations is fortunately gaining international recognition. Indeed, the United Nations Conference on Population and Development held in Cairo in September 1994 emphasized women's reproductive rights and the means by which they could be protected and promoted. But there is more to the population problem than gender inequalities. Even when both parents participate in the decision to have a child, there are several pathways through which the choice becomes harmful to the community. These routes have been uncovered by inquiring into the various motives for procreation.

Little Hands Help...

One motive, common to humankind, relates to children as ends in them-

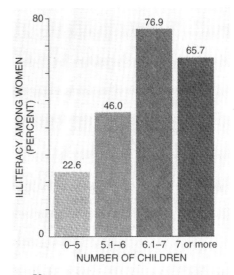

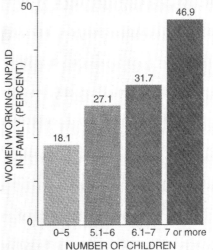

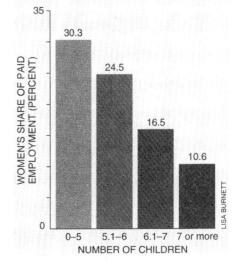

TOTAL FERTILITY RATE around the world (the average number of children a woman produces) generally increases with the percentage of women in a country who are illiterate (*top*) or work unpaid in the family (*middle*). Fertility decreases when a larger share of the paid employment belongs to women (*bottom*). Bringing in a cash income may empower a woman in making decisions within her family, allowing her to resist pressure to bear more children.

selves. It ranges from the desire to have children because they are playful and enjoyable, to the desire to obey the dictates of tradition and religion. One such injunction emanates from the cult of the ancestor, which, taking religion to be the act of reproducing the lineage, requires women to bear many children [see "High Fertility in Sub-Saharan Africa," by John C. Caldwell and Pat Caldwell; SCIENTIFIC AMERICAN, May 1990].

Such traditions are often perpetuated by imitative behavior. Procreation in closely knit communities is not only a private matter; it is also a social activity, influenced by the cultural milieu. Often there are norms encouraging high fertility rates that no household desires unilaterally to break. (These norms may well have outlasted any rationale they had in the past.) Consequently, so long as all others aim at large families, no household on its own will wish to deviate. Thus, a society can get stuck at a self-sustaining mode of behavior that is characterized by high fertility and low educational attainment.

This does not mean that society will live with it forever. As always, people differ in the extent to which they adhere to tradition. Inevitably some, for one reason or another, will experiment, take risks and refrain from joining the crowd. They are the nonconformists, and they help to lead the way. An increase in female literacy could well trigger such a process.

Still other motives for procreation involve viewing children as productive assets. In a rural economy where avenues for saving are highly restricted, parents value children as a source of security in their old age. Mead Cain, previously at the Population Council, studied this aspect extensively. Less discussed, at least until recently, is another kind of motivation, explored by John C. Caldwell of the Australian National University, Marc L. Nerlove of the University of Maryland and Anke S. Meyer of the World Bank and by Karl-Göran Mäler of the Beijer International Institute of Ecological Economics in Stockholm and me. It stems from children's being valuable to their

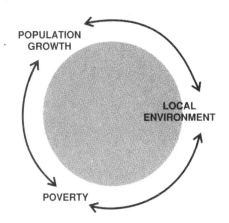

REGION	TOTAL FERTILITY RATE
SUB-SAHARAN AFRICA	6 TO 8
INDIA	4
CHINA	2.3
JAPAN AND WESTERN INDUSTRIAL DEMOCRACIES	1.5 TO 1.9

POVERTY, population growth and environmental degradation interact in a cyclic pattern (*top*). The chart (*bottom*) shows that fertility is higher in countries that are poorer.

parents not only for future income but also as a source of current income.

Third World countries are, for the most part, subsistence economies. The rural folk eke out a living by using products gleaned directly from plants and animals. Much labor is needed even for simple tasks. In addition, poor rural households do not have access to modern sources of domestic energy or tap water. In semiarid and arid regions the water supply may not even be nearby.

Nor is fuelwood at hand when the forests recede. In addition to cultivating crops, caring for livestock, cooking food and producing simple marketable products, members of a household may have to spend as much as five to six hours a day fetching water and collecting fodder and wood.

Children, then, are needed as workers even when their parents are in their prime. Small households are simply not viable; each one needs many hands. In parts of India, children between 10 and 15 years have been observed to work as much as one and a half times the number of hours that adult males do. By the age of six, children in rural India tend domestic animals and care for younger siblings, fetch water and collect firewood, dung and fodder. It may well be that the usefulness of each extra hand increases with declining availability of resources, as measured by, say, the distance to sources of fuel and water.

...But at a Hidden Cost

The need for many hands can lead to a destructive situation, especially when parents do not have to pay the full price of rearing their children but share those costs with the community. In recent years, mores that once regulated the use of local resources have changed. Since time immemorial, rural assets such as village ponds and water holes, threshing grounds, grazing fields, and local forests have been owned communally. This form of control enabled households in semiarid regions to pool their risks. Elinor Ostrom of Indiana University and others have shown that communities have protected such local commons against overexploitation by

Green Net National Production

Some economists believe population growth is conducive to economic growth. They cite statistics showing that, except in sub-Saharan Africa, food production and gross income per head have generally grown since the end of World War II. Even in poor regions, infant survival rate, literacy and life expectancy have improved, despite the population's having grown much faster than in the past.

One weakness of this argument is that it is based on statistics that ignore the depletion of the environmental resource base, on which all production ultimately depends. This base includes soil and its cover, freshwater, breathable air, fisheries and forests. No doubt it is tempting to infer from past trends that human ingenuity can be relied on to overcome the stresses that growing populations impose on the natural environment.

Yet that is not likely to be the case. Societies already use

an enormous 40 percent of the net energy created by terrestrial photosynthesis. Geoffrey M. Heal of Columbia University, John M. Hartwick of Queens University and Karl-Göran Mäler of the Beijer International Institute of Ecological Economics in Stockholm and I have shown how to include environmental degradation in estimating the net national product, or NNP. NNP is obtained by deducting from gross national product the value of, for example, coal extracted or timber logged.

This "green NNP" captures not only present production but also the possibility of future production brought about by resources we bequeath. Viewed through NNP, the future appears far less rosy. Indeed, I know of no ecologist who thinks a population of 11 billion (projected for the year 2050) can support itself at a material standard of living of, say, today's representative American.

invoking norms, imposing fines for deviant behavior and so forth.

But the very process of economic development can erode traditional methods of control. Increased urbanization and mobility can do so as well. Social rules are also endangered by civil strife and by the takeover of resources by landowners or the state. As norms degrade, parents pass some of the costs of children on to the community by overexploiting the commons. If access to shared resources continues, parents produce too many children, which leads to greater crowding and susceptibility to disease as well as to more pressure on environmental resources. But no household, on its own, takes into account the harm it inflicts on others when bringing forth another child.

Parental costs of procreation are also lower when relatives provide a helping hand. Although the price of carrying a child is paid by the mother, the cost of rearing the child is often shared among the kinship. Caroline H. Bledsoe of Northwestern University and others have observed that in much of sub-Saharan Africa fosterage is commonplace, affording a form of insurance protection in semiarid regions. In parts of West Africa about a third of the children have been found to be living with their kin at any given time. Nephews and nieces have the same rights of accommodation and support as do biological offspring. In recent work I have shown that this arrangement encourages couples to have too many offspring if the parents' share of the benefits from having children exceeds their share of the costs.

In addition, where conjugal bonds are weak, as they are in sub-Saharan Africa, fathers often do not bear the costs of siring a child. Historical demographers, such as E. A. Wrigley of the University of Cambridge, have noted a significant difference between western Europe in the 18th century and modern preindustrial societies. In the former, marriage normally meant establishing a new household. This requirement led to late marriages; it also meant that parents bore the cost of rearing their children. Indeed, fertility rates in France dropped before mortality rates registered a decline, before modern family-planning techniques became available and before women became literate.

The perception of both the low costs and high benefits of procreation induces households to produce too many children. In certain circumstances a disastrous process can begin. As the community's resources are depleted, more hands are needed to gather fuel and water for daily use. More children are then produced, further damaging the local environment and in turn providing the household with an incentive to enlarge. When this happens, fertility and environmental degradation reinforce each other in an escalating spiral. By the time some countervailing set of factors—whether public policy or diminished benefits from having additional children—stops the spiral, millions of lives may have suffered through worsening poverty.

Recent findings by the World Bank on sub-Saharan Africa have revealed positive correlations among poverty, fertility and deterioration of the local environment. Such data cannot reveal causal connections, but they do support the idea of a positive-feedback process such as I have described. Over time, the effect of this spiral can be large, as manifested by battles for resources [see "Environmental Change and Violent Conflict," by T. F. Homer-Dixon, J. H. Boutwell and G. W. Rathjens; SCIENTIFIC AMERICAN, February 1993].

The victims hit hardest among those who survive are society's outcasts—the migrants and the dispossessed, some of whom in the course of time become the emaciated beggars seen on the streets of large towns and cities in underdeveloped countries. Historical studies by Robert W. Fogel of the University of Chicago and theoretical explorations by Debraj Ray of Boston University and me, when taken together, show that the spiral I have outlined here is one way in which destitutes are created. Emaciated beggars are not lazy; they have to husband their precarious hold on energy. Having suffered from malnutrition, they cease to be marketable.

Families with greater access to resources are, however, in a position to limit their size and propel themselves into still higher income levels. It is my impression that among the urban middle classes in northern India, the transition to a lower fertility rate has already been achieved. India provides an example of how the vicious cycle I have described can enable extreme poverty to persist amid a growth in well-being in the rest of society. The Matthew effect—"Unto every one that hath shall be given, and he shall have abundance: but from him that hath not shall be taken away even that which he hath"—works relentlessly in impoverished countries.

Breaking Free

This analysis suggests that the way to reduce fertility is to break the destructive spiral. Parental demand for children rather than an unmet need for contraceptives in large measure explains reproductive behavior in developing countries. We should therefore try to identify policies that will change the options available to men and women so that couples choose to limit the number of offspring they produce.

In this regard, civil liberties, as opposed to coercion, play a particular role. Some years ago my colleague Martin R. Weale and I showed through statistical analysis that even in poor countries political and civil liberties go together with improvements in other aspects of life, such as income per person, life expectancy at birth and infant survival rate. Thus, there are now reasons for thinking that such liberties are not only desirable in themselves but also empower people to flourish economically. Recently Adam Przeworski of the University of Chicago demonstrated that fertility, as well, is lower in countries where citizens enjoy more civil and political freedom. (An exception is China, which represents only one country out of many in this analysis.)

The most potent solution in semiarid

FURTHER READING

POPULATION, NATURAL RESOURCES, AND DEVELOPMENT. Special issue of *Ambio*, Vol. 21, No. 1; February 1992.

AN INQUIRY INTO WELL-BEING AND DESTITUTION. Partha Dasgupta. Oxford University Press, 1993.

POPULATION: THE COMPLEX REALITY. Population Summit Report of the World's Scientific Academies, Royal Society, London. North American Press, 1994.

POPULATION, ECONOMIC DEVELOPMENT, AND THE ENVIRONMENT. Edited by Kerstin Lindahl Kiessling and Hans Landberg. Oxford University Press, 1994.

WORLD DEVELOPMENT REPORT. World Bank, annual publication.

POVERTY, INSTITUTIONS AND THE ENVIRONMENTAL RESOURCE BASE. Partha Dasgupta and Karl-Göran Mäler in *Handbook of Development Economics*, Vol. 3. Edited by T. N. Srinivasan et al. North Holland Publishing, Amsterdam (in press).

regions of sub-Saharan Africa and the Indian subcontinent is to deploy a number of policies simultaneously. Family-planning services, especially when allied with health services, and measures that empower women are certainly helpful. As societal norms break down and traditional support systems falter, those women who choose to change their behavior become financially and socially more vulnerable. So a literacy and employment drive for women is essential to smooth the transition to having fewer children.

But improving social coordination and directly increasing the economic security of the poor are also essential. Providing cheap fuel and potable water will reduce the usefulness of extra hands. When a child becomes perceived as expensive, we may finally have a hope of dislodging the rapacious hold of high fertility rates.

Each of the prescriptions suggested by our new perspective on the links between population, poverty and environmental degradation is desirable by itself, not just when we have those problems in mind. It seems to me that this consonance of means and ends is a most agreeable fact in what is otherwise a depressing field of study.

The Future of Populous Economies

China and India Shape Their Destinies

Robert Livernash

A villager looks for fuelwood in a forest. A farm family, forced to sell its small plot of land, wonders what to do next. A government official works on plans for energy development. A successful young executive considers buying a car for the first time.

These everyday events illustrate the numerous connections between people and the environment. And they suggest what could happen on a much larger scale, as an additional billion people join the planet's population in each of the next few decades: resource exhaustion, large-scale migration, and massive pollution from power plants or automobiles.

But these events also suggest leverage points for change. Could community forests be managed to increase wood supplies on a sustainable basis? Could macroeconomic policies be adjusted to increase employment opportunities? Could new technologies reduce power plant emissions? Could public transport systems make private cars things of the past?

Such questions outline the long-running debate that swings from predictions of impending disaster to global prosperity. Here we examine the issue in the context of the world's two most populous countries. Much of the world's growth will take place in India and China, which are already large, poor, and populous. How well they manage growth, poverty, and population will influence not only the condition of their local environments but regional and global environments as well.

In any discussion of population's environmental and resource impacts, China and India logically are paramount. China, which now has about 1.2 billion people, is expected to grow to 1.5 billion by 2025. India's population of 935 million will grow to about 1.4 billion. These population giants are home to 37 percent of the world's population today and will still contain 35 percent of the total 3 decades hence (see Figure 1.)[1]

Size aside, there are important differences in the population outlook for the two countries. With the help of its one-child policy and other factors, China's total fertility rate plunged from 4.8 children per woman during 1970–1975 to below replacement level (less than 2 children per woman) today. However, population growth will continue for several decades because of the demographic momentum of China's large population of women of child-bearing age. In India, fertility also has declined but is currently about 3.6 children per woman. Thus, India will add upwards of 450 million people over the same period that China adds 300 million.

Differing fertility rates also determine the age structure of each nation. China's population is aging: The over-60 contingent will increase from about 10 percent of the population currently to nearly 20 percent by 2020.[2] Unlike most industrialized countries, however, China does not yet have a national social security system for those too old to work.[3] India's over-60 population also will increase but will still comprise less than 15 percent of the whole in 2025.

Both nations will become substantially more urbanized during the next three decades. According to United Nations (UN) estimates, China will be nearly 55 percent urban by 2025, up from 30 percent now; India will be 45 percent urban, up from the current estimate of 27 percent.[4]

A few other key factors illustrate these countries' situations:

Economic Growth: China's economy has been growing at breakneck speed for more than a decade, usually boosting gross domestic product by 9 percent or more per year. The country has had several bouts with inflation; in mid-1994, inflation was running more than 20 percent. The economy is making a swift transition towards private enterprise and market economics, with most of the growth occurring in the coastal regions and in the southeast. Remaining state-run enterprises, which are still a large part of the economy and a major employer, must either become more competitive or

From *Environment*, July/August 1995, pp. 7-11, 25-34. © 1995 by the Helen Dwight Reid Educational Foundation. Reprinted by permission of Heldref Publications, 1319 Eighteenth Street, N.W. Washington, DC 20036-1802.

face the prospect of a shutdown. China has made dramatic strides in reducing poverty. Government estimates, which are limited in scope and do not include urban areas, currently show that about 105 million people (12 percent of the rural population) live below the poverty line.[5]

India managed 5 percent annual growth during the 1980s, which was better than most developing or industrialized countries. The economy slumped during the early 1990s as a result of contractionary policies adopted by the government to counter internal and external deficits but has picked up recently. In India today, roughly one third of the population is impoverished.[6]

Health: In China, life expectancy is now about 71; under-5 mortality is 43 per 1,000 live births.[7] The Chinese government's effort to provide preventive health care in the countryside has significantly improved health. In India, life expectancy is about 60; under-5 mortality was estimated at 131 in 1991. Poverty-related diseases—stemming in part from malnutrition, limited access to safe drinking water, and poor sanitation conditions—are still significant in India.[8]

Politics and Society: China is an authoritarian polity with a relatively homogeneous population. The recent emphasis on market economics also has substantially diminished central political control. The government has allowed some media coverage of domestic environmental developments, but private environmental groups and nongovernmental

organizations (NGOs) are to date a minor factor. India is a democracy with a highly heterogeneous population. Political tensions cut across both economic and religious lines; conflicts between Hindus and Muslims have been particularly difficult. There is a large NGO community, a vigorous press, and a well-developed higher education system.

Geography: China's total land area is roughly 932 million hectares, but it has only about 100 million hectares of agricultural land.[9] (The official count of 96 million hectares is acknowledged to be an underestimate; the actual total is probably about 120–130 million hectares.[10]) Much of China's land consists of mountains and deserts that are not easily amenable to human habitation. India has about 300 million hectares of land and about 170 million hectares of agricultural land. Thus, India has only about one-third the land area of China, but it has more than twice the agricultural land area per person. About half of China's land is irrigated, compared to approximately one-fourth of India's.

Environment: Even ignoring the paucity of data, it is almost impossible to briefly assess the state of the environment in two such vast and diverse countries. To some extent, conditions are in the eye of the beholder: China has embarked on an ambitious tree planting program and reports increases in its forest cover, but the area of mature mixed forests is declining. India's latest assessment shows stable forests, but there is little doubt that forests there are under severe pressures and that forest

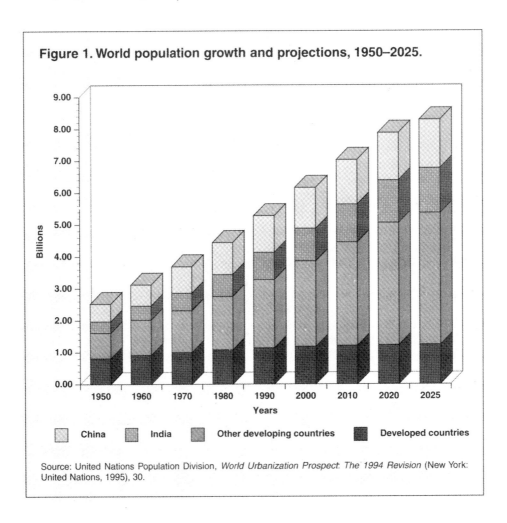

Figure 1. World population growth and projections, 1950–2025.

Source: United Nations Population Division, *World Urbanization Prospect: The 1994 Revision* (New York: United Nations, 1995), 30.

degradation is a continuing problem. Water resources are an acute problem in northern China and in much of India. Air and water pollution are severe in many parts of both countries, though there are some signs of improvements, at least in China. China's economy is growing so rapidly that it is difficult for pollution control programs to keep pace. India's economy is generating less wealth than China's, which is complicating efforts to build support for environmental protection.

There are at least three different ways to approach the population-environment-development interaction: first, in terms of the effects induced by poverty; second, in terms of the constraints posed by development in the context of available resources; and third, in terms of the environmental implications of rising per capita consumption.

Poverty Pressures

Poverty is a vicious circle with many environmental implications. The poor have few options and little ability to make longer-term investments that can improve their situation. Combined with population pressures, poverty contributes to resource degradation and migration.

Until recently, poverty in China was considered exclusively a rural problem, and government estimates focused only on a limited number of rural areas. A 1988 survey of poverty in China, which looked at all rural areas, estimated that 12.7 percent of the rural population, or about 105 million people, lived below the poverty line. The rural poor typically ate less foodgrain, cultivated much less irrigated land, and possessed houses and financial assets of substantially lower value than the nonpoor. Antipoverty programs did not seem to reach them reliably; almost two-thirds were outside of officially designated poor areas.[11] Since 1988, rural poverty has probably declined further, perhaps on the order of 80 to 100 million people, though China's recent period of high inflation (including higher prices for agricultural inputs) may have worsened the situation slightly.

Urban poverty in China is a growing problem. Since the 1980s, controls against internal migration have been loosened, and millions of rural residents have migrated to cities in search of better jobs. In the process, the migrants created an urban informal sector, urban slums, and probably significant numbers of urban poor.[12]

The percentage of Indians living below the poverty line fell from 55 percent in 1973 to 39 percent by 1987–88, according to new estimates by India's Planning Commission. But the absolute number of impoverished remained at roughly 313 million, dropping by only 9 million since 1973. Rural and urban poverty rates are about the same, but the downward trend in poverty rates has been much more pronounced in rural areas. Poverty remains persistent and widespread in Uttar Pradesh, Bihar, Madhya Pradesh, and Orissa (see Figure 2).[13]

By preventing farmers from investing in soil restoration, poverty contributes to soil degradation. Soil erosion in India is extensive, amounting to perhaps 25 billion tons per year,

and nutrient and micronutrient deficiencies are widespread.[14] Many small farms and heavily planted soils lack such micronutrients as zinc, copper, iron, manganese, and boron. Zinc deficiency has been reported in Madhya Pradesh, Tamil Nadu, Andhra Pradesh, Uttar Pradesh, and other states. About 67 percent of soil samples taken in a 1988–89 national survey were low in zinc.[15]

The poor also rely heavily on the resources from nearby forests and grasslands. Such "common property resources" provide animal fodder, organic manures, fuel supplies, edible fruits and nuts, and traditional medicines.[16] Poor rural households obtain up to 20–25 percent of their annual incomes from such resources. Yet, one survey of 82 villages in 20 districts of India's dry region found that from 1951 to 1984 such resources declined in area by 31 to 52 percent.[17]

For centuries, common areas were managed relatively sustainably by local communities. Since Independence, population pressures—as well as logging, the privatization of land for agriculture, and increased grazing—have broken down the old management system and led to resource degradation. As population pressures increased, local councils could no longer manage these shared resources. A survey of 16 Indian states found that since 1970 the common areas have declined by 25 percent.[18]

In the most vulnerable areas, such as Bihar and Uttar Pradesh in the north, the loss of common property resources has hurt the rural poor, especially women who are heavily dependent on them. The decline has also taken a toll on India's biodiversity resources; protected areas have shrunk to just a small fraction of the original ecological zones and are under constant threat of population-induced invasions.[19]

In the late 1980s and early 1990s, the Indian government's approach to forest management changed. The government began encouraging greater participation from village communities and NGOs. In the case of intense grazing pressure, for instance, participatory strategies can help convince villagers of the economic benefits of rehabilitating these areas. Usually, such efforts depend on creating a new management institution and on convincing all subgroups within a village of the benefits of cooperation. Involving women in watershed management is also crucial because women are usually responsible for collecting and processing fuelwood, fodder, food, and water. NGOs too can play a useful role by acting as intermediaries between forest departments and communities.

Throughout India, more than 500,000 hectares of reserve and protected forestland are already under community protection through joint management agreements. By one estimate, communities could help regenerate 30 million hectares of degraded state forestland naturally at only one-twentieth the cost per hectare of establishing tree plantations.[20] So, on most village commons, managing fuel and fodder resources on a sustainable basis will be difficult, but at least sound precedents exist.

Another way to look at poverty is to consider the unevenness of economic development and the challenges that poses for areas that are left behind. In China, for example, eco-

5. POPULATION, RESOURCES, AND SOCIOECONOMIC DEVELOPMENT

nomic growth is proceeding much faster along the coastal areas than in the interior. In the booming city of Guangzhou in China's southeast, per capita gross domestic product (GDP) in 1993 was estimated at about $2,000. In Congqing, a heavily industrialized and severely polluted city of 15 million located along the Yangtze River in Sichuan Province in southeast China, per capita GDP is about $470 (see Figure 3). Chongqing relies on high-sulfur coal as an energy source, which is contributing to an acid rain problem so severe that buildings are visibly deteriorating. Days with no wind and air inversions are a common occurrence. The challenges are formidable and include the problem of generating the capital for environmen-

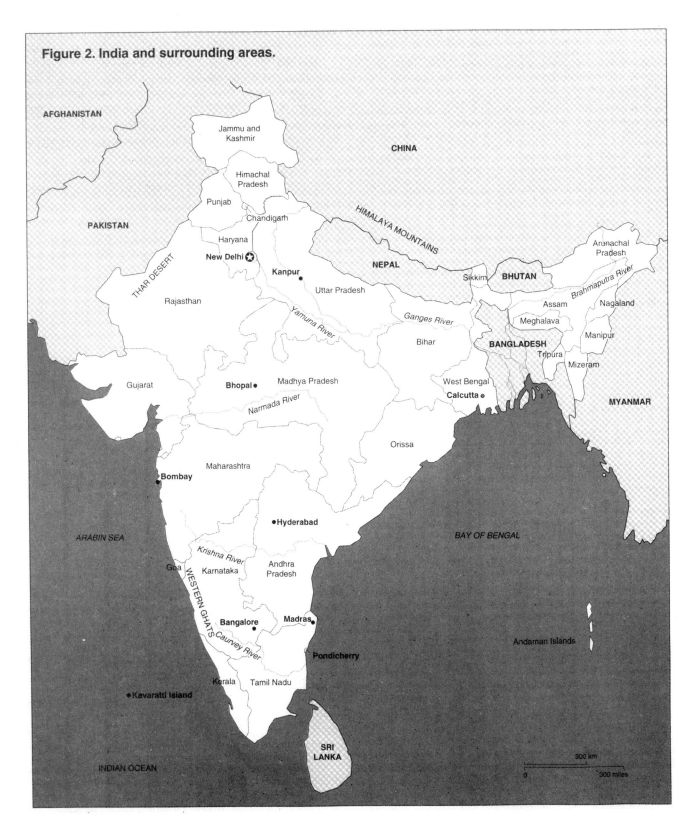

Figure 2. India and surrounding areas.

tal investments in an area that is economically disadvantaged compared to the coastal regions.[21] In short, poverty has ramifications greater than the predicament facing individuals.

Migration

Migration can be an important indicator of demographic and environmental stress. Because so many factors invariably are at work, determining precisely how much population size, growth, or density may contribute to either environmental degradation or internal migration is difficult. But the presence of such factors certainly indicates which countries are at high risk of uncontrolled, large-scale, poverty-induced internal migrations.

One compelling example is the continuing migration of people from Bangladesh to the adjacent Indian states of Assam, Tripura, and West Bengal. Bangladesh has a large absolute population, rapid (though declining) population growth, and very little cropland per capita. Its population density—900 persons per square kilometer—is 3 times that of neighboring Assam.[22] Land scarcity and population growth seem to be the principal factors behind the large-scale migration from Bangladesh to adjacent Indian states. Over the last 40 years, some 12 to 17 million people have migrated; the estimated 7 million migrants to Assam represent one-third of that state's 22 million residents. In several areas in northeast India, including Assam and Tripura, migration has triggered ethnic conflicts. In Tripura, the shift

Figure 3. China and surrounding areas.

in the ethnic balance caused a violent insurgency that lasted through most of the 1980s.[23]

Rural-to-urban migration seems entrenched in both India and China. In every Indian state except Kerala, three of every four members of the rural workforce depend on agriculture.[24] Yet, some 60 percent of all holdings are too small to support an average-sized family.[25] Estimates in the late 1980s indicated that the average value added per agricultural worker was only 27 percent of that in the rest of the economy.[26] So conditions seem ripe for further movement toward the cities.

In China, rural residents in the relatively impoverished interior sections are drawn to the economically robust cities along the coast and in the southeast. By the late 1980s, China's "floating population" numbered 50–70 million; since then, the total has probably increased substantially. In the major cities, "floaters" may constitute anywhere from one-tenth to one-third of the population.[27] Rural laborers are creating de facto ghettos and providing cheap labor in trash collection, sewer cleaning, and the sweatshops that produce apparel and toys. During the next decade, as many as 100–200 million more rural laborers will be looking for work; many, maybe most, will look in cities.[28]

Increasingly liberal government policies in China have fueled this rural-to-urban migration. In the 1950s, the central government set up a household-registration system, dividing the population into urban and rural categories and barring most migration from rural to urban areas. But urban reforms in the late 1980s have made it easier to migrate to cities. Under the old system, for instance, rural migrants living in cities could not get a grain allocation; however, under the new one, anyone with enough money can buy grain on the open market.

Rural migrants also have been an important source of labor for new private businesses and state-run enterprises. State-run enterprises can hire temporary workers with no benefits and fire them at any time.[29] China's rapid growth has allowed the economy to absorb many of these rural laborers; but, by the same token, the newly employed could lose their jobs in an economic slowdown. Furthermore, the use of rural migrants as replacements may pose a potentially serious threat to the economic security of permanent employees.[30]

Development Pressures

Population growth, which adds to the necessity for rapid economic growth, is an important factor for government officials in China and India trying to map their country's economic future. Consider national efforts to control industrial pollution. Even though much evidence shows the benefits of up-front investments in industrial pollution controls, such investments are still widely frowned upon as expensive frills that add burdensome costs to business operations and may slow overall economic growth.

China's pollution-levy system presents a case of a well-designed pollution-control program that follows the polluter-pays principle and, in theory, provides an incentive for pollu-

ters to reduce emissions. Under this system, government environmental protection officials impose a fee on facilities that violate emissions standards. If violations continue, companies may be fined as well. Most of the fees are reabsorbed by businesses, which get grants or low-interest loans for plant-level waste treatment facilities or for operation and maintenance activities that reduce pollution. Yet, the fees are generally so small that most firms choose to pay them rather than invest in pollution control equipment; though raising the fees above the marginal cost of investing in treatment equipment would improve the system, companies would probably resist any such change for the same reason they failed to invest in environmental technology before. The fees and fines can even be lower than the cost of operating and maintaining pollution control equipment; as a result, many companies apparently do not operate pollution control equipment after it is installed. Another problem is that one-fifth of the collected fees go directly into the budgets of local environmental protection bureaus, thus creating a perverse incentive to tolerate pollution in order to continue collecting fees and maintain bureau budgets.[31] In June 1994, China's National Environmental Protection Agency began a two-year study of the pollution-levy system that will look at the system's problems and consider reforms.

Township and village enterprises—the hodge-podge of light industries that have sprung up since the early 1980s—present another conflict between growth and pollution control. Among the most dynamic and rapidly growing segments of the Chinese economy, these enterprises grew by 30 percent annually during the 1980s, and in some provinces they now account for nearly half of industrial output. But most use outdated technology and lack pollution control equipment.[32] Chinese environmental officials are placing a high priority on the worst polluters, which are typically large state-run enterprises. Getting control of township enterprises would require a substantial increase in staff and monitoring equipment at local environmental protection bureaus.[33] Putting a lower priority on these enterprises (or focusing on those sectors that are the worst polluters) may make sense now, when they still account for a relatively small fraction of pollution, but it may create a bigger problem later as their volume of industrial pollution grows.

In the mid-1980s, the Indian government began an ambitious effort to clean up municipal and industrial water pollution in the Ganges River, where most of the 1.4 billion liters of sewage generated every day by cities and towns along the river is dumped without treatment. About $100 million has been spent to date on sewage treatment plants, low-cost sanitation facilities, and other pollution control facilities. Efforts also are underway to expand the program to India's other rivers.

The program has probably helped improve water quality in some stretches of the Ganges. But independent Indian scientists reported in 1994 that many of the waste treatment systems called for by the plan were never built, not commissioned, or not functioning; that few state politicians showed interest in the program; and that public involvement was minimal.[34]

Although domestic waste is the largest source of pollution in the Ganges, industrial pollution is also serious. In Kanpur, some 175 tanneries perched on the Ganges' southern bank are dumping large amounts of toxic heavy metals, such as chrome, into the river. Through an Indo-Dutch program, chrome-recovery plants have been installed at six of the largest tanneries, but owners of smaller tanneries say they cannot afford the new pollution control technologies.[35] Such a case illustrates the difficulties of environmental cleanup when there is limited public and government support and many polluters operate at the margin of profitability.

The Energy Dilemma

Energy development poses an enormous challenge for both China and India over the next several decades. Between 1970 and 1991, commercial energy consumption increased nearly four times in India and more than three times in China. In absolute terms, the growth in China was much greater because China consumes about three times more energy than India.[36] Yet, there is still pent-up demand in both countries,[37] and power outages and brownouts are common: India's electricity short-fall is estimated to be 8.5 percent of total electricity generated and 17.5 percent at peak periods; China's is similar.

Energy demand will continue to be intense because both industrialization and urbanization are energy-intensive. Urban dwellers use more energy than rural: One study found that if India and China were to double the proportion of their population living in cities, per capita energy consumption would rise by 45 percent barring any changes in income or population.[38] China and India, sources of less than 10 percent of today's demand, plan to build about one-fourth of the world's new capacity.[39] China currently plans to build more than 100 new power plants over the next decade.[40]

Both China and India will burn coal to support much of their development over the next few decades. By the year 2000, China's coal consumption will rise from the current 1 billion metric tons per year to about 1.4 billion metric tons—fully one-third of world output in 1992.[41] Coal accounts for roughly three-fourths of China's total energy consumption now, and that share will hold steady through 2010. In India, coal production totaled about 240 million metric tons in the early 1990s;[42] by 2010, production is projected to increase to nearly 600 million metric tons.

The environmental impact of burning coal—in terms of particulate emissions, acid deposition, and carbon dioxide emissions—is potentially immense in these two nations. For one thing, particulate emissions increasingly are recognized as a significant health threat; respiratory diseases, currently 26.5 percent of the total, already are the leading cause of death in China.[43]

Secondly, of course, emissions of carbon dioxide—one of the main greenhouse gases, along with methane and chloro-fluorocarbons (CFCs)—are thought to play a major role in climate change. China and India currently account for about 14 percent of global greenhouse emissions.[44] Over the period 1990–2010, they are forecast to produce a bigger increase in emissions than the entire industrialized world;[45] by 2010, according to the International Energy Agency, China and India will produce about one-fourth of the world's emissions of carbon dioxide.[46] For this reason, China and India will be front and center in all coming debates about coal burning and climate change. Their per capita greenhouse emissions are slight, however, compared to those of the United States and other industrialized countries, so there is a particular onus on the North to assist efforts in India and China to hold down carbon emissions.

From a northern perspective, the key question is whether either country can reduce the growth of coal burning in the next few decades. Price reform can certainly boost efficiency. As part of the Beijing government's economic reform plan, an annual subsidy of $230 million to the coal industry will be phased out by 1995 or soon thereafter, and China's coal producers are already selling more coal at market prices in response. China General Coal Corporation, for example, sold 57 percent of its coal at market prices in 1993, up from 20 percent in 1992.[47]

Continuing advances in efficiency also offer real promise. For example, the United Nations Development Programme and the Global Environment Facility are now studying potential efficiency improvements in the next generation of industrial boilers. The Beijing Energy Efficiency Center—cofounded by the Pacific Northwest Laboratory, World Wildlife Fund, Lawrence Berkeley Laboratory, and the Energy Research Institute of the State Planning Commission of China—is working on a number of energy-efficiency projects. In Shenzen, a booming Special Economic Zone next to Hong Kong, the institute is working with local government officials to develop an energy planning methodology that gives equal priority to energy conservation and new power plant construction investments.[48]

China could substitute natural gas for coal in many areas. Those with the greatest potential seem to be in the South China Sea area and Xinjiang Province in the far west. The government also is pushing ahead with the massive Three Gorges hydroelectric project, which will provide an alternative to coal use but has been roundly criticized for its financial, environmental, and human costs.[49]

India faces similar challenges. The price of electricity has been below the cost of production, so state electricity boards take huge losses and the capacity for new investment shrinks. Particularly thorny is flat-rate pricing for farmers, which encourages energy inefficiency and misuse in agriculture. By the early 1990s, agriculture (primarily tubewell pumps) accounted for more than 24 percent of total electricity consumption. The central government has proposed a minimum 50 paise/kilowatt-hour rate for the sale of electricity to agriculture. But so far only a few utilities have implemented this rate, partly because many state governments are reluctant to upset the longstanding policy of keeping food prices low.[50]

As low-cost electrification has spread, the use of electrified irrigation has grown explosively. The number of diesel and electric irrigation pumpsets rose from 87,000 in 1950 to 12.5 million in 1990.[51] As a result, the extraction of groundwater for irrigation has increased tremendously: the area irrigated from groundwater has increased from 5 million hectares in 1951 to about 23.5 million hectares in 1990.[52] In at least some of this area, groundwater is being heavily overexploited, and if flat-rate electricity pricing continues, farmers have no incentive to conserve groundwater resources.

Demand-side management also could relieve the pressures on electricity production. Adjusting prices to encourage consumption during off-peak hours, for example, has worked in many industrialized and developing countries, but so far no major attempts have been made to initiate such a scheme in India.[53]

> Particulate emissions increasingly are recognized as a significant health threat; respiratory diseases already are the leading cause of death in China.

Further development of natural gas also presents a real energy alternative to coal in India. Gas-fired power plants are cheaper and faster to build than coal-fired plants and substantially less polluting. The problem is that most of the gas is in the relatively undeveloped northeast, where demand is low and where nearly 30 percent of the gas produced every year has been flared (burned off) at the wellhead—a loss of nearly $1 million per day, apart from air pollution costs.[54]

India's coal is generally poor in quality and has a high ash content. One significant and cost-effective policy would be to aggressively invest in equipment to wash noncoking coal; this would remove much of the ash and thus greatly reduce transportation costs. Washing costs are generally about $4–$6 per ton, which is more than offset by transportation cost savings when the distance is greater than 600 miles. Washed coal also emits significantly fewer particulates.[55]

Subsidies for conventional energy make it difficult for renewable energy alternatives to compete, but some developments are promising. Wind power ranks high among them. India has indigenous production capacity, and the private sector is being encouraged to help develop it. The Indian Renewable Energy Development Agency, set up with substantial funding from the World Bank and the Global Environment Facility, is providing soft loans to industries to finance up to 75 percent of project costs. Also, India is now manufacturing photovoltaic cells, supplemented by $55 million over 5 years from the Global Environment Facility earmarked for market development. Photovoltaics are particularly attractive in remote areas where grid extension is difficult.[56]

Consumption Pressures

Consumption issues are an increasingly important factor in the population debate. The average citizen of an industrialized country places a far heavier burden on the environment than one in the developing world, but the North is not doing much to correct this, notes Kamal Nath, India's Minister of Environment and Forests.[57] Key here is the difference in purchasing power: The average GDP per person in industrialized countries is about $19,000, compared with roughly $2,000 in developing countries.[58] The United States, for instance, has only about one-third the population of India but consumes 33 times more aluminum, 183 times more natural gas, and 385 times more pulpwood than Indians. Per capita emissions of carbon dioxide are 19 times those of India.[59]

But consumption is not just a prerogative of industrialized nations; an increasing number of people in developing countries are now joining the ranks of northern consumers. In India, for example, spending on electronic equipment and motor vehicles is much higher among the top 10 percent of urban income earners than in the rest of Indian society.[60] Moreover, the market for future consumption in developing countries, considering expected population growth and rising per capita incomes, is enormous.

Demand for personal transportation in both India and China is potentially gargantuan. India's vehicle fleet increased from 11 million in 1986 to more than 21 million in 1991; nearly 70 percent of these vehicles are motor scooters or three-wheel auto rickshaws. Motor scooters, increasing at a rate of about 20 percent a year, could well number 36 million by the turn of the century.[61]

In China, one planner estimates that there could be 70 million motorcycles, 30 million trucks, and 100 million cars on China's roads by 2015 and that the scope for further growth would still be huge.[62] Automakers are clamoring for access to the Chinese market; in November 1994, 20 major automakers went to Beijing with proposals to build a $1 billion assembly plant that could turn out up to 500,000 cars per year by the end of the century. Some automakers believe that car sales will be in the range of 3 to 4 million per year by the year 2000.[63]

In India, demand for motor fuel is expected to outpace that for all other petroleum products and rise more than 16 percent annually from 1991–92 to 1996–1997, which would double consumption in just 5 years.[64]

Traffic congestion and air pollution, already serious in many cities in India and China, are bound to worsen, taking an even greater toll on economic efficiency and human health. In Delhi, for example, vehicles already account for

70 percent of the total emissions of nitrous oxides, and leaded gas is here to stay until Indian refineries overcome the technical and economic obstacles to production of lead-free gas. To speed the transition, the Central Pollution Control Board is proposing a phaseout by 1997.[65] China produces some unleaded gas, but most is exported to Singapore; whatever is left for domestic consumption is usually mixed with leaded gas because of a shortage of storage tanks. China plans to convert fully to unleaded gas by the year 2000.[66]

In India, air pollution has also been influenced by what one analyst calls a "lopsided" government emphasis on the production of cars and two-wheelers, which are growing by 20 percent a year, over the production of buses, growing at 3 percent a year. Yet, per rider, cars consume 4.9 times more energy, are 9 times more expensive to operate, and emit 5.7 times more pollutants than buses. Two-wheelers consume 2.5 times more energy, are 3 times more expensive to operate than buses, and emit 3 times more pollutants. The benefits of a well-run public transport system in India are enormous. A study by the Tata Energy Research Institute found that increasing the share of public transport from 47 to 80 percent in 83 Indian cities by the year 2000 would reduce air pollution and transport costs by roughly one-third and the total number of vehicles on the road by one-half.[67]

Demand for refrigerators and other appliances will grow in the 1990s and beyond, too. In China, sales of refrigerators, which use ozone-depleting CFCs, jumped from 0.2 per 100 households in 1981 to 42.3 in 1990. China signed the Montreal Protocol on Substances that Deplete the Ozone Layer and is working to introduce CFC substitutes. It has proposed a complete phaseout of ozone-depleting substance by decade's end but seeking $2.1 billion from the protocol's Multilateral Fund to pay for the phaseout and the higher costs of substitute refrigerants. As of December 1994, the fund had allocated $50.2 million to China in support of 107 projects. India has received $11.5 million for 31 projects.[68]

Providing Food and Water

Providing food and water to the growing populations of China and India is a matter of grappling with poverty, development, and consumption issues. In many respects, the delivery of drinking water to urban areas is a current crisis in numerous parts of both nations and could easily become a much graver crisis as urban populations expand.

Water scarcity is commonplace in India. The poor usually suffer the most, typically paying high prices to private suppliers to buy water by the bucket. In many squatter settlements, the poor are forced to use even highly contaminated water—an invitation to outbreaks of such waterborne diseases as jaundice, cholera, and gastroenteritis. In cities where groundwater is available, the poor may dig wells, thus depleting groundwater supplies.[69]

A recent survey of 19 Indian cities cited 3 principal reasons for the water crisis in India: lack of foresight and bad planning, inadequate financial resources, and failure to protect water sources.[70] Most Indian water supply systems, which were designed and installed when city populations were much smaller, are old, poorly maintained, and inefficient. Up to 20 percent of water may be lost due to leakages alone. Most city and state governments lack the financial resources needed to modernize and expand water systems because water charges typically cover no more than one-eighth of actual costs. Artificially low rates also weaken incentives to conserve or recycle water. Finally, in many Indian cities, urban water sources are regularly contaminated by industrial pollutants or municipal wastes.[71] In fact, in many systems, water pipes run alongside sewage networks, adding to the danger of contamination.

Governments—both at the national and local level—typically respond to the crisis with proposals to increase water supplies by constructing expensive new public works. Some 570 Chinese cities, mostly in the north, suffer grave water shortages that officials say cost an estimated $14 billion a year in lost economic output. One solution proposed by the central government is to build an 860-mile-long aqueduct from central China north to Beijing and Tianjin at an estimated cost of at least $5 billion. However, southern provincial officials complain that Chinese cities waste billions of gallons of water per year and that conservation should be tried first.[72]

Similar examples abound in India. The government of Dewas in Madhya Pradesh in central India proposed building a dam on a river 20 kilometers away to relieve scarcity. The project would take 22 years, and the pricetag is so high that the dam is unlikely to ever be built. Meanwhile, under a plan put forth by a voluntary organization, the town's traditional water storage systems could be revived, industrial water and municipal sewage recycled to meet industrial demand for water, and watershed planning improved. This plan reportedly is more cost-effective and much quicker to implement.[73]

Besides slaking their thirst, can China and India feed their growing populations? Several recent attempts to answer this question on a global basis found that food production gains should be able to keep pace with population growth. Most such studies project that yield increases will continue to be the main source of food production growth.[74]

In China's case, agricultural policy reforms have helped spur a food production boom that is one of the great success stories of the developing world's past few decades. But the outlook for further rapid increases in food production is uncertain. Relative to its population, China has little cropland, and most of it lies in its economic powerhouses, the booming eastern and southern regions. Significant amounts of cropland are being converted to other uses, though to date, increases in double-cropping, greater inputs, and mechanization have more than offset the losses.

China's primary strategy in the 1990s will be to raise yields on less productive land by expanding such inputs as fertilizer and high-yield seeds. China also has numerous programs for reducing soil erosion, combatting desertification, reclaiming wastelands (unfortunately including wetlands), promoting integrated pest management and biological pest controls, and reducing the loss of prime farmland. Whether these will offset additional stress in the form of agricultural runoff and intensification of production remains unclear. On some fronts, such as the extent of cropland subject to salinity and alkalinity, evidence suggests that China is winning the battle.

China's rising prosperity is increasing demand for poultry and beef, which in turn requires more grain for animal feed. Combined with population growth, over the next few decades this trend could turn China into a food-deficit country. Some even argue that China's potential cereal shortfall could exceed the world's ability to respond.[75] But such a forecast probably underestimates China's ability to muster additional production. Furthermore, food production could increase much faster than domestic demand in nearby regions such as Eastern Europe and the former Soviet Union. If so, the issue may be largely one of foreign exchange, and the coin of China's realm is much stronger than that of most other developing nations. Sub-Saharan Africa, for instance, is unlikely to have the foreign exchange to import the 250 million tons of cereal that the World Bank estimates will be needed by the year 2020.[76]

In India, per capita food production has increased almost as impressively as it has in China. But poverty and lack of purchasing power make the outlook fundamentally different. Chronic undernutrition is likely to continue to be a major problem in India; for the south Asian region as a whole, the Food and Agriculture Organization of the United Nations estimates that there will still be about 200 million people suffering from chronic undernutrition by the year 2010.[77]

Opportunities for expanding cropped area in India are limited, but the potential for better production is abundant. The average yield of 2 tons of cereals per irrigated hectare, though more than twice that of rainfed land, is low compared with the average yield of irrigated cropland in other countries. Solutions appear to depend mainly on improved water management and the greater involvement of local farmers. The management systems now in use rely too heavily on top-down administrative structures that limit the role of farmers. Furthermore, coordination among support agencies is poor, and some methods of water distribution are inefficient and inequitable.[78]

Production in India's rainfed areas could be improved, too. In demonstration projects, grain yields have reached 4,000 kilograms per hectare, compared to 600 to 800 kilograms using traditional practices. New seed varieties also hold promise: Within 5 years the International Rice Research Institute plans to release a new rice variety that has provided 50 percent higher yields in test plots, with fewer inputs.[79] Although increases in farmers' fields are likely to be far less than in test plots, this could still be a significant development for both China and India.

Meanwhile, India grows increasingly dependent on groundwater for irrigation. Groundwater is typically twice as productive as canal irrigation, and it is now used to provide water for a larger area than canals. Yet, in many areas groundwater is being pumped at unsustainable rates, so aquifers and reservoirs could become less reliable as production pressures increase. One option is to raise prices to create conservation incentives. Another is to encourage the use of groundwater in conjunction with canal irrigation to prevent waterlogging and groundwater depletion. Giving farmers reasons to switch from 3 consecutive rice crops to doublecropping in an agroforestry system would reduce pressures on groundwater resources but would also eliminate about 12 jobs per hectare.[80]

Conclusion

In both China and India, economic growth is both a legitimate aspiration and an overwhelming reality. Given this context, the logical first step is to look for "win-win" opportunities: programs and policies that contribute both to growth and environmental protection.

Fortunately, there are many such opportunities. Improving energy efficiency, for example, can reduce both emissions and production costs. Designing pollution prevention into new plants, though entailing up-front costs, should reduce costs and provide significant health benefits in the long run. Carefully conserving cropland could keep food prices down and enable foreign exchange to be used for more productive investments. Improving water-use efficiency could make construction of costly new water supply projects unnecessary.

In a few critical sectors such as coal, however, win-win strategies are less apparent. Using coal for energy development is generally the cheapest option. Coal washing and the installation of electrostatic precipitators are relatively cost-effective ways to reduce coal's environmental and health impacts, but they do not fully address a critical global concern—carbon dioxide emissions. In areas such as coal and the phaseout of CFCs, the fundamental challenge is for industrialized countries and global institutions to assist China and India.

Population growth could stabilize in the next century because the political consensus about what needs to be done to achieve this objective is now fairly clear. But many obstacles remain. Deep-rooted cultural and economic factors in-

> The poor are forced to use highly contaminated water—an invitation to outbreaks of waterborne diseases.

fluence family size. For example, a preference for sons is still strong in many regions of India. Children in rural areas can help overburdened parents by fetching water or fuelwood. And children often remain the only form of old-age security for their parents.

How well these problems are resolved depends largely on economic growth, urbanization, and a shift in the labor force from primarily agriculture to manufacturing and service. As vital as job creation and poverty reduction are, in their absence progress is possible by providing effective family programs and investing in education for women.

In short, population can be stabilized in many areas of the world. Over the next half century, however, several billion more people will likely be added to the global total. Unless the environmental impact of these additional numbers is reduced, the cumulative environmental stress could be catastrophic.

On consumption, consensus is much weaker. Few industrialized countries regard consumption as an issue, and real uncertainty about how much efficiency improvements and technological innovation can reduce consumption's environmental impacts remains.

As long as industrialized countries preach to developing countries about consumption without restraining their own, the hole we are collectively digging will deepen. But if people in industrialized countries reduce their consumption and governments in all countries set policies that would increase resource-use efficiency, consumption could be kept at safer levels. For example, European countries have taxed petroleum steeply to restrain demand. Similar taxes could also help reduce solid waste, encourage recycling, or reduce traffic congestion. Further implementation of the polluter-pays principle and incentives to prevent pollution also would help improve the efficiency of resource use and reduce pollution. Perhaps at some point, nations will also see the merit of using the price system to account for the environmental costs of consumption.

The outlook for India seems substantially more difficult than for China. Population is growing faster and could double before stabilizing; poverty is widespread and persistent; neither rural nor urban economic growth has been sufficient to accommodate the mushrooming labor force; the status of women remains low, especially in the northern states; and common property resources, linchpins in the rural economy, will be increasingly threatened by development and population pressures. Pressures on the agricultural resource base will continue. Room for improving irrigation efficiency and boosting production on drylands is great, but so are institutional bottlenecks. Fortunately, India has a resilient political system, a respected higher education system, and a vibrant NGO community that can help meet the coming challenges. In both countries, however, the margin for error over the next few decades is slim, especially in terms of economic growth and job creation.

The complexity of the linkages among population, poverty, development, and environmental degradation remains greatly underappreciated.[81] So, for that matter, is the extraordinary potential of the human race to shape its own destiny with intelligence, foresight, and compassion. There will be no greater need for such qualities than in India and China.

NOTES

1. United Nations Population Division, *World Urbanization Prospects: The 1994 Revision,* (New York: United Nations, 1995), 30–33.

2. United Nations Population Division, *Urban and Rural Areas by Sex and Age: The 1992 Revision* (New York: United Nations, 1993), 42–43, 91.

3. S. R. Conly and S. L. Camp, *China's Family Planning Program: Challenging the Myths,* Country Study Series No. 1 (Washington, D.C.: Population Crisis Committee, 1992), 43.

4. United Nations Population Division, *World Urbanization Prospects: The 1992 Revision* (New York: United Nations, 1993), 76–77.

5. United Nations Development Programme, *Human Development Report 1994* (New York: Oxford University Press, 1994), 134.

6. R. Repetto, *The "Second India" Revisited: Population, Poverty, and Environmental Stress over Two Decades* (Washington, D.C.: World Resources Institute, 1994), 26.

7. World Resources Institute in collaboration with the United Nations Environment Programme and the United Nations Development Programme, *World Resources 1994–95* (New York and London: Oxford University Press, 1994), 272.

8. Ibid., pages 270–73.

9. Ibid., pages 94–95, 284.

10. V. Smil, *China's Environmental Crisis* (Armack, N.Y.: M. E. Sharp, 1993), 53–55.

11. C. Riskin, "Income Distribution and Poverty in Rural China," in K. Griffin and Z. Renwei, eds., *The Distribution of Income in China* (New York: St. Martin's Press, 1993), 163.

12. Ibid., page 136.

13. Repetto, note 6 above, page 26; and Planning Commission, Government of India, *Report of the Expert Group on Estimation of Proportion and Number of the Poor* (New Delhi, 1993), 37–40.

14. Repetto, note 6 above, page 37.

15. Indian Institute of Soil Science, *All-India Coordinated Scheme of Micro and Second Nutrients and Pollutant Elements in Soils and Plants,* Annual Report 1988-89 (Bhopal, 1990), 16–18.

16. Repetto, note 6 above, page 49.

17. N. S. Jodha, *Common Property Resources: A Mission Dimension of Development Strategies,* World Bank Discussion Paper No. 169 (Washington, D.C., 1992), iii, 14.

18. Repetto, note 6 above, page 52.

19. Ibid., pages 53–55.

20. M. Poffenberger, ed., *Forest Management Partnerships: Regenerating India's Forests,* Executive Summary of the Workshop on Sustainable Forestry, New Delhi, September 10–12, 1990 (New Delhi: The Ford Foundation and Indian Environmental Society, n.d.), 1–2.

21. W. Spofford, senior fellow and director, Environment and Development Program, Resources for the Future, Washington, D.C., remarks at a seminar on integrating environment and development in China, 29 March 1995, Washington, D.C.

22. World Resources Institute, note 7 above, pages 94–95, 284.

23. T. F. Homer-Dixon, "Environmental Scarcities and Violent Conflict: Evidence from Cases," *International Security* 19, no. 1 (Summer 1994): 21–23.

24. H. R. Sharma, "Distribution of Landholdings in Rural India, 1953–54 to 1981–82," *Economic and Political Weekly* 29, no. 39 (24 September 1994): A-118.

25. Repetto, note 6 above, page 37.

26. Ibid., page 22.

27. D. J. Solinger, "China's Urban Transients in the Transition from Socialism and the Collapse of the 'Urban Public Goods Regime,'" *Comparative Politics,* January 1995, 127–28.

28. L. H. Sun, "The Dragon Within," *The Washington Post,* 9 October 1994, C1; and S. Mufson, "Chinese Leader Presses Call for 'One Couple, One Child,'" *The Washington Post,* 21 March 1995, A11.

29. X. Meng, "China: The Challenge of Urban Migration," *The Urban Age* 2, no. 4 (October 1994): 18.

30. Solinger, note 27 above, pages 139–40.

31. H. K. Florig and W. Spofford, "Economic Incentives in China's Environmental Policy," *Environmental Science and Technology* (forthcoming).

32. World Resources Institute, note 7 above, pages 76–77.

33. Florig and Spofford, note 31 above, page 14.

34. S. Hazarika, "Plan to Clean Holy River Fails to Stem Tide of Filth," *The New York Times,* 18 October 1994, C1.

35. Ibid.

36. United Nations Statistical Division (UNSTAT), UN Energy Tape (New York, 1993).

37. "Energy: The New Prize," *The Economist,* 18 June 1994, 4; and Repetto, note 6 above, page 73.

38. D. W. Jones, "How Urbanization Affects Energy-Use in Developing Countries," *Energy Policy* 19, no. 7 (September 1991): 628.

39. "Energy: The New Prize," note 37 above, page 7.

40. D. C. Esty and R. Mendelsohn, "Powering China: The Environmental Implications of China's Economic Development" (draft manuscript, February 1995), 36–37.

41. "Energy: The New Prize," note 37 above, page 15.

42. Tata Services, *Statistical Outline of India 1992-93* (Bombay, 1992), 62; and Tata Energy Research Institute, *Environmental Considerations in Energy Development,* Final Report Submitted to the Asian Development Bank (July 1992), 49.

43. Esty and Mendelsohn, note 40 above, page 28.

44. World Resources Institute, note 7 above, pages 201–02.

45. "Energy: The New Prize," note 37 above, page 15.

46. Ibid.

47. J. Hamburger, "Linking Energy and Environmental Policy in China" (paper prepared for the Global Studies Program, Battelle Pacific Northwest Laboratory, Washington, D.C., May 1994), 9.

48. Ibid.

49. S. Mufson, "China's Li Breaks Ground for Vast Dam on Yangtze," *The Washington Post,* 15 December 1994, A43.

50. R. K. Pachauri, "Energy Scene in India: Last Two Decades" (background paper prepared for the Second India Reassessment Project, World Resources Institute, Washington, D.C., 1994), 8.5, 8.7, 12.10–12.

51. Ibid., page 8.5.

52. B. B. Vohra, "Agenda for Water: Myth and Reality," in N. Ravi, *The Hindu: Survey of the Environment, 1994* (Madras: S. Rangarajan, 1994), 73.

53. Pachauri, note 50 above, page 4.7.

54. Ibid., page 3.2.

55. Ibid., page 2.4.

56. Ibid., pages 6.1, 6.4, 6.11.

57. K. Nath, "Poverty is the Priority," *Our Planet* 6, no. 3 (1994): 20.

58. World Resources Institute, note 7 above, page 5.

59. Ibid., page 17.

60. Ibid., page 22.

61. D. Biswas and S. A. Dutta, "Vehicular Pollution: Combating the Smog and Noise in Cities," in N. Ravi, *The Hindu: Survey of the Environment, 1994* (Madras: S. Rangajaran, 1994), 41.

62. "Energy: The New Prize," note 37 above, page 11.

63. R. Johnson, "China Gets Concepts 20 Times Over," *Automotive News,* 21 November 1994, 4.

64. Pachauri, note 50 above, page 3.12.

65. Biswas and Dutta, note 61 above, pages 41–45.

66. Michael Walsh, international transportation consultant, remarks made at a meeting on China's environment, Council on Foreign Relations, New York, 6 February 1995.

67. Pachauri, note 50 above, pages 9.2–9.3.

68. Multilateral Fund for the Implementation of the Montreal Protocol, *Inventory of Approved Projects as at December 1994* (Montreal: United Nations Environment Programme, 1994), 103, 115.

69. "Water, Water, Nowhere," in N. Ravi, note 61 above, page 87.

70. Ibid., pages 85–139.

71. Ibid., pages 85, 87.

72. P. E. Tyler, "Huge Water Project Would Supply Beijing by 860-Mile Aqueduct," *The New York Times,* 19 July 1994, A8.

73. C. R. Reddy, "Dewas: A Plan to Turn Deficits into Water Surpluses," in N. Ravi, note 61 above, pages 137–39.

74. D. O. Mitchell and M. D. Ingco, *The World Food Outlook* (Washington, D.C.: World Bank, 1993); Food and Agriculture Organization (FAO) of the United Nations, *Agriculture: Towards 2010* (Rome, 1993); and V. Smil, "How Many People Can the Earth Feed?" *Population and Development Review* 20, no. 2 (June 1994): 255–83.

75. L. Brown, "How China Could Starve the World," *The Washington Post,* 28 August 1994, C1.

76. P. Pinstrup-Andersen, *World Food Trends and Future Food Security* (Washington, D.C.: International Food Policy Research Institute, 1994), 20–21.

77. Food and Agriculture Organization, note 74 above, page 64.

78. The World Bank, *Indian Irrigation Sector Review 2,* Supplementary Analysis, (Washington, D.C., 1991), 4, 10, 33–43.

79. Consultative Group on International Agricultural Research, *Current CGIAR Research Efforts and Their Expected Impact on Food, Agriculture, and National Development,* (Washington, D.C.: CGIAR Secretariat, March 1994), 35.

80. M. S. Swaminathan, "Population and Food: A Crisis on the Horizon," in N. Ravi, note 61 above, page 8.

81. M. Oppenheimer, "Context, Connection, and Opportunity in Environmental Problem Solving," *Environment,* June 1995, 10.

Vicious Circles

African Demographic History as a Warning

TIMOTHY C. WEISKEL

Timothy C. Weiskel is Director of the Harvard Seminar on Environmental Values at Harvard Divinity School.

The terms of debate on global population issues have changed significantly in the last several decades. Theories which tried to isolate simple causes and define simple solutions have been discarded; we have come to recognize that the causes of population growth can only be found in the complexities of the international political economy and the ways it affects the cities and villages of the Third World. The "Developing World" is not developing along Western lines, nor does its demographic history mirror Europe's. Intelligent population policies must be informed by a thorough understanding of population dynamics and of the complex historical, cultural and economic circumstances within which they operate.

Human population growth was identified as a contemporary problem in the 1950s, with the advent of the post-World War II population surge. Initially, the use of birth control pills, condoms and other contraceptive techniques was thought to be the key to slowing population growth. Attention was thus focused on making these new technologies more widely available, especially in the Third World. Contraceptive technologies, however, proved less effective than originally promised. They were difficult to deliver and were resisted by local populations, who considered limits on their reproductive behavior to be limits on their potential livelihood. Rural populations in many parts of the Third World had come to depend upon large families to supply labor, create wealth and provide for the elderly. Thus, attempts to limit family size were regarded with mistrust and suspicion.

Attention eventually shifted to development and economic growth. The general correlation between higher levels of economic prosperity and lower birth rates seemed clear from analyses of global economic and demographic data—poverty appeared to cause excessive population growth. The strategic conclusion was that the population problem would solve itself if significant economic development occurred. With economists in the lead, population experts intoned in mantra-like fashion, "Development is the best contraceptive."

This thinking was guided by the model of "the demographic transition," a phenomenon observed in Europe as it underwent industrialization. One country after another moved from a pattern of high mortality and high birth rates to one of lower mortality and lower birth rates. This same demographic transition, it was thought, would occur throughout the world. The popularity of this model caused the goal of population stabilization to be subsumed by that of economic development. The problem with this approach, however, soon became clear: industrial development according to the European model was not inevitable or even probable in the Third World. Instead, many regions, particularly in Africa, experienced a decline in real GDP per capita. Unless unforseeable rates of economic growth were to spring forth miraculously in these regions, this demographic transition could not occur.

Furthermore, researchers have begun to notice that the presumed correlation between economic growth and declining birth rates is not as absolute as originally believed. Recent studies indicate that, despite a lack of economic growth, selected regions of India and Kenya have witnessed a marked decline in fertility. These studies challenge the idea that economic development is the primary cause of population stabilization. Women's status and education now appear to be far more significant than overall economic growth as a correlate of declining fertility. Many population experts have now embraced this insight, and it is likely to join economic development as a guiding

5. POPULATION, RESOURCES, AND SOCIOECONOMIC DEVELOPMENT

Patterns of production based on cash crops impoverish developing nations.

principle in the formulation of population policy at the International Conference on Population and Development in Cairo this September.

Years of research and debate on population issues have failed to produce convincing mono-causal explanations or successful, unidimensional interventionist strategies; it is finally being accepted that there is no silver bullet. Neither birth control technologies nor development programs alone promise a solution to the population problem. Even programs aimed at improving women's education are not sufficient in themselves; they must be combined with sensitively designed family planning services and facilities.

The case of Bangladesh is instructive: in a poor, male-dominated society that deprives women of access to education, birth rates have been significantly slowed by family planning efforts. This led Jessica Tuckman Mathews of the Council on Foreign Relations to conclude in the *Washington Post* that, "the debate over which is more important, economic development or family planning, can finally be laid to rest. The slogan 'Development is the best contraceptive' stands exposed as the mindless rallying cry of people whose real agenda is opposition to family planning." It is now clear that more attention needs to be devoted to voluntary programs that address the reproductive needs of women.

Population growth is a bio-social problem embedded in the particular history and culture of a society. This realization leads to the awareness that simple mechanical models of causation ("A" causes "B") are inadequate tools

for devising population policy. Such models posit that in order to effect a change in "B" one must attempt to change "A." This logic dominated both the contraceptive technology phase and the economic development phase of population policy discussion, but it is fundamentally unsuited to the problem.

We are coming to realize that population dynamics are not based on such simple relationships; their causality is cumulative, reciprocal and nested. It is *cumulative* in the sense that cultures are strongly bound to tradition. Accepted habits and norms of behavior change slowly and are influenced by the past at least as strongly as by prevailing contemporary circumstances. The causation of population growth is also *reciprocal*: while "A" may cause "B," it is equally true that, over time, "B" causes "A." For example, while having many children may reduce a family's welfare, declining family income may lead to a decision to have more children in an attempt to gain labor and eventually expand household income. Finally, this causation is *nested* because patterns of micro-behavior are conditioned by, and in turn, affect shifts in macro-behavior; local conditions are shaped by global circumstances and vice versa.

Population Growth in Africa: A Case Study

African demographic history provides an illustration of this three-fold framework for examining population dynamics. The magnitude of Africa's population expansion in recent decades is staggering. In 1950, the entire continent had an estimated population of 199 million.

By 1992, this figure had reached 682 million. The United Nations projects that by the year 2000 the continent will be home to 856 million people, and by the year 2025, 1.583 billion. How we account for this remarkable population surge will clarify some of the complexities of the population dilemma confronting us today.

At least five historical components have fueled African population growth. First, Africa's population grew during the slave-trade period. Very little is known about African demographics before the era of the European slave trade, but there is no doubt that the slave trade itself was a significant impulse for population expansion. The warfare and disorder involved in slave acquisition led to a state of generalized conflict in which maximum reproductive performance was highly valued and rewarded. All else being equal, larger families, villages and kingdoms survived more successfully in this state of insecurity than smaller ones.

We have blithely ignored the global patterns of economic integration, urbanization and migration that have conditioned and shaped local reproductive norms for the last five hundred years.

A further consequence of Europe's trade with the Americas was the introduction of foodstuff crops from the New World, like maize, groundnuts and cassava to West Africa. This new food supply made possible the growth of families and villages that, for reasons of self-defense, had become a necessity. Thus, the slave trade launched a fertility boom in Africa. But the fertility boom did not manifest itself as a population boom at the time for two reasons: mortality rates increased during the warfare engendered by the slave trade, and much of the added population was exported as slaves in what became known to demographers as "the largest non-voluntary migration in human history."

The slave trade and the warfare that it fueled lasted from roughly 1500 to 1850, establishing a pattern of large families; however, the impulse to have many children did not end with the close of the slave trade. Rather, European and American interactions with Africa in the latter half of the 19th century placed new demands on the continent's economy. These burdens motivated the second phase of African population growth. The "legitimate commerce" in palm oil, groundnuts, wild rubber and other tropical products put a premium on families that could mobilize large numbers of dependents in order to increase their household production. Thus, the cash-cropping boom of the 19th century—prior to formal colonial rule—maintained and extended the cultural logic that rewarded maximum reproductive performance.

The period of colonial conquest, from approximately 1885 to 1910, generated a third major component in Africa's population history. Much of this conquest was accomplished through destructive warfare. Moreover, in the wake of military intervention, African populations experienced a measurable decline from famine and epidemic disease. As is generally the case with catastrophes caused by famine, disease and warfare, Africa experienced a quick demographic rebound from these early colonial traumas. Thus, in many regions during the 1910s and 1920s a "baby boom" occurred which restored local populations to their pre-colonial numbers. International trade catalyzed this recovery. Based on the labor-intensive export of agricultural commodities, colonial cash-crop regimes—which continue to dominate African economies today, decades after the demise of colonial rule—gave even more support to the well-ingrained cultural preference for large families.

A fourth factor in Africa's population surge involved the gradual expansion of access to elementary hygiene and rudimentary medicine. Infant mortality rates were brought down by the investment in wells and sanitary water supplies for emerging African cities and the instruction in the use of that clean water. Large families (which, over the previous 400 years, had become culturally valued and economically rewarded) were now easier to maintain, since fewer infants died from childhood diseases.

The fifth historical factor contributing to Africa's contemporary population expansion was a remarkable period of urbanization. Whereas fewer than 12 percent of Africa's population lived in cities in 1950, nearly 25 percent did in 1980. This trend has continued; United Nations demographic indicators project that by the year 2010 more than 45 percent of Africa's population (440.9 million people) will be living in cities. In many parts of the world, urbanization is linked to declining fertility rates in the cities, but the impact upon the remaining rural populations is quite different. Many rural households view the loss of young adults to the cities as a "death," or at least as an export of labor. The net effect is to motivate rural households further to expand their dependent labor force by having more children.

Thus, a pattern of significant rural "out-migration" to the cities has actually served to motivate increased reproductive performance in rural areas. The growth of cities with their incessant demands for land, food, fuel and fodder has in turn accelerated the degradation of surrounding rural regions, driving more people off the land and into the cities, and further encouraging the rise of rural fertility rates. In Africa and elsewhere in the Third World, the growth of cities has had a very different impact on the demographics of society than it had in Europe. European urbanization, accompanied by industrialization, has led to marked *declines* in fertility on a society-wide basis. In the contemporary Third World, however, rapid urbanization may actually serve to stimulate society-wide *increases* in fertility, as rural areas seek to replace "lost" labor with more children.

Africa finds itself in what ecologists would call a massive "positive feedback loop." Having more children creates a vicious circle, the only perceived solution for which is to have even more children. Mobilizing greater amounts of dependent labor appears to be the only means households have to work their way out of poverty. The apparent solution is thus the source of the problem in the first place, and the vicious circle manifests itself as a cycle of decline.

African Demographics and the Global Economy

From an analytical perspective, Africa's contemporary population dynamics are best understood within the larger context of the continent's relation to the global economy. Mono-causal explanations do not account for Africa's population dynamics, and neither can these issues be adequately regarded as simply Africa's problem. Responsibility for Africa's population growth may be traced back hundreds of years; it is shared and should be acknowledged by those nations in Europe and the Western hemisphere whose economies have benefited from Africa's demographic history.

Once rural populations were drawn into this pattern of primary production, the local calculus of reproduction became intimately linked to the dynamics of the global economy.

Europe's expansion into Asia and the New World triggered massive demographic dislocations. The New World's population collapse, caused by the disease, famine and warfare engendered by early European encounters, created resource-rich but labor-scarce economies. Slaves from Africa supplied these economies with the means to build prosperity, and Africa became the specialized source for the production of human labor over a period of several hundred years. People were its most valued export commodity.

As European economies stopped demanding unskilled plantation labor and started demanding natural resource inputs for a growing industrial structure, Africa's expanding labor force was put to work in a succession of cash-crop booms. While the objects of this commerce may have changed from palm oil to wild rubber to coffee and cocoa, the underlying logic of expanding the household to expand prosperity was constantly reinforced.

In a broader sense, this pattern came to characterize the entire Third World, even those areas that were not formally absorbed into European colonial empires. While no other region became as involved in the export of labor as Africa did during the slave trade, cash-crop export economies linked to European industrial demand spread throughout Latin America, Asia and the Pacific. Once rural populations were drawn into this pattern of primary production, the local calculus of reproduction became intimately linked to the dynamics of the global economy.

Ironically, the very success of household production units has pressured them to expand their size. The Third World has produced surpluses of coffee, cocoa, tea, so high that the international glut of these commodities has led to a decline in their unit value. The result is what economists call "the primary producer's squeeze." The "squeeze" is simply this: in the face of the declining unit value of its commodity, the surest means available for a peasant household to maintain its income is to expand its production of that same commodity. This requires more labor, hence larger families. Yet, by expanding production in this manner, the primary producer contributes to an even greater glut of their particular commodity on world markets, which, in turn, leads to a further decline in its unit value. Receiving still less for the same volume of production, the peasant household is "squeezed" into expanding its production still further, and the vicious circle of population growth and subsequent emmiseration starts once again.

Urbanization and Population Growth

It is now becoming apparent that global patterns of urbanization are echoing those already manifest in Africa. Urban populations are increasing at rates that exceed average population growth. On a global scale, populations are continuing to grow, but, at an even faster pace, they are agglomerating in massive urban concentrations.

The evidence from Asia is the most dramatic in this regard. A recent report of the United Nations Economic and Social Council for Asia and the Pacific claimed that "by the year 2000, the population of Dhaka is expected to double to 12.2 million; Bombay, Calcutta, Delhi, Jakarta, Karachi, Manila and Shanghai [will] each gain four million people; and Bangkok, Bangalore and Beijing [will each gain] three million." There will be 21 cities with populations in excess of 10 million by the turn of the century, with 13 of these in the Asia-Pacific region. By the year 2020, the report estimates that 1.5 billion more people will be living in Asian cities: the equivalent of creating a new city of 140,000 people every day for the next thirty years.

In a similar vein, recent studies conducted by the Peace and Conflict Studies Program at the University of Toronto in cooperation with the American Academy of Arts and Sciences have drawn attention to rural out-migration in China. Citing Dr. Thomas Homer-Dixon, the author of one of these studies, the *New York Times* reported, "tens of millions of people are already trying to migrate to coastal cities from the country's rural north and interior which...cannot possibly support the next few decades' booming population." The result is the growth of these cities in a locally unsustainable manner; China's growing urban population will have to be supported by 25 percent less arable land per capita by the year 2010.

Chinese cities may therefore become dependent upon an international trade in surplus grains produced in Europe and the United States, as many African cities are today. Any sudden interruption of supply to these cities or continued environmental decline in rural areas could well rekindle age-old regional tensions or trigger ethnic conflict in Asia, as it already has in Africa. Dr. Homer-Dixon's

Population Council

Are growing cities one cause of rural population growth?

study suggests the emergence of a global pattern characterized by "falling grain prices and regional food surpluses in Western countries occurring simultaneously with scarcity-induced civil strife in parts of Africa and Asia." Recently reported rural strife in China is particularly troubling in this regard.

A newly published report of the International Food Policy Research Institute delivers another sobering message to population planners: "Over the next 20 to 30 years, farmers and policy-makers in developing countries will be challenged to provide food at affordable prices for almost 100 million [new] people every year—the largest annual population increase in history." Dr. Per Pinstrup-Anderson, the author of the Institute's study, *World Food Trends and Future Food Security*, quite bluntly claims, "Failure to significantly reduce population growth, particularly in sub-Saharan Africa, [within] the next 20 years will render all other development efforts insufficient to avoid greater human misery in the future." The report suggests that unless immediate commitments are made to undertake accelerated agricultural research, food production will not keep pace with population growth.

The problem we as population analysts face is our failure to develop a global understanding of population dynamics. Instead, we proceed with country-by-country demographic studies, expecting in each case that demographic change will mimic Europe's experience. We have blithely ignored the global patterns of economic integration, urbanization and migration that have conditioned and shaped local reproductive norms for the last five hundred

years. In other words, we divide the world into the "West" and the rest—all those other people who are just waiting to pursue economic and social development on the West's terms.

However, Europe's "demographic transition" may prove to be the exception, not the rule. Similarly, while cities in the Western world have generally stabilized, this is surely not the trend in Third World areas. In the next twenty years 97 percent of world population growth will occur in what we now call the Third World—but perhaps should more accurately name the "Nine-Tenths" World.

Effective population policy can only emerge from a new understanding of the cumulative, reciprocal and nested character of population dynamics on a planetary scale. This expanded understanding of causation necessarily entails an enlarged sense of responsibility and a renewed sense of commitment to this issue on the part of all peoples and all nations. In effect, we face a global population problem without a global understanding of it. We persist in thinking that Africa or Asia have population problems—someone else, somewhere else, not us, not here. In reality, the world now has a human population problem that is most dramatically apparent in its weakest economies and most vulnerable ecosystems.

If we wish to survive as a global species, we must begin to think of ourselves as global citizens. In this context, who is "we"? Who is "they"? What is in our "national self-interest"? These are all concepts that will need to be re-cast as we struggle to forge a morally responsible world community.

RUSSIA'S POPULATION SINK

In the former heart of the Soviet empire, deaths are far outpacing births.

Toni Nelson

Toni Nelson is a staff researcher at the Worldwatch Institute.

In Nadvoitsy, a small Russian town near the Finnish border, an estimated 4,000 children have been poisoned by fluoride, which replaces calcium in the body, leaving its victims with blackened, rotting teeth and weakened bones. Although the town's aluminum plant no longer dumps fluoride into unlined landfills, the contamination persists because neither the authorities nor the company can afford a full-fledged clean-up. Today, 5 to 10 percent of the town's kindergartners continue to exhibit signs of fluorosis.

Nadvoitsy's experience provides a glimpse into the myriad problems facing the countries of the Former Soviet Union (FSU). Years of environmental contamination have combined with economic instability to push the region into a public health crisis, and several FSU countries are now experiencing the most dramatic peacetime population decline in modern history. In Russia, which has more than half the FSU's population, the situation may be at its worst. As the country's birth rate falls and its death rate climbs, the population is expected to shrink by some 9 million between 1992 and 2005. More important, perhaps, is the rising incidence of birth defects and other health problems whose effects may linger for generations.

Russia's demographic decline began in the mid-1980s, well before the collapse of the Soviet Union in 1991 (see graph). Total live births in Russia dropped from a peak of 2.5 million in 1987 to 1.4 million in 1994, while total deaths climbed from 1.5 million to 2.3 million over the same period. The year 1994 brought the most precipitous decline on record, with deaths exceeding births by more than 880,000 and the population falling by 0.6 percent (excluding immigration, which compensated for two-thirds of the decline). Life expectancy, which provides the best general measure of a country's health conditions, also dropped sharply between 1987 and 1994, from 65 to 57 years for men, and from 75 to 71 years for women. This decline has no precedent in industrialized societies; Russian male life expectancy is now the lowest of all developed countries.

Russia's deteriorating social and ecological conditions have had serious consequences for the country's children as well. Infant mortality has climbed to at least 20 deaths per 1,000 live births, although some experts suggest the figure could be as high as 30 per 1,000—more than three times the U.S. rate and double that of Costa Rica, one of the most advanced developing countries. Birth defects occur in 11 percent of newborns, and 60 percent exhibit symptoms of allergies or the deficiency disease known as rickets, caused by a lack of vitamin D. Children's health tends to decline throughout childhood; scarcely one-fifth of Russia's children can be considered healthy by the end of their school years.

Maternal health, and the health of women of reproductive age in general, is also declining—a trend that will almost certainly intensify problems with infant health. Gynecological pathologies have been found in 40 to 60 percent of women in their child-bearing years, and even girls in their early teens are showing signs of reproductive abnormalities. Fully 75 percent of Russian women experience complications during pregnancy, and the death rate during childbirth is 50 per 1,000 births—more than six times the U.S. rate. Only 45 percent of Russian births qualify as normal by Western medical standards.

The factors underlying these trends are complex and numerous, but most can be traced to some combination of environmental contamination and economic instability. In part, the fertility decline is a matter of simple demographics: the number of marriages has decreased, and there are fewer women of childbearing age in the population due to a brief decline in births after World War II. But life in the FSU is still haunted by the abrupt transition from communism, which provided work and housing for nearly everyone, to a capitalist system driven by competition and characterized by insecurity. The uncertain economic situation has prompted many couples to forego childbearing, according to Carl Haub, Director of Information and Education at the Population Reference Bureau. In a survey of 3,000 Russian women in 1992, 75 percent cited insufficient income as a factor discouraging childbearing. As Haub observed in a 1994 report, "The recent birth dearth, not surprisingly, is a direct result of the collapse of the economy and a general lack of confidence in the future."

The rise in Russia's death rate illustrates even more dramatically the extent to which the country's social fabric is fraying. The incidence of stress-related conditions such as heart attacks and alcoholism has risen sharply. When the death rate jumped from 12.1 per 1,000 persons to 14.5 between 1992 and 1993, for example, three-quarters of the increase was due to cardiovascular disease, accidents, murder, suicide, and alcohol poisoning. According to Gennadi I. Gerasimov, a former spokesman for Mikhail Gorbachev, 100,000 Russians have killed themselves in the past two years—a suicide rate more than three times that of the United States. A sharp rise in alcoholism is causing increases in both alcohol poisoning and fatal accidents at work. And lack of adequate health care has exacerbated the problem—treatable conditions are increasingly fatal, and people often die after a relatively mild heart attack.

The death rate also has a clear environmental connection. According to Murray Feshbach, a professor of demography at Georgetown University in Washington, D.C., and an expert on Russia's environment, pollution plays a role in 20 to 30 percent of

the country's deaths. In the most affected areas, that percentage is much higher. Feshbach cites the example of Nikel, a town of 21,000 on the Norwegian border in Russia's extreme north. For employees at

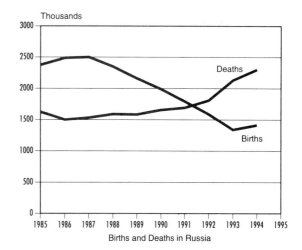

Births and Deaths in Russia

Source: Goskomstat, Russia (Moscow: 1995)

the local smelter, life expectancy is just 34 years; for the town in general, it is 44 years.

Contamination, in one form or another, is undermining public health throughout the FSU. Water in as many as 75 percent of the region's rivers and lakes is unfit for drinking, according to Alexey Yablokov, chairman of a Russian Federation commission on the environment and a former environmental advisor to both Gorbachev and Boris Yeltsin. And at least 50 percent of tap water fails to meet sanitary norms for microbial, chemical, and other forms of pollution. Waterborne infectious diseases are epidemic (see "Environmental Intelligence," November/December 1995), and children are often the principal victims. Yablokov has classified about 15 percent of Russia's land area as ecological disaster zones.

Presumably, economic improvements will eventually stabilize Russia's demographic picture. But economic recovery alone will not erase the effects of decades of gross environmental abuse. Russia's public health crisis is a lesson in the human costs of unbridled development—a lesson that may have particular relevance for the most rapidly developing countries. In China, for example, where the economy has grown by 57 percent in the past four years, coal accounts for more than three-quarters of the commercial energy supply. Yet, nearly 1 million people a year may already be dying from lung diseases related to air pollution—and China plans to double its coal use over the next two decades.

ASSAULT
OF THE EARTH

THE APPETITES OF GROWING POPULATIONS ARE SQUEEZING THE LIFE OUT OF THE EARTH'S FINITE SUPPLY OF GOOD SOIL. NOW THE QUESTION IS WHETHER WE CAN REBUILD IT FASTER THAN IT DISAPPEARS.

Elena Wilken

Elena Wilken is a staff researcher at the Worldwatch Institute.

To be human is to be a creature of the soil: that message is contained in creation stories from all over the world. In Genesis, for instance, man is formed "from the dust of the ground." The soil's mysterious vitality is a subject for science too; in the lightless world beneath our feet, death becomes life, and the renewal of the soil itself—a process so slow it's usually indiscernible in a human lifetime—proceeds in rhythms still largely unknown. But in the developed world, at least, those creation stories seem to be lost on us. By and large, we no longer honor our relationship to the soil. Soil has become simply one more resource—a substance necessary for crop production and for holding up buildings. We take it for granted, and fail to notice that it's disappearing.

For most of human history, we could afford to remain ignorant of how the soil worked. When farmers exhausted the productivity of a field, they could usually bring another one into production. But now that human populations are pushing into every nook and cranny of the globe, we no longer have the option of moving on. Virtually all of the world's most produc- tive cropland is already in cultivation. It's true that in many areas, some of the best land is producing cash crops instead of food for local consumption. But even so, the basic trends are clear: if the amount of land in production remains constant over the next 40 years, farmers will nearly have to double their yields to feed the growing population. And as we try to grow more and more food—by cultivating marginal cropland, by intensifying production, by using more powerful tech- nologies—our soils deteriorate. And our ignorance of how to heal them becomes increasingly dangerous.

In general terms, soil seems a pretty simple affair: it consists of a large mineral component and a small measure of organic material, plus water and air. The mineral content comes from bedrock, which is broken into particles by chemical reactions and the movement of water. Decaying material on the surface and dead roots underneath make up the organic matter, which is broken down by microbes and invertebrates into a web of debris, or humus. Worms, roots, rodents, and the soil's other denizens tunnel through it, mixing the minerals from below with the organic matter from above. This process give the soil its density and texture, or "structure." Good structure requires a high proportion of organic material and a loose, porous consistency; it allows for drainage, aeration, and a high nutrient load.

Most erosion is insidious, and the loss of colossal amounts of material very difficult to detect. A complex set of factors, including rainfall, slope, and farming practices past and present, determine the rate of erosion.

The surface of the earth looks inert and solid, but soils are in constant flux. Just as soil formation is a continuous process, so is degradation. Soils erode; their nutrients leach out; their complement of life waxes and wanes. In undisturbed systems the rate of formation is slightly higher than the rate of erosion, allowing for soil build-up. But human activity, particularly agriculture, increases degradation without enhancing formation.

Degradation has been a part of agriculture from its beginnings. Archaeologists have, for instance, been able to trace the development of farming in the Mesoamerican civilization around Mexico's Lake Plázcuaro by studying the lake's sediments, which eroded off the surrounding farmland. By the 13th century, the sedimentation rate was six times its pre-agricultural level.

Today, farmers face the challenge of slowing the processes of degradation and incorporating their corollary—soil creation—into agriculture. But despite the consensus on the need for conservation, planning is hampered by a high degree of uncertainty. It's very difficult to assess the scope of the problem, or to predict the effect that various solutions might have on agriculture and the environment. Degradation is measured in terms of compaction, erosion, nutrient loss, loss of organic matter, and decreased microbial activity. These points of reference are the same for all soils, but the cumulative effect may vary widely over even a small patch of ground. A single hectare can hold three or four different soil types, each with its own set of vulnerabilities. One area might be especially susceptible to water erosion and compaction, for instance, while another might suffer from a drop in microbe populations. A global measurement of degradation would have to account for the role of each variable within each agricultural system.

The problem is further complicated by our ignorance of natural changes: not every form of degradation is caused by human activity, and large natural cycles are probably futile to combat. In 1984, for

example, the U.N. Environment Programme claimed that the sands of the Sahara were being pulled southward by excessive livestocking, deforestation, and over-grazing around watering holes. But satellite photographs eventually showed that this instance of desertification was largely the result of a sustained drought. In marginal climates, a few centimeters of rain can make the difference between relatively lush vegetation and a barren landscape. Certainly much of sub-Saharan Africa is under increasing pressure from grazing and agriculture, and some areas are severely degraded. But the simple *appearance* of degradation is not a sufficient basis for policy.

On the other hand, it would be a costly mistake to allow our uncertainty to forestall action. Conserving healthy soil is much easier and cheaper than repairing ruined soil. In the western United States, for instance, saltation is a widespread yet largely preventable problem. Saltation occurs in poorly drained fields, where irrigation raises the water table to just below the soil surface. Salts and minerals, from fertilizer and from the soil itself, are dissolved in the water and deposted at the surface as the water evaporates. The results can be dramatic: in Utah, for instance, a highway outside Salt Lake City offers a view of barren fields crusted in white. Rejuvenating such fields costs from $1,000 to $2,000 per hectare, and the effort often fails. But saltation can be prevented with just a simple set of underground pipes to draw excess water off the field.

The components of degradation are interconnected. Loss of soil structure, for instance, tends to increase erosion, which will lower nutrient levels, which will in turn decrease microbial activity. But it's often possible to approach the problem by looking at the relationship between a particular type of soil degradation and the farming practices most often associated with it.

Erosion is one of the most obvious forms of degradation. In dry climates, wind will erode unprotected, fine soils. Water erosion is a greater concern in humid climates and on steep slopes. In both cases, erosion increases with the loss of vegetative cover. Cover slows wind speed, decreases the impact of raindrops, and stabilizes soil with root systems. Just clearing a forest or plowing a grassland may drastically increase the rate of erosion.

In some parts of the Third World, erosion is part of a fundamental social problem. In Latin America, for instance, wealthy land owners are increasing their cash crop production for growing export markets. Subsistence farmers, forced off their rented plots, have no choice but to clear less arable land, often in sloping, forested highlands. Once stripped of trees and plowed, the soil in such areas erodes rapidly, forcing its tenants off in search of yet more land. Under such conditions, soil erosion exacerbates social erosion.

Although obvious in its extreme forms, most erosion is insidious. The loss of colossal amounts of material can be very difficult to detect: 6 metric tons of soil coming off of 1 hectare would reduce the topsoil level by only 1 millimeter. A complex set of factors, including rainfall, slope, and farming practices past and present, determine the rate of erosion, and variation in any of the causes may greatly affect that rate. Erosion rates can vary by a factor of 100 in a single agricultural area. In parts of Poland, erosion in a dry, windy year has been shown to be four times greater than in a wet year. In eastern Kenya, a study found that rangeland with more than 20 percent vegetative cover erodes at a rate of 6 to 12 metric tons per hectare per year, while the rate for land with less than 20 percent cover is several times higher. Even within the same plot of earth, the forces of erosion do not act equally on all parts of the soil. Small particles—the ones most often bonded with nutrients—erode easily; large particles are more stable.

On the other side of the cycle, soil formation is just as difficult to measure. Depending on a host of conditions, it takes between 200 and 1,000 years to form 1 inch (2.5 centimeters) of topsoil. Under natural conditions, at least, soil is practically a nonrenewable resource.

Agriculture has developed several stock responses to this problem. One is to enhance the rate of soil formation. Farmers cannot affect the rate at which minerals are ground out of bedrock, but they can increase the amount of organic matter in a soil by amending their fields with manure and field waste. Unfortunately, many farmers in developing countries depend on field waste for fodder, and on manure for fuel. Removing this material from the agricultural cycle exacerbates the problems that erosion is already causing. As yields drop, farmers are forced onto ever more marginal, more erodible land.

Another remedy is to make up for nutrients lost to erosion by increasing fertilizer applications. In China, some 30 percent of the nitrogen and 22 percent of the potassium applied each year on cropland goes to replace nutrients that have eroded out. Still, research has shown that fertilizing eroded soil does not fully restore lost productivity: it will improve yields, but not enough to match those of uneroded fields.

Despite the obvious need for a more aggressive approach to erosion, conservation techniques have not generally been brought into play on a scale that would allow for real progress. A major obstacle to conservation is that many of the techniques cause at least a short term decline in yields—and farmers are generally reluctant to take the loss. Converting to a different regime may also require capital or technical expertise that can by hard to come by. Such problems have plagued even the most ambitious attempts to counter erosion.

The United States has perhaps the world's most comprehensive erosion control program. A monitoring system combines satellite photographs with ground-level measurements to estimate local rates of erosion and monitor change over time. In 1985, the Conservation Reserve Program (CRP) was enacted to counter excessive erosion, much of it caused by the agricultural boom of the 1970s: in response to lucrative subsidies and high commodity prices, American farmers had expanded their cropland by 20 million hectares between 1972 and 1981. Much of this land was highly erodible, and the national rate of topsoil erosion rose to over 3 billion metric tons a year. The first phase of the CRP paid farmers to convert almost 40 million hectares of cropland to grass and trees. Erosion declined by as much as 25 percent in some regions.

But the target rate for soil loss, set at 12 tons per hectare per year for deep soils, and at 2 tons for shallow soils, has yet to be achieved on land still under production. The CRP's second phase requires farmers to implement conservation practices such as no-till cultivation, contour plowing, or residue management (the practice of leaving crop debris on the field after harvest), on especially erodible cropland still in production. This phase has proven more difficult to monitor and evaluate, since the conservation incentive is poorly connected to the profit incentive.

The biggest problems usually involve a reduction in yield, but productivity can be as difficult to evaluate as erosion. It's clear, for example, that no-till cultivation decreases yields at least over the short term. In no-till regimes, farmers plant seeds in holes punched into the field's surface, instead of plowing. The soil remains covered, by a mixture of wild plants, stubble, and crop plants that survived the previous year's harvest. Weed control is accomplished only with herbicides: no mechanical cultivation is used. Canadian field tests comparing crop performance on a no-till and a conventionally tilled field found the no-till yield 20 percent lower during a year of average rainfall. But the following year happened to be dryer than usual; yields from both fields fell, but the conventionally plowed field suffered the greater drop, and the two yields were equal.

Given the thin margins on which farmers operate, many see any drop in productivity as an unacceptable cost, no matter what the long term trend may be. That kind of reluctance is making the economics of conservation as difficult as the science. Part of the problem is that farmers do not generally account for the full effect of erosion on yields.

Some of the decrease in soil productivity is usually compensated for by non-organic fertilizers, but fertilizers are expensive. Some types of conservation farming, like low-input production, eliminate non-organic fertilizers, thereby lowering yields, but lowering production costs as well. No-till methods greatly reduce machinery requirements, another major operating expense. In the United States, farmers have used no-till practices to cut production costs by 25 to 30 percent, mostly by scaling back on machinery use.

Some farmers are managing to make the economics of conservation work, but many farmers and policy makers are concerned that widespread adoption of low-input systems would greatly reduce U.S. grain exports. That would force up global grain prices and could cause food shortages in importing countries. They're right in a broad sense: mass conversion to new agricultural systems would be very disruptive. But that objection does not take into account the long term costs of soil erosion.

In the United States, farm subsidies would be an obvious place to begin accounting for those costs, and recent developments hold out some promise of constructive change. American farmers have generally been subsidized in proportion to the amount of grain they produce—an arrangement that has encouraged maximum production. But in 1985, the policy began to shift: that year's Farm Bill began requiring conservation plans from every farmer tilling highly erodible land and receiving subsidy payments. Bill Richards, a former Ohio farmer and now chief of the U.S. Soil Conservation Service, estimates that a quarter of the country's cropland is now under some conservation system, from simple residue management to the more complicated no-till cultivation. That percentage is expected to increase during the current year. By encouraging farmers to conserve soil without losing income, Richards claims the legislation is causing a revolution on the farm. "It is beyond science and technology," he says. "It is a cultural revolution." Unfortunately, the program is under fire in Congress, and this year's budget threatens a 50 percent funding cut. Even if funding isn't lost, a rise in grain prices—a likely prospect over the long term—would undercut the program's effectiveness by providing a strong incentive to increase production. And of course, few other countries have the resources to subsidize farming to the degree that the United States does. Even where conservation technologies exist, economics may block their widespread adoption.

Erosion is not the only problem affecting the soil. The topsoil houses countless micro-organisms and small invertebrates—one teaspoon of fertile soil may contain over a million of them. Biologists know little about these creatures. At the current rate of study, it would take eight centuries just to complete an inventory of them. Most have not been isolated because they cannot be kept alive outside their soil habitats. We do know, however, that many are decomposers, converting the "death, dung, and detritus," as soil scientists call it, to humus and nutrients that can be taken up by other organisms. Others play a direct role in nutrient uptake by plants, performing a useful chemical reaction in exchange for a share of the energy that plant metabolism stores. It's generally agreed that the vast diversity of microbial life enhances soil productivity, but there is as yet no way of quantifying the level of diversity that is necessary for crop production. Nor do we know what effect various agricultural techniques have on microbial life.

Fixing agriculture will take more than simple policy reform: it will require us to reconcile the diverging imperatives of conservation and production.

But in South and Southeast Asia, recent trends point to a suppression of soil life that is as ominous as the erosion in the American midwest. The International Rice Research Institute (IRRI), a research organization devoted to increasing rice production, maintains a string of carefully managed test plots throughout the region. Test plot yields have begun to decline, in part, researchers believe, because of decreased microbial activity. It is possible that the IRRI test plots have hit some sort of ceiling for rice production.

The problem has its roots in the mid 1960s, when IRRI released a set of new rice varieties that had shorter maturation times. In Indonesia, Thailand, the Philippines, India, and Japan, farmers responded to increasing demand by using the new varieties to grow two or even three crops a year. Initially, at least, this approach also seemed to make sense as a soil conservation measure: concentrating production in the fertile lowlands reduced the pressure on the highly erodible and less fertile highlands.

For 20 years or so, the strategy worked. Southeast Asia's rice yields rose from 1.1 metric tons per hectare in 1961 to 1.8 tons in 1982. Production increased at 2.7 percent annually, edging out the region's 2.1 percent population growth. Since then, however, increases in yields have slowed. And in the IRRI test plots, where yields regularly surpassed what most farmers achieved, production has begun to decline—in some cases, by as much as 15 percent. Farm and test plot yields are converging: about a third of the region's farmers can now match the test plots. The trend looks ominous to many researchers, who worry that the test plot declines might mean the farm yields have peaked as well.

New rice strains continue to be developed, but none have reversed the test plot declines. Careful testing has ruled out problems with the genetic potential of the strains, and with the input regimes, which means that the problem must involve environmental degradation. No one knows exactly what is happening, but scientists theorize that the community of soil micro-organisms is ill-adapted to the continually flooded soil. As microbial activity declines, the rate of decomposition slows and fewer nutrients are available for plant growth. The irrigation water is richly furnished with nitrogen by the algae growing in it, but the soil is not supplying that nitrogen to the rice. Attempts to inoculate the test plots with foreign microbes have been largely unsuccessful: apparently, the paddies are no more hospitable to foreign microbes than to native ones.

Meanwhile, the demand for rice is increasing, driven by expanding populations and incomes, and the region's governments face an ugly dilemma. Persisting at current levels of production will likely lead to a decline in yields, which could force farmers onto the more fragile highlands. Yet farmers are loathe to cut back to one harvest per year, which would allow soils to dry out and rejuvenate. For the present, the remedy seems worse than the disease. Nor does crop rotation offer an obvious way out. Planting the paddies in wheat or legumes during the dry season has yielded indifferent results, because continually flooded soils form a hard layer of clay below the topsoil, decreasing water absorption. Rice plants thrive in such an environment, but the dry season crops do poorly, since they prefer deeper root space and better drainage.

One of the first lessons in a typical soil science class is a demonstration with two handfuls of soil, one from a field that hasn't been plowed in five years, the other from a field subjected to at least eight tractor crossings a year for several years. Eight crossings is typical in conventional agriculture—two for plowing, one for seeding, two for fertilizing, two for weeding, and one for harvesting. The plowed handful of soil is dense and breaks up into hard chunks; a cup of water thrown on top runs off the surface. The fallow sample is looser and clumps together. It absorbs the water, which runs out the bottom in a few seconds. The differences are a matter of structure.

In undisturbed soil, it's mainly the top layer that stores nutrients, sustains microbial life, and supports roots. Most of the soil's organic matter is found here. Humus is light and bulky—it's measured at only 6 percent of the soil's mass, but up to 25 percent of its volume. Structure determines a soil's ability to "breathe" and drink. The surface is pocked with tiny pores that exchange gasses with the atmosphere and absorb water. A maze of tunnels dug by worms, insects, and rodents allows for drainage and aeration. But plowing collapses the pores and tunnels. Water absorption drops and the gas exchange—an important part of the soil's ecology—slows. Soil can repair itself in time, but not if repeated compaction with heavy tilling equipment decreases its resiliency.

The communal farms of the former Soviet Union may have taken this process to an extreme. The communes averaged 5,000 hectares and were supplied with the world's largest tractors—considerably heavier than the largest American models, which weigh as much as 20 tons. Continual use of these machines compacted the country's most productive soil. Commune harvests also usually removed all the crop residues for fodder, further undermining soil structure by depriving the soil of its organic component. The effects of this assault on the land were partly masked by extremely heavy applications of non-organic fertilizer: from 1975 through 1991, the region's farmers had the world's highest rate of fertilizer use.

The communes were privatized after the collapse of the Soviet state, and the average size of a farm is now under 50 hectares. The huge tractors are no longer necessary, and farmers are demanding more appropriate technology. Fertilizer use has decreased by 50 percent since 1988, because the cost of inputs is rising faster than farm profits. Although yields have not changed noticeably during this transition, farmers will be dealing with the legacy of Soviet agriculture for years to come. An eventual decline in yields is probable unless farmers address the extensive compaction that their soils have suffered.

The cure for compacted soils is relatively simple: planting perennial crops, such as alfalfa and legumes, makes annual tilling unnecessary, so the soils have a chance to rebuild. But Russian farmers want to continue producing wheat and other annuals, because those are the crops that have well-defined markets. Selling an alternative crop requires a capitalist's skill, which is still hard to come by on the Russian farm. In the meantime, additions of organic material—manure, or just crop residues—could boost the soil structure immediately. To farmers struggling with unfamiliar markets and economic instability, any soil management plan more elaborate than that might seem like a luxury.

The task of rebuilding the world's cropland must be done by the world's farmers, but it's up to governments to set the policies that will make that effort possible. Policy specifics may vary as widely as the soils themselves. Formulating them will require a great deal more research and planning, but some basic principles are clear. Broad conservation standards—for erosion, say, or for drainage—could encourage change while allowing flexibility in the methods used to achieve it. That would let farmers experiment and adjust to local conditions. Agricultural subsidies that contain a soil conservation element could reward long-term planning instead of the short-term pursuit of maximum yields. Reforming wasteful procedures for storing and transporting grain would produce a "second harvest" that could take some pressure off the land. Finally, more equitable land distribution would ease the strain on the most marginal land, and perhaps on higher quality land as well, since owning a productive field from which one can feed one's own family is a strong incentive to conservation.

But fixing agriculture will take more than simple policy reform: it will require us to reconcile the diverging imperatives of conservation and production. The latter concern still dominates agricultural policy, which often treats the soil as just a "given," without considering the costs of losing it. But clearly, the way to a sustainable agriculture begins with the study of ecology. And where the economics allow, some farmers are trying to build agricultural ecosystems that resemble natural ones.

Such efforts are still fraught with problems, and no one knows for sure where they might lead. But there is little doubt where our current practices will take us if we persist in them. Our destination can be read, for instance, in the abandoned cities of North Africa—in places like El Jem, on the plain of Tunisia, and Timgad, in northeastern Algeria. These cities once supplied imperial Rome with grain, olive oil, wine, and wood. Now they lie abandoned and partly buried beneath the dust from eroded hillsides and barren fields. There were many reasons for the decline of Rome, but few have had an effect as lasting as the loss of the Empire's soil. If our own societies are to avoid this fate, we must learn to watch over our soils as carefully as we watch over our harvests. And ultimately, we will have to find ways to farm that create at least as much soil as is lost. If this sounds utopian, that's a measure of how far we have yet to go.

We're All Minorities Now

SUMMARY   Racial and ethnic diversity increases the differences between urban, rural, rich, and poor Americans. Children are most likely to be nonwhite or Hispanic, but the aging of diversity will have profound effects on consumer markets in the 1990s. Businesses can respond by using consumer information to unite diverse niches into profitable markets.

Martha   Farnsworth   Riche

Martha Farnsworth Riche is director of policy studies at the Population Reference Bureau in Washington, D.C.

The United States is undergoing a new demographic transition: it is becoming a multicultural society. During the 1990s, it will shift from a society dominated by whites and rooted in Western culture to a world society characterized by three large racial and ethnic minorities. All three minorities will grow both in size and share, while the still-significant white majority will continue its relative decline.

Whites represent eight in ten Americans, the 1990 census found, down from nine in ten as recently as 1960. Subtract white Hispanics, and you discover that only about three out of four Americans are non-Hispanic whites.

During the 1980s, the U.S. received 6 million legal immigrants, up from 4.2 million during the 1970s and 3.2 million during the 1960s. Few immigrants now are of European origin. Immigrants also tend to have more children than the non-Hispanic

All Americans are now members of at least one minority group.

white population, as do Hispanics and blacks. Together, these two factors are boosting the share of minorities in the population.

These trends are also creating diversity within the minority population. According to the Census Bureau, the 1990 census missed 1 in 20 blacks and Hispanics. Nevertheless, it gives an accurate picture of the rapid growth in their numbers. In 1990, 12 percent of Americans identified themselves as black, 9 percent as Hispanic origin (some of whom are also black), 3 percent as Asian or Pacific Islander, 1 percent Native Americans, and 4 percent "other." The first three groups will continue to grow faster than the white population. As each group grows, diversity within them will grow too.

These trends signal a transition to a multicultural society. If you count men and women as separate groups, all Americans are now members of at least one mi-

nority group. Without fully realizing it, we have left the time when the nonwhite, non-Western part of our population could be expected to assimilate to the dominant majority. In the future, the white Western majority will have to do some assimilation of its own.

Government will find that as minority groups grow in size relative to one another, and as the minority population gains on the dwindling majority, no single group will command the power to dictate solutions. The debate over almost any public issue is likely to become more confrontational. Reaching a consensus will require more cooperation than it has in the past.

The new demographic transition may be particularly difficult for business because it parallels an equally momentous economic transition. As the economy moves away from manufacturing and phys-ical skills and toward services and knowledge skills, a real danger emerges. The economic transition is increasing inequality in both incomes and opportunities. This inequality happens within and across racial and ethnic groups, and it has the potential to polarize both consumers and employees.

DIVERSITY DIFFERENCES

Immigration will add more Americans in the 1990s than it did in the 1980s, due to legislation enacted in 1990. The Immigration and Naturalization Service projects that legal immigration will exceed 700,000 per year starting in 1992. That compares with 600,000 immigrants per year as recently as the late 1980s. Illegal immigration will push the total even higher.

The 1990 law will also increase diversity among immigrants—notably at the upper end of the income scale. It allows people who have no family here to immigrate if they have highly prized work skills, or if they are ready to make a significant business investment. The law nearly tripled the number of visas (to 140,000 a year) for engineers and scientists, multinational executives and managers, and other people with skills in demand. This includes 10,000 visas a year for investor immigrants who will put at least $1 million into the economy and create ten jobs. (The entrance fee drops to $500,000 in rural areas and areas of high unemployment.)

Immigrants tend to join their peers, and their peers tend to live in large coastal cities. California, New York, Texas, Florida, Illinois, and New Jersey are expected to get three of every four new immigrants, who will be joining already-large minority populations in those states. In California, non-Hispanic whites will become a minority within the next two decades.

Central cities are still the front line for processing immigrants into society, and native-born minorities and older immigrants are also moving into suburban areas. Asians are most likely to integrate into white suburbs. Suburban blacks are still relatively segregated, according to research by Richard D. Alba and John R. Logan of the State University of New York at Albany. Hispanics fall somewhere in between.

These locational patterns ensure that multiculturalism will evolve unevenly across the country. As a result, many

YOUTH *equals* **DIVERSITY**

Most immigrants are young, and minorities generally have more children than whites. As a result, minorities are a progressively larger share of the population at younger ages.

(percent of population in each group by age)

	white	black	Hispanic	Asian/ Pacific Islander	American Indian	other races
0 to 9	74.8%	15.0%	12.6%	3.3%	1.1%	5.9%
10 to 19	75.1	15.1	11.6	3.3	1.1	5.4
20 to 29	77.3	13.1	11.5	3.3	0.8	5.5
30 to 39	79.9	12.0	8.9	3.3	0.8	4.0
40 to 49	82.9	10.4	7.1	3.1	0.7	2.9
50 to 59	84.4	10.1	6.4	2.6	0.6	2.3
60 to 69	87.4	8.8	4.8	1.9	0.5	1.5
70 to 79	89.3	7.9	3.5	1.4	0.4	0.9
80 or older	90.4	7.5	3.2	1.0	0.3	0.8
All ages	80.3	12.1	9.0	2.9	0.8	3.9

Note: Hispanics may be of any race; therefore, the percentages do not total to 100.

Source: 1990 census data

states and cities will become increasingly unlike the rest of the country.

Multiculturalism is not monolithic, either. The difference among Hispanic subgroups has been well documented; Cuban Americans are an economic and political dynasty in Miami, but no similar clout exists for Puerto Ricans in New York or Chicanos in Texas and California. One-quarter of the Hispanic population in 1990 was the product of immigration during the 1980s, if you include the children of immigrants. And 43 percent of Hispanics are immigrants from the 1970s and 1980s, according to Jeffrey Passel and Barry Edmonston of the Washington, D.C.-based Urban Institute.

Differences are even more pronounced in the fast-growing Asian American population. Passel and Edmonston report that 43 percent of the Asian American population in 1990 came from immigration during the 1980s, and 70 percent from immigration during the 1970s and 1980s. In 1970, the Asian American population was dominated by the Japanese. In 1980, the top group was the Chinese. Thanks to new immigration, the 1990 census found the Fili-

pino American population had grown almost as large as the Chinese American population, and both grew far beyond Americans of Japanese origin. Both the Asian Indian and the Korean populations now rival the Japanese population in size.

Different patterns of childbearing also play a role in creating a more diverse society. Fertility rates are still higher for minority groups than they are for non-Hispanic whites. In 1988, Hispanic women had the highest rate, with 96 children per 1,000 women aged 15 to 44. Black women had a rate of 87 per 1,000, compared with 63 per 1,000 for white women. As a result, two-thirds of minority families had children in 1990, compared with fewer than half of non-Hispanic white families.

Hispanic and nonwhite women will still have higher fertility rates in the 1990s, primarily because they come from younger populations, according to Juanita Tamayo Lott, president of a Washington, D.C. consulting firm. But these rates should diminish as these populations age. Nonwhite and Hispanic fertility rates should resemble white rates by the mid-21st century, she says.

5. POPULATION, RESOURCES, AND SOCIOECONOMIC DEVELOPMENT

The trend is clear. If current conditions continue, the United States will become a nation with no racial or ethnic majority during the 21st century. This may happen as early as 2060, according to demographer Leon Bouvier of the Center for Immigration Studies.

THE AGING OF DIVERSITY

The engine driving the diversity trend is the relative youth of minority populations. In 1988, non-Hispanic whites were older than any minority group, with a median age of 31.4 years. Hispanics were the youngest, with a median age of 24 years. Blacks were second youngest, at 25.6, while "other" races (mainly Asians) had a median age of 27.

The median age is increasing for all racial and ethnic groups, but Hispanics and blacks will remain younger than non-Hispanic whites. According to Census Bureau projections, non-Hispanic whites will have a median age of 41.4 years in 2010. That's ten years older than the median age for blacks in 2010 (31.4 years) and 12 years older than for Hispanics (29.3). "Other" races will have a median age of 35.6.

As a result, different age groups are becoming multicultural at different rates. In 2000, 72 percent of Americans will be non-

> **Immigration will add more Americans in the 1990s than it did in the 1980s.**

Hispanic white, according to Decision Demographics, a Washington, D.C. consulting firm. But fewer than two in three children will be non-Hispanic white. Non-Hispanic whites will account for 63 percent of children under age 8, 65 percent of children aged 8 to 13, and 66 percent of children aged 14 to 17. In contrast, nearly 80 percent of Americans aged 45 or older will be non-Hispanic white. Multicultural milestones show up first in the youngest ages.

These differences in the composition of age groups combine with differences in life expectancy to make the elderly population disproportionately white. However, with the notable exception of black men, the gap in life expectancy between whites and nonwhites has been narrowing. All these trends will eventually increase the multicultural character of the older population.

Multiculturalism is seeping into every aspect of American society, including language. The battle to make English the official language of the United States seems to have fizzled out, as Spanish-speaking Americans make it clear that they intend to retain their native language. As a result, many English-speaking Americans are discovering with a shock that they cannot communicate when visiting certain sections of California, Florida, or Texas. Bilingual signs and forms are becoming commonplace in many parts of the country.

Next spring, the Census Bureau will release the first data on "linguistically isolated" households. These are households in which no member aged 5 or older reported speaking English "very well." The numbers of such households did not merit a separate tabulation in previous censuses. But the 1980 census found 23 million households that spoke a language other than English at home. It also found 10 million households that had a less-than-adequate command of English. These numbers will be considerably larger in the 1990 count, thanks to immigration, according to Census Bureau demographer Paul Siegel.

Other factors are influencing the evolution of racial and ethnic identities. More and more Americans are of mixed parentage, and they are demanding to be recognized as multiracial.

Communications technologies are also changing the way people identify with their ethnic roots. For example, African films are gaining a significant audience here, particularly among African Americans. VCRs, fax machines, and other new technologies create important opportunities for cultural exchange in both directions. At the same time, it reduces the impetus for immigrants to assimilate into the "mainstream."

More than ever, the way for minorities to gain broader opportunities in American society is to get a college education. But relative to whites, college enrollment rates

> **In a multicultural society, businesses can thrive by finding common ground across racial and ethnic groups.**

actually declined for blacks and Hispanics during the 1980s.

As educational attainment becomes increasingly important to individual success, differences in educational attainment will produce sharply different socioeconomic profiles for different racial and ethnic groups. This trend could create a population polarized by both race and economic opportunity. Whites and Asians could increasingly dominate high-income high-status occupations, leaving blacks and Hispanics with low-income low-status occupations.

Even if employment discrimination suddenly ceased to exist, the lower educational attainment of minorities would keep many of them from entering newly opened doors. Poorly educated young black men are already shut out of the broader society; nearly one in four of those aged 20 to 29 is behind bars or on probation or parole.

As America participates increasingly in the world economy, business leaders could use a multicultural work force as a powerful competitive edge. But the opportunities will not be distributed equally among different racial and ethnic groups. The challenge is to maximize our comparative advantage in the world economy while still offering upward mobility to all Americans.

HOW BUSINESS CAN RESPOND

"The typical consumer-citizen of California in the late 1990s may be a 38-year-old professional who does Zen meditation. At home, she listens to Celtic folk music because her grandparents were Scottish. But she spends her vacations in northern Mexico to study Tarahumara culture, after picking up a taste for ranchero music," says Paul Saffo, who follows technology for the Institute for the Future in Menlo Park, California.

In a multicultural society, businesses

thrive by finding common ground across racial and ethnic groups. Businesses that try to target each group separately will be stunted by prohibitive marketing costs. Others will meet this challenge by helping multicultural consumers mix and match their lifestyles. Multicultural consumers will take discrete cultural pieces and mix them into custom-tailored wholes.

Another common need is information and entertainment that explains the world to multicultural consumers from their point of view. Last year, a widely publicized journalism study faulted young Americans for their ignorance of important news figures and news events. But

> **On every dollar bill is the phrase E pluribus unum, "from diversity comes unity."**

given their increasingly multicultural nature, it's no surprise that today's youth had little interest or knowledge in what was going on in Eastern Europe, but were up-to-the-minute on developments in South Africa.* Consumer information and entertainment businesses are going to have to reposition both their content and their advertising to appeal to today's multicultural youth as they become tomorrow's multicultural adults.

Education is a major common need. The educational establishment has not adequately responded to the multicultural challenge, and that creates an opportunity for business.

Communications technology is building a new common ground for an increasingly multicultural population. We saw this during recent events in China and in Eastern Europe. We are going to see more of it as

*See "What's News with You," American Demographics, *November 1990, page 2.*

technological evolution lets our most recent arrivals keep close contact with their roots instead of cutting them off.

These developments create new opportunities for consumer businesses that can unlock culture from its origin and allow others to share in it. One example is the Japanese adoption of the Wild West, as Tokyo executives import log cabins from Montana and vacation on American dude ranches. As the world's first multicultural society, the United States is uniquely positioned to both understand and profit from the emerging global culture.

All this means that consumers are becoming simultaneously part of a global culture and a local community. It also means that these ties are based on common interests. Moreover, technology increasingly allows Americans to switch readily and frequently from one viewpoint to another. The marketer's new challenge is to find not only the right person with the right message but also to find them at the right moment.

Some of those moments will be global moments, as everyone in the world watches a soccer match, or a war. Some will be culturally specific moments, as Muslims or other groups share a moment that is invisible to everyone else. Some will be purely and simply local. But in every case, the common ground will be interests, concerns, and lifestyles.

Without necessarily realizing it, businesses have been preparing to meet this challenge by building detailed consumer information systems. Combined with attitude and behavior research, these systems can efficiently unite niches into markets. The systems' geographic specificity will extend marketing efficiency by allowing marketers to pay attention to the geographic variations in diversity.

For example, a Nissan television campaign featured a multicultural design team engineering cars "for the human race."

The tag line made sense nationally, because it was broadly targeted image advertising. More directly targeted messages have to identify their audiences more closely. An ad that takes a multicultural society as a given is right for Los Angeles, but it might strike a strange note in rural Indiana.

Retailers can use locally based information systems to efficiently target specific demographic and market segments. Mark London is president and CEO of Equity Properties in Chicago, a firm that remodels and re-leases shopping centers whose trade areas have changed significantly. He recently analyzed an anchor store that was doing badly in a repositioned Miami mall. The store managers hadn't understood two crucial concepts. First, upscale Hispanic women don't have the same fashion preferences as other upscale women. Second, they don't have the same preferences as other Hispanic women. When the store learned to feature upscale Hispanic fashions, sales rebounded.

On every dollar bill is the phrase *E pluribus unum*, "from diversity comes unity." If this fundamental American belief can survive, our country will become a microcosm of an increasingly interdependent world. America can still offer hope to other countries, and to all of its citizens. But it can only work if we meet the multicultural challenge.

TAKING IT FURTHER

For more information about the changing makeup of minority populations, contact the Bureau of the Census's Data User Services Division at (301) 763-5820. A good general source of information on immigration is the *Statistical Yearbook* of the Immigration and Naturalization Service; telephone (202) 376-3066. For more on the impact of multiculturalism, contact the Institute for the Future at 2740 Sand Hill Road, Menlo Park, California, 94025; telephone (415) 854-6322. Reprints of this article may be purchased by calling (800) 828-1133.

Preventive Medicine

A Broader Approach to the AIDS Crisis

By J. Mann and D. Tarantola

INFECTION BY THE Human Immunodeficiency Virus (HIV), the virus that causes Acquired Immune Deficiency Syndrome (AIDS), has been spreading at an alarming rate. The HIV/AIDS crisis has progressively intensified worldwide, yet the global response to the pandemic has plateaued and even declined in many areas. Currently, however, a new UN AIDS program is being launched. This event provides a unique opportunity for serious reflection upon the status of the pandemic and the lessons that have been learned from more than a decade of efforts to

Jonathan M. Mann is François-Xavier Bagnoud Professor of Health and Human Rights at Harvard School of Public Health. Daniel J.M. Tarantola is Director of the International AIDS Program at Harvard School of Public Health.

confront it. The experience and knowledge that have accumulated worldwide must be transformed into a new, more effective, more coherent global AIDS strategy.

One of the more important discoveries that has emerged from this body of knowledge is that populations which, prior to the arrival of HIV/AIDS, were marginalized, discriminated against, or stigmatized have a higher risk of becoming infected with HIV. Discrimination and societal marginalization are evidence of a lack of respect for human rights and human dignity. Therefore, the failure to respect human rights can now be identified as a major cause, or even a root cause, of societal vulnerability to HIV/AIDS. It is now clear that HIV/AIDS is as much about society as it is about a virus. This new understanding of the societal basis for vulnerability to HIV/AIDS has the potential to provide strategic coherence to efforts in HIV/AIDS prevention and control.

While the details of the origins and emergence of HIV are unknown, it is clear that the current worldwide epidemic began in the mid-to-late 1970s. By 1980, an estimated 100,000 people worldwide were HIV-infected; this number increased one-hundred-fold during the 1980s, to reach a cumulative total of approximately 10 million people by 1990. The Global AIDS Policy Coalition (GAPC), an independent, international, multidisciplinary organization based at the Harvard School of Public Health estimates that, as of January 1, 1995, 26 million people worldwide were infected with HIV. Of these, about 23 million were adults, including 13.2 million men, 10 million women, and 2.7 million children. The largest number of HIV-infected adults were in sub-Saharan Africa: 17.3 million, about two-thirds of the global total. Overall, over 90 percent of HIV infections have, thus far, occurred in the developing world; only about five percent of HIV-infected people worldwide have been from North America.

The average time between becoming infected with HIV and the onset of clinical AIDS is approximately 10 years. Therefore, as the pandemic is a relatively new phenomenon, there are presently many more people infected with HIV than have developed AIDS. The worldwide cumulative total of people with AIDS, as of January 1, 1995, was 8.5 million, of whom seven million were in sub-Saharan Africa, about 700,000 were in Latin America and the Caribbean, and over 550,000 were in North America, Western Europe, and Oceania combined. The estimate of 8.5 million people with AIDS includes 1.9 million children, 92 percent of whom are from sub-Saharan Africa.

Epidemiological Trends

The pandemic remains dynamic, volatile, and unstable, and its major impact is yet to come. HIV continues to spread in all already affected areas of the world. It is estimated that in recent years, 40,000 to 80,000 new HIV infections have occurred each year in the United States. While in some areas the rate of increase in the number of people newly infected each year may have slowed, new infections continue

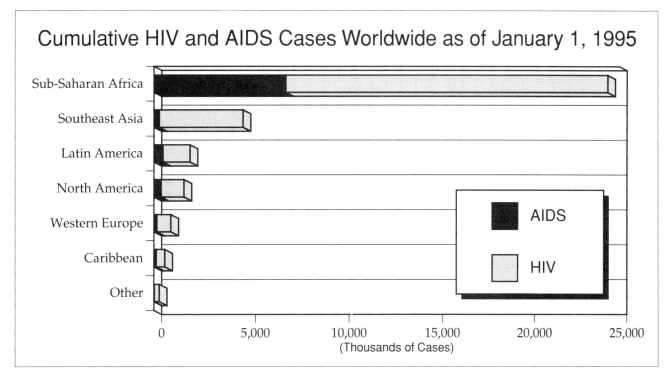

Cumulative HIV and AIDS Cases Worldwide as of January 1, 1995

(Thousands of Cases)

to occur; there is no HIV-affected community or country in which HIV transmission has stopped. During 1994 alone, an estimated four million people worldwide became newly infected with HIV, a daily average of nearly 11,000 people; this is more than the total number of people infected during the entire period between 1975 and 1985.

HIV also continues to spread to countries and communities that were previously unaffected or little affected by the pandemic. For example, while very few people in Asia were HIV-infected prior to the late 1980s, countries such as India, Thailand, and Burma are now experiencing major HIV epidemics and epidemics have begun in other Asian countries, including Malaysia, Nepal, and Vietnam. The cumulative number of HIV-infected people in Southeast Asia, 4.5 million, is now more than twice the total number of HIV-infected people in the entire industrialized world. GAPC estimates that as of 1995, the annual number of new HIV infections in Southeast Asia exceeded the number of infections in sub-Saharan Africa.

As the pandemic continues to spread and accelerate, it is becoming increasingly more complex. The routes of HIV spread have remained constant and quite limited: sexual intercourse, blood contact, and mother-to-fetus or newborn. However, regardless of where and among whom the epidemic starts in a particular community, the combination of available routes of spread and the long period during which infected people remain potentially capable of transmitting HIV provide it with the capacity to spread within a community in increasingly complex ways. For example, the epidemic in Brazil started among gay men from the social elite, yet it is now centered among heterosexual men and women living in the large slums around Rio de Janeiro and Sao Paolo.

In the United States in 1985, women accounted for about seven percent of AIDS cases; during 1994, 18.1 percent of AIDS cases were women. The proportion of AIDS cases in the United States attributable to intravenous drug use or heterosexual contact has also steadily increased. Therefore, with time, the epidemic in any community becomes a composite of many different smaller epidemics; within large urban areas worldwide, multiple, simultaneous community HIV epidemics are generally underway. Accordingly, the global epidemic must be seen as a composite of all of these individual epidemics.

Due principally to the long average period of about ten years between initial infection with HIV and development of clinical AIDS, the major impact of the pandemic will be delayed. The situation in Thailand illustrates the magnitude of this feature of the HIV/AIDS pandemic. Assuming conservatively that at least 500,000 Thais are HIV-infected, it can be projected that the number of AIDS cases in Thailand will increase from perhaps several hundred over the past five years to at least 100,000 during the next five years. The long period of potential transmissibility combined with the time-lag between HIV infection and onset of disease gives the pandemic tremendous momentum. Even if the spread of HIV stopped immediately, the effects of the pandemic would continue through those who have already been infected.

The Impact of AIDS on Society

Even a brief review of the status of the HIV/AIDS pandemic must outline the enormous range of societal impacts that it has. Economic impacts of the pandemic include direct health care costs, which are estimated at more than $US11 billion worldwide in 1993. There are also indirect economic costs that result from the loss of productive young adults. In 1994, AIDS became the leading cause of death among 25- to 44-year-olds in the United States. In Thailand, the direct and indirect costs of AIDS during the 1990s were estimated at US$8 billion, not including the probable decline in tourism, which is currently a US$5 billion industry, or the decline in foreign investment because of the prevalence of the disease.

At a more individual and household level, the consequences of HIV/AIDS are diverse and profound. In large part, this stems from the disproportionate concentration of HIV infection and mortality among young and middle-aged adults. Few diseases other than AIDS target these age groups, and the deaths of these people mean the loss of mothers and fathers, active workers, and supporters of families. HIV/AIDS is a disease affecting many families. For example, by 2000, there will be an estimated 220,000-300,000 AIDS orphans in the Ivory Coast, 380,000 to 580,000 AIDS orphans in Kenya, and from 70,000 to 125,000 AIDS orphans in the United States.

Whether for homosexual men, commercial sex users, intravenous drug users, adolescents, or heterosexual men and women, the Global AIDS Strategy's approach proved to be as successful, or more so, than any other public health program seeking to change individual behavior.

In Tanzania, affected households spend an average of one year's per capita income on care and funerals—two-thirds of this expenditure for the funeral alone. The loss of adult workers also has a transgenerational effect as the children in an affected household are less likely to attend school. Even in industrialized countries, the economic impacts of HIV/AIDS are substantial. For example, in Canada in 1994, estimated production losses due to HIV/AIDS amounted to more than ten percent of market output among men aged 25 to 64 years old. From 1987 to 1991, the average production loss per death for Canadian men was US$558,000, more than for any other cause of death. Similarly, in the United States in 1991, estimated foregone earnings associated with AIDS deaths was US$28 billion to US$36 billion.

In addition to economic and family dislocation, HIV/AIDS has often provoked serious expressions of discrimination and stigmatization. Public policy debates are often dominated by fear and demagoguery. For example, the US Congress refused to drop restrictions on the entry of HIV-infected people into the United States despite the unanimous opinion of public health experts that such rules have little or no impact on the epidemic and, in fact, mislead US residents into thinking that the HIV threat is an "outside" one. Issues such as mandatory testing, reporting, and even, in the case of Cuba, mandatory isolation of HIV-infected people, continue to arise despite the World Health Organization's (WHO's) clear statement that dis-

crimination and coercion are counter-productive to efforts to prevent and control HIV infection.

The history of the global response to HIV/AIDS can be divided into four periods. During the first period, from the mid-1970s until 1981, there was no response, for the pandemic was spreading silently and unnoticed. Then, from 1981, when AIDS was first recognized, until 1985, enormous amounts of scientific knowledge were accumulated. Yet, during this period of discovery and initial response, there was little public health awareness or action. Nearly all of the important work in HIV prevention during this period was carried out by community organizations or nongovernmental organizations (NGOs). Few governments became actively involved in HIV/AIDS prevention, and no international organizations targeted HIV/AIDS for particular attention.

Finally, in the mid 1980s, AIDS was recognized to be a global threat, affecting both the industrialized and developing world. WHO launched a major effort, catalyzing a global mobilization, from 1986 to 1990. During this time a global AIDS strategy was created, national AIDS programs were developed in most countries, and community-based efforts were further expanded and intensified. The speed, intensity, and scope of this mobilization to confront this truly global health problem was unprecedented.

While the AIDS effort became the largest component of WHO and as resources committed to confronting the pandemic in the developing world increased dramatically from less than US$1 million in 1986 to over US$200 million in 1990, the major challenge became developing a coherent analysis of and approach to controlling the pandemic. In 1986, WHO developed the Global AIDS Strategy, which arguably can be considered the world's first truly global strategy in the fight against AIDS. The Global AIDS Strategy encouraged each country to develop its own comprehensive national AIDS program based on a common understanding of the basis for effective prevention programs. WHO then worked to assure human and financial resources and technical support for the implementation of prevention programs in each country.

Prevention was based on three vital components, two of which were drawn from the traditional vocabulary of public health, while the third was strikingly original. The first element was an information and education campaign, which had to be developed with the participation of its intended audience. However, knowledge about HIV/AIDS was not enough, therefore the second element involved health and social services, which were closely linked with prevention messages. For example, information about condom use had to be accompanied by programs to ensure that condoms were readily available, affordable, and of good quality. Similarly, recommendations about HIV testing were only meaningful where confidential counseling and high-quality testing services were available.

The third key element of successful HIV prevention—preventing discrimination against HIV-infected people and people with AIDS—was highly innovative in public health terms. The rationale for anti-discrimination emerged from field experiences, through which it became evident that when those most likely to be HIV-infected were threatened with severe social consequences, such as loss of work, inability to marry, or expulsion from school, they would "go underground" to avoid contact with the public health system. Thus, societal support for infected and ill people was identified to be just as important for successful prevention as information or health services.

When this "prevention triad" was applied and adapted to local cultural and other circumstances, it was highly effective. Whether for homosexual men, commercial sex users, intravenous drug users, adolescents, or heterosexual men and women, the Global AIDS Strategy's approach proved to be as successful, or more so, than any other public health program seeking to change individual behavior.

However, despite the global mobilization and successful prevention programs at the pilot project and community level, the fourth and most recent period in the history of HIV/AIDS, from 1990 to present, has been deeply disappointing. Unfortunately, while the global epidemic has intensified and expanded, the global response has stagnated or even declined. Successful pilot projects have not been replicated. The gap between the rich and poor widens, as currently about 90 percent of resources for prevention and care are spent in the industrialized world, while the developing world bears about 90 percent of the HIV/AIDS burden. The political and social commitment to fight HIV/AIDS has not kept pace with the pandemic. Because the WHO Global AIDS Strategy failed to evolve and develop based upon its experiences, the current period has been characterized by confusion, fragmentation of efforts, and inaction.

Despite the increasing gap between the pace of the pandemic and the global response, it is now possible to revitalize and rekindle global, national, and community efforts. This opportunity derives from a recent discovery about the pandemic. Study of the evolving epidemic in countries around the world has uncovered a powerful and previously unrecognized risk factor for HIV infection at a societal level. Populations that are marginalized, stigmatized, and discriminated against are at higher risk of infection. For example, in the United States, the epidemic is increasingly concentrated in inner-city and poor African-American and Latino populations.

In another example, it is now considered a risk factor for women in East Africa to be married and monogamous. Even if a woman knows that her husband is HIV-infected, she cannot refuse unwanted or unprotected sexual intercourse, for fear of being beaten without civil recourse or for fear of divorce, which effectively results in social and economic death for the woman. Therefore, despite knowledge about HIV/AIDS and despite the availability of condoms in the marketplace, these women cannot protect themselves. They lack the equal rights that alone would enable the translation of knowledge into protection. Efforts to change the laws governing divorce, marriage, and inheritance are now underway—as part of a broad strategy to slow the spread of HIV.

Emergence of a New Global AIDS Strategy

The discovery of this connection between marginalization and vulnerability to infection provides potential

strategic coherence to efforts in HIV/AIDS prevention and control. The lack of acknowledgment and respect for human rights demonstrated by the existence of discrimination and stigmatization is almost certainly a major risk factor for HIV-infection. Indeed, it may be argued that the existence of such marginalizing conditions is the most important risk factor. It is essential to emphasize that this understanding emerged through concrete and practical experience, not from simple theoretical considerations; it was discovered in communities, not in governmental bureaucracies or universities. This phenomenon has been empirically proven, and it indicates that the AIDS problem is part and parcel of broader social problems.

The extraordinary and dramatic increase in the movement of people, goods, and ideas worldwide has truly made this world a "global village." Therefore, whether it involves old diseases or previously unrecognized pathogens, it is merely a matter of when, not a matter of if, the next global epidemic will occur.

This insight regarding the inextricable connection between the promotion and protection of health and the promotion and protection of human rights offers a new avenue for work against HIV/AIDS. It suggests that a two-pronged strategy is now needed. The first part of such a strategy would involve an effort to strengthen existing programs around the world that are based upon the "prevention triad" concepts. These efforts require and deserve continued support at the community, national, and global levels.

The second, truly innovative, part of such a new global AIDS strategy would require that the societal roots of the pandemic be addressed directly. This will require a commitment, within each society, to promoting and protecting the basic human rights of people currently marginalized and discriminated against. This effort may initially seem unusual for or beyond the scope of public health. Yet public health has been defined as "ensuring the conditions in which people can be healthy"—and the major determinants of health status are societal. Therefore, concrete efforts to help transform society by promoting increased respect for human rights can be understood as a vital way to help ensure the "essential conditions" both for HIV prevention and for health more generally.

The challenge today is to convert this critical insight into the societal dimensions of vulnerability to HIV/AIDS into policy. Yet, since how a problem is defined determines what is done about it, this new understanding of the pandemic and its central dynamic is the most important and potentially useful lesson derived from over a decade of work against HIV/AIDS. Hope arises also from the recognition by the United Nations that a truly coordinated global effort is required to confront the diverse challenges of HIV/AIDS prevention and care. Starting in January 1996, a new Joint and Co-Sponsored UN AIDS program will exist. This program will link together the six major UN agencies involved with HIV/AIDS: WHO, the

---

We can no longer believe that our borders will protect us; the health of the world is bound together.

UN Children's Fund, the UN Development Programme, The UN Educational, Scientific, and Cultural Organization, the UN Fund for Population, and the World Bank.

A Global Village in Every Sense

Projections for the HIV/AIDS pandemic are grim. While estimates for the number of people HIV-infected by the year 2000 vary widely—from 40 to 110 million people worldwide—it is clear that the years to come will be much more difficult than the nearly 15 years since AIDS was first recognized. Even as new insights, strategies, and programs are developed against HIV/AIDS, the experience of this pandemic serves as a warning for the future. For today's world is more vulnerable than ever before to the global spread of new and emerging diseases. The extraordinary and dramatic increase in the movement of people, goods, and ideas worldwide has truly made this world a "global village." Therefore, whether it involves old diseases or previously unrecognized pathogens, it is merely a matter of when, not a matter of if, the next global epidemic will occur.

Aside from a new understanding of the inextricable connection between health and human rights—which applies to all major health problems of the modern world, including cancer, heart disease, injuries, violence, and infectious diseases—perhaps the most important lesson to be learned from the "age of AIDS" is the message of global interdependence. For we can no longer believe that our borders will protect us; the health of the world is bound together. In order to respond to this phenomenon, the basis of our approach to the world's health will have to be reconsidered. It will be necessary to view every disease and epidemic as a potentially global phenomenon. It will also be necessary to evaluate health concerns within the larger context of societal conditions and circumstances. WHO may literally have to be re-invented, and the shape of our future may be in the balance.

Index

Credits/Acknowledgments

Cover design by Charles Vitelli

1. Geography in a Changing World
Facing overview—NASA photo.

2. Land-Human Relationships
Facing overview—United Nations photo by R. Marklin.

3. The Region
Facing overview—United Nations photo. 143-146—Contact Press Images photos by Greg Girard.

4. Spatial Interaction and Mapping
Facing overview—State of California Department of Public Works photo.

5. Population, Resources, and Socioeconomic Development
Facing overview—United Nations photo by Shelley Rother.

ANNUAL EDITIONS ARTICLE REVIEW FORM

■ NAME: _____ DATE: _____

■ TITLE AND NUMBER OF ARTICLE: _____

■ BRIEFLY STATE THE MAIN IDEA OF THIS ARTICLE: _____

_____

■ LIST THREE IMPORTANT FACTS THAT THE AUTHOR USES TO SUPPORT THE MAIN IDEA:

_____

_____

_____

_____

_____

■ WHAT INFORMATION OR IDEAS DISCUSSED IN THIS ARTICLE ARE ALSO DISCUSSED IN YOUR
TEXTBOOK OR OTHER READINGS THAT YOU HAVE DONE? LIST THE TEXTBOOK CHAPTERS AND
PAGE NUMBERS:

_____

_____

_____

_____

_____

_____

■ LIST ANY EXAMPLES OF BIAS OR FAULTY REASONING THAT YOU FOUND IN THE ARTICLE:

_____

_____

_____

_____

_____

■ LIST ANY NEW TERMS/CONCEPTS THAT WERE DISCUSSED IN THE ARTICLE, AND WRITE A SHORT
DEFINITION:

_____

_____

_____

_____

We Want Your Advice

ANNUAL EDITIONS revisions depend on two major opinion sources: one is our Advisory Board, listed in the front of this volume, which works with us in scanning the thousands of articles published in the public press each year; the other is you—the person actually using the book. Please help us and the users of the next edition by completing the prepaid article rating form on this page and returning it to us. Thank you for your help!

ANNUAL EDITIONS: GEOGRAPHY 97/98
Article Rating Form

Here is an opportunity for you to have direct input into the next revision of this volume. We would like you to rate each of the 39 articles listed below, using the following scale:

1. **Excellent: should definitely be retained**
2. **Above average: should probably be retained**
3. **Below average: should probably be deleted**
4. **Poor: should definitely be deleted**

Your ratings will play a vital part in the next revision. So please mail this prepaid form to us just as soon as you complete it.
Thanks for your help!

Rating	Article	Rating	Article
	1. The Four Traditions of Geography		21. Indigenous Cultural and Biological Diversity: Overlapping Values of Latin American Ecoregions
	2. The American Geographies: Losing Our Sense of Place		22. Does It Matter Where You Are?
	3. Apocalypse Soon, or, Why Human Geography Is Worth Doing		23. Low Water in the American High Plains
	4. The Coming Anarchy		24. The Long River's Journey Ends
	5. The Global Tide		25. Russia and Japan: Drifting in Opposite Directions
	6. Has Global Warming Begun?		26. Transportation and Urban Growth: The Shaping of the American Metropolis
	7. What's Wrong with the Weather? El Niño Strikes Again		27. High-Speed Rail: Another Golden Age?
	8. The Tortured Land		28. The Spread of Early Farming in Europe
	9. The Environmental Challenges in Sub-Saharan Africa		29. Raising the Dead Sea
	10. Human Encroachments on a Domineering Physical Landscape		30. The New White Flight
	11. Past and Present Land Use and Land Cover in the USA		31. Hispanic Migration and Population Redistribution in the United States
	12. Global Fever		32. Raster Data for the Layman: Just What Is GIS?
	13. The Deforestation Debate		33. Population, Poverty, and the Local Environment
	14. Threat of Encroaching Deserts May Be More Myth than Fact		34. The Future of Populous Economies: China and India Shape Their Destinies
	15. The Decade of Despair		35. Vicious Circles: African Demographic History as a Warning
	16. The Importance of Places, or, a Sense of Where You Are		36. Russia's Population Sink
	17. The Rise of the Region State		37. Assault of the Earth
	18. Megacities: Bane—or Boon?		38. We're All Minorities Now
	19. Regions and Western Europe		39. Preventive Medicine: A Broader Approach to the AIDS Crisis
	20. Two-Way Corridor through History		

(Continued on next page)

ABOUT YOU

Name _____ Date _____

Are you a teacher? ❑ Or a student? ❑

Your school name _____

Department _____

Address _____

City _____ State _____ Zip _____

School telephone # _____

YOUR COMMENTS ARE IMPORTANT TO US!

Please fill in the following information:

For which course did you use this book? _____

Did you use a text with this *ANNUAL EDITION*? ❑ yes ❑ no

What was the title of the text? _____

What are your general reactions to the *Annual Editions* concept?

Have you read any particular articles recently that you think should be included in the next edition?

Are there any articles you feel should be replaced in the next edition? Why?

Are there other areas of study that you feel would utilize an *ANNUAL EDITION?*

May we contact you for editorial input?

May we quote your comments?

ANNUAL EDITIONS: GEOGRAPHY 97/98

BUSINESS REPLY MAIL
First Class   Permit No. 84   Guilford, CT

No Postage Necessary if Mailed in the United States

Postage will be paid by addressee

**Dushkin Publishing Group/
Brown & Benchmark Publishers**
Sluice Dock
Guilford, Connecticut 06437